Dance Research Methodologies

Dance Research Methodologies: Ethics, Orientations, and Practices captures the breadth of methodological approaches to research in dance in the fine arts, the humanities, the social sciences, and the natural sciences by bringing together researchers from around the world writing about a variety of dance forms and practices.

This book makes explicit the implicit skills and experiences at work in the research processes by detailing the ethics, orientations, and practices fundamental to being a researcher across the disciplines of dance. Collating together approaches from key subdisciplines, this book brings together perspectives on dance practice, dance studies, dance education, dance science, as well as dance research in cross-, multi-, and interdisciplinary fields. Practice-based chapters cover methodological approaches that provide rich examples of how research design and implementation are navigated by practicing scholars. *Dance Research Methodologies* also includes a practical workbook that helps readers to decide upon, refine, and enact their research, as well as develop ways in which to communicate their process and outcomes.

This vital textbook is a valuable resource for research faculty interested in interdisciplinary conversation and practice, emerging scholars honing their methodological approaches, graduate students engaged in research-based coursework and projects, and advanced undergraduates.

Rosemary Candelario, PhD, is an Associate Professor of Dance at Texas Woman's University.

Matthew Henley, PhD, is an Arnhold Associate Professor of Dance Education at Teachers College, Columbia University.

"Both inspiring and instructive, *Dance Research Methods* captures the diversity of today's dance scholarship and offers an array of methodological possibilities that will surely lead to research trajectories yet to be discovered. Reminding us that dance theory and dancemaking practices are always intersecting and shaping the myriad ways that we create and present new knowledge, experienced and aspiring researchers using this text will enter into an ever-widening conversation about praxis inquiry, artful research practices, the importance of ethical decision-making, and the joys of pursuing research as a creative and artistic enterprise."

Penelope Hanstein, *MFA, PhD, Cornaro Professor of Dance Emerita, Texas Woman's University, USA*

"While some of the meticulous and rigorously curated essays contain pre-requisite standard approaches that are nourishing, there are many where scholarship itself is critiqued and stretched to include an invaluable selection of voices, grammars, registers, provocations, and contexts, making this a standout book for scholars in the pursuit of inclusive (as yet elusive) dance research methodologies. Imbuing this impressive assembly of work with a sustained call for pervasive ethics is a compelling masterstroke for our times."

Jay Pather, *Director, Institute for Creative Arts, Professor, Centre for Theatre, Dance and Performance Studies, University of Cape Town, South Africa*

"*Dance Research Methodologies* includes comprehensive and detailed step-by-step methods, conversations, and personal reflections on 'how to' do dance research across myriad themes. Providing a wealth of different approaches in an accessible format, it is an invaluable resource for dance researchers, from undergraduate to post-doctoral."

Sarah Whatley, *Director, Centre for Dance Research, Coventry University, UK*

"The book functions like a set of hyperlinks that organize leaping off points to follow up in references and ideas across the diverse field of dance research. This wide-ranging collection highlights differences between 'research' versus 'creating work' or 'rehearsing,' and introduces archival research for where no archive exists, prompts for writing as dancing, ethics as research method, and other gems."

Jonathan W. Marshall, *Western Australian Academy of Performing Arts, Edith Cowan University, Australia*

Dance Research Methodologies

Ethics, Orientations, and Practices

Edited by
Rosemary Candelario and
Matthew Henley

LONDON AND NEW YORK

Designed cover image: Sarah Christine.

First published 2023
by Routledge
4 Park Square, Milton Park, Abingdon, Oxon OX14 4RN

and by Routledge
605 Third Avenue, New York, NY 10158

Routledge is an imprint of the Taylor & Francis Group, an informa business

© 2023 selection and editorial matter, Rosemary Candelario and Matthew Henley individual chapters, the contributors

The right of Rosemary Candelario and Matthew Henley to be identified as the authors of the editorial material, and of the authors for their individual chapters, has been asserted in accordance with sections 77 and 78 of the Copyright, Designs and Patents Act 1988.

All rights reserved. No part of this book may be reprinted or reproduced or utilised in any form or by any electronic, mechanical, or other means, now known or hereafter invented, including photocopying and recording, or in any information storage or retrieval system, without permission in writing from the publishers.

Trademark notice: Product or corporate names may be trademarks or registered trademarks, and are used only for identification and explanation without intent to infringe.

British Library Cataloguing-in-Publication Data
A catalogue record for this book is available from the British Library

Library of Congress Cataloging-in-Publication Data
Names: Candelario, Rosemary, editor. | Henley, Matthew, 1978– editor.
Title: Dance research methodologies: ethics, orientations, and practices / edited by Rosemary Candelario and Matthew Henley.
Description: First Edition. | New York: Routledge, 2023. | Includes bibliographical references and index.
Identifiers: LCCN 2022043734 (print) | LCCN 2022043735 (ebook) | ISBN 9780367703080 (Hardback) | ISBN 9780367703073 (Paperback) | ISBN 9781003145615 (eBook)
Subjects: LCSH: Dance—Research—Methodology.
Classification: LCC GV1589.D3877 2023 (print) | LCC GV1589 (ebook) | DDC 792.8072—dc23/eng/20230109
LC record available at https://lccn.loc.gov/2022043734
LC ebook record available at https://lccn.loc.gov/2022043735

ISBN: 9780367703080 (hbk)
ISBN: 9780367703073 (pbk)
ISBN: 9781003145615 (ebk)

DOI: 10.4324/9781003145615

Typeset in Goudy
by codeMantra

For the teachers, who journey with us.
For the students, who are also our teachers.
For the communities, with whom we practice.

Contents

List of Contributors	x
Acknowledgments	xviii

Part 1 Introduction — 1

1. Dance Research in/as Communities of Practice — 3
   ROSEMARY CANDELARIO AND MATTHEW HENLEY

2. Research Ethics, Orientations, and Practices — 20
   ROSEMARY CANDELARIO AND MATTHEW HENLEY

Part 2 Dance Practice — 39

3. Introduction to Research in Dance Practice: Practice-as-Research — 41
   VIDA MIDGELOW

4. Choreographies of Presence: Improvisation as Feminist Practice — 48
   JO POLLITT

5. Community Dance and Collective Creation: Art, Health, and Social Development across the Hemisphere — 61
   AURELIA CHILLEMI AND VICTORIA FORTUNA

6. FutureBlackSpace: Weaving Art, Healing, and Activism — 79
   JOHN-PAUL ZACCARINI

7. Practice (or) Research: A Conversation with Eiko Otake — 94
   ROSEMARY CANDELARIO AND EIKO OTAKE

Part 3 Dance Studies — 105

8. Introduction to Research in Dance Studies: Dance as a Humanity — 107
   THOMAS F. DEFRANTZ

9 Choreographic Analysis as Dance Studies Methodology: Cases,
   Expansions, and Critiques 113
   HARMONY BENCH, ROSEMARY CANDELARIO, J. LORENZO PERILLO,
   AND CRISTINA FERNANDES ROSA

10 Global South Archives: Listening and Acknowledging
   Authorship 134
   ANA PAULA HÖFLING

11 Cyphering with Oral History 147
   MIRI PARK

12 To the Motion Itself: Toward a Phenomenological Methodology
   of Dance Research 164
   NIGEL STEWART

Part 4 Dance Education 183

13 Introduction to Research in Dance Education: New Pathways to
   Discovery 185
   LYNNETTE YOUNG OVERBY

14 Toward a Decolonial Dance Research Paradigm: Ubuntu as
   Qualitative Hermeneutic Phenomenology 191
   ALFDANIELS MABINGO

15 Ethnography for Research in Dance Education: Global,
   Decolonial, and Somatic Aspirations 212
   OJEYA CRUZ BANKS

16 Conducting an Experiment: How Quantifying Answers to a
   Research Question Can Promote the Value of Dance Education 228
   LYNNETTE YOUNG OVERBY AND MATTHEW HENLEY

17 Classroom as Laboratory: Teacher Self-Study and Dance Education 243
   ILANA MORGAN

18 Mixing Methods and Approaches in Dance Education Research 259
   MATTHEW HENLEY

Part 5 Dance Science 277

19 Introduction to Research in Dance Science: The Science
   of Movement and Choreography of Research – Evolving
   Methodologies in Dance Science 279
   MARGARET WILSON

20 Mentoring Dance Science Research: Circling the Square – Edel Quin in Conversation with Margaret Wilson 286
EDEL QUIN AND MARGARET WILSON

21 Thinking Statistically for Dance Research 304
GREGORY YOUDAN JR.

22 A Dance/Movement Therapy Approach to Interview Analysis 326
TOMOYO KAWANO

23 Carving an Innovative Space for Dialogic Intersections: Dance, Disability, and Design 345
MERRY LYNN MORRIS

Part 6 Dance Research beyond Disciplines 363

24 Introduction to Dance Research beyond Disciplines: Extending Dance-based Ways of Knowing 365
ROSEMARY CANDELARIO AND MATTHEW HENLEY

25 Strange Bedfellows: Dance Studies, Academic Disciplines, and Truth in Crisis 368
JANET O'SHEA

26 Keeping Movement at the Center as We Dance into Interdisciplinary Research 389
ADESOLA AKINLEYE

Part 7 Creative Workbook 401

27 A Creative Workbook for Rehearsing Ethics, Orientations, and Practices 403
ROSEMARY CANDELARIO AND MATTHEW HENLEY

Index 427

Contributors

Adesola Akinleye, PhD, is a choreographer and artist-scholar. She is an Assistant Professor in the Dance Division at Texas Woman's University. She has been an Affiliate Researcher, MIT, Arts Culture and Technology, CAST Visiting Artist at MIT, and a Theatrum Mundi Fellow. She began her career as a dancer with *Dance Theatre of Harlem Workshop Ensemble* (USA) later working in UK companies such as *Green Candle* and Carol Straker. Over the past twenty years, she has created dance works ranging from live performance that is often site-specific and involves a cross-section of the community to dance films, installations, and texts. Her work is characterized by an interest in voicing people's lived experiences in Places through creative moving portraiture. A key aspect of her process is the artistry of opening creative practices to everyone from ballerinas to architects to women in low-wage employment to performance for young audiences.

Harmony Bench is an Associate Professor of Dance at The Ohio State University and the author of *Perpetual Motion: Dance, Digital Cultures, and the Common* (2020). Harmony has an ongoing collaboration with Kate Elswit to bring the digital humanities and dance history into greater dialogue, most recently with *Dunham's Data: Katherine Dunham and Digital Methods for Dance Historical Inquiry* (Ref: AH/R012989/1; www.dunhamsdata.org), which won the 2021 ATHE/ASTR Award for Excellence in Digital Scholarship. Former co-editor of *The International Journal of Screendance* with Simon Ellis, Harmony guest-edited the special issue *This Is Where We Dance Now: COVID-19 and the New and Next in Dance Onscreen* with Alexandra Harlig in 2021, and has a new book in progress on dance film. For further information on Harmony see: www.harmonybench.com

Rosemary Candelario, PhD, writes about and makes dances engaged with Asian and Asian American dance, butoh, ecology, and site-specific performance. She is the recipient of the 2018 Oscar G. Brockett Book Prize for Dance Research for her book *Flowers Cracking Concrete: Eiko & Koma's Asian/American Choreographies* (Wesleyan University Press, 2016). Rosemary is also the co-editor with Bruce Baird of *The Routledge Companion to Butoh Performance* (2018). Rosemary is an Associate Professor of Dance at Texas Woman's University, where she coordinates the PhD in Dance, and is affiliate faculty with Multicultural Women's and Gender Studies. She holds a PhD in Culture and Performance from UCLA.

Aurelia Chillemi is a choreographer, dancer, and movement therapist with degrees in dance and psychology. She is a Professor of Dance at the National University of the Arts in Buenos Aires, Argentina where she teaches undergraduate and graduate courses in Corporeal Expression, community dance, and dance therapy. She is the founding director of Dancers For Life, a community dance project based in Buenos Aires. Her book, *Danza Comunitaria y Desarollo Social: Movimiento Poético del Encuentro* (Artes Escénicas, 2015) explores community dance practice and pedagogy. She currently serves as President of the Argentine Association of Art Therapy.

Ojeya Cruz Banks, PhD, is an Associate Professor of Dance at Denison University. A dancer anthropologist grounded in her Pacific Islander (Guåhan/Guam) and African American heritage (Alabama, Kentucky, and Louisiana). Her specialization includes West African dance (Guinea, Senegal), African diaspora dance, and Contemporary Pacific Island Dance. For over a decade, she worked as a Senior Lecturer at the University of Otago in Aotearoa/New Zealand. This is where she developed a research area in indigenous Pacific contemporary dance and Black Pacific dance intersections. She has published widely and is a member of the Studies in Dance editorial board. Her short dance film shot in Fiji *Ocean in the Blood* premiered at Duke University in 2020. Recently, Cruz Banks gave a keynote address to celebrate the establishment of the new doctoral program dedicated to Dance Education at Teacher's College.

Thomas F. DeFrantz directs SLIPPAGE: Performance | Culture | Technology. DeFrantz received the 2017 Outstanding Research in Dance award from the Dance Studies Association and contributed concept and voice-over for a permanent installation on Black Social Dance at the Smithsonian National Museum of African American History and Culture. DeFrantz has taught at the American Dance Festival, ImPulsTanz, Ponderosa, and the New Waves Dance Institute, as well as at MIT, Stanford, Yale, NYU, Hampshire College, Duke, Northwestern University, and the University of Nice. DeFrantz believes in our shared capacity to do better and to engage our creative spirit for a collective good that is anti-racist, proto-feminist, and queer affirming.

Victoria Fortuna, PhD, is an Associate Professor of Dance at Reed College in Portland, OR. Her interests include Latin American concert and dance as a mode of community engagement. She founded and directs the Community Dance at Reed project, which brings together members of the Reed and broader Portland communities. Her book, *Moving Otherwise: Dance, Violence, and Memory in Buenos Aires* (Oxford University Press, 2019), examines the relationship between Buenos Aires-based contemporary dance practices and histories of political and economic violence in Argentina from the mid-1960s to the mid-2010s.

Matthew Henley, PhD, MFA, is an Associate Professor in the Dance Education Program and Affiliated Researcher at the Arnhold Institute for Dance Education Research, Policy & Leadership at Teachers College, Columbia University. Henley focuses his research on describing cognitive and social-emotional skills associated with dance education. He takes a phenomenological approach, analyzing how dancers in diverse communities describe the experience of learning concepts in the dance classroom. Henley's related interests include enactive cognition in the arts, developmental and neuroscientific approaches to embodied knowing, research methods for pedagogy, and the pedagogy of research methods. Henley danced professionally in New York City with Sean Curran Company and Randy James Dance Works. Henley earned his doctorate in Educational Psychology: Learning Sciences from the University of Washington, and MFA in Dance from the same institution. Previously, he served as Associate Professor of Dance at Texas Woman's University, where he coordinated the BA program and taught in the MFA and PhD programs.

Ana Paula Höfling, PhD, is an Associate Professor and Director of Graduate Studies in the School of Dance at the University of North Carolina, Greensboro. She is the author of *Staging Brazil: Choreographies of Capoeira* (Wesleyan University Press, 2019), winner of the 2021 Dance Studies Association Oscar G. Brocket Book Prize. In 2021–2022 she was a fellow at the National Humanities Center, where she conducted research on Brazilian dancers Eros Volúsia, Felicitas Barreto, and Mercedes Baptista for her second book manuscript, *Dancing Brazil's Other: Choreographies of Race, Class, and Nation*. She was an Andrew Mellon Postdoctoral Fellow at the Center for the Americas at Wesleyan University (2012–2014).

Tomoyo Kawano, PhD, BC-DMT, NCC, LCAT, is an Associate Professor and director of the Master's in Dance/Movement Therapy Program at Antioch University New England. As a dance/movement therapist, she worked primarily with adults and adolescents with mental illness, addictions, and dual diagnoses in inpatient and outpatient settings. She serves on the

American Dance Therapy Association's Board of Directors, the Education Committee Chair; and on the editorial board of the *Arts in Psychotherapy* journal. She formerly co-led the Asian/Asian Pacific Islander Desi American Affinity Group. Her scholarship reflects her interest in dance epistemology and its explication with research methodology, pedagogy, and ritual and ceremony.

Alfdaniels Mabingo, PhD, is a dance researcher, scholar, performer, educator, and co-founder of AFRIKA SPEAKS. Born and raised in his ancestral village, Mbuukiro, on the shores of Lake Victoria in central Uganda, East Africa, he has taught dance courses at Makerere University in Uganda, New York University in the US, the University of Auckland in New Zealand, and Edna Manley College of the Visual and Performing Arts in Jamaica. A recipient of the prestigious Fulbright fellowship, Mabingo's research sits at the intersection of decolonization, interculturalism, postcolonialism, dance pedagogy, African philosophy, and creative arts economies. Mabingo has published more than 20 peer-reviewed scholarly articles and book chapters. His latest book is titled 'Ubuntu as Dance Pedagogy: Individuality, Community, and Inclusion in Teaching and Learning of Indigenous Dances in Uganda'. Mabingo has taught African dances and drumming in schools and community settings and has delivered presentations in the United States, Australia, China, South Sudan, Rwanda, Jamaica, Germany, Uganda, and New Zealand.

Vida L. Midgelow is a Professor of Dance and Choreographic Practices at Middlesex University. As an artist-scholar, she works on practice-as-research methodologies, improvisation, and ethics and has published widely in these areas. She is the editor of the Oxford Handbook of Improvisation in Dance and is the principal researcher for the Artistic Doctorates in Europe project www.artisticdoctorates.com (Erasmus+ funded). With Professor Jane Bacon, she co-devised the Creative Articulations Process (CAP) and co-edited Choreographic Practices (2010–2020). She co-directs the Choreographic Lab www.choreographiclab.co.uk and is currently an associate research artist at i4C4/ Dance4.

Ilana Morgan, PhD, an Associate Professor of Dance at Texas Woman's University, researches dance education as social justice with incarcerated and detained youth, focusing on dance experiences and choreography as an expressive and restorative practice. Her research in dance education and advocacy considers issues of confinement and freedom, governmental approaches to rehabilitation, juvenile justice, autonomy, democracy, and trauma-informed pedagogy. She has published articles in the *Journal of Dance Education*, the *Journal of Emerging Dance Scholarship*, and has a chapter in *Dance Education and Responsible Citizenship: Promoting Civic Engagement through Effective Dance Pedagogies*. At TWU she teaches dance pedagogy and theory courses, coordinates the MA in Dance and the BA in Dance with Teacher Certification, and mentors student teachers.

Merry Lynn Morris, PhD, MFA, is currently an Assistant Director and a Professor at the University of South Florida Dance Program. Dr. Morris applies her movement expertise in novel and diverse ways, pursuing interdisciplinary endeavors that yield innovative products. In 2002, she began exploring the area of integrated/inclusive dance, and her experience as a caregiver to her disabled father over a 21-year period fostered a personal connection to disability needs/advocacy. This motivation led to collaborative work with engineers to invent new mobility devices. Dr. Morris's research spans disability, design, and dance-science/somatics. Publications include five U.S. Patents and over 25 print publications.

Janet O'Shea, PhD, is the author of *Risk, Failure, Play: What Dance Reveals about Martial Arts Training* (Oxford University Press, 2019) and *At Home in the World: Bharata Natyam on the Global Stage* (Wesleyan University Press, 2007), and the co-editor of the *Routledge Dance Studies Reader* (2nd edition). She is currently writing a book on emotion, corporeality, and activism entitled *Bodies on the Line: Physicality, Sentiment, and Social Justice*. Her essays have been published in five languages and seven countries. She is a Professor in the Department of World Arts and Cultures/Dance at UCLA.

Eiko Otake was raised in Japan but has been a resident of New York since 1976, and is a movement – based interdisciplinary artist. She worked for 42 years as Eiko & Koma, receiving many awards, including the MacArthur Fellowship and the Samuel H. Scripps American Dance Festival Award. Since 2014 Eiko has worked as a solo artist. Highlights include a month-long Danspace Project Platform in 2016, three full-day performances at the Metropolitan Museum of Art, and the ongoing *Duet Project* in collaboration with a diverse group of artists. During the pandemic Eiko has been working in her Virtual Studio, creating new media works, with which she performs for her new project, *I invited myself*. For more information on Eiko see: www.eikootake.org.

Lynnette Young Overby, PhD, is a Professor of Theatre and Director of the Community Engagement Initiative at the University of Delaware. Overby is a Teachers College, Columbia University Fellow in the Arnhold Institute for Dance Education Research, Policy, and Leadership. Overby's leadership roles include serving as President of the National Dance Association, and the Delaware Dance Education Organization. She is the author or editor of over 60 publications including 14 edited and authored books. In 2018, she received the Lifetime Achievement Award from the National Dance Education Organization and in 2021, she was appointed to serve on the National Council on the Humanities.

MiRi Park is a Lecturer in the Performing Arts – Dance Studies Program at Cal State University Channel Islands. MiRi completed her MA thesis *Dancing Like a Girl: An Oral history of NYC B-girls in the 1990s* under the tutelage of Mary Marshall Clark. MiRi went on to serve as the inaugural program coordinator to help launch the Columbia OHMA program.

J. Lorenzo Perillo, PhD, is currently an Assistant Professor of Theatre and Dance at the University of Hawai'i at Mānoa. He has taught at UC Berkeley, UCLA, the University of Illinois at Chicago, and Cornell University. As a Fulbright scholar, he researched Hip-Hop in Asia, which resulted in his first book *Choreographing in Color: Filipinos, Hip-hop, and the Cultural Politics of Euphemism* (Oxford University Press, 2020), the first transnational monograph on hip-hop by a practitioner. He utilizes bilingual ethnography, choreographic analysis, and community engagement to examine Black dance in relation to Filipino racialization. Learn more about his research, teaching, and community engagements here: http://choreographingincolor.com.

Jo Pollitt, PhD, is an interdisciplinary artist and research fellow at Edith Cowan University. Jo's work is grounded in a twenty-year practice of improvisation across multiple performed, choreographic, and publishing platforms. She has worked with several Australian dance companies and lectures in dance Improvisation at the Western Australian Academy of Performing Arts. She is a co-founder of creative arts publication BIG Kids Magazine and feminist research collective The Ediths, is an artist-researcher with #FEAS (Feminist Educators Against Sexism), and a core member of ECU's Centre for People, Place, and Planet. Her novella *The dancer in your hands < >* was published in 2020.

Edel Quin, MSc, danced professionally with *Riverdance* before completing a BA (Hons) in Dance and MSc in Dance Science. Edel has transitioned from dancer to renowned dance science practitioner, educator, and researcher, with extensive international experience, specializing in the application of dance science to the practice of dance, across styles, ages, and settings. Edel currently leads the BSc (Hons), and masters (MSci and MSc) programs in dance science at the University of Chichester, UK. Edel is an Associate of Safe in Dance International, an active member of the International Association for Dance Medicine & Science (IADMS), and co-author of *Safe Dance Practice*. Edel is currently enrolled in PhD studies and was awarded the IADMS Dance Educator Award in 2021.

Cristina Fernandes Rosa is an artist-scholar making work at the intersection of somatic practices, dance studies, and ecologies of care. Rosa is currently a Visiting Professor at Universidade Federal da Bahia (UFBA), in Brazil. Dr. Rosa has previously taught at Roehampton University in the UK and various universities in the United States. She was a Postdoctoral Fellow at Freie Universität's IRC Interweaving Performance Cultures in Berlin (Germany, 2012–2013) and a Visiting Professor at UFBA's School of Dance, in Salvador (Brazil, 2021/22). Dr. Rosa is currently involved in two projects, *Movements of Sustainability* and *CosmoAngola*.

Nigel Stewart is a dance artist and scholar. He is a Senior Lecturer at the Institute for Contemporary Arts at Lancaster University, UK, and the Artistic Director of Sap Dance. His written publications follow two lines of inquiry. The first uses descriptive, existential, and hermeneutic phenomenology to explore the relationship between choreography and the visual arts in twenty-first century contemporary dance. The second theorizes environmental dance, including his own rural site-specific dance works, in terms of environmental aesthetics and values. He is co-editor of *Performing Nature: Explorations in Ecology and the Arts* (Peter Lang, 2005). Nigel has danced and choreographed for various European companies.

Margaret Wilson, PhD, is a Professor of Dance at the University of Wyoming where she teaches dance technique, kinesiology, history, and supervises the BFA in Dance Science. She and Neil Humphrey teach and choreograph Vertical Dance, both an artistic and scientific pursuit. Her research has been presented at the International Association for Dance Medicine and Science (IADMS), and she has published in the *Journal for Dance Medicine and Science, Journal of Dance Education, Research in Dance Education, Sports Biomechanics, Medical Problems of Performing Artists* and the *Journal of Dance and Somatic Practices*. With Glenna Batson, she co-authored *Body and Mind in Motion: Dance and Neuroscience in Conversation*.

Gregory Youdan Jr. is a visiting research scholar at Brown University and adjunct lecturer at Lehman College. Greg performed with NY Baroque Dance Company, Sokolow Theatre/Dance Ensemble, and Heidi Latsky Dance, where he is now a board member. He is a Westheimer Fellow through Mark Morris Dance Group's Dance for PD® program and serves on the development committee for the International Association for Dance Medicine and Science and the research committee for the National Organization for Arts in Health. Greg graduated from Hofstra University and has master's degrees in Motor Learning and Applied Statistics from Teachers College, Columbia University.

John-Paul Zaccarini is a Professor of Performing Arts at the Research Centre, Stockholm University of the Arts. A practitioner in theatre, dance, mime, and circus with a focus on poetry and the spoken word he has been both performer/auteur and director/dramaturge/choreographer since 1992. He is currently researching the intersections between art, therapy, and activism in his project FutureBrownSpace which is a creative space for BIPOC to work with Radical Healing and decolonizing artistic research in majority white institutions and fields.

Acknowledgments

We must begin by acknowledging the faculty, staff, and students in the Dance Department at Texas Woman's University who first inspired us to put into practice many of the ideas we articulate here. In particular, this book would not have been possible without our beloved colleague, Linda Caldwell, who directed the PhD Dance Program at TWU when we both arrived, and who through her leadership created a space for interdisciplinary dialogue. Though she passed in 2018, her presence is felt in this book.

Credit and thanks are due to Dagmar Spain, Charlotte Hathaway, and Hetty King for their crucial administrative and editorial assistance that enabled this book to come together on time and all in one piece. We also thank the Department of Arts and Humanities and Dance Education Program at Teachers College, Columbia University for direct and indirect funding that supported the writing, editing, and publishing of the book.

Our friend and colleague Erika Record helped us find the perfect cover image from the Texas Dance Improvisation Festival that conveys dancers as researchers, even though in the end it meant using the work of a photographer other than herself. Thank you to Sarah Christine for giving us permission to use her striking image of TWU alum Irving Maldonado and Eli Webb, and to the dancers for graciously agreeing to appear on the cover of this book.

We are grateful to have generous colleagues who have listened to our ideas and read this work in various stages of development. In particular, we thank Penelope Hanstein and Juliette McMains for providing thoughtful feedback on early drafts of the book proposal that helped shape this project. Additionally, Juliet McMains, Mary Williford Shade, and Margaret Wilson generously read and commented on early drafts of our chapters. We are thankful, too, to our Routledge Editor, Ben Piggot, for encouraging us to foreground ethics, and to be expansive in our conceptualizing of the book. Finally, appreciation goes to the anonymous reviewers of both our proposal and manuscript; this book is far better for their labor.

Part 1
Introduction

1
Dance Research in/as Communities of Practice

Rosemary Candelario and Matthew Henley

Introduction

A lone woman pops into view in silhouette in front of a row of New York brownstones, punching, grinding, thrusting, and shadow-boxing with a bounce that accentuates the beat, and yet remaining grounded. Her movement is fierce, hard, and controlled, but with the feeling that things could blow up (or her joints could blow out) at any moment. Stark red and yellow lighting evokes heat and flames. Anger, frustration, rage fly off her limbs, torso, and hips toward the viewer, as Public Enemy exhorts the dancer and the viewers to "Fight the Power." Her energy explodes beyond the bounds of her body and her punches fill the screen. She is pushed to the limit, whether that's the limit of her torso flexion and extension as she pushes her rib cage as far forward as it can go and then equally far back, or the limits of exhaustion. She is working hard, fighting with every fiber of her body. Her face reflects the struggle, grimacing, showing contempt. When hints of fatigue begin to show, she grounds herself in a wide stance, and wines like her life depends on it. Whether wearing a form-fitting short-sleeved red dress with a broad black 80s belt and chunky earrings; white boxing shorts, black sports bra, red boxing gloves, and a cropped boxing robe; or electric blue lycra tights and matching high cut leotard topped with a cropped motorcycle jacket, she shadow boxes with the finesse of a dancer, and performs the Charlie rock, salsa rock, typewriter, Lindy twist, and the Mike Tyson with the ferocity of a heavyweight world champion.[1] Dances like the cabbage patch and the running man that may otherwise evoke fond memories of parties become vehicles of rage and frustration as they push against the confines of the screen.

Watching Rosie Perez in the opening credits to Spike Lee's 1989 film, *Do the Right Thing*, we could be curious about many aspects of the dance. For example, we could wonder about the popular dances of the late 1980s that she performs, their genesis and connection to earlier popular dances, and who commonly danced them at the time. We could consider the cultural and political contexts of race, gender, and class in New York City in the late 20th century. We could be curious about how to measure markers of expert performance of popular dance and how to ensure dancers in these forms have healthy bodies for long careers; Rosie Perez was after all a featured dancer on *Soul Train*. We might want to find methods for the culturally sustaining teaching of these African diasporic popular dances. We could question how popular dance theorizes about the world. Or we could employ our own popular dance practice as a way to explore our research questions. One short dance can prompt many different inquiries.

Curiosity inspires and guides inquiry. We search and then we re-search because we want to know more, to look beyond the surface, and find patterns, motifs, resonances, and dissonances that help us make sense of, or disrupt, the world around us.

> Anything (material or non-material) can be the object of our awareness, attention, or questioning mind. Whenever we ask "what is this?" we enter into an inquiring frame of mind. When we research something, we formalize this intuitive process to establish a definition for qualitative discourse or quantitative testing. We define the thing we seek to know more about. Then we have a basis for communicating the findings. The results of the research will rest on our basic understanding and definition of the thing we are investigating. The activity of defining underlies all other aspects of research.
>
> (Fraleigh 1999, 3)

In this opening quote from *Researching Dance* (Fraleigh and Hanstein 1999), a book that has inspired this one, Sondra Fraleigh argues that how we define something (in her case she is seeking to define dance) influences how we approach studying it, what we are open to seeing, and even what we are capable of understanding or conceptualizing. In the case of our inquiry about Rosie Perez's dancing, curiosity about the markers of expert performance or curiosity about the implications for race, class, and gender will lead the inquirer to attend to different aspects of the performance. This will, in turn, lead to different questions asked, observations made, connections formed, and explanations shared.

In academia, these practices of inquiry are formalized as research methods. When methods are part of a cohesive system for conducting research, we call them methodologies. The cohesive systems are disciplines. Dance is an academic discipline that historically has had affinities with other disciplines, such as kinesiology, anthropology, and physical education, to name a few. Over time, dance in academia has developed along multiple sub-disciplinary lines with different conceptual frameworks, epistemologies, and inquiry practices. What draws our attention, what we are curious about, how we frame questions, how we generate observations, how we make connections between those observations, how we make sense of those connections, and how we choose to share what we have found, are all influenced by the disciplinary communities with which we identify. The actual dancing, though, is always more than any of these alone. In this book, we bring together researchers from different disciplinary communities across the field of dance in order to describe and discuss their approaches to research methods. The goal is not to reify disciplinary boundaries and hierarchies that might already exist, but to encourage a perspective that frames research design and methods as porous, creative, and fluid, and to indicate that beneath our differences, we have much in common and that beneath our commonalities there is quite a bit of difference.

Who Are We?

It is impossible for us to talk about what it means to research dance and be dance researchers without telling the story of how we—a dance studies scholar and a dance education researcher who are both active dancemakers—came to be working together. We joined the Department of Dance at Texas Woman's University within a year of one another. TWU is a public regional doctoral university with a long history of dance research and the longest continuously running dance PhD in the United States, awarding the first doctorate in 1958. The TWU program also has BA and MA programs in dance education (Dance BA with education minor), a BA in dance, and an MFA program focusing on choreography. Led for close to three decades by Penelope Hanstein, co-editor of *Researching Dance* (1999), the department has a strong sense of dance as knowledge production with an orientation to all forms of dancemaking as scholarship (improvisation, performance, choreography, and production), providing a rich ground from which to consider what we mean when we talk about dance research.

As we two worked together advising PhD students, teaching Master's and Doctoral research methods courses, and supervising Doctoral qualifying exams and dissertation research, we found ourselves confronting differences in terminology, basic assumptions, and even expectations of what research can or should do stemming from our backgrounds in dance studies, dance practice, and dance education. At times it was as if we spoke different languages or were from different cultures (a point to which we will return shortly). And yet there was something about the pragmatic nature of having to extend beyond our silos in order to be collegial and student-centered that led us to begin to find significant commonalities of practice, even if these were traditionally called by different names or taught as methods exclusive to a particular kind of inquiry. For example, for many years Rosemary taught the MA/MFA first-year research and writing course. Many of the students in these programs had only recently earned their BA and were still discovering their choreographic voice. Most had never thought of themselves as researchers before and were nervous about reading theory and writing. In these classes, Rosemary began to emphasize that the skills the students already have as dancers—watching, making (including both choreographing and rehearsing), and performing dance—are in fact research skills of close observation or close reading; gathering data and analyzing it; and organizing findings to share research with a public. Even more specifically, the rehearsal context could be understood as a field site where qualitative research is conducted (documentation, participant observation, memoing, even interviewing). Similarly, Matthew began to frame the activities within dance practice classes (what the program called technique classes), as a series of experiments. For each movement exercise, before the music starts, the students create hypotheses about how they are going to accomplish the task set by the teacher (or peers). While dancing, students generate data. After the exercise is complete, students analyze the data for successes and opportunities for growth, then reformulate their hypotheses for the next performance, and the cycle continues.

By paying attention to our own pedagogical framing of research alongside our personal research practices, while being in close conversation with our colleagues, we were pushed to shift our understandings of what research is, which had been based on our own disciplinary training. Instead, we came to see that despite the wide diversity of disciplines, methodologies, and reporting formats involved in dance research, even within our own small program, the processes and steps are remarkably similar, and all are creative. There was, as Sondra Fraleigh puts it, quoting Wittgenstein, a "family resemblance" (1999, 5).

Emerging out of the context of our experiences together at TWU, we learned important lessons we wanted to share. This prompted us to design a book that could be used in graduate and advanced undergraduate research courses, by individual emerging and even established dance researchers, and among and across research communities. We see this book as a methodological, theoretical, and pedagogical intervention that brings together dance practice, dance studies, dance education, and dance science.[2]

What Is Research?

Depending on the context, "research" can have different meanings. A friend might ask you to research the best restaurant for an upcoming birthday party, or a secondary or undergraduate teacher might ask a student to write a research paper by locating secondary sources in the library and synthesizing them. These definitions are not incorrect, but they are context-specific. In this book, we are generally referring to research within the context of graduate education and professional academic practice, and how these connect out to contexts of professional artmaking, clinical practice, teaching, community engagement, and activism. Revisiting Penelope Hanstein's definition of research from *Researching Dance* provides a starting point.[3] She writes,

> Scholarly research is a process of creating new knowledge, and as such, it seeks to expand the realm of human knowing and understanding. It is a way of thinking and acting; a way of posing and responding to questions; a way of expressing and communicating ideas. It is the search for truth and meaning rooted in our capacity for astute observation, critical analysis, meaningful interpretation, rational understanding, insightful contextualization, and defensible judgment. The researcher as scholar engages in careful study, examination, and observation of facts, which often include what people say and do. Through a rigorous and systematic process using appropriate research methodologies and procedures, he or she gathers, scrutinizes, and assesses the credibility of information. The researcher analyzes the data by seeking relationships and making connections between often seemingly unrelated pieces of information. During this process of gathering and analyzing data, themes emerge, ideas take shape, and meaningful interpretations are discovered. The researcher considers these interpretations within the context of the existing body of knowledge, advances new theories, and considers the significance of her or his discoveries.
> (Hanstein 1999, 23)

In this rich description of the research process, we see openings for all kinds of research related to dance, regardless of disciplinary affiliation. For example, whether Rosemary is writing a book about the choreography of Eiko & Koma or creating site-specific ecological dance performances, she collects information, generates material, sorts through it and searches for patterns and relationships, and coheres what she has found into a form that can be shared with others through a conference paper, a book, a workshop, or a live performance. Similarly, whether Matthew is designing a new curriculum or crafting an empirically-based theory of kinetic concepts, he observes students and teachers and talks to them about their experiences. He organizes this information into themes, finds connections between the themes, and considers how they impact teaching and learning. He then shares the work through publication, presentation, and the development of new content and strategies for teaching.

From our experience conducting research, performing, and teaching research methods and choreography, we began to see that what these endeavors have in common is that they all engage in systematic and ethical inquiry that generates new knowledge that is publicly shared. Below we contextualize each of these terms in order to unpack this definition.

What Does It Mean to Be Systematic?

In one sense, a system is a collection of interconnecting parts that when combined form something more complex (e.g. a cardiovascular system or ecosystem). For the system to function, all parts must work together. In research, then, to be systematic is to align the parts (epistemological stance, conceptual framework, literature review, research questions, data generation, data analysis, and modes of sharing) and ensure they work together.

In another sense, to be systematic is to engage in "interpretation...; critical reflection; thinking about, through, and with... contemplation and comparison; concentrated attention and contextualization..." (Conquergood 2002, 152). To be systematic is to go beyond casual observation, to look beyond the first thought, and to corroborate your thoughts with others. In the intellectual climate of post-Enlightenment academia, systematicity takes the form of deductive and inductive reasoning about empirical evidence. Deductive reasoning is the prediction of empirical evidence based on theoretical suppositions. Inductive reasoning is the development of theoretical positions based on empirical evidence. This is, though, a particular worldview, that knowledge emerges from the observable. There are other knowledge systems that embrace spirit, dream, intuition, and other non-empirical sources of evidence, which are not amenable to deduction or induction but have a systematicity of their own. There are also other forms of knowledge production, such as art making that don't necessarily seek logical consistency, but emerge from systematic practice. In our definition of research, we don't intend to endorse a particular type of systematicity, but encourage researchers to understand how systematicity, reasoning, evidence, and knowledge are defined and enacted in their own community.

In the development of a research design, a great deal of attention is often given to the research questions. From our perspective, this is because research questions are a succinct realization of the systematic nature of the research. An appropriate research question emerges from an epistemological stance, conceptual framework, and literature review, while simultaneously pointing toward methods of data generation, analysis, and sharing. For instance, a research question that presumes the existence of inequity in a particular context would be written differently than a question that seeks to determine if inequity exists, reflecting transformative and constructivist epistemological stances respectively. A question that will be answered through interviews should be different from a question that will be answered through interviews and observations.

What Does It Mean to Be Ethical?

Ethics are the principles and conventions that guide a person's relational interactions. Dance is relational; therefore, all dance research is relational and has ethical implications. When ethical considerations are siloed into the process of applying for institutional research approval, as they often are, they are reduced to procedural ethics. Researchers can sometimes see them as a set of bureaucratic hoops to jump through in order to begin the research process. This is problematic in two ways. First, not all dance research is subject to institutional approval, which might lead the researcher to believe their work does not have ethical implications. Second, researchers who do seek and receive institutional approval might believe that approval indicates no further consideration of ethics is necessary. By broadening considerations to include not only procedural but also situational and relational ethics (described in Chapter 2), we aim to encourage researchers to evaluate the relational implications of their work regardless of whether they are required to seek institutional approval or not.

What Does It Mean to Generate Something New?

In our teaching, we often liken research to the experience of attending a party. A newcomer might join a circle of party-goers who are in the middle of a conversation. After passively listening for a while, the newcomer begins to understand the contours of the conversation: What is the topic? What are the different beliefs about the topic that different members of the group hold? What kind of rhetoric is used to engage in the conversation? Eventually, the newcomer feels they have something to add and so they speak up. They will learn quickly, based on the reactions of the group, whether this comment is a new and useful contribution to the conversation. This party-goer could then float to another group, who, even if they are discussing a similar topic, might have different beliefs or different modes of discourse, and so the process starts again. This points to the important question related to novelty: New to whom? Rather than seeing novelty as absolute ("I have to do something no one has ever done before!") We see "new" as subjective and relational. As Wendy Laura Belcher (2019) suggests, research that makes a contribution can be a new way to look at something old, an old way to look at something new, or a new combination of old information and old approaches. In any case, if it advances the knowledge or practice of the community with which you are engaging, it can be thought of as new.

What Is Knowledge?

Oftentimes, knowledge, particularly academic knowledge, is reduced to that which can be languaged. Three perspectives from psychology, performance studies, and philosophy, though, reinforce what we know in dance: knowing extends beyond language. Psychologist Jerome Kagan (2009) describes schematic, semantic, and procedural knowledge. Schematic knowledge is sensory-perceptual in nature. A blueprint, for instance, is a visual schema, a recipe has a gustatory (and textural and olfactory) schema. Semantic knowledge is abstracted from experience and organized and represented in symbolic forms such as language and mathematics. Procedural knowledge is knowledge of actions, of how to successfully manipulate and adapt to the environment. Performance ethnographer Dwight Conquergood provides a similar description of knowledge as practical knowledge, propositional knowledge, and political savvy, or knowing how, knowing that, and knowing who, when, and where (2002, 153). Along the same lines, philosophers of epistemology, Mattias Steup and Ram Neta (2020), claim knowledge includes knowing individuals, knowing facts, and knowing how. These three examples help us as dance researchers expand not only the types of knowledge that dance, dancing, and studies of dancers can produce but also help us articulate more clearly the nature of our contribution to knowledge.

What Does It Mean to Share Publicly?

Typical academic models for publication include journal articles; conference papers, presentations, and posters; and books. According to some rubrics, performance is also a form of scholarly publication. Teaching, as well, could be considered a public presentation. These forms, though, hearken back to a limited definition of knowledge that is only "knowing that." If we expand our understanding of knowledge to knowing who and how, then the making public of that knowledge could similarly be expanded to practices such as "activism, outreach, connection to community; applications and interventions; action research" (Conquergood 2002, 152) and other forms of community collaboration.

Research in Disciplinary Communities of Practice

In the previous section, we defined research as systematic and ethical inquiry that leads to the generation of new knowledge that is shared publicly. Though this offers a general answer to the question "What is research?," as each of those terms is operationally defined we are left with part of the answer being: It depends. In particular, it depends on the context in which "research" is being used, and the practices and conventions of that particular context. In other words, the definition of research will depend on what we refer to as communities of practice.

We understand communities of practice through the work of situated learning theorists Jean Lave and Etienne Wenger. For them,

> A community of practice is a set of relations among persons, activity, and world, over time and in relation with other tangential and overlapping communities of practice. A community is an intrinsic condition for the existence of knowledge, not least because it provides the interpretive support necessary for making sense of its heritage. Thus, participation in the cultural practice in which any knowledge exists is an epistemological principle of learning. The social structure of this practice, its power relations, and its conditions for legitimacy define possibilities for learning.
>
> (1991, 89)

We relate Lave and Wenger's theory of communities of practice to academic disciplines represented broadly as dance practice, dance studies, dance education, and dance science. These fields generally fit into the larger academic traditions of arts, humanities, social sciences, and natural sciences. These designations are not simply different buildings on campus or ways to create administrative structure. They represent communities of practice that engage in different modes of knowledge production. They use different theoretical frameworks. They accept different types of evidence and use different methods of analysis.

It is beyond the scope of this book to discuss these differences exhaustively from historical and international perspectives. However, Kagan (2009) describes useful contrasts between these academic traditions in the United States academy, primarily, in the 20th century. And though we recognize that these differences might not apply to all contexts, we find the distinctions valuable enough to share in order to understand the implications of dance research historically emerging out of a number of different disciplinary communities.

Kagan's text takes as its starting point a 1959 lecture given by British physicist and novelist C.P. Snow, who describes how the humanities and natural sciences have evolved into distinct cultures in the academy. Kagan updates this argument by describing how the social sciences, which first emerged at the end of the 19th century, have come to be a third culture in the academy. These traditions, Kagan argues, constitute cultures because "each perspective has consistency and coherence within each of the language communities, but not always across communities" (2009, 15). Siloed away from one another, Kagan's "three cultures" are each distinguished from the others in the following nine dimensions.

1. The primary questions asked, including the degree to which prediction, explanation, or description of a phenomenon is the major product of inquiry.
2. The sources of evidence on which inferences are based and the degree of control over the conditions in which the evidence is gathered.
3. The vocabulary used to present observations, concepts, and conclusions, including the balance between continuous properties and categories and the degree to which a functional relation was presumed to generalize across settings or was restricted to the context of observation.
4. The degree to which social conditions, produced by historical events, influence the questions asked.
5. The degree to which ethical values penetrate the questions asked and the conclusions inferred or deduced.
6. The degree of dependence on external financial support from government or industry.
7. The probability that the scholar works alone, with one or two others, or as a member of a large team.
8. The contribution to the national economy.
9. The criteria members of each group use when they judge a body of work as elegant or beautiful.

(Kagan 2009, 2–3)

Based on these dimensions we could imagine a Dance Department with a scholar from each of the subdisciplines. The dance science scholar is working as part of a large well-funded research team that advances the prediction and explanation of physical phenomena that are minimally impacted by historical conditions. Their research involves controlled observation and is validated through mathematical formulas. The dance education scholar works as part of a small group, with moderate external funding, in order to predict or explain behaviors or psychological features of individuals or groups that are moderately impacted by historical conditions. Their research includes the collection and analysis of empirical evidence that advances theoretical views of human behavior. The dance studies scholar works as an individual, with little external funding, to pursue an understanding of human (or posthuman) responses to sociohistorical conditions. Their research describes human behavior, including the creation of artistic artifacts and processes, and is valued for its semantic coherence and elegant prose. We consider the performing and visual arts as a fourth culture in Kagan's framework. Accordingly, the dance practice scholar works alone or as part of an interdisciplinary team, with minimal external funding, uses dancing and dancemaking to generate written and performed ideas in response to personal and/or sociohistorical conditions. Their research involves the generation and organization of kinetic, visual, and audial materials which might or might not be languaged and are valued for their aesthetic or conceptual coherence and impact. In this imaginary department, scholars teach the same students and attend the same faculty meetings, but their research situates them in different cultures.

Kagan claims that in different fields the same word can mean wildly different things. Because of the differences in practice and vocabulary, we end up ignoring the ways in which our work interpenetrates. Kagan helpfully traces how some of these seemingly deeply entrenched beliefs developed, but also shows the usefulness of an approach that seeks out connections across these differences. Indeed, after defining the dimensions that distinguish these academic cultures, Kagan goes on to review research from across the natural sciences, social sciences, and humanities that disrupt or defy these boundaries. Similarly, when we (Rosemary and Matt) began the shared responsibility of teaching and advising graduate students, we each brought language, informed by our research backgrounds in the humanities and social sciences, that at first seemed to divide us. When we stepped back, though, and looked at the bigger picture, we found that what we wanted the students to do had many similarities, disrupting the disciplinary differences that language seemed to impose. We include Kagan's framework with a similar goal, to bring awareness to some of the aspects of research cultures that might divide work among dance researchers while recognizing that research will, and already does, contradict these boundaries. Deep disagreements and differences in orientations exist and we are not arguing that these should be dissolved, or that they are insignificant. Rather, we are arguing that there is value in bringing dance researchers together despite differences in practice and language use.

Dance Research in/as an Expansive Community of Practice

Dance is a product of human culture, a creative practice, a physical science, a mode of expression, and a tool for knowledge generation. Dance is meaning-making, yet operates in a modality different from spoken or written language. Meaning in dance is multiple, being both individually and culturally situated. These qualities of the field complicate what counts as data, how it can be collected, how to hold space for multiple meanings in data analysis, and how to translate kinetic knowing to textual knowing in the writing process. Dance researchers bring all this complexity to the research process as embodied knowledge; they often collect and analyze data through moving, sensing, and observing in ways that are not attended to in most existing methodology texts. Though many dance researchers recognize and value this multiplicity, the structures of the academy guide them into silos that prioritize one, or possibly two, of the cultures over the others.

As the above examples illustrate, dance crosses disciplinary boundaries, sometimes in the same department. Instead of guarding these divisions, why not cross them and see what happens? If we rethink how dance as a community of practice unites us, even across disciplinary or academic culture divisions, what then becomes possible? How could it be productive to cohere around dance instead of, or in addition to, separating around academic cultures? As Janet O'Shea writes in Chapter 25 of this book, "Dance, by its very nature, brings together the symbolic, material, and the experiential. As such, it has the potential to trouble binaristic distinctions between materialism and idealism, discourse and phenomenology, and constructivism and realism" (370–371). Within the subdisciplines, like dance science, dance is troubling distinctions. As Quin and Wilson write in Chapter 21, "dance science is more than 'sport science applied to dance,' it is a way of knowing about dance through dance that embraces theoretical, scientific, and practical perspectives" (290). We are reminded of Dwight Conquergood's call to collapse binaries of theory and practice in academia. Although he was writing about performance studies rather than dance, his passionate call for a "radical move" to "turn, and return, insistently to the crossroads" (2002, 154) of practice, analysis, and civic engagement informs this book.

To do so means to return to some of the deep divergences exposed by Kagan's framework, and to see what happens when we attempt to hold them together in new ways. We return to some established debates or binaries in dance (intentionally posed as both/and rather than either/or) as an example of what this process could open up.

- Ephemerality/Persistence: In what ways does the dancing disappear as it is being danced and in what ways does the dancing remain?
- Universal/Situated: What in your dancing is shared with all other dancers and what is unique to your community or even you alone?
- Subject/Object: In what ways do you conceive of yourself or another as being a body and in what ways do you conceive of yourself or another as having a body?
- Everyday/Rarified: How is dancing embedded in and intertwined with all aspects of life and how is dancing a unique and rarified experience?
- Mundane/Sacred: In what ways is dancing of the earthly world and in what ways is dancing of the spiritual world?
- Discursive/Non-discursive: How is dancing part of ongoing public and private discourse and how does dancing resist participation in public and private discourse?
- Agent/Instrument: In what ways is dancing empowering through invited spectatorship and in what ways is dance disempowering through unwanted spectatorship?

The above binaries are imposed by the culture (and communities of practice) around us. From within a dance community of practice, though, those binaries become embodied and dynamic tensions that are productive for ongoing dialogue. Only when we put all of our subfields together can we unearth the complexities and explode the binaries. We need the ethnography and the experiment. The philosophical and the practical. The deeply historicized/contextualized and the generalizable. Instead of reducing what we do in order to be legible to those outside the practice of dance, what if we embrace our practice in all of its complexity and explore ways to reimagine research practices that are better aligned with dance as a community of practice?

The Stakes of Teaching and Learning Dance Research Methodologies

Teaching people how to become researchers is not, we believe, a simple transferal of steps to be followed, a prescriptive imposition of a model, or a straitjacket into which students are put. We argue that becoming a researcher is about joining an active community of practice that seeks answers, frameworks of understanding, and new knowledge about dance, dancers, and dancemaking. At the same time, recognizing that knowledge, and knowledge production via research, is situated in particular communities of practice invites us to interrogate the ways in which practices of research may reinforce the social structure and power relations inherent in the community, or possibly reshape or reimagine them.

Lave and Wenger suggest that, if particular voices are not "at the table" it is not because they are incapable of engaging in the practices of the community, it is because they have been implicitly or explicitly made to feel that they are not legitimate members of the community. They argue, "'Transparency' of the sociopolitical organization of practice, of its content and of the artifacts engaged in practice, is a crucial resource for increasing participation" (1991, 91). By increasing the transparency of the inner workings of research for novice researchers, experienced researchers invite them to the community of practice.

At the same time, we must be aware of how the use of established methodologies may in fact interfere with underrepresented scholars being able to adequately research their communities of practice. To continue the table metaphor, we have to seriously consider not only who is at the table, but also if the table's materials are in fact applicable to all research. In this book, we suggest that frameworks for analysis should emerge from the culture being studied rather than from frameworks imposed from the outside. For instance, much of academic research is rooted in Euro-American scientism, a framework for knowledge-making that privileges observable and measurable phenomena as the foundation of reality, marginalizing spiritual and intuitive phenomena. Similarly, Laban Movement Analysis (LMA) was developed in relation to Euro-American modern dance practices, and thus attends to the values of occupying and moving through space and time, missing other energetic or spiritual values that are at the heart of many dance practices, and that can't be delimited to an analysis of force, time, and space. Part of changing who is at the table involves a willingness to change the table's composition, and accept that there are no universal (nor universally implemented) methods.

Although we are arguing for ways that dance and dance research is well-positioned to creatively push against some established ways of working by recognizing ourselves as a community of practice, we also acknowledge that research, as we discuss it, is largely (but not exclusively) conducted by people working in institutions, most often universities, and that research practices are embedded in these structures. In these contexts, researchers must adopt theoretical frameworks and procedures, as determined by disciplinary communities and institutional policies. Inquiry moves from an informal human process of experimentation, discovery, and sensemaking to a mode of public knowledge production, with attendant implications for the accrual of financial and professional capital, for the individual, department, and even the institution. It is done by someone, with someone, for someone in order to produce, reproduce, reify, problematize, disrupt, deconstruct, etc. existing knowledge and practice. Its output, knowledge, is not an abstract ideal but a tangible commodity tied to professional, and therefore class, status. Jobs, promotions, tenure, grants, guest speaking gigs, book contracts, and the like are all products of research (as well as the conditions which make future research possible).

Dwight Conquergood reminds us, and we agree, that there are many possible research outcomes that are not product-based (2002), but these are not always recognized by institutions when it comes to promotion and job security. While many universities recognize choreography or performance (especially in national or international venues) as research products, much of the process-based work described particularly in Part II of this book may be illegible to funding or promotion-granting bodies. In her chapter, Eiko Otake provides a much-needed reminder to maintain a healthy questioning of the imposition of frameworks or terminology that could compromise the integrity of the work or change its nature. The fact is that research projects that often develop from our passions and deep commitments are also tied up in requirements, standards, and expectations that are typically established from outside our own control or that of our research participants.

It is not only knowledge as a commodity that is implicated in maintenance of these structures, but also the "technologies" through which that knowledge is generated, that is, research methodologies and methods.

Becoming a full participant certainly include[s] engaging with the technologies of everyday practice, as well as participating in the social relations, production processes, and other activities of communities of practice. But the understanding to be gained from engagement with technology is especially significant because the artifacts used within a cultural practice carry a substantial portion of that practice's heritage… Thus, understanding the technology of practice is more than learning to use tools; it is a way to connect with the history of the practice and to participate more directly in its cultural life.

(Lave and Wenger 1991, 101)

The ways in which technologies are shared and with whom, that is, the teaching of research methods, matters. If methods are not explicitly addressed then novice researchers are left to intuit the expectations for rigorous and ethical practice on their own. We believe that it is an equity orientation to be transparent about methodologies in order to provide access to those modes of production.

Overview of the Book

Rosemary's mentor, Susan Leigh Foster, would often say, "the dance will tell you how to write it." We suggest that the dance can tell you how to research it. Accordingly, this book focuses on orientations, practices, examples, and activities that can help researchers develop a container–a research design in which they find, adapt, or even develop research methods that make sense for their theories, values, and ethics as well as the theories, values, and ethics of their research subject(s) and the dance and research communities with whom they are in dialogue.

Part 1 of this book sets the frame for how we conceive of and define research, how we approach teaching novice researchers, and the ethics, orientations, and practices that support dance research. Parts 2 through 5 focus on the subfields of dance practice, dance studies, dance education, and dance science. Each Part is introduced by a senior scholar in that field. These Part introductions identify the subfield, what research means to the subfield, what methodologies it typically uses, and to what end. They introduce the Part chapters and situate them in current practice and developing trends. Each Part then includes a curated collection of chapters in which dance researchers describe the research practices and decision-making processes in their unique contexts. In the curation of these chapters, we gathered researchers working across the globe and in diverse dance genres. We specifically sought out authors who were pushing the boundaries of research in their subfield; therefore these chapters do not represent canonical methodologies and methods, but rather what we think are exciting new directions in dance research. Moreover, rather than describing how to conduct research, authors reflect on the challenges and opportunities of their methodology. Part 6 widens the scope with chapters from two authors who contemplate the role of dance research in the broader world of academic scholarship and contemporary issues beyond the academy. Finally, Part 7 is a workbook that contains a variety of activities appropriate for the classroom or individual usage to cultivate the various aspects of research ethics, orientations, and practices established in Chapter 2, and elaborated throughout Parts 2 through 5.

The chapters in this book are not meant to provide the reader with a prescriptive set of steps to be followed, rather the text is an impetus to think critically and reflectively about how methodological practices best serve the researcher, the subject of inquiry, and the field. By featuring chapters that describe *how-I* rather than *how-to*, we provide the reader with rich narratives of research practices by authors who let the dance tell them how to research it, and create new methodological containers that are creative, mutable, porous, and permeated by ethical care. By providing examples of how dance researchers have adapted methods for specific situations, we encourage the reader to do the same.

We recognize that, given the scope of this book, its readers will be diverse in their areas of dance expertise and familiarity with different aspects of and approaches to research. A chapter that is straightforward to some readers might be opaque to others, at least initially. Likewise, certain practices described in the book might not even be recognized as research by some readers, depending on their current community of practice. Rather than seeing this as a barrier, we offer this as an invitation to readers to check their own biases about what is and is not research, and be challenged to immerse themselves in the community of dance research assembled herein. We hope that novice and experienced researchers across the subdisciplines of dance will find entry points to deepen and broaden their knowledge, within and beyond their current community of research practice.

Notes

1 Thank you to Jonathan Pattiwael for help with identifying these dances.
2 These subdisciplines are expanded upon in the Part introductions.
3 Although Hanstein retired before either of us joined the faculty at TWU Dance, her lasting impact in that department, and the status of the book she co-edited with Fraleigh as one of the few dance-specific research books until the late twenty-teens, are both significant influences on this book.

Works Cited

Belcher, Wendy Laura. 2019. *Writing Your Journal Article in Twelve Weeks, Second Edition: A Guide to Academic Publishing Success*, 2nd ed. Chicago: University of Chicago Press.

Conquergood, Dwight. 2002. "Performance Studies: Interventions and Radical Research." *TDR: The Drama Review* 46, no. 2 (Summer): 145–156.

Fraleigh, Sondra Horton. 1999. "Family Resemblance." In *Researching Dance: Evolving Modes of Inquiry*, edited by Sondra Horton Fraleigh and Penelope Hanstein, 3–21. Pittsburgh: University of Pittsburgh Press.

Fraleigh, Sondra Horton and Penelope Hanstein. 1999. *Researching Dance: Evolving Modes of Inquiry*. Pittsburgh: University of Pittsburgh Press.

Hanstein, Penelope. 1999. "From Idea to Research Proposal: Balancing the Systemic and Serendipitous." In *Researching Dance: Evolving Modes of Inquiry*, edited by Sondra Horton Fraleigh and Penelope Hanstein, 22–61. Pittsburgh: University of Pittsburgh Press.

Kagan, Jerome. 2009. *The Three Cultures: Natural Sciences, Social Sciences, and the Humanities in the 21st Century*. Cambridge: Cambridge University Press.

Lave, Jean and Etienne Wenger. 1991. *Situated Learning: Legitimate Peripheral Participation*. Cambridge: Cambridge University Press.

Steup, Matthias and Ram Neta. 2020. "Epistemology." In *The Stanford Encyclopedia of Philosophy*, edited by Edward N. Zalta. See https://plato.stanford.edu/archives/fall2020/entries/epistemology/.

2
Research Ethics, Orientations, and Practices

Rosemary Candelario and Matthew Henley

Introduction

In the previous chapter, we defined research as a process of systematic and ethical inquiry that leads to the public sharing of new knowledge, and articulated the ways in which this definition applies to dance research across the arts, humanities, social sciences, and natural sciences. We situated research, for the purposes of this book, within institutional academic communities of practice and argued that teaching research methods, or making the modes of knowledge production transparent to students, is vital to fostering a more equitable and just research community. We also proposed there is value in bringing dance researchers together as a cohesive community of practice, not to homogenize research practices across the field but to highlight and celebrate what is unique about dance research.

As we discussed in the previous chapter, the learning of research methods is a process of novices deepening their participation in a sociocultural practice. Framing learning as cultural participation "provides a way to speak about the relations between newcomers and old-timers, and about activities, identities, artifacts, and communities of knowledge and practice" (Lave and Wenger 1991, 29). Learning research methods does, indeed, involve the transfer of skills, for instance, the skills of data collection and analysis. However, when new researchers join research communities, they also learn ways of attending and relating that are a part of the culture. What practices, concepts, and theories are part of the discourse and which are not? What tools, resources, and technologies are used and which are not? What does the community value and how do members relate to each other? Depending on the context, some of these might be taught as part of the explicit curriculum while others are relegated to the implicit or null curricula. When learning is reframed as participation in cultural practice, relating, attending, and acting become inextricably intertwined; participation "dissolves dichotomies between cerebral and embodied activity, between contemplation and involvement, between abstraction and experience: persons, actions, and the world are implicated in all thought, speech, knowing, and learning" (Lave and Wenger 1991, 51–52). In this chapter, then, we turn our attention to explicitly considering how members develop ways of (1) relating, or ethics; (2) attending, or orientations; and (3) acting, or practices.

Relating, attending, and acting (ethics, orientations, and practices respectively) are interconnected parts of participation in communities of dance research. We seek to make explicit the implicit skills and experiences at work in the research processes by detailing the modes of participation that we find fundamental to being a researcher across the disciplines of dance. Serving on graduate admissions committees together and teaching research methods to graduate students over many years, we found that students were often intimidated by the idea of Research, to which they seemed to assign a capital "R" as if there was a daunting gap between the practices of inquiring, noticing, sensemaking, and responding developed in everyday life and those same practices embedded in a research project. This prompted us to begin to more carefully identify existing orientations and practices in potential students, and nurture them in current students. We think these can be learned and cultivated in incremental and repeated ways, rather than existing as essential traits. Research is not something one is or is not good at; rather, it is a system of interconnected processes that are developed through repeated and regular practice. Together these modes of participation facilitate the development of ethical, critical, and responsive researchers who make significant contributions to their sub-discipline as well as the field of dance as a whole. Here, we draw out in broad strokes what these practices are, while in the workbook we offer specific activities for the classroom or individuals where these may be experienced and rehearsed.

Research Ethics

Simply put, ethics are principles, established and enacted within communities of practice, that guide our actions. Yet, too often ethics are relegated to the end of the methodological discussion, or as a step required by institutions that can be checked off a to-do list. We argue that ethics—including a consideration of bias, systemic racism and other -isms, and equity—must form the foundation of any research process. Further, they must be recursively reconsidered throughout the process, including the sharing phase of performance and publication, and beyond. Being ethical is not optional; it's a prerequisite to being a researcher. As we suggested in Chapter 1, all research is relational, and therefore has ethical implications; ignoring those implications is not an option. In fact, we see it as so foundational to conducting research that we discuss it first.

As researchers in dance, the ethical issue with which we are continually confronted is that our main research subjects and participants are bodies in motion, whether they are live in a studio, lab, classroom, or community setting; on stage; or present in traces in documentation in an archive. Dancing bodies are bodies on display in both private and public settings. This has led in many cases to assumptions about the availability of those bodies for critique, objectification, touch, sex, etc. Bodies are not neutral, nor are the lenses with which we interpret bodies. Different bodies are valued differently depending on where we live, on our own positionality, and the intersectionality of race, ethnicity, class, caste, gender, sexuality, geographic location, and so many other things in our lives. Bodies move and dance and are seen and studied in the context of specific societal beliefs and stereotypes about various bodies. Dance performance depends heavily on long-established codes and conventions of representation that inform how we understand what we see, not only the movement but also the bodies doing the moving. Dance—whether performance, technique, education, theory, social event, or therapy—is imbricated with the body, with specific bodies in specific times and places, with specific cultures and histories, and as researchers, we must be able to articulate these things on their own terms and in relation to how our own backgrounds and biases and understandings influence what we are able to see. The codes and conventions of the researcher might not match the codes and conventions of the dancer. The impact on every aspect of the research process is significant, whether it's whose bodies are studied in relation to which technique, whose dance culture is valued in scholarship, whose pedagogy is considered valid, etc.

In many cases, particularly in the social and natural sciences, research ethics are thought to be reducible to a series of safeguards for human subjects: articulate risks, avoid coercion, and actively seek consent, what Marilys Guillemin and Lynn Gillam (2004) call procedural ethics. Although institutional ethics compliance is an important baseline, there are many research situations in our field that provide opportunities to consider situational ethics (Guillemin and Gillam 2004) and relational ethics (Ellis 2007). These categories invite us to think deeply and recursively about the micro and macro ethical implications across our research practices. In what follows, we first review procedural approaches to ethics, since much of dance research is conducted within institutional contexts including but not limited to universities. We then turn our attention to how the dance field is grappling with current issues in order to establish broader parameters for thinking about ethics.

Procedural Ethics

Ellis explains that procedural ethics "ensure procedures adequately deal with informed consent, confidentiality, rights to privacy, deception, and protecting human subjects from harm" (2007, 4). In the community of practice of higher education, procedural ethics in research involving humans, particularly biomedical and social/behavioral research, are governed by institutionally situated ethical review boards and committees.[1] These review boards follow principles that were developed in response to egregious racist, classist, and ableist research practices that led to direct harm and even death. For instance, the Nuremburg Code (1947) was developed following World War II in response to torturous biomedical research conducted on concentration camp prisoners by Nazi doctors. The Belmont Report (1979) was developed in response to research by American doctors that deceived African American men into believing they were receiving treatment for syphilis, when, in fact, they were not.

In the Belmont Report, three ethical principles guide procedural considerations: respect for persons, beneficence, and justice. According to the principle of respect for persons, research participants must be interacted with as autonomous self-determining individuals who are given adequate information in order to make considered opinions and choices as well as have the freedom to act on those opinions and choices. Research, therefore, that is conducted with persons who are incapable of acting as autonomous persons, either through coercion, being provided misinformation, or because of developmental or disability status would be considered unethical unless protections are put into place to safeguard their personhood. Procedurally, respect for persons is protected through the informed consent process, in which potential participants are provided with information about the project, their comprehension is checked, and it is made clear that participation is voluntary. Although this process might be clear in biomedical and social science research, it might be less clear in other areas. For instance, if a college professor is working with students to create a dance that will be part of the professor's scholarly profile, what level of autonomy or personhood do the dancers have? Or what does respect for persons mean if the main subject of research has passed away, but people who knew and worked with them are still alive?

The medical maxim "first, do no harm" is extended to research practice in the principle of nonmaleficence. Research practices should not cause immediate or long-term harm to the participants. The Belmont Report extends this principle, though, beyond lack of harm to a consideration of the benefits to the participant, referred to as the principle of beneficence. When considering the ethics of a research design, the two principles are considered in relation to each other: beneficence should be maximized and the potential for maleficence should be reduced. In a biomedical context, this comparison is often more concrete with research interventions leading to improved health or wellness outcomes for the participant, in addition to generalized knowledge about the disease or condition that will improve treatment for the population at large. The comparison of beneficence and nonmaleficence is often more abstract in social science and humanities contexts. There is often no direct benefit to the participant (or the subject of analysis) for engaging in the research; instead, the benefit is the potential for a future intervention for other members of the population. It is also less likely, though, that the research procedures will lead to direct harm to the participant as research interventions are primarily interviews, observations, and the completion of other non-invasive research instruments. Though not often considered, this comparison becomes even more complicated in a performance-as-scholarship context. Though dancers performing in a scholar's work are not usually considered research participants, they are participants in a scholarly project that benefits the choreographer's professional profile. It is worth considering, then, the relationship between the benefits and risks of participating in the project. The benefits for participants/dancers are often articulated as "exposure" or "a good learning" experience, which are certainly true, if not sometimes exaggerated. The risks for participants/dancers, though not often explicitly articulated or discussed, are, depending on the work, physical injury, continuous wear and tear on joints and muscles, as well as mental and emotional stress. How can dance researchers in all of their scholarly endeavors maximize beneficence while reducing risk?

The principle of justice extends the evaluation of benefit and risk, by prompting a consideration of their distribution. Who receives the benefits and who bears the risks? Historically, research risks have often been borne by marginalized populations (e.g. racial and ethnic minorities, individuals with developmental differences, and prisoners), whereas the benefits of the research are enjoyed by the majority or a privileged minority. The principle of justice demands that these imbalances be considered and corrected. If there is a risk to be borne then it is to those who bear the risk that the benefits must flow. Procedurally, the principle of justice is evaluated through an explicit articulation of the recruitment procedures. This focus, however, misses other opportunities to pay attention to issues of justice. For example, in dance practice, justice includes fair pay, safe working conditions, and credit for authorship. In dance studies, justice includes paying attention to who/what is written about, by whom, and from what framework. Moreover, it includes noting to whom benefits flow as a result of the research (e.g. tenure and promotion for the researcher).

Situational and Relational Ethics

Situational ethics, or "ethics in practice," are "the kind that deal with the unpredictable, often subtle, yet ethically important moments that come up in the field" (Ellis 2007, 4). Relational ethics "[recognize and value] mutual respect, dignity, and connectedness between researcher and researched, and between researchers and the communities in which they live and work" (ibid). Although Ellis is specifically focusing on ethnographic and autoethnographic situations involving "intimate others" (e.g. friends and family members), her formulation is helpful in dance research situations where we might be researching with our colleagues, students, dancers in our own community, or alongside regular clients. Whether we are in community, social, or professional dance settings, there is an ethics specific to each community of practice of how we (usually implicitly or tacitly) agree to be together as moving bodies, whether in rehearsal, in the club, or on the stage. And as we are in the process of moving together, situations arise with which we need to ethically grapple.

Recently dancemakers have been taking the lead around ethics in performance settings and the presenter/choreographer/performer relationship, particularly in relationship to white supremacy. The *Creating New Futures: Phase 1: Working Guidelines for Ethics & Equity in Presenting Dance & Performance* "living document," for example, was collectively written by arts workers in the wake of COVID-19 closures and cancellations, and in the midst of the #BlackLivesMatter uprisings in response to the murder of George Floyd by police. The document is described as

> 1) a house for testimonials so that we can hear the voices of individuals, 2) a handbook for transparent conversations including putting forward principles for equity in our relations, and 3) a tool for change, for radical reinvention of the field and how we work together.
>
> (2020, 8)

Creating New Futures can be seen as an example of both situational and relational ethics in practice as it grapples with a developing situation of the twin pandemics of COVID-19 and racism, values the voices of those in the situation,[2] outlines principles for interaction, and calls for changes moving into the future based on just relations.[3]

In addition to thinking through the relational ethics of the performer/presenter relationship, dancers are also developing ethics for (re)emergent issues like physical contact in the studio between teachers and students, and among dancers in jams or rehearsals.[4] In some places, working toward situational and relational ethics has led to an expansion of procedural ethics. In Australia, for example, it has become standard practice for dancers in the premieres of task-based choreographed works to be listed as contributing authors, and for choreographers to be liable for at the very least acknowledging those dancers in publications and remounts, but often including them in rights, too. Also, in Australia, there is a standardized information for participants letter, and a permission to participate (i.e. be interviewed or dance) letter, to be signed by participants and archived. There's usually also a separate risk review for rehearsal processes, in which choreographers indicate if they are mitigating risks and how (e.g. first aid training, warm downs, etc.).[5] Taken together these practices suggest that although many institutional review boards do not consider rehearsals, jams, or performances to be "research" governed by procedural ethics, dancers themselves, guided by situational and relational ethics, have begun developing their own procedural ethics.

Dance history research, including oral history, may or may not involve living participants, but even when it does, it often falls outside the purview of procedural ethics (oral history, for example, is considered exempt from institutional review in the United States). Even in cases, such as ethnographic research, where procedural ethics are required, researchers often develop further situational and relational ethical guidelines, whether formal or informal. In Chapter 15 of this volume, for example, Ojeya Cruz Banks centralizes "establishing relationships and respect" as the goal of ethnography, and characterizes data collection as "community engagement" (218). Even when there may be no live human participants with whom a researcher comes into direct contact, for example in archival research or choreographic analysis,[6] there are still situational and relational ethics to consider. Dance studies, for example, as a field is concerned with the intersections of race, gender, sexuality, class, and socio/historical/political contexts and therefore considers ethics through the lenses of relationships and power, bringing in issues such as access to knowledge, sharing of resources and benefits, and being conscious of who speaks for whom. In the case of dance history, especially that of indigenous communities, VK Preston reminds us that history is entwined with living communities with whom we need to develop just relations. Examples of how dance historians (both Indigenous and non-Indigenous) working in First Nations contexts address this include "lots of work on repatriation,…community boards advising historians,…and letters of intent/understanding taken up by university indigenous advising circles and also by elders/chiefs."[7] In these cases, situational and relational ethics call on researchers to attend to issues beyond the purview of procedural ethics, and are therefore crucial to incorporate throughout the research process, whether or not institutional review is required.

Research Orientations

Learning research methods orients us to what a community of practice values. In the essay "Orientations Matter," Sara Ahmed says that orientations not only show us what is "significant and important" (what *matters*), but they also ask us to attend to "physical or corporeal substance" (they are themselves matter).

Orientations, she writes, "affect how subjects and objects materialize or come to take shape in the way that they do" (2010, 235). Orientations are not only personal, they are spatial (and we would add, embodied). They determine what is "here," but also what is "out of place." Moreover, they are about beginnings, the "point at which the world unfolds" (2010, 234). For us, research orientations are different from research practices (detailed in the following section); they both precede and suffuse practices. They don't tell us how to conduct research. Rather they are ways of attending that are fundamental to engaging in research throughout the process. Moreover, orientations are something we have in common across methodologies and academic cultures.

Through our experiences teaching dance research methods and coordinating graduate programs and admissions, we identified the following as important dance research orientations:

- Connecting outward to communities of practice
- Working from curiosity
- Carefully questioning assumptions and engaging in self-reflexivity
- Valuing care, intuition, spirit, affect, relationality, emotion
- Critically observing
- Being willing to try out different lenses and scopes
- Noticing when to slow down and when to leap

In this section, we detail these orientations. Exercises to further explore and practice the orientations can be found in the workbook.

Connecting Outward to Communities of Practice

Being in touch with what the community of research is saying and doing in relation to one's interests is an essential orientation for researchers. D. Soyini Madison calls this being part of an interpretive community, from whom one learns, to which one contributes, and in relation to which one is willing to both be critical and be inspired (2012, 22). This community includes senior scholars whom you've never met, peers you meet through a conference panel, or even strangers who find your email. Often this is thought of solely as a literature review, but we suggest that reaching out happens throughout all the stages of research. Reaching outward to communities of practice (whether academic or non-academic) is not only about connecting to existing scholarship or supportive colleagues. It also involves being brave and vulnerable enough to share one's work (at the in-progress and completed stages), and being able to take in critique from one's community.

One of the most exciting aspects of the dance field is how much still remains to be researched and written about. For students and emerging researchers, however, this aspect of the field can be frustrating. If it seems like no one has researched your specific topic, how do you connect to a community of practice in the literature, at conferences, in writing groups, etc.? Sometimes we have to do the work of cobbling together our own community of practice. For Rosemary this meant working with a few other colleagues researching Asian American and Asian diasporic dance to consistently propose dance panels to the Association for Asian American Studies conference over a number of years, slowly building up a network of colleagues, and supporting each other's writing projects. This led over time to a small and growing body of literature and an increasing number of affinity and working groups. For TWU PhD students working on dance education in postcolonial countries (e.g. Beatrice Ayi in Ghana, Aadya Kaktikar in India, to name a couple), it meant looking for parallel situations outside their home countries to compare and contrast approaches. Or as Merry Lynn Morris details in Chapter 23 of this volume, her work constructing mobility devices for dance required her working at the intersections of many different communities (disability dance, engineering, business, design, to name a few).

Working from Curiosity

Curiosity is an engaged and motivated state in which one experiments and explores in order to figure something out (Opdal 2001; Silvia 2017). This orientation is foundational not only to research but to learning in general. How many of us, though, have heard our colleagues complain—or have complained ourselves—that our students lack curiosity? After years of participating in educational systems where they were subjected to and evaluated by standardized tests at the primary, secondary, and even undergraduate levels, many students have oriented toward producing correct answers rather than engaging in critical thinking. It is no surprise, then, and is not their fault, that curiosity hasn't been cultivated. And yet, it is perhaps the foundational quality of research: the desire to know the who, what, why, where, how, and to what end of a choreographic puzzle, technique, dance form, or dancing community.

Rosemary remembers one student in her first year Master's level research and writing class complaining that hip hop was not included in her university dance history or technique curricula; but when pushed to identify existing hip hop materials she would like to see included, the student could not, not because they didn't exist, but because she had never sought them out. This student was incidentally a straight-A student, used to excelling in classes; but she realized she had never ventured beyond the syllabus or the material presented by the teacher. She later confided that this was a transformational moment in her own education. Simply being asked the questions and then being given a structure through which to explore the answers was the spark this student needed to open up her research.

Carefully Questioning Assumptions and Engaging in Reflexivity

The so-called reflexive turn in the social sciences in the 1980s, inspired by feminist and critical theory and postcolonial critiques, challenged the myth of the researcher as an objective, neutral observer, and emphasized that the researcher's position is key to understanding how knowledge is constructed. Identifying one's positionality as a researcher, particularly in the setup and sharing stages of research, has become a matter of course in qualitative research, and in some quantitative research. Being reflexive about our life experiences and our intersectional identities is key to explicitly identifying how our worldview shapes the kinds of questions we ask, the kinds of data we seek out, and how we approach making sense of what we learn. Orienting to one's positionality and the impact thereof on all stages of the research process, is essential to ethical and rigorous research. For dancer researchers, who often come into the research process with years of training and experience in their research areas, reflexivity and attending to positionality is especially important to explicitly tease out this implicit knowledge that will deeply shape what and how one researches.

For example, dance training (in whatever form or genre) inculcates strong beliefs in what dance is, what it means, what constitutes quality or talent or technique, the role of dance in society, and who and what dance is for. At the same time, this kind of embodied knowledge is not always taken seriously in academia. Eugenia Zuroski's challenge to think of positionality as "where do you know from?" (rather than "where are you from?") is a powerful shift. She writes, "Academic intellectual authority—what we think it looks, sounds, and feels like; where we think it *comes from*—is precisely the problem, the structure that perpetuates imperialism in our spaces of learning and intellectual engagement" (2020, n.p.). For Zuroski, challenging this starts in the classroom, in students being able to recognize "the real, unquestionable presence of knowledge and intellectual agency in every person in the room" and allows students "to identify themselves as intellectual subjects in whatever terms they [wish]" (ibid.). These ideas help dance researchers not only identify where they know from, but also to see their research participants as individuals who also know from particular positions.

Valuing Care, Intuition, Spirit, Affect, Relationality, Emotion

At the same time that it is absolutely essential to examine one's assumptions and put into play structures that help researchers account for their own biases, we rarely talk about trusting one's intuition as a part of the research process. D. Soyini Madison shares,

> It is important to honor your own personal history and the knowledge you have accumulated up to this point, as well as the intuition or instincts that draw you toward a particular direction, question, problem, or topic—understanding that you may not always know exactly why or how you are being drawn in that direction.
>
> (2012, 21)

From ideas for research projects, to getting the sense that a participant is not sharing the whole picture, to how the pieces fit together, trusting intuition is a way of honoring the analytical processes that happen outside of our conscious awareness and are reflective of our emerging expertise.

This attention to intuition to inform the process is often discouraged in many research practices that aim toward objectivity and the requirement to validate analysis with empirical data. Authors that seek to decolonize research methods, though, call into question this need for objectivity, leaving space, not only for intuition, but for spirit and emotion in the research process. Gregory Cajete, for instance, claims that for Native Americans

> science has always been a broad-based ecological philosophy, based not on rational thought alone but also incorporating to the highest degree all aspects of interactions of "man in and of nature," i.e. the knowledge and truth gained from interaction of body, mind, soul, and spirit with all aspects of Nature.
>
> (2004, 46)

In dance research, one might be part of a research tradition in which these sources are not considered valid evidence, but that does not mean they do not exist. An orientation to one's intuitions and emotions in the moment can be a valuable tool for honing one's attention in research practice. What does your gut tell you? How did you feel? What ideas came to you even if you can't explain where they came from? Though this might be uncomfortable in some cases, Ruth Behar (1996) also calls on researchers to be "vulnerable" at the point of sharing their research by incorporating emotion and personal experiences relevant to the work into their writing and presentation.

Critically Observing

Although participant observation is a standard ethnographic method adopted by qualitative researchers in dance studies and dance education, critical observation is also key to artistic research in the studio and performance, as well as to dance science research in the laboratory. In fact, it is vital to almost every activity we can think of, from reading texts, to examining archival materials. By critically observing, we mean taking the care to understand and represent a text/situation/event in depth on its own terms before taking a stand. David Rosenwasser and Jill Stephen emphasize that learning to notice (what they call "notice and focus") requires that we get out of our habitual minds and suspend judgment so that we can stay open to what is there in front of us (2019). Similarly, Liz Lerman's Critical Response Process (2003) asks audience members to begin by stating only what they have noticed about a work (reserving questions and opinions for later stages of the process).

Being Willing to Try out Different Lenses and Scopes

As James Clifford has shown (1981), the surrealist dictum to "make the strange familiar and the familiar strange" has been operative in ethnography since the 1920s. Given the pressures of the academy and publishing, however, many researchers feel they must avoid ambiguity or diminish the complexity of their data in favor of being more accessible or taking a definitive stand. We argue, however, that being open—to surprise, ambiguity, complexity, change—is a fundamental orientation of research. Our late TWU colleague Dr. Linda Caldwell used Istvan Banyai's picture book *Zoom* (1998) to teach about how changing our perspective leads us to see radically different things. Johnny Saldaña, a noted scholar and author of methodology textbooks, emphasizes the importance of being willing to try something else if what you're doing is not working, writing, "If you notice that your methods choices may not be working for you or not delivering the emergent answers you need, be flexible with your approach and try a modified or different method altogether" (2016, 38–39).

Noticing When to Slow Down, When to Leap

When Matthew was completing his doctoral degree, he would notice times he sat down at the computer to generate text for a course paper or his dissertation, and no words would come. He would sit for periods of time with ideas swirling around but none of them seemed ready to make it onto the screen. In these times he would step away from the computer and return to reading texts, seeing the authors as mentors and guides who could help provide structure and language for what he was trying to communicate. At other times, he would be reading scholarly material and have the sensation that his mind was full, like a gas tank that's topped off even though you keep trying to add those last few drops. Like the gas, the ideas needed to be put to use to make room for more. At these times he would step away from reading for a while and put the ideas into practice, in his teaching, in conversations with peers, and in his writing.

Noticing this pattern helped Matthew realize that, in a broader sense, there are ebbs and flows in the research process, times for input and times for output, times to slow down decision-making and times to leap boldly. This happens at each stage of the research process. In designing the research, it is essential to carefully and judiciously think through all aspects of the research so that they fit together as a cohesive and coherent system, but decisions eventually need to be made or the research will never proceed. Data collection with human participants is often an exercise in patience as you are forced to slow down when waiting to hear back from participants, then rushing to meet them when they are available. There is also a sense of ebb and flow in the sharing phase of research. Making a public claim can be one of the most intimidating aspects of the research process for novice researchers (experienced researchers too!). As the final product begins to come together, it is important to slow down, follow procedures to check the validity of the data, check for biases or assumptions in the analysis, and run tentative conclusions by peers and advisors. There comes a point, though, when, unless you are willing to take the leap, it all will have been for naught. There is no standard time for how long these phases take, but part of developing a research practice is attending to these shifts in oneself, particularly orienting to when one has stayed in a phase too long and is no longer being productive.

Research Practices

Ethics and orientations are enacted through practices. The practices of a research project are typically described as reviewing literature, forming research questions and designs, collecting data, analyzing data, and reporting findings. But as we discussed in the first chapter, when we were teaching in a department in which the students aspired to be dancemakers, dance educators, and dance researchers among other professional pathways, the above terms for the research process were used in courses, but without consideration for what they actually meant for developing dance practice, dance studies, and dance education researchers. We sensed, however, that, though different language might be used in each of these areas, there was a commonality to what we actually did. Literature review was used when planning a new course or lecture. Data collection via participant observation was used in the choreography class when students wrote in choreographic journals. Data analysis happened in the technique class when students rehearsed phrases. This led to a pragmatic interdisciplinarity in which we sought to make course content and activity relevant to inquiry in these modes of professional practice.

As we de-emphasized the language used to describe and teach research methods, and focused more on the practices researchers should be engaged in, verbs became important motifs. We adopted a succinct list of verbs from Ritchhart, Church, and Morris' *Making Thinking Visible* (2011) that we felt supported the systematicity needed in research but was flexible enough to apply to a variety of settings:

- Set Up
- Generate
- Sort and Connect
- Elaborate
- Share

We propose these as a common set of practices across dance research. Though the list is succinct, there is a constellation of ideas behind each verb[8] as shown in Table 2.1, which provides examples of what the practices may look like for different research communities or approaches.

Though these verbs are in a vertical order, we are not suggesting that research proceeds linearly; indeed, most often, it does not (see Figure 2.1). For instance, a qualitative research project might begin when a teacher casually *sorts and connects* everyday experiences from the classroom on the journey home. They might decide to *generate* more systematic observations of the classroom, only to realize after *sorting, connecting, and elaborating* that they need to *set up* their inquiry with more knowledge about classroom dynamics and *generate* additional observations. They might *sort and connect* those observations, *elaborate* on them by telling a story about the classroom which is *shared* with other educators at a conference. Or a choreographer might *set up* a new work by *generating* movement material and then going through a process of *elaborating* on that material. Later the choreographer might *sort and connect* the movement phrases into spatial and temporal configurations *generating* additional movement in order to *elaborate* and build internal coherence. They might then *share* the work as a public performance.

Contributors to this book were invited, but not required, to adopt this framework and to reflect on how it might or might not uniquely manifest in their own practice. Following are the questions we sent to all contributors:

Table 2.1 Brief descriptions of research practices in four different disciplinary approaches

	A Practice as Research Approach	A Science or Social Science Quantitative Approach	A Social Science Qualitative Approach	A Humanities Qualitative Approach
Set up	Physical practice; establishment of conceptual or esthetic framework	Justification of hypothesis through literature review	Establishment of conceptual framework through literature review	Establishment of conceptual framework through literature review or historiographic work
Generate	Generate movement	Measure	Observe and interview	Observation or "reading" of performances, texts, or events
Sort and connect	Organize movement in space, time, community, context	Statistical analysis	Coding	Analysis, often with and through critical theory
Elaborate	Revise for internal coherence, world-building, theory building	Interpret statistics	Interpret experience through thick description of codes	Crafting of rich prose that performs the analysis on the page
Share	Perform, publish, or present	Publish or present	Publish or present	Publish or present

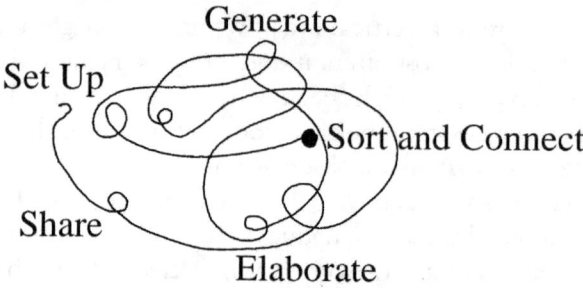

Figure 2.1 A non-linear path through the practices.

- Set up
    - What disciplinary practices or conversations inform your research?
    - What counts as knowledge? What themes pervade?
    - How is your work in conversation with the work of others?
    - How do you decide what to explore?
    - How do you position yourself in relation to the inquiry?
    - What ethical issues arise during the setup phase of the inquiry?

- Generate
  - What counts as data/practice?
  - How is it generated, collected, and documented?
  - What ethical issues arise during the generation phase of the inquiry?
- Sort and Connect
  - How do you make sense of the information you've collected or practices in which you've engaged?
  - How do you test, perceive, or generate relationships in and among the practices and/or data you've collected?
  - What ethical issues arise during the sort and connect phase of the inquiry?
- Elaborate
  - How do these processes lead to new explanations, practices, and/or questions?
  - How do you ensure your work is good/valid/believable?
- Share
  - How do you share your work?
  - What ethical issues arise during the sharing phase of your inquiry?

By thinking of dance research as a recursive process of engaging in these practices, phrased as verbs, we focus on what we do, pointing to alignments across our subdisciplines. By asking questions, rather than proscribing steps, we become and remain curious about what we do at each stage of the process. Readers will notice that authors throughout this book engaged these questions in part or as a whole, and addressed them explicitly or implicitly. In some cases, authors even renamed steps in line with the ontologies or practices of the dances being researched. This type of divergent engagement with research practices outlined above aligns with our suggestion, via Foster, that the dance tells the researcher how it should be researched.

Conclusion

We suggest, in this chapter, that becoming a researcher involves repeated, incremental engagement with the ethics, orientations, and practices of disciplinary communities. As you read Parts 2 through 5 we invite you to keep these procedural, relational, and situational ethics; orientations; and practices in mind and become curious about how the authors situate them (or don't) in their own work. Where are commonalities and differences? How do they resonate or dissonate? When is there a theme and variation? What are the motifs? Where is there point and counterpoint? How do other worldviews bump into these practices and orientations in order to create a productive space for moving the practice of research in dance forward (or inward, or outward, or toward, etc.) in meaningful ways? How do these chapters invite you to think creatively about ethics, orientations, and practices to and with your own shifting, malleable, porous dance research?

Notes

1 It is not our intention to review international and national research ethics codes and enforcement mechanisms in detail here, but rather to gesture to what these generally cover. The US Department of Health and Human Services Office for Human Research Protections publishes an exhaustive "International Compilation of Human Research Standards" that lists agencies responsible for providing ethical guidance and compliance for international and national research, including general guidance, as well as that for medical and social/behavioral research. See https://www.hhs.gov/ohrp/sites/default/files/2020-international-compilation-of-human-research-standards.pdf, accessed July 23, 2021.
2 In addition to the statements in *Creating New Futures*, open letters detailing specific experience of white supremacy in arts organizations published by Nana Chinara (2020) and Emily Johnson (2021) have circulated widely on social media.
3 Other organizations addressing these issues include Dance Artists' National Collective (DANC), "advocating for safe, equitable, and sustainable working conditions for dancers in the U.S." (https://danceartistsnationalcollective.org) and The Dance Union podcast (@TheDanceUnion).
4 See, for example, Contact Improv Consent Culture. See https://contactimprovconsentculture.com/
5 Thank you to Jonathan W. Marshall for this personal communication.
6 Of course archival research and chorographic analysis both may also involve live participants. See Höfling, Chapter 10, and Candelario et al., Chapter 9.
7 Personal communication July 22, 2021. Preston recommends the History of Indigenous Peoples Network (HIPN) at York University for more information: https://robarts.info.yorku.ca/research-clusters/hip/.
8 For example, Ritchhart et al. also include this list of skills: observing closely and describing what's there, building explanations, reasoning from evidence, making connections, considering different viewpoint and perspectives, capturing the heart and forming conclusions, wondering and asking questions, uncovering complexity and going below the surface (2011, 11). Rosenwasser and Stephen suggest Five Analytical Moves: (1) suspend judgment, (2) define significant parts and how they are related, (3) make the implicit explicit. push observations to implications, (4) look for patterns of repetition and contrast for anomalies, (5) keep reformulating explanations and questions (2019, 2).

Works Cited

Ahmed, Sara. 2010. "Orientations Matter." In *New Materialisms: Ontology, Agency, and Politics*, edited by Diana Coole and Samantha Frost, 234–257. Durham, NC: Duke University Press.

Banyai, Istvan. 1998. *Zoom*. New York: Puffin Books.

Behar, Ruth. 1996. *The Vulnerable Observer: Anthropology That Breaks Your Heart*. Boston: Beacon Press.

Cajete, Gregory. 2004. "Philosophy of Native Science." In *American Indian Thought: Philosophical Essays*, edited by Anne Waters, 45–57. Malden, MA: Blackwell Publishing Ltd.

Chinara, Nana. 2020. "An Open Letter to Arts Organizations Rampant with White Supremacy." *Medium*, May 27. See https://medium.com/@nanachinara/an-open-letter-to-arts-organizations-rampant-with-white-supremacy-4540f8f0e45f. Accessed January 20, 2022.

Clifford, James. 1981. "On Ethnographic Surrealism." *Comparative Studies in Society and History* 23, no. 4 (October): 539–564.

Creating New Futures: Phase 1: Working Guidelines for Ethics & Equity in Presenting Dance & Performance. 2020. See https://drive.google.com/drive/folders/1B6bbiFTBP1UAvt9qFchr7nLUndh7zorA. Accessed January 20, 2022.

Ellis, Carolyn. 2007. "Telling Secrets, Revealing Lives: Relational Ethics in Research with Intimate Others." *Qualitative Inquiry* 13, no. 1 (January): 3–29. https://doi.org/10.1177/1077800406294947.

Guillemin, Marilys, and Lynn Gillam. 2004. "Ethics, Reflexivity, and 'Ethically Important Moments' in Research." *Qualitative Inquiry* 10, no. 2: 261–280. https://doi.org/10.1177/1077800403262360

Johnson, Emily. 2021. "A Letter I Hope in the Future, Doesn't Need to be Written." *Medium* January 22. See https://emily-72967.medium.com/a-letter-i-hope-in-the-future-doesnt-need-to-be-written-52e1d6fd5350. Accessed January 20, 2022.

Lave, Jean and Etienne Wenger. 1991. *Situated Learning: Legitimate Peripheral Participation*. Cambridge: Cambridge University Press.

Lerman, Liz and John Borstel. 2003. *Liz Lerman's Critical Response Process: A Method for Getting Useful Feedback on Anything You Make, from Dance to Dessert*. Takoma Park, MD: Dance Exchange.

Madison, D. Soyini. 2012. *Critical Ethnography: Method, Ethics, and Performance*, 2nd edition. Thousand Oaks: SAGE Publications, Inc.

Opdal, P.M. 2001. "Curiosity, Wonder and Education seen as Perspective Development." *Studies in Philosophy and Education* 20: 331–344. doi.org/10.1023/A:1011851211125

Ritchhart, Ron, Mark Church, and Karin Morrison. 2011. *Making Thinking Visible: How to Promote Engagement, Understanding, and Independence for All Learners*, 1st edition. San Francisco: Jossey-Bass.

Rosenwasser, David and Jill Stephen. 2019. *Writing Analytically*, 8th edition. Boston: Cengage.

Saldaña, Johnny. 2016. *The Coding Manual for Qualitative Researchers*, 3rd edition. Thousand Oaks: Sage.

Silvia, P.J. (2017). "Curiosity." In: The Science of Interest, P. O'Keefe and J. Harackiewicz, eds., 97-108. Cham, Switzerland: Springer. doi.org/10.1007/978-3-319-55509-6_5

Zuroski, Eugenia. 2020. "'Where Do You Know From?': An Exercise in Placing Ourselves Together in the Classroom." *MAI: Feminism and Visual Culture* 5 "Feminist Pedagogies" (Winter 2020). See https://maifeminism.com/where-do-you-know-from-an-exercise-in-placing-ourselves-together-in-the-classroom/?fbclid=IwAR0txEmdqF8eCsQ9UmuI3cW1IxGnYtb-SMyYGCR4wUbqP73pta_bYQU7UtM. Accessed July 23, 2021.

Part 2
Dance Practice

3
Introduction to Research in Dance Practice

Practice-as-Research

Vida Midgelow

Practice-as-Research (PaR) (with its variants, artistic research, practice-based-research and performance-as-research, among others)[1] has been driven largely by the perceived need to challenge conventional university paradigms.[2] At the same time, PaR is part of the wider shift toward "choreographic thinking" and the development of what have been called "choreographic objects," emboldening us to extend our understanding of the choreographic (see, e.g. Forsythe website, Joy 2014, Lepecki 2006, McGregor website).[3]

As such, the insights and potentialities of PaR can be seen to be part of contemporary choreographic developments more broadly and there are many parallels to be found between the practices of contemporary dance makers and the practices developed more explicitly and intentionally as research activities emerging from within universities. Indeed, the synchronous developments of PaR and contemporary dance-making through the 1990s onward are clear. Both evidence increasing interdisciplinarity and deep levels of contextual awareness, including the relatedness of the wide field of choreographic practice to cultural and critical discourses, encompassing reflexive and rigorous processes that extend the choreographic field within and beyond notions of dance and dancing. These parallel developments can be seen to be co-constituting a field in which dance-making is being re-figured as an epistemic practice: a field no longer defined in a disciplinary fashion, by style or genre for example, but by an approach in which the choreographic reaches out from its associations with dance as a set of language possibilities and production protocols, becoming instead a research practice that finds many modes of articulation in the world.

Inherently concerned with aesthetic and experiential embodiments, choreographic researchers can be seen to elaborate what Jenn Joy has described as the "possibility of sensual address" (Joy 2014, 1). Such sensual address can perhaps reveal "less visible, less legible moments of art, of history, and of knowledge production" to offer a "productive disciplinary and discursive intervention" (Joy 2014, 4). Such interventions can be seen in the chapters that follow to encompass the blurring of dancing, writing, and feminism (Jo Pollitt), the development of inclusive and situated community dance (Aurelia Chillemi and Victoria Fortuna), the use of the creative practice to make spaces for blackness (John-Paul Zaccarini), and the development of creative methods (Eiko Otake).

This is not to say that all dance-making is research and, whilst blurring many boundaries, there are often different structures and agendas at work for choreographers and choreographers-as-researchers as the interview with US-based Japanese dance artist Eiko Otake attests in Chapter 7. She asks: "What do we gain by saying that choreography is research?" (Otake 96) suggesting that the prevalence of research is an invasion of academic vocabulary. Her resistance to the language of research and discourses of the academy usefully reminds us that undertaking choreography as research whilst entailing related creative processes also entails differences, not the least of which is the intention of the endeavor. A researcher may not always foreground the producing of artworks. Instead, a research-driven approach to practice foregrounds processes of inquiry and the knowledges embedded in and generated through dancing and dance-making.

Otake considers her work to involve aspects of research, particularly in relation to the subjects of her dances. Her processes of making entail exploring in the studio, continually monitoring her own practice, as well as publishing about her work. In relation to the work *Attending* (2020), she describes practicing dying which she explored following the death of her mother. Through practicing and rehearsing, words she prefers to researching, she explains how she gets closer to the feeling of dying. Through practicing and repetition over long periods—be it dying, closely watching one person, or screaming—she creates memorable experiences for audiences.

The notion of practicing that arises in Otake's interview chimes with the writing of performance scholar and practitioner Ben Spatz. Spatz points out that the term "practice" (as key to practice-as-research) entails embodied repetition (2018). This practicing is the basis for experimentation wherein techniques of the bodily arise from the body as the first affordance. Embodied technique is everywhere, notes Spatz; it "is the very stuff of life, the fabric of practical knowledge" and it provides the "epistemic threads along which life is lived and experienced" (2015, 47). Working with/through the bodily as a method of practice-as-research in dance is core. This bodily endeavor, whilst commonplace in dancing and dance-making, gives rise to PaR's radical intervention into conventional academic work by placing the lived in-motion experience of the researcher at the center of research.

This approach and the centrality of embodiment are not without difficulties as Jo Pollitt's chapter "Choreographies of Presence: Improvisation as feminist practice" elucidates in Chapter 4. She positions writing as dancing and improvisatory research in terms of her white settler status in Australia, acknowledging the integral practices of attunement in First Nations communities. In doing so she calls upon the notion of mid-embodiments. These mid-embodiments are "unfixed, can rupture binaries of (western) positionality, and engage in the partial and relational as a feminist practice of our times" (52). Bringing this rupturing to improvisations she articulates how she attends to the potential of instability and the margins in her work *comma piece*. Using the practice and the metaphor of the grammatical comma, she articulates this as a place of turning. *comma piece* is part of her writing as dancing practice in which writing is re-figured, becoming a "mid-embodied continuation of dancing." This writing is emergent rather than a tool for reflection or analysis, and contributes to expanded choreographies, exemplifying, cultural attunement, and partial knowings.

This work, akin to PaR more generally, implicitly entails the reassessment of the status of and relationships between processes of making and processes of theorizing, wherein the research is not (only) thinking *about* art (as external object), but is engaged in materially creative thinking *within and through* the practices of art making, and, in this case, improvisation and writing. In doing so, choreographic researchers usurp the traditional character of knowledge, by "a refusal to distance thinking from moving, knowing from being, thought from the material specificity of bodies" (Brown 2019, n.p.).

Increasingly PaR addresses ethico-political and societal problems for, as Canadian dance dramaturg Pil Hansen has argued, the potential of PaR lies in bringing something anew into the world, making "jumping points" (2018, 27) from which their audiences/participants can experience the world differently. Such an approach to research provides a strong foundation from which to activate change—acting in what artist researchers Paula Kramer and Stephanie Misa describe as a "tool of critique." Whilst work explicitly engaged in social change addressing social injustice has been until recently less common in choreographic PaR,[4] practice researchers often "have a strong impetus for questioning dominant modes of sense-making and knowledge creation" (2019, n.p.). They point to the work of Mika Elo, University of Arts Helsinki, who argues that practice researchers "not only *facilitate* cultural processes, but furthermore *embed* them in a setting that shapes and transforms these processes, and, at the same time, *shows* something of the effects of their embedding" (see Kramer and Misa 2019, n.p.). Yet whilst potentially transformative, PaR, like other areas of academic research and professional dance leadership, has been dominated by

English-speaking, white, able-bodied, male voices. Challenging this normative position by asking, which bodies, which voices, which cultural practices are present, which are heard, is crucial to the development of PaR.

The work of John-Paul Zaccarini and Aurelia Chillemi and Victoria Fortuna starts to address this gap. Zaccarini, a black diasporic cross-disciplinary performer-researcher, currently based at the University of Stockholm, charts the project FutureBlackSpace, presenting artistic research methods for establishing creative space for artists of color in predominantly white institutions. He describes how the preliminary workshops for the project, conducted in the aftermath of George Floyd's murder, highlighted the urgent need to create research spaces relevant to the specific needs of black practitioners. Articulating the excess labor and resultant silencing of artists of color, FutureBlackSpace connects art, activism, and healing outside of the white gaze and unhindered by neocolonial structures. Generating a space/time for what he calls "weaving," the work is grounded in the specificity of the artist of color experiences. Using creative processes such as free association, automatic writing, memoir, imaginary letter writing, poetry, singing, and dancing, Zaccarini describes facilitating a disentanglement from whiteness to sketch afro-futurist fictions. Markedly not intended for viewing in a public, white, space, participants are invited to share their processes—contributing to the fabric of the weave—creating a resistant and healing space of community. Researching how to prototype FutureBlackSpaces, rather than what artworks this might generate, Zaccarini expands PaR, generatively providing a path through which to navigate racism and institutional contexts, enabling artistic self-care and critical evaluation, through connectedness and reflection for participants, as well as tools for the future.

Aurelia Chillemi and Victoria Fortuna also engage in dance-making as activism by responding to the specific situatedness of their communities. Their chapter "Community Dance and Collection Creation: Art, Health, and Social Development Across the Hemisphere" discusses two community/pedagogy focused collectives—Bailarines Toda la Vida (Dancers for Life) and Community Dance at Reed. Addressing themes of social injustice, both collectives seek to inculcate ethical values through the creation of inclusive class structures and flexible choreographic approaches. Reflecting the very different socio-geographical context of the two collectives, Dancers for Life, located in Buenos Aires, have explored the memories of Argentina's last civic–military dictatorship (1976–1983), colonial histories of violence, and accompanying concerns of land and borders. Community Dance, based at Reed College in Portland, Oregon, focuses on racial justice and the unequal distribution of resources, in response to the elite institution in which it resides. Articulating the decision-making processes that underpin the collectives, Chillemi and Fortuna seek to support the future of community-based dance research.

Promoting self-management and horizontality, they acknowledge the difficulty of retaining openness whilst promoting community. Bringing people together as "neighbors" that are in proximity rather than subsumed into sameness, they draw together movers across different ages, communities, and backgrounds. They describe their embodied research as developing across four areas: movement education, creativity, community, and collective creation. The enacting of these approaches embeds social justice into the processes of dancing and dance-making and reaches beyond the immediate participants through performance and writing.

The diverse, participatory, and embodied encounters described in this Part are each deeply informed by the authors' specialist knowings as dance makers and artists. Recognizing the situated nature of their work, they evidence the following of rigorous yet often internally derived creative processes. They each use embodied experiences and movement as a means to understanding, each in different ways asking questions about the nature and processes of arts practice, as well as articulating and sharing their experiential insights through artistic and written means. As such, what we read here shows ways in which creative practices make a difference, reaching audiences such that the commonly defined routes for the knowledges generated in universities become diversified.

In summation, to engage in PaR is to be responsive to embodied and emergent knowledge. It is also to cultivate an essentially material, esthetic, and experiential attitude that requires a reconsideration of how we undertake and communicate research, transforming the scholarly task of doing research into dance-making. These approaches are profoundly different from the prevailing models for conducting research, based as they are upon a quest for certainty, whereas dance-making appeals to uncertainty. This is both the difficulty and strength of PaR. Breaking through the illusion of certitude, and its oft-sensuous excess, is perhaps the very pleasure of this work and core to what PaR has to offer to the wider research community.

Notes

1 There has been extensive mapping and vigorous debate about the naming of this mode of research. See the introductory chapters in Arlander et al. (2018) for a good account and contrasting views. I have selected to use the term "Practice-as-Research" (PaR) as it is the most commonly used in my own context here in the United Kingdom and it has been the term used at several international dance / performance conferences (including the Dance Studies Association and International Federation for Theatre Research). Whatever the term used however, what

is important to me, and what is articulated here, is the view that dance-making in PaR be positioned as both the site of research enquiry and a significant mode of dissemination.

2   In the United Kingdom debates about the acceptance of arts practices within the academy have also been shaped by the government Research Excellence Framework (REF). The requirements of this national audit of research means that arts researchers have needed to not only gain acceptance within their own universities, but also engage with the auditing system to ensure their practice was valued equally to other forms of research.

3   This introduction borrows from the author's previous writing to frame the new contributions that appear in this collection. If you wish to explore these ideas more deeply they can be found in Midgelow "Practice-as-Research" (2019).

4   This observation by Kramer and Misa was derived from recent Society of Artistic Research Conferences (SAR 2017 and 2018) and works recently published and peer-reviewed in artistic research platforms such as JAR (http://jar-online.net/), VIS (https://www.en.visjournal.nu/), OAR (https://www.oarplatform.com/), or Ruukku (http://ruukku-journal.fi/home). They suggest that these show that only a few are overtly critical or political in terms of explicitly seeking social change, engaging with injustices and demanding equal access.

Works Cited

Arlander, Annette, Bruce Barton, Melanie Dreyer-Lude, and Ben Spatz. 2018. *Performance as Research: Knowledge, Methods, Impact.* London: Routledge.

Brown, Carol. 2019. "A Field Guide for Choreography as Research." In *Researching (in/as) Motion: A Resource Collection, Artistic Doctorates in Europe.* https://nivel.teak.fi/adie/field-guide-for-choreography-as-research/. Accessed January 14, 2021.

Forsythe, William. "William Forsythe: Choreographic Objects." www.williamforsythe.com. Accessed February 2, 2018.

Hansen, Pil. 2018. "Research-based Practice: Facilitating Transfer across Artistic, Scholarly, and Scientific Inquiries." In *Performance as Research: Knowledge, Methods, Impact*, edited by Arlander, Annette, Bruce Barton, Melanie Dreyer-Lude, and Ben Spatz, 32–49. London: Routledge.

Joy, Jenn. 2014. *The Choreographic.* Cambridge, MA: The MIT Press.

Lepecki, André. 2006. *Exhausting Dance: Performance and the Politics of Movement.* New York: Routledge

McGregor, Wayne. "Studio Wayne McGregor." www.waynemcgregor.com. Accessed February 2, 2018.

Kramer, Paula and Stephanie Misa. 2019."Artistic Research as a Tool of Critique." In *Researching (in/as) Motion: A Resource Collection, Artistic Doctorates in Europe*. https://nivel.teak.fi/adie/field-guide-for-choreography-as-research/. Accessed January 14, 2021.

Midgelow, Vida. 2019. "Practice-as-Research." In *The Bloomsbury Companion to Dance*, edited by Sherril Dodds, 111–144. London: Bloomsbury Academic.

Otake, Eiko. 2020. "Attending." https://www.eikootake.org/attending.

Spatz, Ben. 2015. *What a Body Can Do: Technique as Knowledge, Practice as Research*. London: Routledge.

———. 2018. "Introduction III: Mad Lab – or Why we can't do Practice as Research." In *Performance as Research: Knowledge, Methods, Impact*, edited by Annette Arlander, Bruce Barton, Melanie Dreyer-Lude, and Ben Spatz, 219–223. London: Routledge.

4
Choreographies of Presence
Improvisation as Feminist Practice

Jo Pollitt

Introduction: Improvising Presence as a Method for Attending to Unstable Futures

This chapter begins with a score borrowed from a performance 20 years ago at the Perth Institute of Contemporary Art in Western Australia. Dancer and friend Jonathon Sinatra began a solo dance performance sitting in a chair on the stage and quietly addressed the audience:

> I'm just going to take a few moments for you to get used to me and for me to get used to you
>
> , , , , , , , , , , , , , ,
> , , , , , , , , , , , , ,

Twenty years after that performance, I walked into Dr. Roma Winmar's office—Noongar artist and elder-in-residence at my university—to ask her thoughts on a news broadsheet called Feminism 101 I was creating in collaboration with fellow feminist researchers specifically for academics in higher education. In that exchange, I experienced a similar, albeit unannounced, score. *the heft and weave of presence.* Nan Roma delayed. She unpicked time and expected I would meet her in the quiet and uncomfortable charge. In the ensuing moments, linear time dismantled and the experience of presence was voluminous and reverberating. I noticed my body participating in improvised adjustments of response and felt an inviting of unsettling and an aliveness of relations. The active practicing of not knowing and remaining behind the urge to propel into comfort and surety created an expanded space for attending differently. The exchange brought me back to thinking with the pedagogical application of presence in a return to the question I asked repeatedly during my doctoral studies several years ago: *What is it our bodies know before we do?* And further to this, how can activating choreographies of presence provoke more nuanced

DOI: 10.4324/9781003145615-6

receptivity and response-ability inside the complexity and flux of emergent relations in an unstable world?

> practicing staying in the moment you know is leaving
> / practice staying with leaving /

The dominant paradigms of knowledge production are becoming increasingly unstuck amid an unstable world of perpetual disruption and crisis linked to physical disconnection, global pandemic, and climate change—the intersections of which are gendered, raced, classed, and far from equal (Gray et al. 2021). One way to make visible these inequities is by attending to one's own body through understanding presence as a practice of improvisation—not to persist with an individualist logic, but as a method for attuning to an ever-changing present and prioritizing embodied knowledge and other ways of sensing/being/knowing. Choreographies of presence are engaged through the practice of scores that position not knowing, unhiding, and relationality as a mid-embodied (Myers and Dumit 2011) and feminist practice.

Writing as Dancing

In writing like I dance (Pollitt 2017), I work with attention to energetic state, associational response, and the continuum of dancing. I trick myself to try and catch up with what my body knows before I can name it. As content retreats in time before I can catch it, my body becomes more deliberately attuned in the noticing and the pace of writing. Similarly, the paradox of *writing as dancing* works with an actively improvised decision-making process while simultaneously trying to catch content in words which enables a straddling of worlds. Improvisation is an emergent form by its very process and this project of transparency is a pressured place, locating the practitioner as both an agent of form and a host of not-knowing.

1. *Dance yourself into writing*
   Dance for four minutes and, while maintaining momentum and energetic state, continue this dancing as writing on the screen or page
2. *Write yourself into dancing*
   Begin writing with pen or keyboard, and write for as long as it takes until the writing can only be continued in movement off the page

Writing as dancing serves as a methodology to expand platforms for dancerly knowledge in generating more transparent texts around what the body knows before we can recognize or frame it. In the interdisciplinary worlds I inhabit,

I believe more than ever that dancers are at the forefront of tangible ways of thinking that have applications in expanded studios as well as in the everyday. As Vida Midgelow writes, "Through leaky excessiveness disciplinary bounds are broken, as improvisation is understood here as un/disciplinary practice that proceeds toward a productive (un)knowing" (2017, n.p.).

Writing as dancing, as a practice that insists on writing as a *continuation* of dancing rather than representation, can be applied to other disciplines and processes to uncover hidden stories and ways of unsettling dominant paradigms. For example, in a 2020 project focused on children and climate futures called *Conversations with Rain*,[1] experiments of *writing as raining* or, "rainwriting," imagined a continuation of rain in poetic form that ignited a textual downpour of climate, drought, scale, momentum, and movement. In another example, I applied *writing as dancing* to a practice called Drawing Breath by Lilly Blue,[2] where I worked with an undergraduate dance class to establish the practice of making a single mark for every in-breath and a mark for every out breath and then continued these marks made from breathing into words. The collective presence and attention of the group became tangibly amplified. As dancer Becky Hilton notes, "The newness is in the way we perceive things; it is there in the time and in the responsibility, we take to notice, to comprehend and to acknowledge our constant transformations" (2017, 6). We then continued this score of *writing as drawing breath* into dancing off the page and into the studio.

The premise for each of the *writing as dancing* scores in this chapter is to continue on the page the experiential dynamic of dancing and to practice choreographies of presence that invite transparency. I work on a laptop as it involves the physicality and specificity of both hands; the keyboard is for the most part divided with the left taking t and g and the right hand taking the b. The left hand is responsible for 14 letters, the right for 12. An unequal responsibility given I am right-handed. But the right hand is responsible for both, and.; the comma and the full stop. For the most part, my dominant hand is responsible for punctuation. And for returning to the next line. The activation of fingertips is an integral part of the practice. The limitations of the keyboard act as palette and collaborator in generating a kind of naïve notation I use as a poetic device to expand range rather than as static translation. The decisions between the pressing of letters, the making or dividing of room with a tiny parade of forward slash markers /// /, the turn of an elbow <. The throw of arms in the air \ o /. The lineage of experimental poetry, performance writing, and sound art makes room for a dancer to viscerally enter the page as "something you pass through" (Hall 2013, 84).

I work with the same process of decision-making in performance to compose each word and mark made in the pace, tone, and mid-embodiment of writing.

The borders between dancing and writing are porous and my practice remains in the slippage of page and/as studio/stage.

3. *How long is the life of a movement?*
   a) Attempt to dance the length of the life of a movement /// // / do this for a continuous period of time notice differing lengths and lives. b) Attempt to write the length of the life of an idea, thought, or energetic shift. //// / /// / do this for a continuous period of time notice differing lengths and lives on the page.

Presence, Improvisation, and Mid-Embodiment

Working as an interdisciplinary artist during a three-year postdoctoral fellowship situated in environmental education, I came to understand the deeply relational practice of dance improvisation as keenly relevant in thinking with the paradigm of global instability and precarity. Improvisation is a practice of attending to and being in relation with the world through a perpetual response system (Pollitt 2019), activated in a mode of what Natasha Myers and Joe Dumit call, "mid-embodiment." Following a series of haptic experiments with scientists, they posited that,

> Where "embodiment" risks a tendency to naturalise and take for granted bodies as a kind of pre-existing substrate, we insist on partial and tentative mid-embodiments in such a way as to evoke the ongoing and never ending process scientists participate in as they search for a place to stand and speak about their findings. A responsive body is one uncommitted to one mode of embodiment over another; it is a willing to move with and be moved by another.
> (2011, 249)

Posthumanist and feminist new materialist scholars (see particularly Alaimo 2010; Barad 2007; and Haraway 2003), support the urgency and relevance of improvisation as a practice of mid-embodied attention in grappling with cultivating practices of being in better relation. The need for different kinds of strategies and processes for mobilizing relations is increasingly vital as it becomes no longer possible to continue with anthropogenic business as usual models. Paying attention to, and with, the body helps to bring attention to the spaces and difficult histories we inhabit. Listening with the physical imagination of the whole body can help to slow down the immediacy of flight or fight responses and make room for a wider and perhaps more collective response system. Bodies are unstable and this instability directly connects us with other human and more-than-human processes. The concept of mid-embodiment offers a less fixed form of engagement "hovering in a space of not knowing" with others and the world and acknowledges embodied responses that are "partial, incomplete, and labile" (Myers and Dumit 2011, 246). This understanding of lability acknowledges that relational spaces are not without tensions.

Understanding presence as a process that is always in flux, and thus always improvisational, sees it operate in the interstices of people, place, politics, and things, as a practice of relationality. In returning to my encounter with Nan Roma, I notice how my own staying with the energetic state of not knowing enabled connection by expanding the intersections that grapple with difference and complexity. Rather than focusing on the body as a human-centric agenda, I argue that paying attention to the body and the nuance of physical imagination through improvisation can dismantle the edges of the personal kinesphere (as described by Laban as the peripheral space around the body) to better understand the body as part of the unseparated naturecultures (Haraway 2003) we live with. Here, I bring attention to acknowledging that I live and practice on Whadjuk Noongar Country, and that the idea of naturecultures has been integral to First Nations practices and of elders past and present; in the Noongar language "ngarnk" is the same word for both sun and mother. In First Nations communities there is an inherent understanding of Country as kin, and kin as Country, and as a white settler in Western Australia, I understand these long-standing practices of attunement existed before the thinking-in-moving (Sheets-Johnstone 1966) paradigm of Western dance improvisation came to the fore in the 1960s. When we engage in movement improvisation we sense differently. I am interested in how applying the expanding of senses can deepen relations with the more-than-human world. It is here that presence as mid-embodied and unfixed can rupture binaries of (western) positionality, and engage in the partial and relational as a feminist practice of our times. Indeed, as Kramer writes, "Such a repositioning of the human seems to become growingly relevant in the context of the humanly caused ecological, economic, and political crises we are currently facing" (2016, 108).

4. *Writing with shifting focus*
   a) *write with an internal focus for one minute, b) write with a focus on the surface of the body for one minute, c) write while focusing beyond the horizon for one minute, d) write while maintaining focus in the room for one minute, e) write with all of the foci states at once*

Presence as Mid-Pause: The Comma Piece

My book, *The Dancer in Your Hands* < > (2020) developed from an experimental piece of *writing as dancing* that composer Cat Hope named as a score she called *the comma piece*. I performed the work as a solo accompanied by a small artist book called "this book has elbows" at Performing, Writing 2017 in New Zealand. Initially, I worked with the comma not as a device for tripping or interruption, but as a tool toward continuum. I used the comma as a bridge or extension between, rather than as a manufactured pause comma comma comma and to disrupt hierarchies of breathing and pace. *There is no state that can retrain the order of breathing* (Pollitt 2020, 25). I used the comma to extend the between as a way to undo (and draw attention to) the value and impossible volatility of beginnings and endings.

The comma became a turn and the use of "turn" in the work became synonymous with "comma," in that it is a physical encounter, a bend at the elbow, a lift of the knee. Turn as comma. Comma as elbow. The space extended between each change of direction. Turn comma turn. The eros of a turn toward. The angle of each turn, each elbow, each comma. Poet Marcella Polain responded to this thinking in a personal email adding that:

> The comma links, creates meaning, is integral to meaning. Repetition (of comma, or anything else) defamiliarizes so that it is made strange, becomes something other than itself. So, for me, comma stands in for something insisted, difficult to articulate or unspoken/silenced/taboo - the lived, embodied experience.
>
> (April 12, 2017)

Comma becomes a turn. Turn as a directional shift. Turn as a conceptual hinge. Turn as a waiting of time. Turn as changing the page. Turn as queer. Turn as repetition. Turn as a sickness. Turn as a righting of wrongs. Turn as deviation. Turn as revelation. In all of the corners, turns, and elbows a multi-directional and dancerly sensing is evident; turn as reorientation. My early training as a dancer involved the technique of spotting; focusing on a single fixed point to orient yourself in space in order to achieve multiple turns while not losing your place or falling over. However, Judith Butler posits "'turning around' as keeping open the possibility of not returning to the same place" (cited in Ahmed 2016, 483). And as Diana Taylor reiterates "Being with, in motion, accepts knowledge as a practice developed in transit with others not knowing what lies around the bend, always developing, never arriving" (2020, 26). The possibility that multiple turns could be otherwise navigated in the absence of a single fixed point of focus opened a possibility for a different kind of presence and a different kind of practice. And perhaps a different kind of academy.

> and then she comma recorded comma the sound comma of scoring comma in the base of her spine comma where fingers comma print comma attention comma differently comma soundly comma tearing comma any comma precedent comma of love comma into tiny comma repetitions comma commitment comma and comma while comma staying comma she opens comma in hallways comma countries comma perfect ovation of pages comma bird call

feelers comma scar sung antlers comma creases comma carbon kept sense comma split comma by range comma not axe comma gusts comma

, , , , , , , , , , , , ,

Presence-in-Moving: A Feminist (Dis)Orientation

Contributing to Haraway's concept of staying with the trouble (2016), my personal proposal of *staying with leaving* works to enact a kind of *radical impermanence* (Pollitt 2019) that enables a commitment to choreographies of presence that are immediate but unfixed. *Staying with leaving* takes the pressure off the individual to be "sure" and instead invites a state of deepening and perpetual arrival in each unstable moment. This, for me, ignites a more rigorous presence that acknowledges the unfixity of attention and connects with the ongoing feminist project of activating other knowledges and paradigms of noticing inequities and intersections (see Ahmed 2006, Mauro-Flude 2021, Puig de la Bellacasa 2017, Tsing et al. 2017). It takes effort and practice, and this is where dancerly embodied knowledges can be practically applied across difficult conversations of our times as a feminist politics of presence that contributes to more expansive relations with human and more-than-human figurations.

Proponents of dance improvisation (see, e.g. Albright 2019; Albright and Gere 2003, Forti 1974; Midgelow 2013; Monson/iLand 2017; Raheem 2019) practice various modes of situated embodied responsiveness, which, as Susan Leigh Foster describes, "[entail] a vigilant porousness toward the unknown, a stance that can only be acquired through intensive practice" (2003, 7). This practice of presence through the mid-embodiment of improvisation is not an autotelic becoming "one" with the world but rather is keenly aware of differences and inequities and requires a perpetual effort of attention and decision-making. This engagement with the politics of presence makes it a feminist practice that demands risk and a commitment to being in relation through not-knowing. Such jostling and redressing of the patriarchal silencing by challenging the status quo and power of dominant paradigms of practice (including codified western dance forms) activates choreographies of presence that are nonlinear, relational, and embodied. Choreographies is used as plural here in an attempt to include and invigorate practices of presence that further contribute to this discussion and feminist activations of distributed and mid-embodied presence as resistance to patriarchal fixity. Practicing presence in this way unsettles and disorientates in ways that shift perspective "from a focus on visibility and stability to a sensibility energized by proprioception and instability" (Albright 2019, 50). Attending to instability in this way "can help to destabilize the positions of center and margin allowing us to attend to the shifting currents of political or cultural contexts differently" (Albright 2019, 50).

Turning: Moving into Writing

Western Australian Noongar author Kim Scott speaks of the "readiness of oral tradition to move into language" (2018, n.p.) as he communicates the vital importance of retaining oral stories and forgotten language in connecting with identity. The volition with which the improvising dancer is able to apply their practice in a written form relies on a viscerally honed readiness or state of preacceleration (Manning 2012) to continue the move into writing. Imperative to this "move into language" is acknowledging, contributing to, and propelling the discourse and practice in the growing field of dancing and writing. Simone Forti's logomotion (1974), L. Martina Young's dancing on the page (1996), Vida Midgelow and Jane Bacon's writing-dancing (2019), Alys Longley's movement-initiated writing (2014, 2015), Paea Leach's kinesthetic data (2020), Nancy Mauro-Flude's performing codes (2020), and Tru Paraha's choreopoetics (2020) all "unsettle the notion that methods of documentation are about taming and containing creative practices in tidy, conventional forms" (Longley 2014, 77). Dalisa Pigram's Listening to Country lab (2018), Vicky Van Hout's Plenty Serious Talk Talk (2018), and Trevor Ryan's Noongar performances connecting to waterscapes (Bracknell et al., 2021), are examples of Australian First Nations dance voices leading and further unsettling this discourse.

5. **Resistance**
   Begin writing with your dominant hand then switch to your non-dominant hand and continue this compositional state into dancing that inhabits the attention of the non-dominant.

In my own practice of *writing as dancing*, the paradox of working with both an actively improvised decision-making process while simultaneously trying to catch content is central to the project. Such a paradox enables the slippage between worlds (of attention to moment/movement and emergent content) to manifest on the page. The emergence of new creative texts can expand knowledge about what dance can transfer of lived experience in written form. *The dancer in your hands < >* (Pollitt 2020) is an experiment in queering the embodied states of dancerness (Hilton 2017) embedded in printed pages. In *writing as dancing*, I tend to the compression and attention of lived experience with the mantle of dancerly intelligence enabling an "outing" of hidden narratives of the body toward activating presence as a feminist practice.

6. **Spot-lit solo**
   Practice entering the screen or paper page as a spot-lit stage and perform a three-minute solo there.

Writing as dancing is a state of intent and a specifically located physical practice that began as an extended attempt to write like I dance. By working with attention to associational shifts, compositional rigor, and practiced energetic states, the work proposes that the dancer begins on the page from the vantage and experience of entering the stage as a solo improvising performer. The words and form are forged from the body in a "State of Dancingness" (Pollitt 2019) with the dancer as author in the process of *writing as dancing*. Emergent content is thus revealed as textual bodies of evidence, as dance documents you can hold in your hands. Rather than creative response, reflection, analysis, commentary, or archive, *writing as dancing* is the practice of writing, configured as a mid-embodied continuation of dancing. It proposes publication as performance.

Writing as dancing generates new creative texts written in the liminal spaces between the embodiment of professional dance practice, performance writing, and visual poetry. Working in this transcorporeal (Alaimo 2010) space makes room for the dancer-writer to apply the embodied compositional strategies of making decisions in the moment of performance to inhabit *writing as dancing*.

I practice *writing as dancing* as rigorously and immediately as live performance "to find a translation of form to make myself clear" (Winterson 1996, 105). *Writing as dancing* is a project to challenge ambiguity, not to reduce mystery but with an overarching score of inviting transparency. It hopes to make the dancerly ways in which I am practiced at accessing experience, fictive renderings, and physical imagination, communicable in a wider context. The presence of thinking-doing through *writing as dancing* does not knit together in the process of "printing" the dancer on the page; but rather extends beyond metaphor with its mediated materiality now in the hands of the reader as choreographer.

A Long Form Score Written as a Portal into the Practice of *Writing as Dancing*

Dancing is never solo; multiple idiolectic histories locate in a single body through the accumulated influence and distinct lineage of practice. In *writing as dancing*, emergent content arrives from the state of double embodiment as both dancer and writer, experienced as a rolling overlap of unfixed mid-embodiments. Here I work with the tools of solo improvisation, understanding that it is a deeply relational practice; practicing acute perception, heightening associational response, increasing range of energetic and compositional states, and honing receptivity through accessing physical imagination:

> Compress the tone in your body so that density is simultaneously porous and pressing. Listen to the sound of dancing, the sound of pace. Write inside pace, with the undersound. Write with it, type with it, bring your weight slightly

forward, be critical. Edit as you go, but keep going. Write in the middle of moving, with the same associational shifts as solo-ing. Perpetually arrive in each portal, choreographing in the moment of movement, rigorous, with applied directional shifts, following the life of one movement and then staying for longer. Tripping up. Turning. Staying when there is too much to say, write underneath the overwhelm. Work acutely, this is decision overlapping with decision, undercutting decision, building on decision, honing decision. Write in the awake. Write like you are looking into one of those 3D hidden pictures; simultaneously activate and relax your surfaces, concentrate and open the edges of your seeing to not knowing but press the keys with clarity, notice each pressing, turning. Write with your whole body, not about your body, not because of your body, just with your body comma comma comma. Be generous with each departure, there will be another and another, stay with leaving.

Mid-Embodied Conclusions

As Clare Croft argues, "Treating bodies like instruments rather than social forces forecloses queer possibility, which is often intertwined with the unspoken and the felt" (2017, 15). Presence as a social force has the potential to invite different kinds of relations necessary for living in an unstable and unequal world. Choreographies of presence as a feminist practice activates bodies as social forces in flux. These dancerly practices can be used across platforms to support a more active collective presence that can help people better connect and address the video conferencing glitches of our times by tending to moments of the unfamiliar or awkward with increased nuance and awareness of the potential of such moments of mid-embodiment. *Writing as dancing* is one method for practicing presence through improvisation and sense-making that challenge normative fixtures in both codified contemporary dance and in language to extend the interval   // ////   /   the turn   ,
   the comma   ,   ,   ,

"Bodies never do one thing or mean one thing. By embracing a messy, heterogeneous, even possibly contradictory queer, dance forges community, not in spite of, but through and with challenges and contradictions" (Croft 2017, 10).

\   o
/
|
/ \

To return to the introductory score, and turn to Roma—what of her thoughts of the feminist broadsheet? She appeared more interested in the space between us—in the wider world of each moment that was leaving, and in unsettling normative neoliberal paradigms of paying attention. When she offered her mother's words "no one above no one below" for printing, there was an authoritative dismissing of binaries and divisions, and a generative undoing of the status quo. The exchange was a subtle improvisation of attuning to the not-knowing of relations and staying with instability as a feminist practice and politics of presence. An urgent comma. An urgent practice. An urgent presence.

7. **Write like you dance**
"these are not words to hide behind" (Winterson 1996, 95).

Notes

1 See https://artgallery.wa.gov.au/learn/artist-activation/conversations-with-rain
2 See https://artgallery.wa.gov.au/learn/drawing-breath

Works Cited

Ahmed, Sara. 2006. *Queer Phenomenology: Orientations, Objects, Others*. Durham, NC: Duke University Press.

———. 2016. "Interview with Judith Butler." *Sexualities* 19, no. 4: 482–492. https://doi.org/10.1177/1363460716629607.

Alaimo, Stacy. 2010. *Bodily Natures: Science, Environment, and the Material Self*. Bloomington: Indiana University Press.

Albright, Ann Cooper. 2019. *How to Land: Finding Ground in an Unstable World*. New York: Oxford University Press.

Albright, Ann Cooper, and David Gere, eds. 2003. *Taken by Surprise: A Dance Improvisation Reader*. Middletown, CT: Wesleyan University Press.

Barad, Karen. 2007. *Meeting the Universe Halfway: Quantum Physics and the Entanglement of Matter and Meaning*. Durham, NC: Duke University Press.

Bracknell, Clint, Pierre Horwitz, Trevor Ryan, and Jonathan Marshall. 2021. "Performing *kayepa dordok* Living Waters in Noongar boodjar, South-Western Australia." *River Research and Applications*, 1–8. https://doi.org/10.1002/rra.3868.

Croft, Clare, ed. 2017. *Queer Dance: Meanings and Makings*. New York: Oxford University Press.

Forti, Simone. 1974. *Handbook in Motion*. Halifax: Press of the Nova Scotia College of Art and Design.

Foster, Susan Leigh. 2003. "Taken by Surprise: Improvisation in Dance and Mind." In *Taken by Surprise: A Dance Improvisation Reader*, edited by Ann Cooper Albright and David Gere, 398–404. Middletown, CT: Wesleyan University Press.

Gray, Emily, Jo Pollitt, and Mindy Blaise. 2021. "Between Activism and Academia: Zine-Making as a Feminist Response to Covid-19." *Gender and Education*, 1–19. https://doi.org/10.1080/09540253.2021.1931045.

Hall, John. 2013. *On Performance Writing*. Bristol: Shearsman Books.

Haraway, Donna. 2003. *The Companion Species Manifesto: Dogs, People, and Significant Otherness*. Chicago: Prickly Paradigm Press.

Hilton, Rebecca. 2017. "DANCERNESS." *Performance Paradigm* 13: 196–200.

Kramer, Paula. 2016. "Working with Physical Exposure in Contemporary Outdoor Movement Practice." *Art Research Journal* 3, no. 1: 107–128. https://periodicos.ufrn.br/artresearchjournal/article/viewFile/8458/6825.

Leach, Paea. 2020. "I Came Here to Dance." https://whalerider.hotglue.me. Accessed September 1, 2021.

Longley, Alys. 2014. *The Foreign Language of Motion*. Winchester: Winchester University Press.

———. 2015. *Radio Strainer*. Winchester: Winchester University Press.

Manning, Erin. 2012. *Relationscapes: Movement, Art, Philosophy*. Cambridge, MA: MIT Press.

Mauro-Flude, Nancy. 2021. "Caring about the Vast Non-Existent Horizon: Cosmographic Infrastructures and Performances of Care in Twenty-First Century Feminist Art Practice." In *Care Ethics and Art*, edited by Jacqueline Millner and Gretchen Coombs, 212–225. London: Routledge.

Mauro-Flude, Nancy, and Jo Pollitt. 2020. *Expanding Liminality: We Live Inside the Interstices of the World Located between Folds of the Red Fibres*. https://indeterminacy.ac.uk/conference-panels-11-12-videos/

Midgelow, Vida. 2013. "Sensualities: Experiencing/dancing/writing." *New Writing* 10, no. 1: 3–17. https://doi.org/10.1080/14790726.2012.693098

———. 2017. *Everywhere and Nowhere*. Choreographic Lab. https://www.choreographiclab.co.uk/everywhere-and-nowhere-performance-lecture/)

Midgelow, Vida L., Jane Bacon, Paula Kramer, Rebecca Hilton. 2019. *Researching (in/as) Motion: A Resource Collection*. Helsinki: Theatre Academy of the University of the Arts Helsinki.

Monson, Jennifer and iLAND. 2017. *A Field Guide to iLANDing: Scores for Researching Urban Ecologies*. New York: 53rd State Press.

Myers, Natasha, and Joe Dumit. 2011. "Haptics: Haptic Creativity and the Mid-Embodiments of Experimental Life." In *A Companion to the Anthropology of the Body and Embodiment*, edited by Frances E. Mascia-Lees, 239–261. Malden, MA: Wiley-Blackwell.

Paraha, Tru. 2020. "A Choreopoetics of Te Pō." *Ka Mate Ka Ora: A New Zealand Journal of Poetry and Poetics* 18: 29–41.

Pigram, Dalisa, and Rachael Swain. 2018. "Cut the Sky: Traces of Experimentation in Dance and Dramaturgy in the Age of the Anthropocene." *Global Performance Studies* 1, no. 2, https://doi.org/10.33303/gpsv1n2a4.

Pollitt, Jo. 2017. "She Writes like SShe Dances: Response and Radical Impermanence in Writing as Dancing." *Choreographic Practices* 8, no. 2: 199–218.

———. 2019. "The State of Dancingness: Staying with Leaving." *PARtake: The Journal of Performance as Research* 2, no. 2. https://doi.org/10.33011/partake.v2i2.419.

———. 2020. *The Dancer in Your Hands*. Perth, WA: UWA Publishing.

Puig de la Bellacasa, María. 2017. *Matters of Care: Speculative Ethics in More Than Human Worlds*. Minneapolis: University of Minnesota Press.

Raheem, Amara. 2019. "Speaking Dancer in-residence." In *Researching (in/as) Motion: A Resource Collection, Artistic Doctorates in Europe*, edited by Vida Midgelow, Jane Bacon, Paula Kramer, and Rebecca Hilton, n.p. Helsinki: Theatre Academy, University of the Arts. nivel.teak.fi/adie.

Scott, Kim. 2018. "Keynote Address." Presented at Australasian Association of Writing Programs Conference, Perth, Western Australia, November. https://aawp.org.au/annual-conference/23rd-annual-conference/.

Sheets-Johnstone, Maxine. 1966. *The Phenomenology of Dance*. Madison: University of Wisconsin Press.

Taylor, Diane. 2020. *¡Presente!: The Politics of Presence*. Durham, NC: Duke University Press. https://doi.org/10.2307/j.ctv14t48hf.

Tsing, Anna Lowenhaupt, Nils Bubandt, Elaine Gan, and Heather Anne Swanson, eds. 2017. *Arts of Living on a Damaged Planet*. Minneapolis: University of Minnesota Press.

Van Hout, Vicky. 2018. "Plenty Serious Talk Talk." https://www.youtube.com/watch?v=bVZ0v4IpAck

Winterson, Jeanette. 1996. *Art Objects: Essays on Ecstasy and Effrontery*. London: Vintage.

Young, L. Martina. 1996. *Swan: A Poetical Inquiry in Dance, Text & Memoir*. Self-published: A Poetic Body Publishing.

5
Community Dance and Collective Creation

Art, Health, and Social Development across the Hemisphere

Aurelia Chillemi and Victoria Fortuna

Despite robust conversations around community theater and performance, scholarly work documenting and/or analyzing community-based dance pedagogy and creation methods is relatively sparse.[1] Even less attention has been paid to work happening outside of the United States and Europe. This article explores the background and methodology behind two community dance projects, founded and directed by the co-authors, that share a model despite markedly different cultural and institutional contexts: Dancers for Life (National University of the Arts, Buenos Aires, Argentina, directed by Aurelia Chillemi) and Community Dance at Reed (Reed College, Portland, Oregon, USA, directed by Victoria Fortuna).[2] Dancers for Life directly inspired Community Dance at Reed; Fortuna founded the Portland-based project following her participation with Dancers for Life between 2010 and 2011. Both projects integrate community-based collectives that focus on the collective creation of original choreography with university classes that advance training in community dance pedagogy. Both projects assert dance—and artistic practice more broadly—as a social right capable of transforming, nurturing, and sustaining individuals and communities alike.

Dancers for Life and Community Dance at Reed meet for weekly movement sessions that are free and open to the public and strive to welcome a diverse group of participants with or without previous dance experience. Participants are welcome to attend one or every session and may join the collective creation process at any point. The choreographic structures of the works themselves are designed to expand and contract with the number of dancers who happen to be present at a particular performance. In their radical openness and flexibility,

DOI: 10.4324/9781003145615-7

both collectives aim to construct reparative, meaningful spaces for gathering among neighbors—old and new. They foster values of tolerance, empathy, solidarity, and respect through the creation of works that address salient social and political themes. Dancers for Life's works have focused on themes including the memory of the violence that marked Argentina's last civic–military dictatorship (1976–1983) and the relationship between land, borders, and colonial histories of violence. Community Dance at Reed's works have engaged with racial justice activism and the unequal distribution of resources.[3] As these themes indicate, the process aims to build critical awareness of how race, class, ability, nation, gender, sexuality, and place impact the ways that we relate to ourselves and one another in public (see Figures 5.1 and 5.2).

This article explores the practices and decision-making processes that shape these projects' shared model for community-based dance practice and pedagogy. Through movement education and collective creation, this methodology mobilizes dance's subversive and transgressive potential to foster the production of subjectivities and identities that sustain the individual as well as the group. By demonstrating how these projects' practices function in different sociocultural contexts, each shaped by different political exigencies, we hope that this chapter galvanizes and supports current and future community-based dance research projects.

Figure 5.1 De la Tierra, Dancers for Life, 2019. Copyright Aurelia Chillemi.

Figure 5.2 Eat Well, Community Dance at Reed, 2019. Copyright Jim Coleman.

Two Community Dance Projects: A Brief History

Chillemi, a contemporary dancer, dance/movement therapist, and practicing psychoanalyst, founded Dancers for Life in 2002 through the National University for the Arts' university extension courses.[4] The project expanded to include the "Community Dance" open university course and the Community Dance Movement-Therapy graduate research group. Dancers for Life emerged alongside a wave of collaborative activist and artistic projects that aimed to address social and economic upheaval caused by Argentina's 2001 economic crisis. While liberalization measures first began during the dictatorships that marked the 1960s, 1970s, and early 1980s, the neoliberal policies advanced throughout the 1990s concentrated class power and formed the immediate context of the economic collapse. In the midst of protests and widespread police violence following currency devaluation and an attempted run on the banks, workers, artists, and middle-class professionals alike turned to cooperative politics not only as a means of sustaining themselves but also to contest neoliberal emphases on individual achievement and financial gain. As activist-scholar Marina Sitrin (2006) points out, the concepts of *autogestión* (self-management) and *horizontalidad* (horizontality) became key to cooperative activism and art-making alike. *Horizontalidad* "implies democratic communication on a level plane and involves—or at least intentionally strives toward—non-hierarchical and anti-authoritarian creation rather than reaction. It is a break with vertical ways of organizing and relating" (2006, 3).[5]

In response to the economic, physical, and psychological precarity that formed the immediate context of the crisis as well as existing forms of social exclusion, Chillemi framed her project around the promotion of health and the prevention of disease. Notably, as a publicly funded research project, the formal title is Community Dance: Art, Health, and Social Development. Dancers for Life made their home in a space made possible by post-crisis practices of self-management and horizontality: a breadstick factory that was reopened by the labor cooperative La Nueva Esperanza (The New Hope) following the factory's closure during the 2001 crisis. The Grissinopoli factory (*grisines* are breadsticks in Argentine Spanish) is one of the longest-lasting worker cooperatives to emerge from the National Movement of Worker Recuperated Factories, a cornerstone of post-crisis labor mobilization. Many factories, including Grissinopoli, reopened as hybrid cultural centers where manual and creative labor joined forces to support alternative management configurations. Grissinopoli, in turn, deeply shaped the collective creation method at the core of Dancers for Life. Dancers for Life rehearsed in the factory until March 2018, and as of this writing, meets weekly in the Mutual Sentimento's Sexto Kultural (itself a cooperative initiative) and virtually during the COVID-19 pandemic. Dancers for Life performs regularly in theaters, schools, and cultural centers across Buenos Aires (Fortuna 2019, 141).

Fortuna, a dance studies scholar and contemporary dance practitioner, founded Community Dance at Reed in 2016. Based in Portland, Oregon, in the United States, Reed College is a private, small liberal arts college. Community Dance at Reed meets on campus in the state-of-the-art Performing Arts Building—a space with a very different history and infrastructure than the recuperated factory. Reed College, historically, has not centered community engagement within its curricular or institutional priorities. A common narrative shared by students as well as the Portland community is that of the Reed "bubble," a description of the College as intentionally separate from non-Reed bodies and spaces. This narrative hinges on the privileges attached to and cultivated by elite institutions of higher education in the United States: monied, selective, and predominately White. In line with community performance practice's emphasis on attending to the politics of place and mobilizing existing resources, engaging with this narrative was the first step in launching a community dance program. Community Dance at Reed aims to redefine the Performing Arts Building as a public space for gathering where people with and without official Reed affiliations feel a sense of access and ownership over it. Welcoming the "outside" community to Reed (rather than "reaching out" to "them") and sharing its considerable resources (rehearsal space, live musical accompaniment, participation in fully produced Dance Department concerts) strives for a redistributive politics necessary for securing dance as a social right. Each semester that the program runs, Community Dance at Reed develops a new work presented as part of the Dance Department's biannual concerts.

As is well-considered within the literature on community performance, invoking the concept of community—even in the context of projects conceived to be radically non-exclusive, anti-racist, and trauma-informed—by nature implies exclusion. In aiming to draw people together, "community" inevitably draws bounds around itself and brings with it the weight of (sometimes violent) projects waged in its name (Creed 2006, 4–5). With this in mind, both Dancers for Life and Community Dance at Reed take as their central research question one posed by Petra Kuppers (2007) in the context of her own community performance work: "How can a community politics that keeps openness, provisionality and respect for difference alive be mobilized" (2007, 37)?

The concept and practice of *vecinidad*, or neighborliness, is central to Dancers for Life and Community Dance at Reed's understanding of community as continually made and remade, and characterized by difference rather than sameness. Dancers for Life's preferred term for participants, in fact, is "neighbors." We understand *vecinidad* to encompasses the literal bringing together of people who live in a particular area as well as Marta Savigliano's (2009) notion of *vecinidad* "as instances of proximity—which do not constitute an idyllic relationality, but rather a permanent negotiation based on the encounters among others, without (and outside) the 'same' as an identitarian foundation" (2009, 184). In this spirit of *vecinidad*, we also value transparency—to our participants, students, and ourselves. Though we are committed to minimizing barriers to participation and potential harm, we can never completely eliminate either, and promising to do so would be disingenuous. However, by holding *vecinidad*, provisionality, and reciprocity at the core of our embodied work, movers of a wide range of ages, identities, classes, and backgrounds find new ways to live and engage socially through movement.

Dancers for Life and Community Dance at Reed fall within a broad tradition of community-engaged research that is done *with* rather than *on* a given community. The dialogical nature of community-engaged research "creates and disseminates knowledge that is beneficial to the discipline as well as the community" (Welch and Plaxton-Moore 2019, 21). These projects create knowledge relevant to the dance field by generating translatable models for social justice-oriented approaches to dance-making and analysis that emphasize non-exclusion and critical engagement with the politics of place. For the participants involved in these projects—a majority of whom have no stake in the university and its investment in expertise and authorship—the research process allows for experiences of embodiment, community, and critical reflection that translate into engaged citizenship outside of the practice and performance space. The embodied research at the core of both projects develops across four interconnected areas: (1) the body (movement education and sensoperception), (2) creativity development, (3) communication and community building, and (4) collective creation with an ever-changing cast. In the following, we detail the research questions and decision-making processes that shape our approach within these four areas, offering examples of how this work manifests in our respective contexts. As readers consider these four areas, we encourage imagination around how these areas—as well as the exercises themselves—might be adapted for different contexts.

The Body: Movement Education and Sensoperception

Work with the body—or more specifically movement education and sensoperception—forms the cornerstone of weekly movement sessions. Dancers for Life's approach to movement education is strongly informed by *Expresión Corporal Danza* (Corporal Expression Dance), a practice developed by Argentine dancer Patricia Stokoe (2005) in the 1950s. *Expresión Corporal Danza* aims to cultivate movement creativity through structured improvisation, freeing it from the confines of codified technique, and putting "dance within everyone's reach" (2005, 132). Dancers for Life's movement education methodology elaborates six main principles that emphasize building the body-mind connection: *eje* (axis or centering), support, flexibility, physical comportment/bodily movement, respiratory capacity, and movement language construction.

Eje, or centering, relates to the body's ability to support and root itself, and determines posture. In the community dance context, we understand there to be a dialectic relationship between a mover's interior emotionality and physical posture. Centering work develops support, which reflects participants' individual histories and constructions of subjectivity. Support, beginning from the rooting of the feet into the earth, allows for alignment or displacement. It also facilitates the investigation of new points of support, from physically changing levels to encounters with other bodies. Support builds an understanding of how weight is shared, and prompts movers to ask: How do I share weight? Partially or fully? What do I share in my point(s) of contact with others? Can I receive the other? The ease or difficulty with which movers share weight offers insight into how they relate to themselves and others. Explorations of support, in turn, help develop physical flexibility and deepen understanding of the body's protective mechanisms and occupation of space.

Relatedly, learning to work with breath is a fundamental aspect of movement education. Breathing is our first act at birth. It is also our first social act because it connects us to the external world and our last biological act and final point of connection to the external world before death. Inhalation and exhalation occur through the nostrils, which as Austrian psychiatrist Paul Ferdinand Schilder (1935) notes, "are of particular importance as zones of contact with the outside world" (1935, 28).[6] The processes of inhalation and exhalation externalize interior experiences of joy, stress, relaxation, etc. No matter how much an ill person might withdraw into themselves, they cannot evade their respiratory system, which is a permanent and uninterrupted point of contact with the surrounding world. Of course, it is the whole person that breathes, not only the lungs. The full body expresses itself, biologically, through breath. Given that breadth is biological, psychological, and social, training attunement to it is a critical aspect of the embodied research that drives community dance work.

Within our movement education methodology, understanding and exploring the individual histories that shape our everyday habits of postural attitude and quotidian bodily movement is key to developing a creative movement language. Postural attitude refers to how the corporeal participates in the structuring of the psyche, expressing emotional states and aspects of identity. Quotidian body movement is the socially, culturally, and politically informed repertoire of organized movements that shape how bodies move through the world.[7] *Expresión Corporal Danza* conceptualizes the interrogation and expansion of existing postural attitudes and quotidian bodily movement as a creative process that expands the movers' ability to communicate. In this way, community dance is defined by diversity, with as many in-progress creative body languages as there are participants.

Exercises that open movement sessions are designed specifically to help participants reflect on the postural attitudes and quotidian bodily movement that they bring into the room on a given day. A common prompt asks participants to reflect on the route they took to arrive to the session, and to explore the postures and movements associated with that route. Dancers first work individually and are then prompted to interact with each other, modifying their postures/movements while seeing their own reflected in those around them. In this way, work with postural attitudes and quotidian bodily movement offers the opportunity to expand the group's movement language through interaction, in turn enriching its symbolic world and modes of expression. Work with postural attitudes and quotidian movement generates both self-awareness of the body and often a palpable energetic shift. Frequently, participants report hurried, stress-ridden journeys to movement sessions that are reflected initially in hunched shoulders, frantic paces, and lack of eye contact. Following the exercise, however, participants express an increase in energy and focus that is reflected corporeally across the group.

The second branch of the body area of focus is sensoperception. Neuroscience defines sensoperception as the process through which we integrate stimuli from our external and internal environments so that they can be processed by our brains. Western concert dance forms—which dominate dance training in Argentina as well as the United States—favor training techniques that emphasize attention to and discipline over one's own body in relationship to an external image of "correct" movement. *Expresión Corporal Danza* moves away from a mimetic model of technical training, and instead understands sensoperception as a discipline based in embodied research that builds awareness and facilitates the integration of sensations and perceptions that typically go unnoticed—within quotidian movement as well as formal studio training. *Expression Corporal Danza*'s understanding of sensoperception resonates with the work of Moshe Feldenkrais, Gerda Alexander, Inx Bayerthal, and other Argentine dancers including Violeta de Gainza, Oscar Fessler, and Iris Scaccheri.

For Argentine social psychologist Daniel Calmels (2001), "the body provides us with the primary materials for forming images of the world" (2001, 24). Calmels specializes in *psicomotricidad*, or the study of the relationship between the construction of the body and its environment in the subject formation of children and adults. For Calmels, the body makes sense of the world around it and constructs knowledge from bodily experiences shaped by specific sociocultural contexts; this knowledge is continually constructed and modified throughout a subject's history. When we move, we do not only move our physical body, but also a symbolic and representative one that makes present these complex processes of subjectification. In the community dance context, sensoperception is most often trained through work with the eyes closed. Lead through verbal prompting, exercises aim to build sensory connections, both to the internal functions of the body (exploration of the shoulder blades, for example) and to the skin as a way of gaining information about the external world. Community dance's emphasis on sensoperceptive work, then, favors the construction of one's own image through bodily research, as opposed to that of an instructor representing a model body. Sensoperception aims to ease the hold of rational control over the body, allowing for forms of bodily attunement that open new possibilities of relating to one's own corporeality and to others.

Developing Creativity: Community Dance as a Practice of and for Daily Life

In the community dance setting, creativity allows for the discovery and formation of identity because it accesses interior spaces often closed off by personal or social pressures. Dancers for Life and Community Dance at Reed conceive of creativity as a practice of and for daily life—not something reserved exclusively for artists. Training creativity through community dance's improvisation-based movement education creates the possibility of accessing deeper aspects of the psyche, enabling innovative responses to daily challenges and encouraging flexibility in conflict resolution outside of the movement session. For participants, creativity emerges as a new facility, made of one's own experiences in a new context and in relationship to the facilitator, the other participants, the group as an entity unto itself, and the external world. Each mover, rooted in their particular historical context, can bring this new ability to bear in any number of daily or artistic activities, from the office to the stage, recreating and transforming external as well as internal realities and understanding conflicts as sites for creative response.

During movement sessions, movement prompts and exercises are not randomly introduced. Rather, they are conceived and deployed in response to the explicit and implicit needs of the group, between the external and the internal. In order to determine how best to foster the developing creativity of the group, facilitators attune to how the movement education principles are functioning (or not) within a given group, making improvisatory adjustments to exercises within the session itself or in subsequent sessions. Additionally, some exercises are designed explicitly to support the collective creation process, addressing both the thematic content of developing work as well as any physical qualities needed to execute it (working in unison, direction changes, etc.). Ultimately, the process of learning to recognize oneself from places and possibilities different than the habitual is a powerful form of self-realization that cultivates new modes of being in the world.

Communication and Community Building: Moving Together in Difference

In his writing on the histories undergirding various conceptions of community, Gerald Delanty (2007) advocates for the redefinition of community as communication. Similarly, Dancers for Life and Community Dance at Reed approach communication through an emphasis on the reconstruction of social and affective networks continually fractured by neoliberal precarity, institutional racism, and global crises. Community dance is, at its core, a mechanism for galvanizing social change. Reconstructing social and affective networks toward political change is a long-term process and takes place with and through the creative process. In addition to the principles of movement education and creativity development detailed above, the collective creation of dance works (explored in additional detail below) is integral to consolidating commitment and recomposing networks. The space of practice—and access to it—is also critical to enacting community as communication.

For Dancers for Life, practicing in nonconventional, cooperative spaces that model new forms of labor organization and relationality foster participants' growth into creative subjects capable of individual and social transformation. As sites for gathering, unconventional spaces democratize access to culture, counteract the elitism that characterizes much formal dance training, and actualize dance as a social right. These values in turn support the creation of work with a focus on human rights issues and social problems that might otherwise feel distant in a conventional studio or training context.

While Dancers for Life developed through activity in and collaboration with unconventional spaces for dance, Community Dance at Reed strives to use a conventional dance space unconventionally. Dismantling "swipe access" that normally bars entrance to buildings and studios to non-Reed community members, and instead insisting on horizontality in a space otherwise governed by vertical logics, Community Dance at Reed denaturalizes the role that institutions of higher learning play in inequitable power structures—even as the project inevitably benefits from these structures. As participants question the use of space and resources in the private university, and reimagine the Performing Arts Building as a community space, they are able to concretely enact social change through movement education and the collective creation of dance works. For students and participants alike, this transforms understandings of the role of the private university in the community and the utility of a liberal arts education.

To create dialogue and action around complex issues, Dancers for Life and Community Dance at Reed emphasize the cultivation of empathy. Learning to sense the movement languages of others through affective attunement—itself a form of embodied research—creates a moving relational fabric, a strong support network for participants' lives as well as those around them. Mirroring, or the prompt to take on the movement generated by other dancers, exemplifies how movement sessions train communication through the body. Based on a relatively common exercise in dance and theater, movers first work in pairs. One partner is the movement "motor" and one is the "mirror." Motors begin to move, often with some structured prompt—for example, to explore the articulation of joints—making choices that allow them to explore how their own bodies work. Mirrors face their partners and follow their movement, taking it on in their own bodies. The aim of mirroring, in this application, is not to replicate the partners' movement perfectly—asking participants to replicate movement exactly would replicate mimetic-based dance training and impede efforts to make the practice accessible to all bodies. Rather, the idea is to learn to anticipate the partner's movement by attuning to embodied cues (breath, weight shifts, rhythms), in order to interpret the essence of the movement in their body. In other words, the emphasis is not on looking the same, but on learning to sense with another body. The aim of this exercise is to build toward partners switching wordlessly between motor and mirror, to the point where it's unclear who is initiating the movement. This exercise is frequently expanded to small groups, and ultimately, to work as a singular group.

As a group, confidence is established as participants learn to recognize each other's ways of moving. Within our improvisation-based method, movement circulates in such a way that it is always relational and never individual. Movement is always for, with, and through the other bodies sharing the space. A shared code of horizontality and non-judgment—where movement exercises and collective creation methods put into action values of solidarity, social responsibility, and taking and ceding leadership roles within a shared democratic space—generates confidence, mutual respect, and the recognition of sociality as a cultural device for and within the community. These gains manifest as micro-transformations, which are not necessarily measurable by institutional metrics, but are articulated in the corporeality of participants and within the shared space itself.

In addition to choreographic works, the outcome of community dance research manifests in new forms of sociality, of being and doing together, that emerge from the creative process's investigation and critique of hegemonic power relationships. Historically, success, beauty, and youth have been measures of achievement in the professional dance field. However, with an integrated cast that is defined by difference (age, background, race, class, nationality, ability, language, sexuality, etc.), we instead value bodies committed to exploring their expressive possibilities, moving outside of the established limits, and understanding social problems. In this way, community dance functions as a form of resistance and militant politics that produces attuned, embodied subjects.[8] As philosopher Cornelius Castoriadis (1999) suggests, subjectivity is not a product, but rather a creation, a continual "self-creation" that takes place within a network of relationships in which the social, cultural, historical, psychic, organic, and biological are linked (1999, 99). Community dance, then, serves as an antidote to social environments otherwise defined by sensory numbing, isolation, and the glorification of over-work. The "community" of community dance is a group of people with shared interests who come together in a particular time and space to achieve their ideals.

Collective Creation and the Ever-Changing Cast *(Elenco móvil)*

Collective creation is the core of Dancers for Life and Community Dance at Reed's work. Like most community performance, the creative process is as important as the final product. Both projects follow a similar methodology, beginning with group improvisations led by facilitators. Typically, the artistic directors will design initial improvisation prompts, though at different points in the process, students enrolled in the corresponding university courses will also lead movement sessions. The creation of original work binds participants and manifests group identity; however, the dance works, like the composition of the collectives themselves, are never stable or permanent. Given that the cast is in continual flux, with participants joining and departing at all parts of the process, the work itself is living. Collective memory carries the work forward, while new participants leave their own mark.

Traditionally, dance composition based on the Western concert tradition emphasizes the creation of solo or group work with a singular choreographer at the helm. Dancers for Life and Community Dance at Reed, typically have between 30 and 60 participants who attend regularly or sporadically, instead work toward a new concept of dance and compositional methodology based on collective creation. The artistic directors of the collectives offer structures and timeframes for decision-making, while all members of the collective participate in the creation and curation of choreography. Rather than framing movement generation as a process based on individual invention, our horizontal process emphasizes oral transmission between participants where experienced members welcome and pass down existing or developing choreography to new members. This enacts solidarity and social responsibility among members of the collective and establishes the dance work itself as a common good.

The concept of artistic-work-as-common-good rejects the single authorship model so fundamental to dance's circulation in a capitalist market. In addition to articulating with the cooperative labor politics of the Grissinopoli factory, it also reflects the main principles of *Expresión Corporal Danza*, whose adaptation to the community dance context is detailed above. The collective creation process focuses on communication and is facilitated by the sensoperception cultivated during movement exercises. The sensing, perceiving body-as-researcher is able to find new ways of moving that break with habitual forms, opening the possibility of relating to others. Relationality occurs through the sharing of new embodied discoveries, mirroring one another, anticipating the movement of others, and responding in turn, thus constructing a new body language marked by the other bodies in the space. Individual creative capacity mobilizes the group, and the group mobilizes the individual, creating the engine for developing movement resonances and phrases born out of improvisation. Every group improvisation is a common good, the result of shared doing that enables tacit agreements and choreographic micro-resolutions.

Group improvisations ultimately form the raw material for choreographic works. Choreographic works, however, are not a mere summation of movement that comes out of group improvisations. Rather, movement's integration into stage works represents a new stage in the embodied research process. It is a gradual process of construction where nothing is individual—everything is with, by, and through others within a network that sustains the individual and supports the group identity. In her book *Moving Otherwise: Dance, Violence, and Memory in Buenos Aires*, Fortuna narrates her experience participating in the collective creation of Dancers for Life's *…Y el mar* (*…And the Sea*), a piece dedicated to family members of *desaparecidos* (those disappeared during the last civic–military dictatorship). In particular, the work aimed to address the dictatorship's death-flight method of killing wherein officials threw detainees (often drugged but still alive) from planes into the Río de la Plata that borders Buenos Aires and empties into the Atlantic Ocean. Many victims' remains subsequently washed up on beaches across the Buenos Aires province. Improvisations for the work centered on the traces (both physical and affective) left by *desaparecidos*, the violent yet tender movements of the sea, the act of witness, and persistence over time (Fortuna 2019). Of the journey from group improvisation to choreography, Fortuna writes:

> My partner and I first began working with the lower body, experimenting with how far we could stretch our legs forward before losing balance. Coordinating our bodies required a shared physical investment in playing with the paradox of wanting to remain and advance at the same time. Our agreement was not determined verbally, but rather felt out through attention to the pace and suspension of the other's movements. The pull of the leg extending before us eventually morphed, releasing into a deep lunge—our extended supporting legs still firmly rooted in place. Kinesthetically agreeing it was time, we slowly shifted forward, dragging our extended legs to bring our feet together, slowly rolling up the spine…[Eventually] my partner and I were asked to teach our sequence to a group of dancers. Though my partner stopped coming to rehearsals soon after the staging process began, I performed the movement sequence with the group for the remainder of my time with the collective. During one of my final rehearsals with the group before leaving for the United States, I taught the sequence and narrated the history of its relational genesis to a dancer who would take my place in upcoming performances. Watching the piece for the first time as a spectator, I experienced not only a mournful release of the movement but also joy as I watched the steps literally "put" another body into a painful, yet hope-filled, reflection on what it means to remember that which can never be whole. In that moment, I experienced movement as a common good not only in the sense of cooperative creation, but also in the sense of its graceful circulation between bodies over time.
>
> (2019, 163)

This passage not only narrates a specific instance of how movement that emerged from group improvisations became incorporated into a choreographic work, but also highlights the role of the facilitator within a horizontal creation process at points when decisions ultimately need to be made. Chillemi asked Fortuna and her partner to share their movement with the larger group, just as Fortuna has gone on to guide Community Dance at Reed members toward decisions at critical junctures in the collective creation process. At such junctures, facilitators function as translators among various groups of dancers working to consider variations in choreography and to solidify sequence and timing, helping multiple viewpoints and contributions to become a multi-vocal whole. This is not a negation of the horizontal process, but rather a necessary step to bring choreographic works to fruition.

Problems of violence, marginalization, and social exclusion, like those addressed by ...*Y el mar*, affect communities at national as well as international levels, and the aim of community dance practice is to respond to specific histories that mark its (literal) neighborhood. Where histories of Argentine political violence have been a frequent focus for Dancers for Life, Community Dance at Reed has focused on issues of racial (specifically anti-Black racism) and economic inequality, issues at the center of mobilization at Reed College and in Portland. Dancers for Life and Community Dance at Reed know that their creative processes and works do not necessarily produce social change in a quantifiable or legislative sense. We maintain, however, the transformative and reparative potential of danced encounters between neighbors that enact values of care, solidarity, and mutual respect. As neuroscientific research has shown, empathy affects other cognitive processes, acting specifically in neural regions that interact with areas affected by violence and trauma (Zambudio 2014). As such, the individual and group experience of community dance produces new modes of embodied subjectivity that have the potential to lower levels of social violence. Respected for their unique capacities and creative contributions, participants become creative subjects capable of effecting micro-transformations outside of the community dance context as cultural and democratic agents. The process of creating original work that generates reflections and critical engagement with hegemonic, hierarchical social orders instills a sense of social responsibility. This responsibility manifests in community dancers' recognition of themselves as social actors and transformation agents within their respective contexts. These outcomes are reflected in the multiple modes of assessment practiced by both groups, including weekly end-of-session discussions; intermittent formal and informal interviews and surveys; and social media conversations. For Dancers for Life, this material has been gathered over the course of 20 years. All modes of the assessment provide vital information around how group members express themselves and grow in their forms of expression over time.

Lastly, we would like to reflect in more detail on the politics of maintaining large and diverse collectives whose composition is always in flux, a structure with a fundamental relationship to the collective creation process. Dancers for Life and Community Dance at Reed operate from an ethic of *No Violencia*, or non-violence. Our conception of non-violence shapes the ways we transmit knowledge, respects the varying levels of commitment participants are able to make to the project, and suspends assumptions around which bodies should (or are able to) perform which movements in a given choreography (participants continually surprise us). Our approach articulates with what Terry Galloway, Donna Marie Nudd, and Carrie Sandahl (2007), writing about their theater work with disabled performers, call the "ethic of accommodation" (2007, 229). For these authors, the ethic of accommodation includes "making room for difference possible, letting go of preconceived notions of perfectibility, and negotiating complex sets of needs," even when these needs come into conflict (2007, 229). Working from a place of non-violence that accommodates participants' various needs means that attendance changes constantly from one rehearsal or performance to the next. This unpredictability feeds the collective creation process as participants learn to self-select for roles that match their capacities, and choreographic structures support the ability of dancers to continually swap into and out of different roles depending on the situation. This is not anarchy (as it may appear to some) but is, in fact, horizontality at work.

Collective creation involves not only the ebb and flow of collective members, but also musicians, artistic directors/professors, and students enrolled in the companion university courses.[9] Along with longtime members who attend rehearsals regularly and perform frequently, these figures provide stability and continuity. Just as the community dance movement education methodology and collective creation process requires participants to break with established modes of being and relating, for directors it demands flexibility and a willingness to let go of plans and respond to situations at hand. The ever-changing composition of the cast necessitates the release of traditional pedagogical structures that situate the professor/director as the primary decision-making agent, allowing for the emergence of a collective imagination that steps in to resolve unforeseen circumstances.

The uniqueness of the ever-changing cast also means that works accrue new meanings with the arrival of new participants while still retaining the collective memory of their origin. Similarly, the repetition of choreography during rehearsals does not take on a mechanistic quality, but itself changes the work with each repetition. As psychoanalyst Donald Winnicot (2003) argues regarding subject formation, a child's recognition of themselves as separate from their mother takes place within the creative, transitional space of play. This transitional space is a kind of waiting period, during which the presence and absence of the mother alternate as the child's sense of self and other constantly changes. Though certainly distinct from Winnicot's decidedly Eurocentric and patriarchal view of childhood development, the time between rehearsals can also be thought of as a kind of waiting period where dancers continue to change in relation to the creative space of the dance work. Each new repetition of the work, then, produces new meanings that are shared during the reflection circles that close movement sessions. These reflections enrich the symbolic world of the developing work. Engaging in collective creation provides a container for this process-based experience, which differs significantly from individual improvisation work in the dance classroom. This process-based work allows for the inclusion of new structures of knowledge with resonances that stretch far beyond the practice room. For Dancers for Life, the creative process is also extended in two critical ways: the creation of site-specific video dance works and the ongoing performance of repertory works.[10] Where the videodance works layer additional place-based meanings onto the choreography and circulate the work to broader audiences, the repetition of repertory works in performances across the years broadens and deepens the meanings of the works themselves, emphasizing further their living status.[11]

Conclusion

For both authors of this chapter, the journey to and within community dance has shaped and redirected our careers in the most unexpected, joyful, and productively challenging ways. It has provided a model for creating work aimed at generating social change while also working to dismantle what we both see as the exclusionary and at times damaging structures that mark conventional dance training within the Western concert tradition. As the dance field strives to be continually more responsive to the political, cultural, and emotional needs of communities of all scales, we hope that community dance practice plays an increasingly more visible role as a form of embodied research capable of effecting social and political change.

Notes

1 From the United States, Petra Kuppers has written extensively about community performance, including community dance. *An Introduction to Community Dance Practice* (2017), edited by UK-based Diane Amans, provides a rich resource for community dance practitioners, though many of the assumptions around government funding structures and infrastructure do not apply outside of Europe.
2 Both authors have written extensively about these projects elsewhere. (see Chillemi 2015 and Fortuna 2019, 142–168).

3 For a complete list and discussion of Dancers for Life's choreographic works, see Chillemi 2015: 90–150. Video dance works can be found at the following links: *La Oscuridad* (*The Darkness*) https://www.youtube.com/watch?v=po3ZYIBdEcA&t=16s, ...*Y el mar* (*...And the Sea*) https://www.youtube.com/watch?v=fbOwRkJ9XmY, and *De la tierra* (*From the Earth*) https://www.youtube.com/watch?v=DXA2YyDVFGY. For a video on the overarching research project, see https://www.youtube.com/watch?v=TDVMaxXJSCU. For video of Community Dance at Reed works in performance, see https://www.reed.edu/dance/community-dance/previous-works.html.
4 Chillemi's psychoanalytic training deeply informs her approach to community dance, as does her work as a dance/movement therapist in clinical contexts. Dancers for Life, however, is not framed as therapy, though participants may find the practice to be a site of healing and mental health support.
5 For broader discussion of Buenos Aires-based contemporary dance's response to the 2001 crisis, see Fortuna 2019: 109–138.
6 All translations of quotes from Spanish-language texts and editions by Victoria Fortuna.
7 Our understanding of postural attitude and quotidian body movement map roughly onto Pierre Bourdieu's understanding of bodily hexis (the tendency to hold one's body in a certain way) as a function of habitus, or the ways in which naturalized habits and ways of moving are functions of individual and collective socialization processes (Bourdieu 1984).
8 In line with its usage in Argentina, we employ "militant" to signify a deep and enduring commitment to a cause with one's own body as well as mind. In this case, community dance fosters a commitment to embodiment itself and to the potential of collaborative work.
9 Both Dancers for Life and Community Dance at Reed collaborate with accomplished musicians who are invested in the ethics and methodological approaches of the projects. Osvaldo Aguilar (Dancers for Life) and Joe Janiga (Community Dance at Reed) regularly accompany movement sessions and compose original scores for choreographic works.
10 At present, Community Dance at Reed is not able to support the production of videodance works, and to date, develops a new work each semester that is presented in dance department concerts.
11 See endnote 3 for links to videodance works.

Works Cited

Amans, Diane (ed.). 2017. *An Introduction to Community Dance Practice*. London: Palgrave.

Bourdieu, Pierre. 1984. *Distinction: A Social Critique of the Judgement of Taste*. Translated by Richard Nice. Cambridge, MA: Harvard University Press.

Calmels, Daniel. 2001. *Cuerpo y saber*. México: Novedades Educativas.

Castoriadis, Cornelius. 1999. *Sobre el Político de Platón*. Madrid: Editorial Trotta.

Chillemi, Aurelia. 2015. *Danza Comunitaria y Desarrollo Social: Movimiento poético del encuentro*. Buenos Aires: Artes Escénicas.

Creed, Gerald W. 2006. "Reconsidering Community." In *The Seductions of Community: Emancipations, Oppressions, Quandaries*, edited by Gerald W. Creed, 3–22. New Mexico: School of American Research Press.

Delanty, Gerrard. 2007. "Critiques of Community: Habermas, Touraine and Bauman." In *The Community Performance Reader*, edited by Petra Kuppers and Gwen Robertson, 28–33. New York: Routledge.

Fortuna, Victoria. 2019. *Moving Otherwise. Dance, Violence, and Memory in Buenos Aires*. Oxford: Oxford University Press.

Galloway, Terry, Donna Marie Nudd, and Carrie Sandahl. 2007. "'Actual Lives' and the Ethic of Accomodation." In *The Community Performance Reader*, edited by Petra Kuppers and Gwen Robertson, 227–234. New York: Routledge.

Kuppers, Petra. 2007. "Community Arts and Practices: Improvising Being-Together." In *The Community Performance Reader*, edited by Petra Kuppers and Gwen Robertson, 34–47. New York: Routledge.

Savigliano, Marta. 2009. "Worlding Dance and Dancing out There in the World." In *Worlding Dance*, edited by Susan Leigh Foster, 163–190. New York: Palgrave Macmillan.

Schilder, Paul Ferdinand. 1935. *Imagen y apariencia del cuerpo humano: Estudios sobre las energías constructivas de la psique*. Buenos Aires: Paidos.

Sitrin, Marina. 2006. *Horizontalism: Voices of Popular Power in Argentina*. Oakland: AK Press.

Stokoe, Patricia. 2005. "Historia y antecedentes de esta corriente, según la experiencia de su creadora." Appendix in *Qué es la expresión corporal: A partir de la corriente de trabajo creada por Patricia Stokoe*, edited by Déborah Kalmar, 131–138. Buenos Aires: Lumen. Welch, Marshall and Star Plaxton-Moore. 2019. *The Craft of Community-Engaged Teaching and Learning*. Boston: Campus Compact.

Winnicot, Donald. 2003. *Realidad y juego*. Buenos Aires: Jedesa.

Zambudio, Nancy. 2014. *Enlaces en Red*. Buenos Aires: Editorial Ricardo Vergara.

6
FutureBlackSpace
Weaving Art, Healing, and Activism

John-Paul Zaccarini

Introduction

FutureBlackSpace (FBS) is an internally funded research project at Stockholm University of the Arts that began in June 2020. It looks to research methods for establishing creative space for artists of color (AOC) in predominantly white institutions/fields to research without the pressure of the "white gaze."

The text that follows is an example of exposition of research, a result of 16 months in a dialectic between the fullness of an FBS and treading on eggshells while presenting the findings in majority white spaces. By majority I mean an average of 1.5% POC to 98.5% non-brown/black identifying people and often that 1.5% being just me. If I focus on the moment of Acceptance/Hope in the stages of grief, which I have come to call The Upward Turn to resonant more specifically with the notion of racial "uplift" coined by such thinkers as W.E.B. DuBois (2007), I have, at a psychic level, the so far 236 participants of FBS within me as good internal objects in those white spaces. I am never alone. The Upward Turn designates a gaze lifted to the future, rather than one mired in melancholic historiography (Best 2018). Regular participant Anna Adeniji, critical diversity consultant, reminds me that we have never, and will never be in an all-white space, because we are also there, albeit as a minority (Zaccarini et al. 2020). "If treading on egg shells is a cliché, then perhaps I should rather say that I negotiate, in those white rooms, the sharp debris caused by the black bull in the white china shop" (Zaccarini 2021, 129). The work is an exercise in stamina, in not shying away from the anxiety and awkwardness on both sides of the so-called color-line that our interracial dialogue can summon. Discomfort, once the condition of the "other," comes to be the default of us all. We are all "othered."

DOI: 10.4324/9781003145615-8

If working with blackness in an artistic research context must always demand excessive historical explanation/contextualization and a disproportionate amount of patient and sensitive pedagogy because of the fear that the work will upset the white cohort, then the AOC rarely gets beyond opening statements. Any statements must then be measured against the potential guilt, shame, denial, or recriminations that their project may induce. Generativity is stunted by the unconscious affects that are brought into play by the presence of a black body speaking or moving in white space on its own terms.

Preliminary workshops conducted in the aftermath of George Floyd's murder highlighted with urgency the necessity for creating artistic research spaces that are relevant to the specific needs of black practitioners. What does it mean to be a diasporic black identity at this intersection in the predominately white institutions and artistic fields of Stockholm? FBS hones in on a Swedish black political identity, embedded in an idiosyncratically racist culture in order to refine precise methods at specific sites to alleviate the minority stress, double labor, micro-aggression, and effects of unconscious racism on Swedish AOC. Looking to instantiate a more agential performance of race, the question is: what would the repercussions be on the artwork that the AOC goes on to generate? This then, is research into methods to develop a space that functions at the intersection of art, activism, and healing to mitigate the subtle violence that these reactions perform on the black psyche.

I was supported in this via an immersion in Black Studies that included the work of Best (2018), Fanon (2017), Harney and Moten (2013), Lorde (2017), Morrison (2020), Moten (2008), Sharpe (2016), Wallace (2015), Warren (2018), Wilderson III (2020) and Wright (2015). Literature becomes a methodological site within which a variety of art practices can weave with and through each other. To be in a writing/thinking/dialogue process that unconceals blackness as neither defined in a relation to whiteness, or indeed to otherness, produces a careful but fraught consideration of how words relating to color and race can de-activate critical thinking and undermine our attempts at a future thinking. Very soon, these words, which are never our own to begin with (white, black, of color, racialized, etc.) leave the room. They don't belong anymore. Without them our being becomes fuller, that is, less defined in relation or as a reaction to its other. Can words be put into diasporic parentheses?

Ana Sanchez-Colberg, choreographer and visual artist and key contributor to the space, wonders what difference would being "'in the weave'" make to and for the artist's process. What contribution would it make to and for the field? And what, in the first place would constitute "difference"? This loaded question, automatically consigning divergence from normativity to "other," was something that needed unpacking in the context of artistic research, in terms of exposition of knowledge, method development, and concepts and practices of documentation and composition (conversation October 15, 2020).

Facilitating the Weave

Working within a variety of literary genres and bodily practices (dancing and singing) to encourage the co-existence of historiography, memoir, theory, and speculative fiction, various clusters of artists and practitioners come together in FBS to explore what it could mean to develop a research practice that manifests primarily outside of the white gaze. We interrogate our current environments by proposing a legitimized space for black artistic processes unshackled from neocolonial structure/practices/knowledge. Posed from inside a majority white institution in an attempt to understand whether institutions can be changed from within, these questions allow participating artists to develop their own anti-racist/activist/decolonial or healing projects within this emergent space without fear of reproach or the need to overly explain that which is already clear to everyone in the room. The subject of the research is not what it might generate, which would require a different methodology and contract with the artist but rather how to prototype an FBS: a space of black artistic identity speaking from a future time of post-racialism: how a curation, or "weave" of individual processes could inform the structure and methodology of such a space: how an FBS could move from being a safely contained separatist space woven of specialized knowledge toward becoming an integrated and necessary part of a large institution of the arts (Sanchez, conversation November 18, 2020).

Writing memoir, poetry, or science fiction with guidance from a facilitator has become the main method in producing unconscious knowledge of how black being operates in white artistic spaces, that is, we produce *what we did not know we already knew* because of internal and ambiguous external censorship. The FBS writing spaces are thus informed by the analytic techniques of bringing the unconscious onto the light of the page, techniques which are already informed by structural linguistics and how language partially reveals the drive that underwrites desire, or as Lacan put it, how the unconscious is structured like a language. Here I posit the notion of a black unconscious as an imaginative prompt to motivate a critical black desire in art-making that releases itself from both the demands of an internalized white gaze and the foreclosure of black desire by the epistemological force of the colonial unconscious of the institution/field/university (Wilderson III 2020, 220–221). If we, as artists, are working with unifying the double consciousness that halts our progress, how can our ensuing work momentarily give pause to the smooth forward progress of work that is not interrupted by race?

It is a supportive platform for the work that persists in my preconscious: a surface of comfort on a hard cold floor: something to give succor as you wrap it around you: a wall hanging that provides an imaginary tapestry of communal history, pain, vitality, pride, magic, and hope: a basket that holds the work and can carry it out into the world, a carrier bag of fiction (LeGuin 1986). In this sense, the weave is also a safety net that can catch negative affect or conflict and hold it so it can play itself out through fantasy, fiction, dance, song lyric, or satirical sketch, rather than express itself in either acting-out or self-damage. And so, the net becomes stronger the more threads are woven into it. Therefore, the net is a metaphor for the analytic space itself and our co-weaving of it.

There are certainly moments of tension or conflict in the weave, as well as release/relief. A rope, a woven being, is bound at both ends keeping its tension and thus its form and usefulness, otherwise it frays, unravels, and falls apart. What is the tension then? What are the contractual binds that keep the woven in place? I think it is an implicit understanding that our intersectional conflicts – black Marxist versus black entrepreneur for example – will, and have always proved to, hold us back as a community. We do not deny conflict, but we bracket it momentarily for the space to function.

The psychic action of weave is predicated on the disentangling and re-weaving of the facilitator's subjectivity, who must use themselves to notice what threads to draw out, or to take care of when they start to fray away from dominant white narratives and might therefore get "lost in the fray." Grounded in specificity of experience, the facilitator provides a space where participants can disentangle themselves from whiteness. This is at once liberating and shameful once we realize how deeply knit we are with it.

I collect my thoughts once the session is over, not during. I do not transcribe the stories told but rather how they affect or contribute to the formulation of new metaphors for the experience that could become new linguistic tools as prompts for new practices. This is where I experience my own artistic process at play which emerges in prototypes of movement, spoken word, memoir, and video which can be found in The Library (Zaccarini et al. 2020).

I listen as they write, even though all I can "realistically" listen to is the meditative sound of pens scratching paper. It's not telepathy, but empathy. I ask myself – where did I just send them, where might they be going, how do I hold, for example, five different participants' narratives, concerns, locations in mind as we, together but on our own, explore this cartography of the black unconscious in the Swedish artistic community? And that map is at the very least four-dimensional since it accounts for genealogies, geographies, extractions, immigrations, and multiple temporalities that are activated when we come together. I am also asking myself – where am I going, in this epiphenomenal experience of blackness that is no longer a performance of race scripted by the white gaze?[1]

The notation and documentation of thoughts after each session is mediated by and interacts with my immersion in the black study. I go back through my black bookshelves and re-trace my steps. I re-read and rewrite in the light of the emerging embodied knowledge, the transformed experiences of increased capacity for authenticity in white spaces due to the project, the movement of affect from, for example, disaffection to hope and the shifting of temporal emphasis from melancholic past to activated future: the Upward Turn, which has resonances with the turn to uplift.

As a facilitator, I gravitate to the gaps in my knowledge or my naivete to different perspectives. I orient myself with my own deficiencies. So, before each session, I allow previous sessions' strands of stories, images, experiences of double consciousness, shared processes, geographies, genealogies, subjects, encounters, dances, songs, and my own black study to weave themselves within me into a kind of preconscious fabric. This interdisciplinary and intersubjective woven fabric functions as a backdrop for me to draw from in order to find our commonality and continuity rather than our potential conflicts.

These steps allowed me to arrange and condense the information from sessions into orientation tools in the form of repeatable workshops for mapping and facilitating the production of the black unconscious and activating forms of artistic sustainability and authentic black persistence in white spaces. The research does not record or extract artists' ensuing output, nor does it require citation within the artists' work. Therefore, examples of outputs arising from these processes are located in The Library, an open-access website we commissioned from participants (https://subcase.se/the-huddle-2022/).

The Sessions

Memoir. (Rankine 2014)

In order to situate artistic research in our own experience we sketch a memoir of micro-aggression. We list unresolved situations within our practice and choose one to focus on. Using automatic writing, we approach it from different perspectives: we change the tense, the pronoun, write it from the point of view of the aggressor, write it as a letter to someone we admire or would seek solace from, write their response, write it from the point of view of a seemingly unimportant object (a coffee cup, or a barking dog in the distance) that is nonetheless part of the scene. We then rewrite the scene with a more hopeful, progressive conclusion, preparing us with methods for the next time.

Genealogy. Geography. Geologies of Extraction. (Yusoff 2019)

We work with our given/family names unpacking and improvising with them, performing a free-associative genealogy of their meanings and locations. It automatically brings us to our various heritages and diasporic geographies. We notice where chains of association flow and when they halt, are cut short. We search for metaphors within this cartography of identity and displacement. We choose one place from which (one of/one part of) our blackness was born, choose an object extracted and transported for the profit of another location. We write an ode to it. We write a eulogy to it from the land it was stolen from. Then we write a poem that begins "I am (gold, bauxite, labor, etc.)."

Community. House. Continuity. Home. (Morrison 2020)

We create a compass with these words at its cardinal points. We create associative word clouds of nouns around each point, i.e. continuity might have "narrative," "vision," "movement" as its nouns. At the intercardinal points we place our practices, and word cloud transitive verbs around them, that is, pedagogy might have "open," "guide," "hold" as its verbs. Between each cardinal and intercardinal point, we choose a song. We dance/sing along to our songs bearing the nouns and verbs of that intersection within our movement/vocalization. We write poems from these movement/vocal meditations. We continue around the compass until we reach the point we began with, creating a poem cycle that ends where it started, but transformed.

Black Utopias. (Zamalin 2019)

We take our practices as a starting point and reduce them to their core ethics – holding, caring for, disrupting, etc. We choose three other fields where these ethics are also visible: health care, agriculture, activism for example. How do these three fields collaborate with our practice? What new field of interdisciplinary practice do they suggest? What has to be left out in order for their function to be utopic? How do they not repeat colonial procedures of violence and extraction? From these inquiries we sketch afro-futurist fictions.

The Seven Stages of Grieving Race – What Do We Lose When We Lose Race?

We work through each stage in relation to how each has affected our artistic practice and output: Shock and Denial, Pain and Guilt, Anger and Bargaining, Depression, The Upward Turn, Reconstruction and Working Through, Acceptance, and Hope. Where are we now? Within what stage do we research and generate new knowledge right now? What is the work to be done to get to Acceptance and Hope?

Writing – *graphy* – works as a generative tool within multiple mediums. With dancers, the space of black embodied expertise gives rise to choreographies previously censored for having to be produced for the interpretative lens of whiteness: in this case, we discover that movement has always been marked and conditioned by the identity qualifiers of race. In a FutureBlack dance space where we write on paper with hand and pen and then write with our bodies through space and time, our unmarked being in space and time gains agency.

Bi-Directional Double Consciousness: An Awkward Dialectic

Issues arise in these workshops concerning the interpretation of an artistic research project or artwork. When we share work in the space, the layers and complexities of racialization are understood, felt, and the feedback we give each other reinforces the truth of our experience; just as when we read Black Studies, we find solace and validation. This reinforcement from the weave gives us the confidence to show the works in predominantly white spaces and not be adversely affected by misinterpretation from an uninformed gaze. Therefore, the research is also in relation to the processes of genesis and production. Artworks created for a predominantly white market can unconsciously be made with the white gaze in mind. Work then is created under the aegis of a harmful double consciousness (DuBois 2007; Fanon 2017) where it is only the minority who embody experiences of alienation and not the majority in whose context they attempt to operate. To analyze and further articulate this harmful, unilateral double consciousness and to attempt a shift toward bi-directional double consciousness, is to pave the way toward creating a critical interracial dialogue and practice within our fields. Central to the aim of FBS is to develop into practice the concept of a bi-directional double consciousness as a critique of the singular, universal consciousness that relegates other perspectives to the unconscious. The effect of this is that we all become racialized and race is no longer a property of those with darker skin tones or non-Western/Caucasian ethnicities.

This practice of facilitating bi-directional double consciousness happens in seminars, workshops, or studio practices for the above-mentioned institutions or fields. The key to the staging of these encounters with the work is that when we are asked to show the outputs of research we, rather than enter white space with the work, invite those who operate in white space into our own self-created space. I should reiterate: this space is the subject of the research, what is important for us about the research is how to create this space within an artistic institution. We invite the institution into FBS in order to speak or show on our own terms. If a solo artist shows their research, they know that the weave has their back. One of these sites of encounter is the online resource The Library of spoken poetic texts and movement pieces commissioned from a curation of participants of the process.

The Library is a tool used in workshops for white-identifying artists. It employs the seven stages of grief as a method for exploring artists' and researchers' relationship to the dawning of their whiteness. Opening the doors of the space to this white gaze confronts that gaze with the bright reflection of its own whiteness because whiteness is now in the dazzle of a racialized spotlight. We find ourselves blinking, watery-eyed at whiteness and it is the deep hue of the weave, the collectedness of black knowledge and experience that softens or dims that painfully bright glare. Then we close the doors to continue our work in the less tense and anxiety-ridden space that we have co-authored.

Back to Black

FBS sessions run for three hours divided into three 45-minute sessions. There are different constellations of artists, researchers, art educators, consultants, psychologists, activists, and AOC student groups. There are three to six sessions as detailed above, but the sessions are oriented by the concerns of each specific constellation. This is especially true of groups that grapple with relationships to, most often well-meaning, authorities that declare themselves inclusive but seem to have no idea what that means in practice – in the practice of dance training or choreography, of theater directing, of the representation of the body of color, of cultural appropriation, etc.

Large groups, of approximately 20–70 provide a comforting environment to work with issues arising in individual projects, so participants sit with their own rising unconscious knowledge but within the supportive swell of many doing the same. Smaller groups, of between two to six, find a life-raft in the sharing of experience, of diving in together on the same subject, or sharing mutual currents of thought. There is a sense of mutual development and caring for the gaps in each other's knowledge. One-to-one sessions allow for a deeper investigation into the specificities of an art practice bound or bracketed by racialization and, as such, approximate a supervisory relationship. Some artists or students drop in just to vent, to have breathing space. Others, such as Anna Adeniji, Hanna Wallensteen, psychologist specializing in minority stress and Afro adoption issues in Sweden, Ana Sanchez-Colberg and Toubab Holmes, circus artist, musician, and perfumier, commit to a long-term investment in the sessions and the development of its tools, methods, knowledge production and thus to this expositional text – a weave of the multiple strands of experience and process shared within these 16 months of research.

As facilitator then, of the work with AOC, I attempt to knit a space of many strands, as mentioned above, wherein the risk of double consciousness would be tempered by the presence of many black knowledges collaborating in the weave. For example, a strand of Afro Pessimism finds a connection with Black Optimism or a focus on vitality within, and as a result of social death (Moten 2008), different experiences of micro-aggression wrap into each other to collaborate on more resilient strategies to counter it, a psychological technique binds to a literary method to produce the black unconscious, a historical revisionist approach or counter-narrative technique makes a mutual knot with a dance practice or a theatrical scripting practice is woven with public performance activism. The hybrid tools that emerge in this improvisation of black togetherness are then available for all, no matter what practices, artistic or otherwise, are attending.

Within this weave, the performance of race is no longer a requirement. Needing to educate people in relation to embodied knowledges no longer slow or prevent one from addressing what is most urgent to a practice. In the process, we educate each other and are nourished by the knowledge that other AOC are doing their own double work in their studios, writing desks, artistic employments, or research milieux. The fear of creating an upset and the possibility of provoking white fragility is no longer an obstacle to getting on with the work at hand. These are not the usual conditions an artist of color encounters within a white institution. Being the embodiment of both the problem and its solution makes for a distinctly unsustainable labor. We have to care for ourselves in the face of ongoing unintentional micro-aggression, while at the same time attending to the basic lack of knowledge surrounding historical issues of race/colonialism while somehow being responsible for both educating and nursing the debilitating shame/guilt or unconscious rage that can often accompany talking about race with non-POC.

Here, can be seen as an example of how the continued use of words such as "white" de-activate critical thinking by reproducing a colonial language of division. Recalling that this project is focused on the specifically diasporic black subject in Sweden, the "black" in FBS will, in later iterations alloy with "brown" inviting a future inclusivity, a collected hope based on a pluriverse of specific struggles, a more decolonial perspective and further attempts at envisioning a post-racial present beyond, but still including US-centric Black Studies.

With the future in mind, a major aim continues to be to promote and chart the journey from unconscious knowledge, that which resides in the unconscious in order not to disturb or interrupt the functioning of white space, to conscious knowledge of and in our practices. Wallensteen reports that the white gaze not only tells what she can and cannot say, but also what she can and cannot think, and so the stories bubbling up from the unconscious allow her to formulate a much more accurate analysis of her present, her context and even of her clients (email to author June 24, 2021).

Participants are under no compulsion to report their content, in order that they feel free to rid themselves of censoring agencies and find a modicum of freedom in thought and affect. They are invited rather to share their process and it is this that creates the fabric of communal thinking, of thinking together, that I have been calling the weave. Therefore, as a lead researcher, I need to find ways to share my subjective experience of being a facilitator in contact/contract with others in the space as they generate their own discourse, so that our work together can be of some benefit to the wider community. So, I share my experience and reflections within the larger frame of the institution and public domain, as a prompt to expand vocabularies, conversations, and understandings around the currently fractious discourse of race in predominantly white institutions.

This delineation of what emerges and why and under which conditions constitutes both an ongoing evaluation and refinement of the psychoanalytically informed literary tools being worked with and also a practical/theoretical contribution to institutional development. It is both a positive contribution to the well-being of the participants in the form of a method of artistic self-care and a critical evaluation of both the lack of provision and scarce recognition of said lack. Its aim is to proactively engage the artistic research community in sustainable, healthy, and generative discourse around the silences or empty rhetoric concerning its homogeneity and colonial unconscious. And to make a case for a psychologically sustainable art practice for minoritized artists and researchers.

In this following section, I collect the metaphors that have struck me as most powerful in the space and weave them through the strands of my study. This writing gives a sense of the weave of theory, memoir, historiography, and embodied recall of my encounters with black anti-racist and support student groups founding their own spaces of safety and activism within arts institutions in Stockholm.

Writing in Black Spaces

Metaphor emerges at the point where there is not enough empirical research to back up a position. If the evidence for such a position is perceived as merely "anecdotal" then metaphor can bind, in this case, those 236 story strands of structural racism into an image that opens up disenfranchised research via one of art's most valuable effects, affect. When Christina Sharpe situates anti-Blackness and white supremacy in the United States as the total climate that produces premature Black death as normative (Sharpe 2016), she is metaphorically inviting us into the effects of this normativity as a hyper-object. Black artists in Sweden feel the fallout of this trans-Atlantic weather acutely, but because they operate in a micro-climate that presupposes a hermetic seal from history and the rest of the world by proclaiming color-blindness and racial equality in an attempt to secure a concept of exceptionalism and good Swedishness, they are left with the ambivalent privilege of coping with indirect, passive-aggressive symbolic violence (Hübinette and Lundström 2014). Therefore, metaphors such as these can break the silence among those habituated to coping rather than thriving in artistic institutions (French et al. 2020).

The practice of metaphor in writing/thinking as a method for producing the conditions of research allows for the translation of those unthought thoughts into our individual practices. It creates the conditions for thinking of a present within which we can start co-creating a post-racial future beyond "wounded attachments" and "melancholic historiography" (Best 2018, 15–17).

AOC can indeed censor thoughts and not only speech in white spaces – cubes, studios, canons – because this is how double consciousness works, always second guessing itself, always at war with itself. That censorship may also be active in the production of movement, image, or sound. This is perceived in Stockholm's AOC as a "minimizing" of the self's expression, whether in the way one walks down a street, speaks to other POC in public or one's dress code. The white gaze does penetrate the black psyche, or more precisely the white gaze does activate itself there, the same way that white presence can press upon the black body as some form of an unspoken law, one that is sensed as curtailing movement or access. White majority presence can impress upon the black body its need for what the black body should be in order not to disturb the smooth functioning of universal space, it demands something that stops black desire in its tracks. And this may well be a projection on the part of AOC, a paranoia that we can be relieved from in FBS allowing us more room to move without self- or imagined external judgment.

Without the reminder of whiteness as the condition-of-being (imagined, symbolic, or real), blackness finds space, blackness can breathe and oxygenate affects that have previously been buried alive in order to exist in oftentimes suffocating social space.

Of course, this breathing space closes down when you leave it, but you exit with certain muscles having been exercised and enlarged – maybe the lungs, and their capacity to oxygenate and allow for speech – affording more space there. Whiteness will, over time, test those muscles till they are unable to keep that space open. We return to the black space to keep active our right to black speech – that enunciation that seems to put white discourse on pause. I experience myself as a discomfort in the discourse, an uneasiness in the use of words, as if I make the free flow of speech stumble: people have to think before they speak or, they just stay silent for fear of saying the wrong thing. It's not easy being the thing in the room that seemingly prevents the "free" flow of speech, but the irony is not lost on me. I have had to get used to measuring my words, if not putting myself completely on mute.

Therefore, in the weave, we attempt a polyphony of our experience of how those spaces silence us, or curtail our movements and analyze how we allow those spaces to do so. This recalls what Audre Lorde called a symphony of anger –

> at being silenced, at being unchosen, at knowing that when we survive, it is in spite of a world that takes for granted our lack of humanness, and which hates our very existence outside of its service. symphony rather than cacophony because we have had to learn how to orchestrate those furies so they do not tear us apart.
>
> (Lorde 2017, 113)

Each individual somehow and in their own way collects the stories shared in the space and weaves those lived and still-living experiences into a backdrop they can bring with them when they enter white rooms again – the dance studio, the conference, the diversity workshop, the token seminar on decolonizing research, the rehearsal. The weave is a metaphor for community, of a resistance against interruption and a support for envisioning a future where race does not feature. In white rooms, even those doubly conscious of themselves and critical of their own whiteness, FBS becomes, for the participants of the weave, a background that continues to hold them. We are all in that room with them, we have each other's back. So, if racism arises, in whatever guise, we all, as internal good-objects, rise too.

Conclusion: Grieving

How participants go on to work after being in FBS is not something the research wants or needs to document. That is as personal a process as when the analysand leaves the consulting room to get on with their life outside, once the transferential hour is over. What I can document is my own experience of that gift of being in the presence of so much blackness in a field populated and silently defined by an experience that is not my own. So, as an artistic researcher what I have proposed and developed is not an artwork, but a prototypical space wherein the potentiality of a perhaps disenfranchised artwork could be considered. The artwork that I myself produce after FBS is not the research either but it can point back to it and can be put into dialogue with it.

I test the results by opening the doors of FBS to a white field. Not to exhibit artworks to it, but to afford it the very same process that AOC have engaged with over the 16 months. As a facilitator of white spaces that either earnestly, or cynically, desire to engage with the construct of whiteness, it has been akin to aversion therapy. I work daily in white spaces where whiteness is invisible, unmarked, unspoken. Here whiteness is in the headlights, as artists and gatekeepers wanting to work with the concept – which is both an abstract epistemological tool of coloniality but also a deeply embedded and embodied mode of living – experience a form of vivisection upon the still-living white body. I could put this even more strongly – a surgery upon the parasitically racist logos getting fat on our denial. This operation is difficult for us all, not least for the POC trying to excise introjected colonial epistemology. To stop feeding it, to draw it out – to articulate it – requires the acceptance of a certain form of grieving. What do we lose when we lose race, and, as in the writing session with this sub-heading, what do we need to do to get to a place of hope?

You and I, in our differing affective attachments to the notion of being racialized – and in this context white folk are as racialized as black or brown folk, albeit in some cases more freshly so – might well be at different stages of that process of grieving which will make for a fraught and fragile dialogue. If I am in denial and you are in rage, if I am in acceptance and you are in guilt, if I am frozen in shock and you are also, albeit differently, immobilized by depression, for example, it will be difficult for us to work together to imagine a post-racial future for ourselves. Only mourning will provide us with the release from lethargic, hopeless melancholia or the over-compensating defensive energy of mania. Both are denials of the need to grieve the obsoletism of race as a construct and how it instructs us still.

Note

1 I use here, the term *epiphenomenal* in reference to Michelle M. Wright's re-working of the term for Black Studies in which

> Our *constructs* of Blackness are largely historical and more specifically based on a notion of space-time that is commonly fitted into a linear progress narrative, while our

phenomenological manifestations of Blackness happen in what I term *Epiphenomenal time,* or the "now," through which the past, present, and future are always interpreted....

(Wright 2015, 4)

Works Cited

Best, Stephen. 2018. *None Like Us: Blackness, Belonging, Aesthetic life*. Durham, NC: Duke University Press.

DuBois, W.E.B. 2007. *The Souls of Black Folk*, edited by Brent Hayes Edwards. Oxford: Oxford University Press.

Fanon, Franz. 2017. *Black Skin, White Masks*. London: Pluto Press.

French, Bryana H., Jioni A. Lewis, Della V. Mosley, Hector Y. Adames, Nayeli Y. Chavez-Dueñas, Grace A. Chen, and Helen A. Neville. 2020. "Toward a Psychological Framework of Radical Healing in Communities of Color." *The Counseling Psychologist* 48, no. 1: 14–46. https://doi.org/10.1177/0011000019843506.

Harney, Stefano and Fred Moten. 2013. *The Undercommons: Fugitive Planning and Black Study*. Wivenhoe/New York/Port Watson: Minor Compositions.

Hübinette, Tobias and Catrin Lundström. 2014. "Three Phases of Hegemonic Whiteness: Understanding Racial Temporalities in Sweden." *Social Identities: Journal for the Study of Race, Nation and Culture*, 20, 6: 423–437. https:/doi.org/10.1080/13504630.2015.1004827

LeGuin, Ursula, K. 1986. "The Carrier Bag Theory of Fiction." The Anarchist Library. https://theanarchistlibrary.org/library/ursula-k-le-guin-the-carrier-bag-theory-of-fiction

Lorde, Audre. 2017. *Your Silence Will Not Protect You*. London: Silver Press.Morrison, Toni. 2020. *The Source of Self-Regard*. New York: Vintage Books.

Moten, Fred. 2008. "The Case of Blackness." *Criticism* 50, no. 2: 177–218. https://doi.org/10.1353/crt.0.0062.

Rankine, Claudia. 2014. *Citizen. An American Lyric*. Minneapolis: Graywolf Press.

Sharpe, Christina. 2016. *In the Wake: On Blackness and Being*. Durham, NC: Duke University Press.

Wallace, Michele. 2015. *Black Macho and the Myth of the Super Woman*. London: Verso.

Warren, Calvin. 2018. *Ontological Terror: Blackness, Nihilism, and Emancipation*. Durham, NC: Duke University Press.

Wilderson III. Frank, B. 2020. *Afropessimism*. New York: Liveright Publishing Corporation.

Wright, Michelle M. 2015. *Physics of Blackness: Beyond the Middle Passage Epistemology*. Minneapolis: University of Minnesota Press.

Yusoff, Kathryn. 2019. *A Billion Black Anthropocenes*. Minneapolis: University of Minnesota Press.

Zaccarini, John-Paul. 2021. "Staging Intersectionality: An Aesthetics of Action." *Lambda Nordica* 25, no. 3–4: 126–138. https://doi.org/10.34041/ln.v25.711

Zaccarini, John-Paul, ed., Anna Adeniji, Andrea Davis-Kronlund, Ana Sanchez-Colberg, Toubab Holmes, and Hanna Wallensteen. 2020. "The Library." FutureBrownSpace February 2020. https://subcase.se/the-huddle-2022/.

Zamalin, Alex. 2019. *Black Utopia: The History of an Idea from Black Nationalism to Afrofuturism*. New York: Columbia University Press.

7
Practice (or) Research
A Conversation with Eiko Otake

Rosemary Candelario and Eiko Otake

When we were planning who to commission for this Dance Practice section, Eiko Otake seemed a clear choice. Not only have I written extensively about Eiko & Koma (2010, 2011, 2014, 2016a, 2016b, 2018) and Eiko's solo work (2016c, 2017), but also Eiko has a long and well-established body of performance, written (2002, 2009, 2021, and translation of Hayashi 2010), and pedagogical work on mourning, atomic bomb literature, nakedness, Fukushima, and place and space. What has drawn me to Eiko's work, and what keeps me coming back time and again, is her insistence upon a willful and persistent questioning: of rules, of issues of concern to her, of how to be an artist. Given all that, I should have known that when we spoke via Zoom on June 15, 2021, that our conversation would not be a straightforward discussion of what I saw as Eiko's research. Indeed, in response to my first question, "Do you think of yourself as a researcher?" Eiko immediately turned around and asked me to define how we are using that term in this book. Throughout our conversation, she not only pressed on the definition of research (especially in relation to artistic creation, practice, and methods), but also questioned the implications of imposing academic language on artistic processes and work. Her objection is not to research in dance, rather it is to unquestioned systems of power. As we talked, she referenced her body of work from 1971 to 2013 as Eiko & Koma, as well as projects from her work as a solo artist since 2014, both solo and in duets with a number of different artists. What follows is an edited version of our conversation. In her editing, as in her artistic work, Eiko insists on precision, and resists simplification.

EIKO OTAKE: The word "research" has been used so often for the past ten or so years, especially in the dance field. I, however, have not embraced the use of the word in speaking about my art-making. Yes, by all means, we do a lot of searching, but why call it research? What's wrong with working? By claiming dance artists are always researching, are we not erasing the differences between finding new knowledge and making art? Twenty-five years ago people did not ask me about "research." They asked me about "work."

That in my mind includes "fooling around" and "being stuck." Now, so many people talk about research in proposals and descriptions of their work. In my recent project with Joan Jonas at Danspace Project, *With the Earth at My Waistline* (2021), we more or less just worked, trying different things. That's what we do as artists. In the process, we get to know each other more, but it's not really a focused research that determines our work.

For me, research starts with questioning and, through various methods, we stumble upon or systematically create new deliverable knowledge. You really get to know more about something. I am not shy about delivering that knowledge. Of course, knowledge can be acquired through bodily experience, and I think that's why many practitioners have started to use the word research. I am ok with that. But what I'm afraid of nowadays is how that colors the way we artists work: we are supposed to be always researching. Why, for example, instead of saying, "we are commissioning you to create this piece," do some presenters now say, "We are commissioning this research process"? I feel a sense of suspicion when certain words are used too often in sweeping ways. Such words do not inspire me. I do not think we should feel obliged to use the same vocabulary, and I have been kind of resisting that.

I'm not saying I don't research. There are some pieces Koma and I made that we clearly researched. For *Fur Seal* (1977), we read everything we could on seals. We went to zoos many times, and we went to the California and Oregon coasts to watch seals. We took our time and talked to many people to find out anything they knew about seals. By the time we premiered the piece, we learned a lot, and some of that knowledge might have been reflected in the movement material and a certain "smell" of another species. But I hesitate to say the movements or the piece were the results of the research. The core of this work came from our desire to focus on torso movement and the time sense that seals represented. Our desire was to create something that challenged the gendered choreography and vocabulary of modern dance, ballet, and traditional Japanese dance, and that was not human-centric; I carry these concerns from childhood to this day.

For *Land* (1991) with Robert Mirabal, we went to the Taos Pueblo many times to be with him and his family there, and we brought him to Japan and took him to Hiroshima. It's not so much that we "conducted" research, but we visited each other's places, and looked within by being a guide to each other. We gained some knowledge of each other and of places, but more importantly, we learned how to be strangers yet trust each other. We did not avoid difficult conversations. We investigated our political and emotional positionality in relation to native people and land. Parts of knowledge might leave us, but emotional experiences stay with us. We cannot turn back the clock.

I love knowing. Knowing defines each of us, and I get to know things along the way as I work. But that's not always the core or purpose of my work as an artist. I like making things. By making and elaborating I find what I like to see. Art-making does not have to be knowledge production. I like performing even when what I produce might be meaningless for most people. Performing also creates a particular time and space. Making, performing, and seeing art hones each of our individual aesthetics. Can we then regard both the differences and commonalities of humanity? Sometimes the art-making process necessitates particular research and sometimes not, depending on the piece, depending on my questions and desires. Sometimes I may make a piece about something I already know. I may shout the same scream. But other times, I might have to really acquire knowledge even in order to know what I want.

With my *Body in Fukushima* project, it's not so much that I had a distinct research period; rather I regularly monitor what's happening there as a part of my accountability as a teacher, as a dancer who remembers that place, and as an artist who published a book (2021). Of course, I found new information each time: which roads or towns opened, or if radiation levels went down or up. Underneath all that lay the fundamental knowledge about which I have been deeply dismayed. Fear and anger made me dance my "No! No! Dance." My photographer collaborator, William Johnston, and I saw and smelled the Fukushima disaster. Being shaken kept bringing us back to Fukushima, and resulted in our book and multiple versions of films, *A Body in Fukushima*. When I improvise in places, I do not think about choreography. I become a body without a plan or words. Then I can better remember the place and what I felt there. I think something is lost if I say I am always engaged in research when working.

I ask you, what do we gain by saying that choreography is research? What are the mindsets and actions where the word research is no longer applicable? What is research? What is not? I do not want to say that every time choreographers are working in a studio they are doing research. They are working. Let's not make the word research too broad. I don't want my work to be defined as research by someone else. I want my process to be mutable and undefined.

Practice versus Research

ROSEMARY CANDELARIO: I've heard you talk about some aspects of your *The Duet Project* (n.d.) as practicing dying. How does that fit into this discussion?

EO: I've thought a lot about death, the non-existence of existence, and the existence of non-existence. Many, if not all, deaths make those who remember the dead feel a new "empty space." From childhood, I have known that I love living and therefore would be afraid to die, to disappear, to lose my body and senses. I don't want to die, and I fear I might cling to life. So I practice dying through performing pieces such as *Death Poem* (2005), *Mourning* (2008), and *With My Mother* (2019). In the media works *Soak* (2017 with DonChristian Jones) and *Attending* (2020 with Iris McCloughan), I practiced receiving help in dying a "good death."

Movements in these pieces came from me observing my mother and a close friend die. I attended to their dying full-time for a month. My mother died at age 93. She opened her eyes really wide right before she died. I do that in *Attending*. Not imitating her, but remembering my experience of that moment of her death and taking it into my own body. I looked at her eyes, my eyes also wide open. It was not "peaceful." She resisted dying a little at the last moment, but was gone soon after. I have thought about this moment many times, and I now say to the audience in my performance, "my mother had a good death." That is relative because so many people die in a more painful manner or are killed. I also say on stage to DonChristian, my younger collaborator, "Working with you makes me know I want to die before you. This is the order. I do not want to break it. Survive me." By practicing dying, I get to remember my experiences more vividly, and feel I am inching toward dying. My body performing this movement changes my sense of distance to dying. I am not researching. I am practicing.

By rehearsing dying, I wonder if when I am actually dying, will it feel more like a deja vu, or here comes the real thing? Will I be clear-headed? Will my body know what to do? So that's my practice of dying, tossing around my own questions. I am not researching dying. In research, one finds new knowledge that is ideally deliverable to others. In practice, one's body learns how it is, how it might be. And one's mind remembers important things and doesn't let them fade. Choreography then is a curation of what not to forget. Deaths of loved ones teach me more deeply than the knowledge that we all die.

In the beginning of the pandemic, I made a short piece entitled *Another Day* (2020). This piece is also about dying. It consists of only six photographs. But I really worked on the lighting and the crossfades and timing of it. There was something rigorous about this work process. I took a long time editing it, even if it's just connecting six photos; I always knew the order, so the choreography was just a matter of trying different durations for each photo and each fade, and determining what kind of light changes to make. Now looking at the piece I feel an absoluteness to it. This is also the case in *Seagull* (2020). In making this piece, by choreographing through editing, I really saw what I had seen. I did not research seagulls. I know nothing more about seagulls. I just changed my sense of distance to their bodies by watching so intently while I edited. Whereas in the video piece with Merián Soto where we throw our shoes (*Practice of Being a Nuisance* 2021), the editing process was fast. That piece doesn't really call me to work on it further. I just had to deliver what happened. The practice of being a nuisance is what I do. Not everything I do has to be rigorously choreographed. Some things just happen, and what happened could be more important than how it is delivered. In other cases, how to deliver affects my understanding of what happened. So I then examine different possibilities and watch myself react. Choices might be made instinctively, but not without examination.

On Methods

RC: When I mentioned methods, you referred to that as "how I know what to do." So how do you know what to do?

EO: When I prepare a solo performance, I arrive at the place, sit, and watch. If there are people there, I also watch their flow. Then I come back with some costumes, and I start to move around. Where could I stand? Why? Who is there? I try to be there at the time of the day when the performance will happen. Which way is the sun facing and where are there shadows? For example, if the setting sun is the performance's backdrop, it is hard to watch the performer for a long time. I decide where to put the audience by determining which direction they will face and how comfortable they might be. I try to be friendly with the security guards so that I can start practicing in a particular site, like when I performed on Wall Street. Working in a studio does not prepare me. I bring my friends or my dramaturg, Iris McCloughan, to the site. They add to what I can see.

In Fulton Center (*A Body in a Station* 2015), practicing at the site was not allowed. So I went there every day, but I could not practice. I would just hold the costume [gestures holding costume up] to see what it looked like. I would chat with the security guards so they would get used to me. I took a slow approach and, finally, I laid myself down on my futon. Some passers-by thought I was ill and called 911. The ambulance came and then the head of security, the one who had previously prohibited me from rehearsing, ran to the ambulance shouting "it's okay! She's an artist, she's rehearsing." So that's my method. I work in and out of the rules. I take time to expand what I can do. I do not readily accept what I cannot do. I do not swallow "No." Breaking a rule, if chosen and done well, can be a creative act.

There are so many things I do in my solo that are rough or raw or left to the moment. Cutting into the audience while performing is one such act. In the graveyard (*A Body in a Cemetery* 2020), due to COVID-19, I couldn't really do what I usually do, like standing right in front of one person so that everybody else sees me watching that person. I've practiced these tools over time, mainly through performing in public places. I've found that intentionally exchanging a gaze with a few people creates an odd density in a performance space. When this happens, I'm aware, and she's aware, that everybody's watching this charged gaze between the two of us. She accepts it and performs it. If I'm dancing around here [lifts arms gently up to her left side, gaze softly to the left] and then suddenly go [lowers arms quickly and turns with a direct, strong gaze into the camera]: time changes. The energy changes. It's not research because I know what I'm doing. I've done that move many times and know when and how to do it. But one time there was a dog near me as I was performing, so I went down to look at the dog, but the dog did not know about my practice, and the dog nearly bit me. I was kind of shocked because, in my performing mindset, I forgot that the dog is a different being. Whereas I know how to deal with kids while performing. I was once a preschool teacher. I also know because I have performed in so many places with kids running around. I can quiet them down. I wouldn't do it this way [shows a direct gaze used for adults]; instead, I kind of go this way [softens face and gaze with the slightest of smiles] and I would gently touch their shoulders. I might smile. I also know how to get the attention of those who are ignoring me. For example, I can scream loudly at a particular tonality that catches people's attention. I use my tools to create something that I feel is worth happening, worth remembering. I learn about the sites where I am working and draft a score. I practice and elaborate on that score. However, once a performance starts, I encourage myself to betray that score as needed, to forget my tools, and stray away from my preparation. This is how I experience each performance as worth happening, worth remembering. With many regrets in the past, I am learning experientially how to trust myself.

I want to be practical but I often overload myself with many desires and commitments. In *The Duet Project* (ongoing) I have collaborated with 24 people! That is not practical. With each one, we had a different way of working together. That's expanding our sense of how we learn to encounter the other person and not just "encounter" [makes air quotes with fingers] but [deepens voice, slows pace] really "e-n-c-o-u-n-t-e-r." I want to learn about the collaborator and myself, through different ways of working, various possibilities, not by doing what is convenient or what I already know works. The point of working together is to come up with something that I cannot do alone or with just anyone. *The Duet Project* has taught me to pay attention to whom I'm working with, and how to come up with a different method/process for each by figuring out what is possible and what is not. I do not look for a completely equal collaboration. Equality doesn't exist in the world except we all die. Because we all die, it is urgent that we collaborate.

In the case of *The Duet Project*, I do not impose the same method on every collaboration. It is not a game with a rule. The process and score come from working together. When I worked with Joan Jonas, for example, we agreed that she would direct me. So that's one way of collaborating. I had not done that with anyone before. Making 50/50 decisions is time-consuming, so we agreed to avoid that. We had worked together before as an experiment, so this was the next thing to try. Talking until we both agreed on every detail was not practical for this occasion. She didn't want to work every day, so we agreed to work for four hours every other day for two weeks to create material. Giving Joan the directorship made her feel more at ease, and she moved with me more as a result. I didn't sit together with Joan as she edited several drafts of our project, but I responded fully to each draft and did not hold back my thoughts. There are many ways to edit and I enjoyed being a responder, which is a rare role for me. At the same time, I interviewed her and edited that footage myself, which was a good complement to our video; we aired them together. We were committed to creating a piece, and this is how we managed to do it.

Working with Merián Soto was an entirely different process. We went to the Indiana Dunes. Ramón Rivera-Servera, host of the residency at Northwestern University, told us about a little boy who was sucked into the sand because the dunes are moving. Of course, the story gave us an emotional tilt. It's one thing to learn from a book that the sand dunes move. It's another to hear that a little boy was sucked into an air pocket. I learned this just by being there and listening to a friend. The choreographic process has so much happenstance. A decision does not always come from knowledge, but sometimes rather from the tactical, strategic, or emotional ways we happen to make a piece. Producing and presenting a work is what we do. Knowledge is not almighty. We know this because humans have failed in so many areas so deeply. With that recognition, I have a renewed commitment, not to "art for art's sake," but for the occasions when people gather together to experience something intense and revealing. That kind of time and space, for those moments of seeing, can potentially have the same weight as the gravest happenings in the world. Without such occasions, we become numb and further fall into helplessness.

Aesthetic Choices and Values

RC: It feels like there are values or commitments that you've demonstrated over the years through your work, like you value being seen by people who wouldn't come see you in a theater, you value your audience literally being able to see you, you value not listening to authority…

EO: Yeah, I'm just trying to change the frame a little bit about the place or about the power structure. Not only do I make a work, or produce an event, but also I perform in many places (*A Body in Places*, ongoing). I want to leave stains of memories in each place. Ever since my twelve-hour first solo in Philadelphia (*A Body in a Station* 2014), people still tell me, "I just passed the station, and I remembered your performance." And that happens to me when I see other people's site work and pass that site years later. That is the beauty of site work. When I performed in each of the three locations of the Metropolitan Museum of Art (*A Body in Places: Met Edition* 2017), I was trying to stain the Met's walls metaphorically. I lingered there as long as I was allowed: seven and a half hours in each of the three locations. I did not get three times more research results, but I maximized the possibility of staining those walls. I cannot change the place or the world, but I can stain the place. Thus, my decisions are not based on or aimed at research, even though I can be fascinated about knowing.

I watched Kazuo Ohno perform in many places and in many videos and photos. So, I do not feel I'm doing something new when I go to Fukushima, for example. I do worry people might see me as simply following what he did in many places, dancing outdoors. Nevertheless, I go to Fukushima because it's an important place for me. I also have long been aware that Tatsumi Hijikata did *Kamaitachi* many years ago [with Eikoh Hosoe in 1968]. I was in Hijikata's studio when he was spreading many of the photos from this series on the studio floor because Hosoe had asked him to select images. At the time, I was stunned by these photos. Who wants to be seen as "Oh you are doing what so-and-so did 50 years ago"? But the pull of Fukushima was strong enough for me to disregard that concern. I couldn't help but go to Fukushima. And I did go there six times.

Producing Knowledge versus Creating Art

RC: Earlier you said that research produces knowledge, whereas an artist's creative process produces an artwork, so I'm wondering about the difference between knowledge and an artwork. Certainly, everything you and William Johnston did, and not just the book, *A Body in Fukushima* (2021), we could call research. Every step of the way since you first started going to Fukushima in 2011, and with Johnston in 2014, 2016, 2017, and 2019, for example – exhibiting the photos, or doing *A Body in Places* at the different sites in New York where you're making connections with different nuclear power plants, teaching the subject with your students – in each of these actions you're producing a very different kind of knowledge than, say, measuring radiation with a tool. You're not producing "usable data" per se, but rather you're producing art that hopefully prompts each audience member, each student, to have their own experience with your images of Fukushima. You're offering them the opportunity to feel something differently.

EO: I hope so. I wish to somehow move, or feel the movement of, something rather than to only show body movement. One important thing is how time moves with a performance. The density of watching something together makes the time move differently. In a theater, most audiences stay until the end. This is not the case when I perform in a public space without ticket sales. Even intentional audiences can easily give up watching, saying "Okay, I've had enough;" more so for passers-by. But even without an audience's commitment to watching from beginning until the end, I hope each performance leaves some marks, or shadows, both on the place and on viewers' minds. When they come again to the place or think about the place, they remember what happened there. Not only is performance memory making, but it is also participating in a history. That itself is a human act, whether researched well or not. There is also movement in an act of resisting, even in a standstill. A gaze is different from a look. A gaze is intense, even disturbing. A gaze asks for decision-making: when to pull away or get more involved. That tension is something I cling to when I have so few answers to mounting problems.

I am not at all against acquiring and delivering knowledge. Research or not, a performance is a powerful experience for a doer and a watcher. The last thing I wish to happen is that people go home thinking "Oh, I wish I didn't come." I'm sad when I feel that way myself when I go to see things. So I try hard to offer something that is worth experiencing in whatever way. Could I be a trusted performer for this person or that person? I do plenty of research when I need to do so, and in my everyday life, I am eager to share what I find profound. I believe in collective learning and my teaching is based on that principle. Seeing, making art, and dancing are profound human experiences. Nobody hates oneself when one is being moved by art or when one dances fully. Well-researched is good, but research is not a deciding factor when we are moved by art. I do not want to be taught. I want to be touched. I want to be shaken.

The uselessness of dancing is human.

Across the interview, Eiko pushes back against the encroaching of an academic term on artistic structures and resists a blanket application of "research" to her artistic process, asking instead for specificity of what dancing and art making do. In calling much of what she does practice or just working rather than research, she emphasizes the undefinable moments of performance, the body, and art making. That is consistent with Eiko's work across decades, both solo and as part of Eiko & Koma, which evidences an activist stance, an unwillingness to codify, a resistance to labels, and a commitment to being radically available. It may then seem contradictory to include Eiko's perspective in a book about dance research that is aimed at people in academia. As we wrote in the introduction to this volume, however, we recognize the structures – and strictures – within which scholarly dance research is conducted. As part of the struggle for legitimacy that dance has faced in the academy, we are often asked to translate our work in dance into language and formulas understood by other fields. Eiko's contribution here cautions us to pay attention to the costs of that (assumption of) legibility to other disciplines, funding bodies, university tenure committees, etc., while urging us to be very clear about what our dance practice and performance does in fact do. This is an important intervention, one that we feel is actually in line with the larger project of this volume, which is to push against the borders between dance practice, studies, education, and science that would keep us separated from one another, while also not glossing over the things that make us unique. Eiko asks for expansive, personal, experiential, and creative approaches to seeing, doing, and talking about dance, while cautioning against the universal application of words such as research just because they are key for certain groups. Most of all, she asks us to remember that the desires and urges of artists often resist clarification and definition.

Works Cited

Candelario, Rosemary. 2010. "A Manifesto for Moving: Eiko & Koma's Delicious Movement Workshops." *Journal of Theatre, Dance and Performance Training* 1, no. 1 (March): 88–100.

———. 2011. "Eiko & Koma: Choreographing Spaces Apart in Asian America." PhD Dissertation, University of California, Los Angeles.

———. 2014. "Bodies, Camera, Screen: Eiko & Koma's Immersive Media Dances." *International Journal of Screendance* 4: 80–92.

———. 2016a. *Flowers Cracking Concrete: Eiko & Koma's Asian/American Choreographies*. Middletown, CT: Wesleyan University Press.

———. 2016b. "An Asian American Land: Eiko & Koma Choreograph Cultural Politics." In *Contemporary Directions in Asian American Dance*, edited by Yutian Wong, 174–190. Madison: University of Wisconsin Press.

———. 2016c. "A Body on the Line." In *A Body in Places: Danspace Project PLATFORM 2016*, edited by Lydia Bell, 39–51. New York: Danspace Project.

———. 2017. "An Interview with Eiko Otake." *International Journal of Screendance* 8: 134–141.

———. 2018. "Choreographing American Dance Archives: Artist-driven Archival Projects by Eiko & Koma, Bebe Miller, and Jennifer Monson." *Dance Research Journal* 50, no. 1: 80–102.

Eiko & Koma. 2005. *Death Poem*. http://eikoandkoma.org/videoofdeathpoemeikosolo.

———. 2008. *Mourning*. http://eikoandkoma.org/index.php?p=ek&id=2525.

Hayashi, Kyoko. 2010. *From Trinity to Trinity*. Translated by Eiko Otake. Barrytown, NY: Station Hill of Barrytown.

Otake, Eiko. 2002. "A Dancer Behind the Lens." In *Envisioning Dance on Film and Video*, edited by Judy Mitoma, 82–88. New York: Routledge.

———. 2009. "Feeling Wind." In *Site Dance: Choreographers and the Lure of Alternative Spaces*, edited by Melanie Kloetzel and Carolyn Pavlik, 188–198. Gainesville: University Press of Florida.

———. 2014. *A Body in a Station*. https://www.eikootake.org/solo-project-a-body-in-a-station. Accessed February 28, 2022.

———. 2015. *A Body in a Station at Fulton Center*. https://www.eikootake.org/solo-project-a-body-in-a-station-at-fulton-center-excerpt. Accessed February 28, 2022.

———. 2017. *A Body in Places: Met Edition*. https://www.eikootake.org/solo-project-a-body-in-places-met-edition. Accessed February 28, 2022.

———. 2017. *Soak*. https://www.eikootake.org/media-work-soak.

———. 2019. *With My Mother*. https://www.eikootake.org/with-my-mother.

———. 2020. *Another Day*. https://www.eikootake.org/another-day. Accessed February 28, 2022.

———. 2020. *Attending*. https://www.eikootake.org/attending. Accessed February 28, 2022.

———. 2020. *A Body in a Cemetery*. https://www.eikootake.org/solo-project-a-body-in-a-cemetery. Accessed February 28, 2022.

———. 2020. *Seagull*. https://www.eikootake.org/media-work-seagull. Accessed August 3, 2022.

———. 2021. *Practice of Being a Nuisance*. https://www.eikootake.org/media-work-practice-of-being-a-nuisance. Accessed February 28, 2022.

———. n.d. "The Duet Project: Distance is Malleable." https://www.eikootake.org/the-duet-project. Accessed December 27, 2021.

———. Ongoing. *A Body in Places*. https://www.eikootake.org/solo-project. Accessed February 28, 2022.

Otake, Eiko, and Joan Jonas. 2021. *With the Earth at My Waistline*. https://danspaceproject.org/2021/07/01/eiko-otake-and-joan-jonas/. Accessed December 27, 2021.

Otake, Eiko, and William Johnston. 2021. *A Body in Fukushima*. Middletown, CT: Wesleyan University Press.

Part 3
Dance Studies

8
Introduction to Research in Dance Studies

Dance as a Humanity

Thomas F. DeFrantz

Dance studies, the disciplinary title assigned to dance research within the general humanities, affords academic scaffolding that allows the ever-present political concerns of the world to orient our research in embodied practice. In this formation, dance studies is the designation outside of artmaking, scientific research, or pedagogical concerns that might align dance with areas like history, cultural theory, theater, visual, or media studies. As a gathering notion, dance studies accommodates critical race theory, feminist theory, and queer theory with urgency, allowing dance to spill out from its practices toward the ways that dance engages in *worldmaking* beyond the stage.

To make a world as a researcher, dance studies encourages the assembly of disparate methods and ideological formations in the narration of dance and dancing. Dance studies allow humanities researchers to make any manner of connections across disciplines. Historians, cultural theorists, philosophers, anthropologists, religious studies researchers all turn to dance to better understand their own topics and to reconsider method. In this, *dance* tends to operate as a lever; as evidence of its own ongoing presence in nearly any construction of culture.

Dance studies encourages a wondering at connections usually elided by practice, physical analyses, pedagogy, or even performance. Dance studies might encourage readers to consider how a studio has been constructed; the sourcing of materials that create dance floors; the labor that cleared the ground for the location; the terms of payment for that labor and for the teachers who lead classes in the dance space. Dance studies encourages the consideration of religious devotions that endorse particular movement patterns, those that inevitably emerge outside of anything like a "dance studio," as well as the political specificities of dictatorial regimes that support and curtail certain "folk dance" practices. Dance studies considers racialized dynamics of classroom settings, as well as the diversities of the audience that might constitute a public for any performance in any circumstance. Dance studies brings questions from "the backgrounds" of dance to bear on a rendering of the fact of dance.

Dance studies has emerged mostly as part of the educational complex that produced dance departments in US-based universities. Often, it ties its histories to the development of so-called "modern dance" in those contexts. The whiteness of both the US university system and modern dance are always up for critique in dance studies, as the field arrives essentially as a remain, or a consequence, of attention paid to "white modern dance." In this, dance studies constantly wonders at its own formations and its possibilities as a colonial formation.

In particular, dance studies offers a wondering at how to value practices that need no translation into academic language to continue, but that sometimes benefit from the activities of discourse and discussion. Dance studies might wonder how social movements are arranged, or choreographed, and offer empirical evidence from a constructed archive that demonstrates the routes of exchange that produce social geographies. Dance studies allows thinkers to consider the choreography of the social justice protest, or the flows of capital from the state to the community arts experience. Generally, dance studies participates in a re-valuing of dance according to the terms of various modes of academic interrogation: economics, religion, fashion studies, and media studies offer just a few routes of exploration that researchers follow.

Histories

Dance studies grew as researchers interested in dance sought out circumstances to explore ideas within established humanities disciplines. "Dance history" became a catch-all category for advanced research in the particularities of practice. Some researchers point toward the mid-1990s when scholars turned toward cultural studies methods that insisted that the "inclusion of social context and acknowledgment of historical contingency were essential parts of the process of doing cultural studies and… interdisciplinarity" (Morris 2009, 94). Dance research "became interdisciplinary by adding such theories and methods to those it already possessed" (ibid). As example, an emphasis on the anthropology of movement allowed dance to emerge as a site of study alongside other forms of cultural practice, such as foodways, letter-writing, or music-making. Considerations of aesthetic valuing in relationship to the social movements of people and ideologies eventually allowed dance to be considered as an aspect of artistic communication worthy of humanistic study in the academy.

Clearly, then, dance studies points to other recent disciplinary formations that grew from twentieth-century shifts in modes of academic inquiry. Performance studies, cultural studies, and media studies each hold resonance for researchers in dance studies, and vice-versa. After all, dance tends to be concerned with performance; dance is always embedded within culture; and dance expands through its affiliations with media. Dance studies distinguishes itself with a concern toward embodied practice and the resonance of gesture *as dance*, imagining a container found in every part of the globe that escapes containment as a singularity because of its rampant diversity. We remind each other often that there might not be a single *unit of dance* to be found in practice, even as there are modes, trends, tendencies, genres, skill sets, and valuings that help dancers recognize their activities as dance. The diversity of dance practice allows dance studies to expand continually, as the gestures of dancers continue to be revealed even amid neighboring disciplines, including feminist studies and queer studies.

Dance studies continues to tussle with its own foundations in relation to its functions as a historical apparatus as well as a theoretical apparatus, the whole always bound up by a practice-based method. Historical method, theoretical method, and practical method are each to be found within dance studies; each mode of inquiry influencing and teasing out ideas in the others. In this, dance studies relies equivalently on analyses of how a thing is done, how it has come to be materialized, and how these movements matter. In this formation, practice, history, and theory become entangled in the action of dance studies itself, as a wondering of the world through dance.

Current Practices

In line with my own research interests, critical race theory holds the urgent potential to transform Dance studies toward its destiny as an essential academic provocation. In critical race theory, researchers begin to wonder at systems of power and domination – the biopolitical – that produce categories of artmaking and social practice. These considerations reveal layer upon layer of the myriad ways that dance circulates, and the infinite variety of manners that circulations of movement allow for social exchange. Critical race theory encourages a wondering across and through difference, toward analytic formations that assume hierarchies of power that might be dissembled through their exposure. As examples, wondering through ethnography to better learn how living people value dance, or through philosophy to align thinking about movement with historical antecedents, each gain immensely by considering racialized formations that produced even the practices of "philosophy" or "ethnography." Critical race theory provides a meta-formation that organizes a way to consider various ideas around how groups of people form, and how those groups might affirm, align with, or disavow one another.

While not always referring directly to critical race theory, the four chapters of this Part refer to assumptive logics that might be foundational to dance studies research now. Bench, Candelario, Perillo, and Rosa contend with choreographic analysis in a polyvocal articulation designed to explore decolonial possibilities of thinking alongside each other toward the ideas of their shared dance studies mentor, Professor Susan Leigh Foster. Wondering together at the fielding of forces that produce movement, the quartet of researchers searches out the inner discourse of the dance itself as a site of theoretical production. Demonstrating an awareness of the limits of method in dance studies, any method perhaps, they argue for dance as argumentation; for the recognition of its ethical epistemologies that emerge in relation to its contents and ambitions.

Höfling opens the space of "archive" to include story circles and transmissions in spaces where people dance together as historical documentation. Working through the sources that hold information for the study of capoeira – daily newspapers, and possibly even bits of gossip – Höfling follows the trail of tiny bits of information to limn a historical narrative that is too often hard to see. The chapter also pays attention to structural inequalities that plague the study of dance in the Global South, where resources have displaced the possibilities of traditional archival orientations.

Park elaborates a different archive, one of oral history, that allows stories of dance to emerge and intertwine in moments of unapologetic presence. Concerned with the entanglements of stories that people might be willing to tell one to the other, Park looks for a "research method to match the practice" (159) of b-girl dance, casting oral history as a cypher to familiarize it to artists used to working in story-circle formations.

Working in a different register, Stewart follows philosophers Husserl and Sheets-Johnstone to wonder at how movement might be animated by bringing philosophical thought to bear on its contents, and translating that thought into textual analyses. Stewart demonstrates how some philosophers conduct research that extends an experience of dance toward unexpected ends of memory and its realization in time, crafted in relation to performance.

In their diversity, these chapters offer a microcosm of debates in the field of dance studies.

Future Trends

Interdisciplinary in its foundational design, dance studies arrives concerned with the worlds where dance emerges, with a broad vision of dance's capacities as spiritual practice, as political formation, as celebration and erotic expression, and of course as art. Questions of central importance to dance research today offer evidence of how dance studies moves. We can imagine many futures for dance studies in the world. Practices of ethnography and oral history predict a manner to engage, for example, questions of access for Black women to gain artistic recognition as prima ballerinas in large, well-resourced dance companies. Concerns of how disabled dancers achieve access to performance venues as well as relatable theoretical models of dance drive researchers to analyze architecture and to promote audio descriptions of movement and visual signing of research delivered through oral discourse. Religious and neo-orthodox dance foment vibrant considerations of how spirituality drives esthetic valuing in dance; researchers wonder at historical strands of faith-based movements and their creative foundations through empathetic prisms of study. Queer dance allows a gathering mode centered in non-normative affiliations of, possibly, sex or gender; dance studies researchers revise considerations of normativity or queer possibility in everyday life that involves dance. Dance as protest predicts emergent strategies for training marginalized people toward places in civic life; dance studies researchers detail how protest emerges as and from dance. And dance continually references ancestral presences that expand how communities might experience time, as predicted by Native and First Nation/Indigenous people and the dance studies researchers who accompany their movements.

These trends, among so many others, demonstrate how dance studies works to elucidate changing social circumstances.

History Returns

I want to lift up the potential for dance studies to operate as a lever for the essential critical race studies that surround performance, and especially dance practices. The first two decades of the 21st century have called for a renewed attention to climate change, resource inequalities, and concerns of social justice and reconciliation of coloniality across the planet. Each of these areas of exploration is entangled with critical race studies, and contemporary dance research continues to arrive within this emergent context. We can only expect this trend to continue, and that more and more researchers will be compelled to analyze how their research is entangled in systems of racialized operands that demand theoretical parsing. Dance studies, as a young discipline, arrives well-positioned to take on this urgent challenge that might analyze the choices that people have made with their embodied practices in alignment with the structuring logics that allow some to move in some ways, but deny others those same possibilities.

In this, dance studies reveals its concern as a historicizing structure that embraces consideration and care for events of the past. Dance holds a remarkable ability to engage first-person narratives in the person-to-person mode of transmission that is at its center. Dancing holds history, and dance studies reveal what has been at stake in gestures, revealed now through intellectual scrutiny. History returns in our dances and in our considerations of how those dances operate. And when history returns, we might share a hope: that the past creates space for unimagined futures.

Works Cited

Morris, Gay. 2009. "Dance Studies/Cultural Studies." *Dance Research Journal* 41, no. 1 (Summer): 82–100.

9
Choreographic Analysis as Dance Studies Methodology

Cases, Expansions, and Critiques

Harmony Bench, Rosemary Candelario,
J. Lorenzo Perillo, and Cristina Fernandes Rosa

Introduction

In their introduction to the third edition of *The Routledge Dance Studies Reader*, Jens Richard Giersdorf and Yutian Wong identify the emergence of dance studies as a field in the United States and Europe in the 1980s with the effort to "recast dance and choreography as a method" in which choreography and dance could "become models for accessing, organizing, and destabilizing political, structuralist, and post-colonial enquiries" (2019, 5). This approach, they argue, provided a methodology for researching gender, race, sexuality, class, and more. In this chapter, we address the formation, continued application, and pedagogy of one such approach – choreographic analysis – in which choreography simultaneously names an object, a method, and an analytic framework. A choreographic lens might interpret, direct, and foreclose possibilities for movement; choreographic analysis may also offer a way to understand and convey the multiple, contradictory, temporal, and particular power relations involved in movement, spatial distributions, or systems of relations.

The stakes of choreographic analysis, both at the beginning of dance studies as a field and today, are significant. Choreographic analysis expanded dance scholarship by showing not only what dances mean but also how they produce meaning. It demonstrated the possibilities of writing complex analyses of a system of representation with verbal and non-verbal signifiers, and advanced notions of embodied knowledge production, especially in terms of writing. It also gave credibility to the field, particularly in relation to other fields also engaged in the interpretive turn. The other side of the coin of validation by the academy is being subject to its constraints and limitations in terms of scholarship, pedagogy, and curricula. Choreographic analysis isn't neutral; it's a framework with a history. It emerged from academic circles in the Global North, spaces historically patriarchal, colonial, and capitalist. While many dance studies texts pushed against these systems of oppression, they have also been pulled in or co-opted by these circles. At colleges and universities, texts that opened up new possibilities for dance research themselves became subject to canonization and codification in order to comply with expectations from the industry of higher education for legible, replicable methods and methodologies. Furthermore, the assumption that such methods could then be applied universally, worldwide, only reinforced colonial paternalism.

To consider these issues, Rosemary invited Cristina, Harmony, and Lorenzo to dialogue about choreographic analysis. In what follows, we discuss choreographic analysis: what it is, what we see as its affordances and limitations, and how we have each employed it differently in our research and teaching. Our discussion uses as its starting point the work of Susan Leigh Foster as a foundational scholar within the development of critical dance studies in North America, its significance to dance studies in the Global North, and its international impact. And since we all earned PhDs in Culture and Performance from UCLA chaired by Foster, we also relate to our experiences learning to work with her approaches and lenses firsthand. Despite this commonality in our training, our research interests vary greatly (broadly: movement practices from Brazil, Filipino and Filipino diasporic hip hop, the diaspora of Japanese butoh, and dance in online and digital spaces), and we have been working in a variety of university departments (dance, theater, ethnic studies) in North and South America, Europe, and the Pacific. Furthermore, we don't necessarily agree on what choreographic analysis is, how or when it can be applied, and what its limitations/affordances are. Yet, our diverse perspectives allow us to attend in our scholarship to many different dimensions of choreography, including its relationships to bodies, societies, political and cultural frameworks, as well as nonhuman situations. Given the challenges of the pandemic and our disparate locations, we came together asynchronously – via email, video recordings, WhatsApp voice messages, Zoom chats, and Google Docs – to forge a "dialogue" on the page out of our individual contributions. Throughout, we assert that choreographic analysis is a useful tool, but one that should not be fixed with a single definition or a prescribed set of steps to follow. Rather, we emphasize choreographic analysis as a productive framework that prompts us to ask questions about the event at hand.

What Is Choreographic Analysis?

ROSEMARY CANDELARIO (RC): Choreographic analysis is often linked to Foster's 1986 book, *Reading Dancing*, even though she does not use that term.

Instead, she proposes "reading dancing" as the name for an "active and interactive interpretation of dance as a system of meaning" based on "a set of choreographic conventions that create and convey what a dance is about" (1986, xvii), including frame, modes of representation, style, vocabulary, and syntax. These codes and conventions are, Foster argues, used by "literate dance readers" (1986, 56) to interpret the dance. She builds this method of movement and semiotic analysis (via a Barthesian understanding of the text) on four paradigmatic examples: Deborah Hay, George Balanchine, Martha Graham, and Merce Cunningham. These four choreographers were all part of the 20th-century American concert dance scene, and more specifically were all active in the 1983–1984 New York season. These examples of white choreographers working in ballet, modern, and postmodern dance provided material for Foster to propose a system for analyzing not only how dances are made and what they mean, but more so how dances make meaning. This semiotic approach paves the way for the elaboration in subsequent texts of choreography as a framework of structural analysis, that exceeds methods of content or movement analysis, such as Laban Movement Analysis.

HARMONY BENCH (HB): To me, choreographic analysis is a form of close reading that employs movement as evidence, but I do not tie it exclusively or even primarily to dancing bodies, nor do I seek "meaning" in my use of choreographic analysis. In that way, my own use and understanding deviate from what Foster laid out in *Reading Dancing*, but are aligned with her overall project of elaborating choreography as a framework. Confession: *Reading Dancing* never resonated with me; I turn to Foster's later essays "Choreographies of Gender" (1998) and "Choreographies of Protest" (2003) for articulations of how choreographic analysis allows me to focus on what arranged, planned, or executed movement achieves or embodies. It illuminates how power (in a Foucauldian sense) is spatialized, temporalized, and corporealized in terms of the development of bodily capacities and the organization of environments to shape or direct certain outcomes. In my mind, choreographic analysis connects to Maussian techniques of the body and Foucauldian anatomo- and biopolitics (inclusive of but not limited to docile bodies as Foster lays out in "Dancing Bodies" [1997]).

This is how I define choreographic analysis in *Perpetual Motion: Dance, Digital Cultures, and the Common*:

> In my view, choreographic analysis foregrounds the forces through which movement is produced, maintained, constrained, accelerated, directed, and made legible. As a social analytic, choreography is concerned with issues of bodily discipline and regimes of movement. It is worth emphasizing, however, that choreography is necessarily plural. Any complex system

simultaneously brings together multiple contradictory forces and pressures, along with multiple structures for organizing movement. These may materialize in the form of dance, or they may materialize in the forms of gestures, postures, mobilities, constraints, pathways, and flows, among other manifestations.

(2020, 13)

I think choreographic analysis really emphasizes how movement is a manifestation or physical expression of underlying structures. Giving movement weight as evidence affirms how bodies are articulate – they are not merely reacting to environments and conditions as "dumb" matter, they are actively reading the scene and making choices. But at the same time, choreographic analysis demonstrates how those choices are circumscribed. In other words, choreographic analysis offers a way to hold the agential and articulate in productive tension with the nonvoluntary and coerced.

How We Learned Choreographic Analysis

RC: Choreographic analysis is at the heart of many dance studies texts. However, scholars using the methodology have primarily learned it inductively by reading texts that analyze choreography. My graduate school training, guided by Foster, involved reading the latest texts by dance studies scholars. In class, she would ask us the following questions about texts we read:

> What in the dance's action is most vividly represented in print? How does the author analyze the choreography? How does the author implement or otherwise dialogue with theories raised in cultural studies and critical theory? What does the author's "body" look like and how is it moving? What does the author envision as the relationship between dancing and writing? How does the writing make you feel?

This approach to noticing other scholars' processes and learning to apply and adapt them, along with Foster's frequent reminder, "the dance will tell you how to write it," provided me with an intuitive process guided by the choreography itself, rather than any didactic list of steps, that worked for me in my own research.

J. LORENZO PERILLO (JLP): I learned about choreographic methods in the mid-aughts primarily through a series of Foster's classes, departmental events, conferences, and one-on-one advising meetings. I don't believe *Reading Dancing* was ever assigned course reading, but rather I read texts by Brenda Dixon Gottschild (1998, 2005), Thomas DeFrantz (2006), Cynthia Novack (1990), Randy Martin (1998), and many others. As a research method, choreographic analysis gave me space to see how a variety of analytical approaches to movement could be less about notation or capturing the dance, and rather serve particular scholarly research functions.

CRISTINA FERNANDES ROSA (CFR): To me, Foster was not proposing that we use her book as a cookie-cutter methodology. This is not a cake recipe. Rather, she offers a semiotic way of reading dances by prominent US-based choreographers. But her texts also reveal to us, dance scholars, her thinking behind it. That way, we could further employ these conventions and/or (re)formulate our own categories of analysis and structure them as we see fit, in a given case or context. Her goal, I think, was to demonstrate that choreography is a system of representation and, as such, could be read or decoded. Behind all that laid acts of perception and translation between what she later called moving and pen-pushing bodies (Foster 1995). She would ask me, "Cristina, tell me, what did you see?"

JLP: The thing that choreographic analysis afforded me that differed from my previous training in American studies and concurrent Asian American studies training was a set of guiding questions to pay attention to in relationship to the body and social, cultural surroundings. How does the subject depict bodily reality? How does the subject conceptualize and organize movement knowledge? In American studies and critical race studies, literary and historical methods that rely on close-textual analysis are dominant; thus choreographic analysis helped legitimize what I was doing as a scholar coming from the hip hop and street dance community. Additionally, it became about the writing of research. How do I write, and how do I translate it onto the page? How will I depict my authorial body in relation to other moving bodies? So choreographic analysis as a method meant as much to me on the back end as on the front end. How do I bring these guiding questions to an interview, or bring a particular awareness to a viewing? How do I get at the internal discourse of the dance? For me, it lies in recognizing the agency of the dance, the interior elements, or the aesthetics of the practice, for example, and allowing them to inform the research process. The ongoing experimentation with writing dance in the field led me to sometimes think about the feeling that the dancer gets or the audience gets from the dance. It could mean being very mindful of the lineage of DeFrantz's "the break" (2006) or what Foster talks about in terms of the agency of the dance, to let it come over you, or to let it take hold of you in the research process, in the reading of the research, and the delivery of the research. It wasn't just "insert movement description here." I think that opened a lot, it destabilized dance as an object. And so I could bring in that mixed insider-outsider feeling that I have in the community and try to replicate that, or try to give the reader of the research that feeling. Not just describe it, but try to give them that vibe, you know.

The question of the multi-dimensional, multi-sensorial, and multi-modal is what was really interesting and generative for me and also what I couldn't find in American studies and critical race studies.

How We Have Used and Adapted Choreographic Analysis

CFR: When writing my book *Brazilian Bodies and their Choreographies of Identification: Swing Nation* (2015), I took Foster's choreographic analysis as a foundational framework for analyzing the repertoire of Grupo Corpo, a ballet-centered company of contemporary dance that utilizes a variety of movement vocabulary materials from Afro-Brazilian aesthetics. What I liked the most about Foster's approach in *Reading Dancing*, and her teaching style, was that it gave me a tangible awareness of how the constructions of categories of analysis could be productive to my examination of Grupo Corpo's dance works *Nazareth* (1992) and *Breu* (2007). But before I could get there, I wrote five previous chapters unpacking their Africanist qualities of movement, and historicizing them, outside and beyond the conventions outlined in *Reading Dancing*. In the end, I developed my own way of seeing and reading those dance works, which was certainly informed by my own historical positionality. Dancing is always already complex, subjective, and circumstantial, and so is watching and trying to make sense of it. However, I was grateful to understand the notion of categories, meaning how categorizing is an artificial procedure that nevertheless supports analytical thinking. The act of recognizing patterns, drawing out particular elements, pulling them apart, and/or sorting them into cognitive boxes clarified what I was looking at. But, and here is the caveat: I was analyzing set choreographies performed on theatrical stages by a company that, despite its specificities, remained centered on a European technique. And that is exactly what afforded them international visibility and legibility.

RC: I remember during graduate school sitting with performance artist and scholar Doran George on the hill next to the dance building at UCLA with our copies of *Reading Dancing*, and discussing whether it was something that could be applied beyond US and European concert dance to our respective fields of somatics and butoh. And even more than can it be, should it be? Foster's specific yet narrow focus on her four paradigmatic examples – all white, US-based, modern and postmodern concert dance – does not address further possible paradigms beyond these Eurocentric examples, as Foster herself acknowledges. We ultimately decided that the method was not exhausted by Foster's selection of material, and that we could take some of her big principles as a way to look at different forms. I think the notion that helped us get there was of "dance as a product of the choreographer's creative process" (1986, xix). More broadly, Foster's articulation that, "Reflected in the organization of the dances and the preparations for them are certain fundamental assumptions about the nature of the body and also the self, or subject, of the person dancing" (1986, 43) helped us see that there was so much room to extend this beyond the event of a dance performance, as well as beyond the construction of meaning, to explore how the world of the dance relates to the world around it, what it effects in the world, and how it is affected by that world in which it is experienced. You can see this in Doran's book, *The Natural Body in Somatics Dance Training* (2020),[1] in which they analyze how somatics dance training both relates to larger aesthetic and political values, and produces a kind of embodied politics. In my book *Flowers Cracking Concrete: Eiko & Koma's Asian/American Choreographies*, choreographic analysis helped me to articulate the pair's profound slowness – often Orientalized by critics and audiences as "Zen" – as a persistent and insistent "adagio activism" (2016, 4–8). In this I depart from Foster's emphasis on semiotic analysis in favor of focusing on what Eiko & Koma's dances do in the world, what I called their "profound corporeal and affective work" (2016, 4). And then it also helped me get at the structural forces – discourses about Japan, the binds of Asian/America, multi-cultural programming policies – that have often occluded the political implications of their performances.

JLP: I approached choreographic analysis not as something that was set in stone or limiting, but more like a launching pad or a stepping stone to my own method that I developed. I think that was what was most useful and meaningful to me to get at my experience with the material and the subject. My experiences doing research in the Philippines opened up a world. It really pushed the limits of understanding a dance from a narrower idea of what choreographic analysis is, that it's just breaking down a dance. For me, it was more about that expansive idea that choreography is not just something for professional dancers. Rather, the military choreographs, or the state choreographs, or there's choreography beyond the concert stage at institutional levels. There are real kinds of dynamics that we can articulate about the body and the self, the social and cultural at that level.

One example in the "Heroes and Filipino Migrations" chapter of my book *Choreographing in Color: Filipinos, Hip-Hop, and the Cultural Politics of Euphemism* (2020) lies in the reality that thinking about dances purely as a form of expression misses out on the dynamics by which dancers were exported by the Philippine state to provide care for the globe, for rapidly industrializing Asian countries, and for institutions like Hong Kong

Disney and Universal Studios Singapore. Multi-national corporations and employment agencies rely on stereotypes that naturalize Filipinos as the world's best dancers and singers. But if we just treat that as entertainment, or as a win for the arts community, then we miss out on how racialized and gendered dancers are part of the global care chain. Now more than ever in the pandemic, we realize how much we have to think about the relationship between choreography and care. We're creating audiences, or you're dancing with others, or you're teaching others to care for themselves and treat their bodies with respect and not dance when they're sick. We're not taught this necessarily with historical and close-textual analysis. However, I think choreographic analysis helped me get there because it revealed all the different dimensions of choreography, of the relationship between body, society, politics, and culture that I wouldn't have seen otherwise if I just relied on interviews with dancers. That helps, of course. But also I needed to see the interlocking pieces. The frequent *despedida* for dancers going away. Awareness of the power dynamics behind the "going aways" or the new arrivals of people coming from the United States, those kinds of things were critical for that community to sustain its scene.

HB: Just as interesting for me are the nonhuman applications of choreographic analysis to, for example, computer hardware and interface design; camera movement, including framing and editing in dance onscreen; built environments and their implications for how humans and nonhumans gather or pass through, and whether their motion is forced or blocked; and so on. Urban planning, computational surveillance, Trump's border wall, red lining – these can all be viewed through a choreographic lens insofar as they interpret, direct, and foreclose possibilities for movement.

Openings for Decolonial Processes?

RC: We have been talking about what choreographic analysis enables and how it may be adapted and expanded. What about its limitations?

CFR: I've come to realize that developing our own categories of analysis is not enough. It is still, as my current students at the Federal University of Bahia in Salvador (UFBA) have argued, reproducing coloniality. Because, if in order to value dancing – not only to bring visibility and clarity to it but to value dancing *otherwise* – we must subscribe to conventions that have been established within Eurocentric cosmologies, that is already negating the possibility of extending what an analysis could be, its function and its productivity, in terms of understanding not only alterity but also pluriversity. In Brazil, for instance, black dance scholars have been empowered by a series of public policies that implemented affirmative action in state institutions and National Curriculum Guidelines for the Implementation of Ethnic-Racial Relations Education and the Teaching of Afro-Brazilian, African, and Indigenous History and Culture. And now, they are asking: What if, instead of clarifying – or whitewashing – our analyses, we were to black them up (*enegrecer* in Portuguese), through Afrocentric perspectivism (Nogueira 2011), *pretagogia* (neologism indicating black pedagogy, Petit 2015) or an Afro-diasporic epistemology (Rufino 2019)?

In a nutshell, the extent to which seminal dance studies texts, such as but not limited to Foster's *Reading Dancing*, are applicable to a wide range of works gives us the false impression that they work for everything. However, that's not the case. And as we expand the field of dance studies to examine other kinds of artistic movement practices from distinct kinds of people circulating in different kinds of contexts, it becomes clear that what we historically know as critical dance studies up to very recently is more like an "area studies." Historically speaking, it's a Eurocentric discipline anchored on epistemologies of the Global North. Another problem with (the notion of) any method is that it assumes that there's some kind of universality or neutrality about it, but there isn't, either. Nothing about Foster's way of thinking is natural or neutral, or somehow critical enough that it's disembodied or not situated. Hence, it's important to not only care for the movements, in and of themselves; to look very carefully and to describe them accurately, or productively. It's equally important to understand the ideas that the people doing those movements have about a variety of things, starting with how they know or perceive their own bodies, both physically and metaphysically. At least, we should try to grasp the nuts and bolts of bodily movements through the eyes of those performing them, their ways of knowing, and how they function in each context. Meanwhile, we should also tend to the effects that those movements produce, here and there, whether they have emotional, cultural, or political implications or legibility. We might also need to scratch and reevaluate our own notions of beauty and correctness, in terms of what is considered to be "good" or "well done." What are the dancers' epistemological parameters for deciding who is doing "that thing" well, in terms of ethics and aesthetics, and so forth? Or even, what is a category or convention? What is a logical argument or is clarifying logic always the ultimate goal? Once you step outside the thinking practices of the Global North, the value of creative movement might also exceed or differ from those within Eurocentric cosmologies. At the same time, I think that any decolonial or anti-colonial exercise in dance studies must also question the coloniality of language, that is, the choices made in communicating your findings in writing, from how you structure a sentence or paragraph to word choice. Do you incorporate vocabulary from a native language to address local key concepts or do you translate and/or approximate them to words in the target language, often English? So, it's a matter of both perception and translation. These two are inseparable parts of a methodology, and its production of knowledges.

RC: That makes me think of one of our UCLA contemporaries, D. Sabela Grimes, who does what he calls a "mash-up" of Foster's concept of the frame (1986), and DeFrantz (2004) and H. Sami Alim (2006) on call-and-response and the cipher to think through Soulja Boy's "Crank That" on YouTube, specifically, and the space and community of the digital cipher more broadly (2008). The way he uses the language, rhythms, and syntax of hip hop to both "read" and communicate his analysis feels very much like what Cristina is talking about. The way Grimes takes Foster's argument and "makes it his own," in writing, seeks to (and perhaps succeeds in) overcoming some of the limits outlined above.

JLP: Thinking about the issues Cristina raises makes me wonder if I am imposing a Western concept into a space where I'm trying to decolonize at the same time? For example, one approach that I considered in response to the predominant positioning of white and European choreographers as paradigmatic of both 20th-century American concert dance and choreographic analysis, was to shift and recenter Filipino choreographers like Francisca Reyes-Aquino, Agnes Locsin, and Myra Beltran. At the same time, a reclamation of the individual genius of choreographers from the Philippines isn't going to cut it. It doesn't have a direct impact on the rules of the game. If we're not cognizant of that definition of choreography being limited in some ways, then we're just replicating some of those unhealthy relationships between the United States and its postcolonial territories. For these reasons, in my book I employed choreographic analysis along with indigenous, ethnographic, and archival methods to rethink the naturalization of colonial relations between indigenous, Black, and Filipino peoples. In order to adapt choreographic analysis and as an initial step toward awareness and action, I find it important to acknowledge and honor the indigenous people and stewards of the land upon which the university is located. This opens up not only the specific settler politics of terms like "choreographic" and thus choreographic analysis, but also highlights how the rise of such terms is embedded within a history of indigenous land dispossession by "land-grab" universities like the University of California, The Ohio State University, and Cornell University (Lee et al. 2020). In a different approach to decolonial choreographic analysis in my article "Embodying Modernism: A Postcolonial Intervention Across Filipino Dance" (2017),

I reveal the white settler colonial genealogies that helped give rise to the landmark *Philippine Dances and Games* (Reyes-Tolentino and Ramos 1927), and the debate between dance as a means of choreographing colonial legitimacy and national subjectivity.

CFR: I agree with Lorenzo. From a decolonial perspective, I think it's necessary to exercise something that Walter Mignolo has called epistemic disobedience (2021). Similar to the black Brazilian authors I mentioned above, the work of other black and brown dance scholars such as Nadine George-Graves, Raquel Monroe, Priya Srinivasan, Melissa Blanco Borelli, Royona Mitra, and María Regina Firmino-Castillo, to name a few, continues to draw on decolonial methodologies and pedagogies as a way of unsettling or unhinging from epistemologies of the Global North, pointing to how they have historically shaped analyses of dances and other movement practices in our field.

HB: I appreciate this discussion of how choreographic analysis isn't neutral. It came from somewhere. But I'm not ready to call choreographic analysis any more or less colonial than other methods; the academy as a whole is a colonial institution. Just like discourse analysis, performance analysis, data analysis, etc., choreographic analysis names the thing being analyzed. So the question becomes: what is the "choreographic" in choreographic analysis? If the choreographic refers only to dances composed in a certain kind of way, that's a big problem. There's a very interesting slippage here where choreography simultaneously names an object of analysis (choreography as composition), a method of analysis (close reading of movement), and an analytic framework (reading "as" choreography in a kind of Schechnerian is/as performance approach). How very postmodern. How very confusing. But I'm surprised by the question of whether or not choreographic analysis can be decolonial. Without myself laying claim to a decolonial method, the question for me would not be "if" a decolonial choreographic analysis is possible, but "how" or "in what ways" is it possible? Foster showed us a feminist choreographic analysis in "The Ballerina's Phallic Pointe" (1996) and "Choreographies of Gender" (1998), and in her "Choreographing Empathy" essay (2005) that preceded her book by the same title (2011), she shows how the project of colonial expansion is situated in the very bodies and practices of 18th-century dancers – not least through their imagination of space as abstract and empty. Foster deconstructs the operations through which worldviews take shape in movement, which seems to me an important step in decolonial critique.

CFR: Indeed, Harmony. How very confusing. On the one hand, scholars such as Marta Savigliano have problematized discourses that uphold the centrality of Choreography, as she puts it, "with a capital 'C,' to connote the privileged status given to the ability to create or read meaningful and/or effective configurations of movement such as space and time" (2009, 187), assigned to dance composition as an art form, in opposition to other kinds of "dancing happening out there in the world" (2009, 181). On the other hand, Foster's scholarship invites us to grasp "choreography," more broadly speaking, as any set of underlying codes or guidelines organizing moving bodies, artistically, socially, politically, ideologically, epistemologically, and so forth. In my book (2015), I use this broader understanding in order to problematize the (perceived) fixity of marked identities. In short, my analyses of various bodily arts (from concert dance to martial arts) as well as practices of daily life, such as walking, pay close attention to the ways in which marginalized bodies circulating in Brazil have negotiated agency through movement. Some articulate, as I argue, empowering "choreographies of identification," even when they continue to be placed or viewed in positions of otherness. I would qualify my analysis as decolonial, in as much as I'm not interested in framing practices such as capoeira angola and samba circles as "choreographic works," for instance. Rather, I deploy choreographic lenses to shed light on discourses articulated from an Afrocentric system of bodily organization and knowledge production cultivated in Brazil. Simply put, my analysis of what I call "ginga aesthetic" across distinct practices acknowledges in writing a black diasporic way of thinking about and moving across the world that differs from and exceeds the epistemologies of the Global North.

JLP: I think a lot of folks who came through our genealogy at UCLA advocate for choreographic analysis to gain recognition as legitimate as historical or ethnographic methods. And I think in order to do that, we do need to think along different lines. What does choreographic analysis mean in terms of self and selfhood? What does it mean in terms of interpersonal relations? What does it mean in terms of institutional dynamics, whether the institution be the state, or the educational institution, or the prison? And then, what does it mean in terms of the world, for the environment, climate change, the cosmos, and more-than-humans?

CFR: In terms of my current research, titled "Movements of Sustainability," I'm approaching the analysis of bodily arts through four categories, three of which are widely addressed in several postmodern dance practices: the care of self, the care of others, and the care for environments. I have added a fourth one: the care for ideas and ways of knowing. For me, any decolonial methodology seeking to support and sustain ways of doing and being otherwise would have to consider those four.

The Ethics of Choreographic Analysis

RC: This decolonial problematization we've been discussing also feels like an articulation of the ethics of choreographic analysis.

JLP: In order to secure the rights, welfare, and dignity of human research subjects, my university has several administrative support systems and ethics review boards that provide policies, procedures, and approval necessary before any investigator can conduct research. As far as I know, the ethics review board doesn't recognize choreographic analysis or question its ethical consequences, as it does ethnography or other methodologies. So if we want to think about it at the policy level, what would it look like if we had an ethics review board consider choreographic analysis? How would that board evaluate the selfhood part that I referred to before, that is, doing justice to the dance, and the ethical relationship specific to choreographies?

RC: Drawing from what Carolyn Ellis (2007) calls relational ethics, what are the ethics of relating to the dance? How do you relate to the dance's agency? How do you engage with the dancemaker, the dancers, producers, audiences? Maybe you're writing about something and as you're going along you realize that it's appropriative and now that you're into it, there's this problem that's being raised. How do you address that? Do you sweep it under the rug, or grapple with it? I had a student who was writing about Maguy Marin's *Groosland* (1989). Her interest in it was thinking with object-oriented ontology – a field of philosophy that rejects anthropocentrism and considers objects to exist independent of human perception – about the relationship of the dancers' bodies to the fatsuits they wore. But I kept urging her to not ignore the element of fat phobia in the performance. What is the choreographic representation saying about abled-bodyism and particular kinds of bodies? On the one hand, the dance is doing these really interesting things with objects, but on the other hand, it's being kind of crappy about people. I pushed her to not let the dance off the hook. The student went into the dance thinking about the analysis one way and as she got into it, she realized that she had to develop how to relate to other aspects of the dance and take that seriously and acknowledge that in the analysis. The resulting article, "Intra-acting fat suits, tutu flesh, and sweaty skins: material-semiotic clashes in Maguy Marin's Ballet *Groosland*" (Mandradjieff 2021), is an example of developing the relational ethics of choreographic analysis. By focusing on the costumes as agential matter that nonetheless function within particular cultural frameworks, Mandradjieff showed how the choreography could reify fat phobia even as it opened up questions about the divide between human and nonhuman.

HB: I find this to be an interesting and complicated space of navigation with my students, who sometimes want to offset the evaluative weight of dance criticism (e.g. newspaper reviews) by being so overly generous and deferential that their scholarship reads like they've been hired as part of a public relations campaign for the artists they analyze. On the flipside, however, sometimes I read scholarship that is little more than a pugilistic take-down, and the author hasn't backed up their assertions with any movement evidence, which again, is central to my understanding of choreographic analysis. I think one aspect of the ethical relation comes through in taking responsibility for our own roles as scholars and writers, and to historicize, contextualize, and interpret – even to offer strong criticism when appropriate – while also recognizing the position of the author in relation to who or what they are writing about, and the power that the written word continues to hold vis à vis embodied practices.

JLP: Beyond the relationship of self to the choreography, the interpersonal relationship would address how you share the dance with others, in the educational realm or in the media realm, like posting on social media, or commodifying your own labor. How do you make peace with those kinds of relationships? The interpersonal leads to questions such as: what are my communication skills and patterns, or how do I care for others? And then, how do I inhabit that role as a teacher?

CFR: I have a quote by Brazilian choreographer Lia Rodrigues, originally posted on her old website, which I wrote down on a piece of paper and I carry around with me wherever I go. It always comes to mind when I think of the ethics of relating to artworks and making sense of them. My translation of her quote is: "How can we relate to that which is different from us? How do you meet the other, in their habitat? And what can you gain, as much as you give, through these experiments and exchanges? Learn to learn from one another?"

My current post-graduate students at the UFBA (a state institution that has implemented a series of successful affirmative action policies) are basically demanding three points. Firstly, when they enter the university, they want to feel included, which might mean different things to different people. But they want to feel acknowledged and embraced by the system. Secondly, they problematize or question notions of representativity in the curricula. Similar to Rodrigues' point mentioned above, I often hear students expressing something like "I don't see myself in this text," or "I don't recognize myself in what this author is saying," in terms of the place from which one speaks or locus of enunciation ("*lugar de fala,*" in Portuguese, see Ribeiro 2019). Finally, in addition to reading authors that are speaking from their historical positionalities, students have expressed the need or desire to engage in topics pertinent to their interest, their sociohistorical backgrounds, and ethno-cultural heritages. They want to be in a program that speaks to, about, and for them, their positionalities, their ancestralities, their systems of beliefs and meaning-making, etc. And, when I assigned Foster's *Reading Dancing* and the recording of one of her performative lectures in my methodology class, they didn't see themselves in it. Several students reacted by canceling her and her ideas, at first sight. In the case of the performative lecture, I presumed that the whiteness of her skin, the foreignness of her accent, her academic rhetoric and voice intonation, and the bodily traces of her ballet training, all obfuscated any cutting-edge thought or problematizing argument her enactment was meant to achieve. After the initial shock – and the embarrassment of showing up thinking that I could fit that North American critique into a discussion useful to decolonial scholarship in Brazil, yet my decolonial approach wasn't deep enough – I was actually pleased with the students' ability to read her work against the grain and point out some things that for me had become invisible. In retrospect, my naiveness lay on my assumption that her long-lived contributions to the Global North dispensed any critical contextualization of their applicability to dance studies in Brazil. Instead, I should have contextualised these readings/viewings with a discussion of how her scholarship has historically pushed against systems of oppression (patriarchy, coloniality, capitalism), but were equally pulled in by them, as it was co-opted into a codified "standardization" of choreographic analysis as a fixed method. I'm teaching this methodology class once again and this time we will begin by looking at works that are currently being published or performed in Brazil, and then we're going to deconstruct that through various decolonial approaches, and in relation to what is being valued abroad, in the Global North. I'm going to ask students to bring examples from their research topics, many of which are rooted in epistemologies of the Global South, and use them to problematize the limits of methodological approaches codified in dance studies, such as choreographic analysis, ethnography, and so forth. That way, I hope to practice, as Vázquez proposes, the task of listening "as an ethical orientation, towards knowledge as *relationality*" (2012, 247).

Pedagogy of Choreographic Analysis

RC: Choreographic analysis then raises pedagogical questions in addition to ethical ones: how can you teach an approach that has this ability that we've been discussing here to really let the movement teach us about how to work with it and how to analyze it, without replicating colonial structures? In my experience, once I began teaching in a PhD program with colleagues trained in qualitative social science research methods, I began to have to articulate the what and how of choreographic analysis in order to prove its validity as a scholarly method. I was, however, reluctant to say definitively "this is what it is," because it necessarily adapts to the event/performance/practice at hand.

JLP: It might be the case that for most methods in higher education, we are taught how to "do" the method rather than how to teach the method. Perhaps this is why our reflections on instructional experiences have been so illuminating. For me, I talk to my students about the opening up of the term "choreography," rather than just the common or popular usage of the term. Within hip hop or street dance communities, it still has limited use. But, it could be about looking at that polyvalent or polysemous nature of choreography – to see it as informing or agentive to your writing, taking control of your authorial body, you know, or to think about those ethical relationships. Or to think about how it can inform your historical approach, it can inform your ethnographic approach, it kind of cuts across all those other methods in a way that's really mischievous. And it points at the disembodiment of historical approaches, and it points at the overemphasis of the interpersonal in ethnography.

CFR: I have developed a few strategies for teaching how to analyze and contextualize movement, extrapolating from what scholars from the Global North have offered, and what their way of reading might have missed. When I was teaching in the United States, I might begin with African American choreographers and ask what is at stake for them, then compare and contrast those with works elsewhere in the African Diaspora. Similarly, in the United Kingdom or in Brazil, I might evoke Akram Khan or Grupo Corpo to ask questions regarding the form and function of hybrid ways of dancing or the effects they produce on global stages, in contrast to process-oriented practices such as capoeira's or hip hop's participatory improvisations in local communities. But, like Foster, I continue to ask my students: "what did you see?" In writing classes, I have drawn attention to etymology, the construction of new concepts between languages, and other translation issues.

JLP: We're saying choreographic analysis is a tool, but we can't just take it and say, "Oh, this is how you do it and it's a formula and it's going to work every time." We have to think about "What does this community need from this tool and then how can we use it best?" So in my Asian and Asian American dance theory class, I asked the students what they are interested in, in terms of Asian dance and performance theories, and how we can look at the field together. I don't want to replicate a canon approach, so I set it up that we had a conversation at the beginning of the class wherein we took a poll and ranked a cross-section of existing literature, that they might or might not know, in order of their existing interests. From that I created clusters of conversations. For example, one week we read the intro to *Dancing East Asia* (Mezur and Wilcox 2020) with my "Heroes and Filipino Migrations" chapter (2020) and "Towards a Chinese Hip-Hop Feminism and a Feminist Reassessment of Hip-Hop with Breakdance: B-Girling in Hong Kong, Taiwan and China" (Chew and Mo 2019). I think the class conversation went in different and more meaningful directions than if I had used a canon kind of approach. Then a few students wanted to explore Asian-Latinx intersections. And I was like, yeah, I want to look at that, too! So, this will open up a space to explore Latinx dance in Asia and Asian diasporas in the Caribbean and then perhaps we will come up with new lessons on choreographic analysis.

Possibilities and Responsibilities

RC: As we continue to apply and teach choreographic analysis ourselves, and as our field grapples with how to decolonize dance studies and to value – in the sense that Cristina mentioned earlier – the Global South, I wonder what possibilities and responsibilities we see for choreographic analysis?

JLP: My critical race studies training keeps nudging me to return to the question of the institution and the possible structural dynamics of "choreographic analysis": How could choreographic analysis work in/as policy? If policy can drive the culture and the culture is not there yet, policy can help people. Of course, you have to implement policy, and people have to abide by it, or be compliant. But what would that look like, choreographic analysis as policy? Right now, it appears in the title of things, potentially that's a doorway. With the UCLA World Arts and Cultures/Dance Department's MFA degree in "choreographic inquiry," rather than "choreography" for example, the front end and research questions appear to be emphasized over the product. Perhaps this relieves pressures of producing "professional dancers." Perhaps this enables more attention to, as Harmony mentioned earlier, the nonhuman applications of choreographic analysis. One might imagine, for example, an American studies scholar researching demilitarization in the Pacific, and they might adopt choreographic analysis as part of their methodology.

CFR: I'm asking myself: what does it really mean when we advocate for the equality, diversity, and inclusion of other ways of knowing in the classroom or the diverse and inclusive ways of approaching movement analysis or dance methodology as a whole? What does it mean to make the effort of incorporating particular writing styles or languages, taking into consideration that both native and target languages are always already creative media? Languages are contextual and have been practiced by certain groups of people differently. So, how can we empower diverse groups of students to create tactics and strategies with which to look at, think, and write about other ways of dancing? In the end, we have to remember that dance is not only an object of study. Dance is also a field of knowledge composed of various ways of thinking and doing things.

RC: What if we extend choreographic analysis beyond the department and the university to the field, for example, to the Dance Studies Association? How is the field being choreographed? I think we're in a really interesting moment of the possibility of structures shifting, priorities shifting, and policies shifting, as a result of that kind of analysis.

HB: To a hammer, everything looks like a nail. Choreographic analysis enables some kinds of considerations and not others – but it's just one tool in the toolbox. I think if you look at any of our scholarship and teaching, you'll see that choreographic analysis is one approach among many, that most projects employ multiple methods simultaneously and are further oriented in terms of political and intellectual investments. I think scholarship is at its most exciting and creative when different approaches are combined to produce a unique analysis that really only that author could thread together from their specific expertise and experiences.

JLP: I'm optimistic that we can use choreographic analysis to change the world. But I'm realistic that there are different circumstances and obstacles in the way, I can have self-doubt, people can be impediments, and institutions can be disciplining, and so understanding these levels is to me part of our job as educators and as scholars.

Note

1 Following Doran George's death, Foster posthumously edited their dissertation and saw it through to publication.

Works Cited

Alim, H. Samy. 2006. *Roc the Mic Right: The Language of Hip Hop Culture*. London: Routledge.

Bench, Harmony. 2020. *Perpetual Motion: Dance, Digital Cultures, and the Common*. Minneapolis: University of Minnesota Press.

Candelario, Rosemary. 2016. *Flowers Cracking Concrete: Eiko & Koma's Asian/American Choreographies*. Middletown, CT: Wesleyan University Press.

Chew, Matthew Ming-tak, and Sophie Pui Sim Mo. 2019. "Towards a Chinese Hip-Hop Feminism and a Feminist Reassessment of Hip-Hop with Breakdance: B-Girling in Hong Kong, Taiwan and China." *Asian Studies Review* 43, no. 3: 455–474.

DeFrantz, Thomas F. 2004. "The Black Beat Made Visible: Hip Hop Dance and Body Power." In *Of the Presence of the Body: Essays on Dance and Performance Theory*, edited by André Lepecki, 64-81. Middletown, CT: Wesleyan University Press.

———. 2006. *Dancing Revelations: Alvin Ailey's Embodiment of African American Culture*. New York: Oxford University Press.

Ellis, Carolyn. 2007. "Telling Secrets, Revealing Lives: Relational Ethics in Research With Intimate Others." *Qualitative Inquiry* 13, no. 1 (January): 3–29. https://doi.org/10.1177/1077800406294947.

Foster, Susan Leigh. 1986. *Reading Dancing: Bodies and Subjects in Contemporary American Dance*. Berkeley: University of California Press.

———. 1995. *Choreographing History*. Bloomington: Indiana University Press.

———. 1996. "The Ballerina's Phallic Pointe." In *Corporealities: Dancing Knowledge, Culture and Power*, edited by Susan Leigh Foster, 1–24. London: Routledge.

———. 1997. "Dancing Bodies." In *Meaning in Motion: New Cultural Studies of Dance*, edited by Jane C. Desmond, 235–257. Durham, NC: Duke University Press.

———. 1998. "Choreographies of Gender." *Signs* 24, no. 1: 1–33.

———. 2003. "Choreographies of Protest." *Theatre Journal* 55, no. 3 (October): 395–412.

———. 2005. "Choreographing Empathy." *Topoi* 24, no. 1: 81–91. https://doi.org/10.1007/s11245-004-4163-9.

———. 2011. *Choreographing Empathy: Kinesthesia in Performance*. London: Routledge.

———. 2016. "Choreography." In *In Terms of Performance*, edited by Shannon Jackson and Paula Marincola. http://intermsofperformance.site/keywords/choreography/susan-leigh-foster. Accessed February 15, 2022.

George, Doran. 2020. *The Natural Body in Somatics Dance Training*, ed. Susan Leigh Foster. New York: Oxford University Press.

Giersdorf, Jens and Yutian Wong, eds. 2019. *The Routledge Dance Studies Reader*, 3rd edition. London: Routledge.

Gottschild, Brenda Dixon. 1998. *Digging the Africanist Presence in American Performance: Dance and Other Contexts*. Westport, CT: Praeger.

———. 2005. *The Black Dancing Body: A Geography from Coon to Cool*. New York: Palgrave Macmillan.

Grimes, D. Sabela. 2008. "Street Scholar Sampler." *Social | *Dance* | Media: Old Shuffles in a New Paradigm* website. http://socialdancemedia.blogspot.com/2008/08/-street-scholar-sampler.html. Accessed February 25, 2022.

Lee, Robert, Tristan Ahtone, Margaret Pearce, Kalen Goodluck, Geoff McGhee, Cody Leff, Katherine Lanpher, and Taryn Salinas. 2020. "Land-Grab Universities: How the United States Funded Land-Grant Universities with Expropriated Indigenous Land." *High Country News*. https://www.landgrabu.org/. Accessed August 21, 2022.

Mandradjieff, Mara. 2021. "Intra-Acting Fat Suits, Tutu Flesh, and Sweaty Skins: Material-Semiotic Clashes in Maguy Marin's Ballet *Groosland*." *Women & Performance: A Journal of Feminist Theory*. 31, no. 1: 43–58.

Martin, Randy. 1998. *Critical Moves: Dance Studies in Theory and Politics*. Durham, NC: Duke University Press.

Mezur, Katherine and Emily Wilcox, eds. 2020. *Corporeal Politics: Dancing East Asia*. Ann Arbor: University of Michigan Press.

Mignolo, Walter. 2021. "Decolonial Research Methods: A Planetary Conversation beyond the North Atlantic (the Global East and the Global South)." Part 4 of the *Decolonial Research Methods: Resisting Coloniality in Academic Knowledge Production* webinar series sponsored by the National Centre for Research Methods. https://www.youtube.com/watch?v=BZfXSs8FioE&list=WL&index=57&t=16s. Accessed February 15, 2022.

Nogueira, Renato. 2011. "Denegrindo a Filosofia: O Pensamento como Coreografia de Conceitos Afroperspectivistas." *Griot – Revista de Filosofia* 4, no. 2 (dezembro): 1–19.

Novack, Cynthia. 1990. *Sharing the Dance: Contact Improvisation and American Culture*. Madison: University of Wisconsin Press.

Perillo, J. Lorenzo. 2017. "Embodying Modernism: A Postcolonial Intervention across Filipino Dance." *Amerasia Journal* 43, no. 2: 122–140.

———. 2020. *Choreographing in Color: Filipinos, Hip-Hop, and the Cultural Politics of Euphemism*. New York: Oxford University Press.

Petit, Sandra Haydée. 2015. *Pretagogia: Pertencimento, Corpo-Dança Afroancestral e Tradição Oral – Contribuições do Legado Africano para a Implementação da Lei no. 10.639/03*. Fortaleza: EdUECE

Reyes-Tolentino, Francisca S. and Petrona Ramos. 1927/1935. *Philippine Folk Dances and Games*. New York: Silver, Burdett and Company.

Ribeiro, Djamila. 2019. *Lugar de Fala*. São Paulo: Editora Jandaíra.

Rosa, Cristina Fernandes. 2015. *Brazilian Bodies and Their Choreographies of Identification: Swing Nation*. New York: Palgrave Macmillan.

Rufino, Luiz. 2019. *Pedagogia das Encruzilhadas*. Rio de Janeiro: Mórula Editorial.

Savigliano, Marta. 2009. "Worlding Dance and Dancing out There in the World." In *Worlding Dance*, edited by Susan Leigh Foster, 163–189. Basingstoke: Palgrave Macmillan.

Vázquez, Rolando. 2012. "Towards a Decolonial Critique of Modernity: *Buen Vivir*, Relationality and the Task of Listening." In *Capital, Poverty, Development (Denktraditionen im Dialog: Studien zur Befreiung und interkulturalität*, no. 33), edited by Raúl Fornet-Betancourt, 241–252. Aachen: Wissenschaftsverlag Mainz.

10
Global South Archives
Listening and Acknowledging Authorship

Ana Paula Höfling

Early on in my research on capoeira, I embarked on what seemed to be the *de rigueur* methodology for Global South movement practices: ethnographic research. A year before I began my PhD studies, I moved back to Brazil to dive head-first into capoeira, the Afro-Brazilian combat form I had practiced on and off for over a decade. Having studied both capoeira regional and capoeira angola with various mestres in the past, my return to Brazil marked my exclusive dedication to capoeira angola, the "more traditional" style, where players listen carefully to each other as they interweave legs and torsos in a series of near misses, striking with the feet or sometimes the head in a calculated game of feints; the aerial acrobatics, high kicks, and fast spins of capoeira regional give way to a calculated, often sly, and sometimes humorous movement dialogue. Capoeira angola just seemed more interesting to me: less competitive, less aggressive, and, most importantly, guided by explicit and implicit rules and principles, referred to as *fundamentos*, which I was eager to learn more about. After almost a year of intensive training with the *Grupo Semente do Jogo de Angola* under the leadership of Mestre Jogo de Dentro and his disciples,[1] attending classes five days a week as well as weekly rodas, I felt I had a good mastery of capoeira angola, although I was fully aware that I needed another decade or so to fully master many nuances of the practice. Most importantly, after this intensive training, I felt I belonged to a capoeira group and could claim a lineage and a mestre, important elements in the capoeira angola community (see Varella 2019).

When I began my graduate studies, I had all the elements at my disposal to continue my research on capoeira from an ethnographic perspective: I would write a dissertation based on my intensive apprenticeship with the *Grupo Semente do*

Jogo de Angola, which would be further supported and legitimated by my own extensive involvement with capoeira, both in the United States and in Brazil. Several capoeira scholars before me seemed to follow this same pattern: one year of field research/intensive training in Brazil complemented by continued involvement in capoeira in the scholar's home country. However, I noticed that most books on capoeira based on ethnographic participant-observation as a primary methodology were not exactly ethnographies in that they were not portraits of capoeira practice at a particular time and place. Instead, these analyses presented capoeira as a practice to be "decoded" with the aid of graphs, charts, and glossaries, the symbolism of its various aspects explained (Browning 1995; Lewis 1992; Merrell 2005; Rosa 2012).

Capoeira scholarship published outside Brazil in the 1990s and 2000s focused on explaining and defining capoeira to an audience unfamiliar with it; some texts explored possible etymologies of the word "capoeira" (Browning 1995; Lewis 1992; Rosa 2015; Talmon-Chvaicer 2008), adding to the mystique of this dance-like Afro-Brazilian martial art that increasingly attracted the attention of Global North scholars. Bits of historical information were interspersed throughout these texts, often anecdotally, and in some cases, a short chapter was devoted to capoeira's history. Only Matthias Röhrig Assunção's 2005 *Capoeira: The History of an Afro-Brazilian Martial Art* offered a thorough and rigorously researched history of capoeira, based on archival sources. After my literature review, it became clear that more archival research was needed – there were still many histories of capoeira out there waiting to be told. My experiences in "the field" as a dancer-scholar-capoeirista and any new revelation based on my ethnographic research did not seem as interesting as the untold experiences of the people who shaped this Afro-Brazilian movement practice throughout the 20th century.

With few secondary sources at my disposal, I would need to rely on primary sources. I realized that I had embarked on a challenging research trajectory when I was faced with the reality that there was no centralized "capoeira archive": no library or research center holds primary source materials related to capoeira.[2] I confess I am jealous of my colleagues who are able to access collections created by archivists and librarians, available for consultation in air-conditioned libraries, by appointment, where documents and photographs are carefully placed in folders and boxes and cataloged by call numbers. In countries where libraries are valued and well-funded, which is unfortunately not the case in Brazil, archival research is not necessarily easier, but it certainly seems less chaotic than when "the archive" does not yet exist, and primary source materials are scattered in inaccessible private collections, damaged by mold, or tied with twine in bundles as if ready for the recycling bin. In this chapter,

I share the lessons I learned in my quite literally uncharted journey through the archive while simultaneously creating that archive along the way. This journey included countless moments of frustration, but also wonderful discoveries that resulted from giving into the messiness of the resources available and allowing myself to spend entire afternoons flipping somewhat randomly through daily newspapers that were nearly 100 years old.

Daily Newspapers: "Losing my rush" in the Archive

Daily newspapers are one of the best starting points for archival research in cases when other resources – such as biographies, memoirs, letters, photographs, or film – are scarce or not available. They can also be the slowest source, especially if the researcher is not looking for a specific known news item on a specific date. Browsing through months, years, and decades of daily news can feel like an endless task and even a waste of time, as it did for me in the beginning. But archival research worth its salt must be slow – it takes time to identify patterns, values, and trends, especially when one's source is daily newspapers.

When I first arrived at the public library known as Biblioteca dos Barris in Salvador, Bahia, I was excited to see banners announcing a recently completed digitalization project, funded by a large public grant, of the Bahian newspaper A Tarde. The scanned newspapers were not available online, so I had to access them from a designated computer at the library. I eagerly sat at the computer and double-clicked to open a test document, selecting the first file on the list. After a few seconds, three or four seconds that felt like an eternity, the digital file opened: the first page of the first edition of the newspaper. I felt excitement and even giddiness – this was my ticket to discovering all the missing pieces and hidden gems of capoeira's history. I scrolled, hoping to view pages two, three, etc., but instead got to the bottom of the same page. That was it! The newspaper was digitized one page at a time, and each page was a separate document that took a few seconds to open. These slow-to-open files were not available online and were not word-searchable; printing was possible but only a limited number of pages per day.[3] This system might work for targeted searches of news items on specific days, but would not work for browsing.

And this is how I ended up sitting and browsing through historical newspapers in the rare periodical section of the library, for hours on end. There is an expression in Brazil used to refer to tasks that demand patience: it is necessary to *perder a pressa*, literally to "lose your rush." After I "lost" my rush and settled into "reading the paper" every day (five to six hours a day for about three weeks), capoeira's history began taking shape: I saw capoeira move from the police pages to the sports pages, and from the sports pages to the entertainment

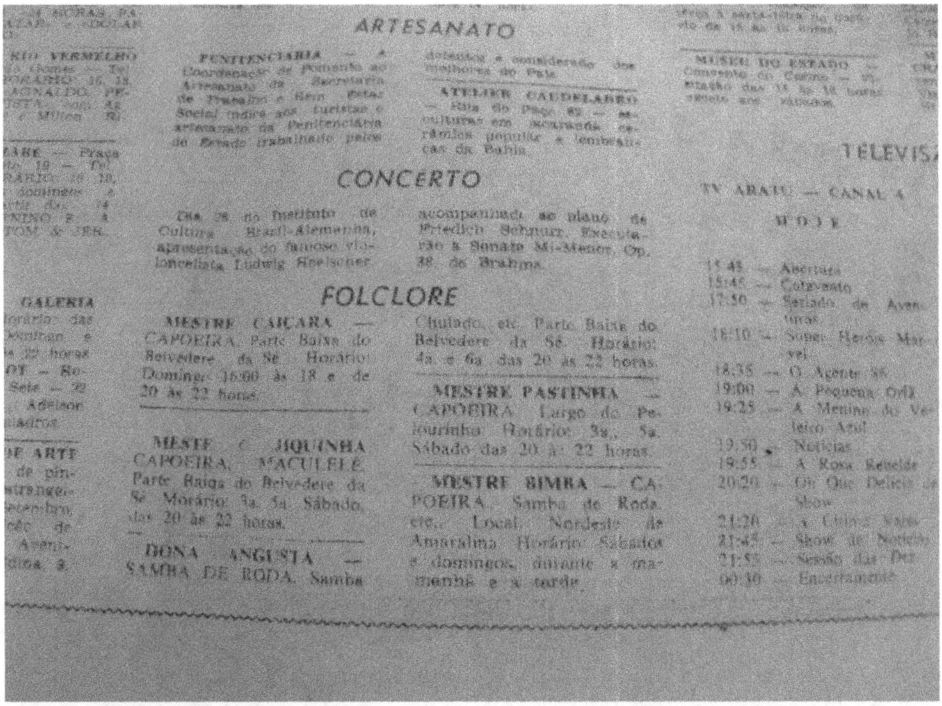
ARTESANATO

PENITENCIÁRIA — A Coordenação de Fomento ao Artesanato da Secretaria de Trabalho e Bem Estar Social indica aos turistas o artesanato da Penitenciária do Estado trabalhado pelos detentos e considerado dos melhores do País.

ATELIER CANDELABRO — Rua do Paço 82 — esculturas em ... cerâmica popular e lembranças da Bahia.

CONCERTO

Dia 28 no Instituto de Cultura Brasil-Alemanha, apresentação do famoso violoncelista Ludwig Hoelscher acompanhado ao piano de Friedrich Schnurr. Execução a Sonata Mi-Menor, Op. 38, de Brahms.

FOLCLORE

MESTRE CAIÇARA — CAPOEIRA. Parte Baixa do Belvedere da Sé. Horário: Domingo 16:00 às 18 e de 20 às 22 horas.

MESTRE CANJIQUINHA — CAPOEIRA, MACULELÊ. Parte Baixa do Belvedere da Sé. Horário: 3a, 5a, Sábado, das 20 às 22 horas.

DONA ANGUSTA — SAMBA DE RODA. Samba Chulado, etc. Parte Baixa do Belvedere da Sé. Horário: 4a e 6a das 20 às 22 horas.

MESTRE PASTINHA — CAPOEIRA. Largo do Pelourinho. Horário: 3a., 5a. Sábado das 20 às 22 horas.

MESTRE BIMBA — CAPOEIRA. Samba de Roda etc. Local: Nordeste de Amaralina. Horário: Sábados e domingos, durante a manhã e a tarde.

TELEVISÃO

TV ARATU — CANAL 4

HOJE

Figure 10.1 *Jornal da Bahia*, August 25, 1969.

pages over time. That was significant! In the early 1960s, capoeira shows began to be advertised in the entertainment listings (often in a section titled "*folclore*"); by the end of the decade tourists could choose from at least four different folkloric shows featuring capoeira on any given day (see Figure 10.1). Also, a significant find! According to listings from the early 1970s, many of these shows, directed by capoeiristas, had become full-fledged folkloric shows that now included various types of samba, *puxade de rede*, *maculelê*, and even "African dance" (see Figure 10.2). My patient browsing had paid off: a clear pattern of legitimization and folkoricization had emerged from the daily news.

The lack of word-searchable, easily accessible digital files forced me to "lose my rush" and browse, and this browsing yielded a clear trajectory of capoeira – from public nuisance to sport and later folklore – that shaped my analysis. These newspaper listings allowed me to understand how central folkloric shows were to these capoeiristas, some of whom performed nearly daily in shows for tourists. They also helped me understand the significance of the work of a capoeira *mestre* who had been relegated to the footnotes of capoeira's history: Washington Bruno da Silva (1925–1994), better known as Mestre Canjiquinha (see Figure 10.3).

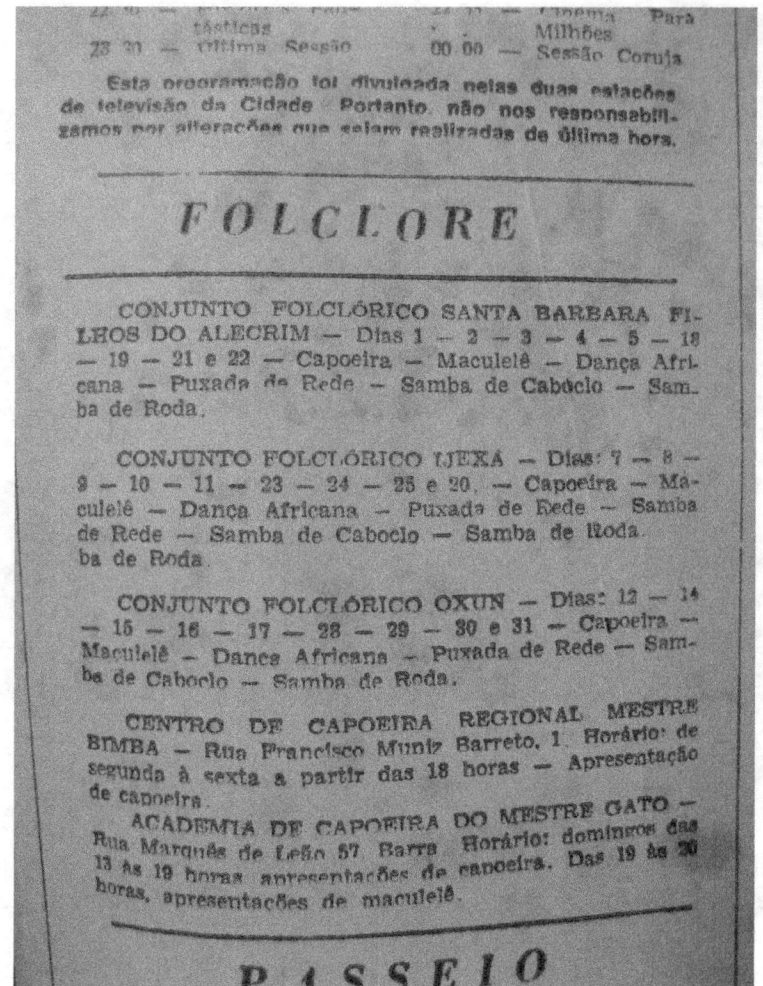

Figure 10.2 *A Tarde*, May 2, 1974.

Acknowledging Authorship: Listening to Mestre Canjiquinha

Historical research on capoeira has emphasized the legacies of Mestre Pastinha (Vicente Ferreira Pastinha, 1889–1981) and Mestre Bimba (Manuel dos Reis Machado, 1900–1974), the two mestres who shaped the practice in the mid-20th century along the binaries tradition/modernity and preservation/innovation (see Assunção 2005; Höfling 2019). Their legacies have become central to the history of capoeira because, in addition to being famous and even iconic during their lifetimes, they both left written documents (published manuals and, in the case of Pastinha, a lengthy illustrated manuscript he hoped

Figure 10.3 Mestre Canjiquinha in undated newspaper clipping, *Diário de Notícias*, c. 1973.

to publish). In addition, they both left lasting, discernible embodied legacies through their students – their distinct styles and pedagogies are recognizable a century later. When establishing the parameters of my own research, I knew I needed to acknowledge these iconic mestres, but I was more interested in those who did not leave such clearly defined legacies, especially those whose work was implicated in the tourism industry.

After coming across Mestre Canjiquinha's name several times, mostly in reference to his participation in capoeira shows and a couple of 1960s films that featured capoeira, I decided to investigate this overlooked capoeira mestre. But where to start? When no biography is available, no memoir, and not that much in the press, how would I begin to put together a portrait of this mestre? A short book self-published in the late 1980s by a group of Canjiquinha's students (Moreira et al. 1989) consists of excerpts from interviews with Canjiquinha in no particular order, in various fonts, with little to no commentary – as confusing as that was initially, it was a start! From these interview excerpts, I gathered that Canjiquinha had attained considerable fame during his lifetime, which made his near-erasure from capoeira history today even more confounding.

Although he did not leave behind manuals, manuscripts, or a clearly defined pedagogy, Canjiquinha's participation in films left a record of his movement style. I was able to view his performances in two films: *O Pagador de Promessas*

(The Keeper of Promises), nominated for an Oscar and winner of a Palme d'Or at Cannes, and *Barravento* (The Turning Wind), both released in 1962. These films allowed me to see, for the first time, Canjiquinha's capoeira: quick and efficient, no frills, even rough-around-the-edges. His *ginga*, the between-strikes back-and-forth motion today taught as capoeira's "basic step" (codified as such by Mestre Bimba in the 1950s and 1960s) is more like a boxer's bouncy footwork. He takes short steps followed by hops, quickly alternating from one side to the other – very different from the smooth rocking motion of present-day *ginga* (Höfling 2019,1940). He strikes quickly and retreats only to come in with a decisive sweep. In *Barravento*, in addition to playing capoeira, Canjiquinha sings and dances a *samba de roda*. His smile reveals dental work in gold, popular at the time and a mark of upward mobility. His voice has an easy-going quality, and he adds a playfulness to the well-known samba song by inserting personalized stanzas into the lyrics: "I'm going to say my full name/Alô Bahia [...] I am Washington Bruno/Alô Bahia." He blends this verse into the lyrics so smoothly it is almost imperceptible–I wonder if the director himself noticed at the time. With this verse, by stating his full name, Canjiquinha guarantees recognition for his singing in the film.

While many documentary filmmakers at the time sought Bimba and Pastinha, those seeking to insert a capoeira scene in their feature films hired Canjiquinha as a performer and, in today's terms, as a "fight choreographer," even though he is never credited as such. Waldeloir Rego, in his 1968 *Capoeira Angola: Ensaio Sócio-Etnográfico* identifies the Salvador municipal tourism department as a kind of "oracle," where filmmakers from elsewhere in Brazil or from abroad would find recommendations of capoeiristas and capoeira groups to participate in their films. In this book, the first monograph on capoeira, Rego mentions Canjiquinha's participation in films and includes a long list of his invited performances and demonstrations throughout Brazil (Rego 1968, 275–278). Rego notes that Canjiquinha

> is a young and agile capoeirista, which makes him stand out among his peers, although what sets him apart are his abilities as a [berimbau] player and a singer. He sings like few others and has a vast repertory, including a great facility to improvise.
>
> (Rego 1968, 275)

Rego was a Bahian self-taught ethnographer and capoeira enthusiast – that much was clear from his publication. When reading about the development of the tourism industry in Bahia, however, I came across relevant information about Rego's "day job": he worked as a public functionary at state and municipal tourism departments in Salvador from the early 1950s until his retirement in the 1990s. In *Capoeira Angola*, he mentions (and even criticizes) the municipal tourism department without ever acknowledging that he worked there. From the published interview excerpts mentioned above, I learned that Canjiquinha also worked at the municipal tourism department (Moreira et al. 1989, 59): in the mornings, he worked in the copy room, running the mimeograph, and in the evenings, he returned not as the low-ranking public functionary but as a capoeira mestre and director of his city-sponsored folkloric show (Moreira et al. 1989, 8, 23, 63). In 1968, the year that Rego's book was published, Canjiquinha still directed his daily folkloric shows at the tourism department's stage at the scenic terrace known as the Belvedere da Sé (see Figure 10.1). And that was when two separate findings in the archive came together to reveal that Rego and Canjiquinha had *worked together in the same office*, precisely during the time Rego was collecting data for *Capoeira Angola* (Höfling 2019, 121). Canjiquinha had clearly been Rego's main informant, a fact that he only briefly acknowledges in the book: "A large portion of the songs in this [book] were collected from Canjiquinha" (Rego 1968, 276). Re-reading the book with the realization that they had worked together, *Capoeira Angola* went from being a secondary source about capoeira to becoming a primary source about the relationship between Rego and Canjiquinha.

Rego's insufficient acknowledgment of Canjiquinha's role in the book also puts in perspective Canjiquinha's repeated claims of authorship, including his claims to selecting the dance and movement practices that make up the Brazilian "folkloric suite" today, such as capoeira, samba de roda, *maculelê*[4] and *puxada de rede*[5] (Höfling 2019, 120). Canjiquinha's insistence on claiming authorship taught me to "listen" to the voices in the archive; as it turned out, he wasn't the only capoeira mestre repeatedly claiming authorship. Mestre Bimba claimed to have borrowed moves from Greco-Roman wrestling, Judo, and Jiu-Jitsu to expand capoeira's movement repertory and allegedly improve its efficiency; Mestre Pastinha was proud of having "organized" capoeira, creating his *Centro Esportivo de Capoeira Angola* (Capoeira Angola Sports Center) – a capoeira "hub" where various mestres also taught, including Mestre Canjiquinha (Moreira et al. 1989, 59). With the guidance of these and other mestres, who repeatedly and in no uncertain terms claimed credit for their innovations in capoeira, I approached writing a history of the practice that challenged the prevailing assumption that capoeiristas were merely "bearers" of tradition.

All evidence countered the idea that capoeira was a static, communally created "traditional" practice that did not value its innovators. In her groundbreaking 1969 article "An Anthropologist looks at ballet as a form of ethnic dance," Joann Keali'inohomoku notes that, although

> some cultures do not place the same value on preserving the names of their innovators as we do [...] we must not be deceived into believing that a few

hundred people all got together and with one unanimous surge created a dance tradition which, having once been created, never changed from that day forward.

(2001, 36)

Canjiquinha helped me understand the importance and indeed the urgency of moving research on Global South dance practices away from implicit assumptions of unchanging traditions waiting to be explained and decoded. Instead, we must begin to listen and acknowledge the claims to authorship and artistry of those formerly understood as "folklore bearers" (*portadores de folclore*).

Acknowledging Authorship: Listening to Living Mestres

My archival research led me to seek out living capoeira mestres who could share with me, in the flesh, their memories of participating in Canjiquinha's folkloric shows; these capoeiristas, quite literally, embody the archive. In his published interview excerpts (Moreira et al. 1989), Canjiquinha identifies several of his star students, many of whom have become well-known capoeira mestres, and as such, were not difficult to track down. The first mestre to grant me an interview was Mestre Brasília.[6] We met at a restaurant in São Paulo in 2013 and talked for over two hours – I turned on my audio recorder and listened attentively, prompting him with a few prepared questions but mostly letting him lead the interview about his early days as a capoeira student and performer with Canjiquinha. In 2015, I returned to Salvador and was able to interview Mestre Geni[7] and Mestre Lua Rasta,[8] who also studied and performed with Canquijinha. Audio recorder and notebook in hand, I met with Mestre Lua Rasta at his percussion instrument store in the historic district of the city, and a few days later met with Mestre Geni at a shopping center in downtown Salvador, a place conveniently located for both of us. All three men made it clear to me how excited they were that, at last, there was scholarly interest in the work of their mestre, and expressed pride not only in having studied with Canjiquinha but also in their participation in folkloric shows. During these interviews, it became clear that these shows were, in fact, formative in their capoeira careers – rather than eroding capoeira's traditions or its "integrity," it was evident that these shows were an extension of their training and creative practice.

From these interviews, I learned that capoeira performers were in their majority young men at the beginning of their apprenticeship, and the stage offered simultaneously a place for tourist spectacle and a safe space for honing one's skills as a capoeira player. Few shows hired choreographers; capoeiristas were the choreographers of their own staged games, which were at least partially choreographed (as opposed to capoeira offstage, which is always improvised).

Performed by capoeiristas themselves, capoeira onstage, in addition to providing income and visibility, included both a creative and a pedagogical aspect. Folkloric shows were often tourist audiences' first introduction to capoeira; however, these shows were as didactic for the performers as they were for their audiences, if not more so.

Canjiquinha's daily shows, which ran from the mid-1950s until the late 1960s, provided a space for capoeiristas to practice strike and defense combinations in a safe space where capoeira's combative aspect was staged. Mestre Brasília, who performed with Canjiquinha from 1959 until 1966, explained that games were choreographed to prevent injury but also to create spectacle. During our 2013 interview, he remembered that

> the sweeps we sometimes staged [...] We would let the other guy complete the sweep, we would fall, get up, the audience would laugh – we *performed*. In the bat's flight we would let [the other player] hit us, we would stagger away, and it was very beautiful, because it was [still] just capoeira.

Mestre Lua Rasta, who performed in Canjiquinha's shows in the early 1960s, remembered that a type of game used in shows, known as *samango*, was actually intended as training, specifically used for improving the performers' lateral kicks. During our 2015 interview, he told me that Canjiquinha would remind his performers that the fight scenes in the show were also an exercise to prepare capoeiristas for situations of conflict offstage. Training and performance co-existed; choreographed games for the stage, in fact, improved capoeiristas' abilities to apply the skills they rehearsed to actual combat situations.

In addition, choreographed games allowed performers to indulge in the aesthetics and artistry of the game and include embellishments such as headspins, backflips, and other virtuosic moves with no combat function, called *floreios* (flourishes). Mestre Geni, who also performed with Canjiquinha in the 1960s, attributes the increased use of *floreios* in capoeira today to the adaptations made for staged performances. Onstage, a "held back" capoeira gives way to a capoeira where players are allowed to drop their guard and be creative, indulging in *floreios* without the need to play defensively. Capoeira on tourist stages, so often blamed for a commodification of the practice and an erosion of its traditions, in fact, offered a space for capoeiristas to be authors and artists.

Conclusion

Rather than approaching capoeira as a practice waiting to be explained or decoded, or drawing conclusions about capoeira as a whole from my own experiences (which could never be representative of all of capoeira), my choice to explore uncharted areas of the history of capoeira proved rewarding, even if at times the research process was trying, slow, and frustrating. This research opened the doors to a rich and complex past where capoeiristas – actual human beings with names, ambitions, preoccupations, alliances, antipathies, and often day jobs – practiced capoeira, and capoeira could only be examined in very specific contexts such as formal classes, informal practice, choreography for film, demonstrations, and shows. Taking in the details present in the archive with no rush, I let the specificity of the lives of capoeiristas of the past lead the way to identifying and interviewing living mestres whose memories and embodied knowledge complemented my archival findings and revealed yet another facet of the development of capoeira: staged demonstrations for tourists were part of these men's capoeira training, part and parcel of the development of capoeira in the 20th century. On stage, these capoeiristas authored capoeira.

Focusing on the histories of movement practices deemed traditional and recognizing their innovators and artists (in the same way we credit artists and authors such as Martha Graham, Isadora Duncan, or George Balanchine) is, I believe, a matter of methodological equity. It would be unthinkable to write an analysis of ballet (all of ballet) based on the embodied experiences of one scholar with some experience in ballet who spent one year in "the field." While such methodology seems ludicrous when applied to a European concert dance form such as ballet, this is a common methodology for studying movement practices of the Global South – a lack of attention to Global South authors that continues to perpetuate the inequities identified by Keali'inohomoku in the 1960s. Writing Global South histories may be challenging and it may seem like an impossible task in places where formal, organized archives do not exist, but we must acknowledge the contributions of authors of "traditional" movement practices.

Notes

1 In addition to classes taught by Mestre Jogo de Dentro, occasionally classes were taught by the group's advanced students Danny Soares, Guga Cacilhas, Ivens Burg, Valmir Maurício, and Daisy Caribé.
2 When I began my research, I had hoped to find capoeira materials at the Instituto Jair Moura, directed by independent capoeira scholar Frede Abreu, who had created his own collection over the years with intermittent government funding. After his passing in 2013, however, this archive was made inaccessible by his descendants.
3 The newspaper *A Tarde* has since removed the computer terminals where the scanned pages of the newspaper had been available to the public, making access to this resource even more difficult. The newspaper does have an archives division but the charges for reproduction of materials are significant.

4 Maculelê is a combat dance of much-debated origins where dancers hit a pair of wooden clubs rhythmically while performing a highly energetic and percussive dance.
5 A dance derived from the rhythmic back-and-forth movement of bringing in a fishing net, when several men join forces to drag a large and heavy fishing net full of fish onto the sand.
6 Antônio Cardoso de Andrade, b. 1942.
7 Also known as Madame Geni, José Serafim Ferreira Júnior, b. 1947.
8 Gilson Fernandes, b. 1950.

Works Cited

Andrade, Antonio Cardoso. (Mestre Brasília). December 28, 2013. Audio-recorded interview by author.

Assunção, Matthias Röhrig. 2005. *Capoeira: The History of an Afro-Brazilian Martial Art*. London: Routledge.

Browning, Barbara. 1995. *Samba: Resistance in Motion*. Bloomington: Indiana University Press.

Fernandes, Gilson. (Mestre Lua Rasta). July 13, 2015. Audio-recorded interview by author.

Ferreira Jr., José Serafim. (Mestre Geni). July 20, 2015. Audio-recorded interview by author.

Höfling, Ana Paula. 2019. *Staging Brazil: Choreographies of Capoeira*. Middletown, CT: Wesleyan University Press.

Keali'inohomoku, Joann. 2001 [1969]. "An Anthropologist Looks at Ballet as a Form of Ethnic Dance." In *Moving History/Dancing Cultures: A Dance History Reader*, edited by Ann Dils and Ann Cooper Albright, 33–43. Middletown, CT: Wesleyan University Press.

Lewis, John Lowell. 1992. *Ring of Liberation: Deceptive Discourse in Brazilian Capoeira*. Chicago: University of Chicago Press.

Merrell, Floyd. 2005. *Capoeira and Candomblé: Conformity and Resistance through Afro-Brazilian Experience*. Princeton, NJ: Markus Wiener Publishers.

Moreira, Antônio et al. 1989. *Canjiquinha: a alegria da capoeira*. Salvador: Editora A Rasteira.

Rego, Waldeloir. 1968. *Capoeira Angola: ensaio socio-etnográfico*. Salvador: Editora Itapuã.

Rosa, Cristina F. 2012. "Playing, Fighting, and Dancing: Unpacking the Significance of *Ginga* within the Practice of Capoeira Angola," *TDR: The Drama Review* 56, no. 3: 141–166.

———. 2015. *Brazilian Bodies and Their Choreographies of Identification*. London and New York: Palgrave.

Talmon-Chvaicer, Maya. 2008. *The Hidden History of Capoeira: A Collision of Cultures in the Brazilian Battle Dance*. Austin: University of Texas Press.

Varella, Sérgio Ganzales. 2019. *Capoeira, Mobility, and Tourism: Preserving an Afro-Brazilian Tradition in a Globalized World*. New York: Lexington Books.

11
Cyphering with Oral History

MiRi Park

Stepping into the Cypher

Back when I started breakin' in 2001 in Williamsburg, Brooklyn, I felt joy, freedom, frustration, and accomplishment. I'd been dancing for most of my life as a competitive studio dancer and was a recent graduate of a BFA dance program, but for the first time in my life I finally felt comfortable in my own skin. This dance, these beats, these people, this environment was something I didn't know I'd been searching for all along. Trying to physicalize the funk with footwork, spins, and freezes became an obsession for me, much like many of the others I practiced with in McCarren Park. The group of people with whom I beat up the linoleum on a regular basis ranged from adolescents to middle-aged people, some grew up in the neighborhood, some were transplants (like me), and were of varying ethnicities, races, and national backgrounds. Of course, in the heat of practice, the only thing that mattered was the dancing. But afterward, over meals, drinks, and just hanging out with the other b-boys and b-girls, we all learned about each other. My mentor Richard "Break Easy" Santiago, a Williamsburg native, shared with us his life experiences that led him to start a free breaking practice. In his many lessons, we learned about the history of immigration to the area, the influence of immigrant parents' jobs on how dancers adorned themselves, and the influence of local motorcycle clubs and outlaw culture on dancers' style.

At breakin' jams and events, OGs[1] constantly implored us to "learn your history," so I listened to as many lessons as the elder dancers were willing to impart. I also picked up books about hip hop culture. Through those texts, I learned about the socio-cultural and historical contexts of hip hop culture's roots in the South Bronx, and how it was borne from black and brown disenfranchised and dispossessed youth.[2] According to the books, the elements of dance, visual art, DJing, and MCing emerged as energetic declarations of existence for these youth. This all vibed with everything I was experiencing. But the more I read, the more I realized that much of the literature focused on literary analysis of rap lyrics, and ignored the experience of dancers. Moreover, I saw nothing of the current moment in breakin' culture I participated in, nor of the networks of local, regional, national, and international jams that dancers from all over the world attended, creating found-family over days and nights of sweating, eating, and getting into it together.

Ever the intrepid student, I decided to heed the call of "learn your history" and enrolled in the liberal studies MA program at Columbia University with the intent of writing about and reflecting on the experiences of fellow dancers in the breakin' scene. Not knowing exactly what academic discipline my research most closely aligned with, I took classes in both anthropology and history and learned about participant-observation and historical research methods. But both methodologies left me with questions: Am I doing cultural work or historical work? How could I "observe" my friends when I was already a participant? How could I become an expert on people who could clearly speak for themselves?

I had the great fortune of taking history with the great Manning Marable who, while stating that a historians' responsibility was to become the expert of a research topic that was narrow and deep, also strongly recommended that we visit the Columbia Oral History Research Office (now the Columbia Center for Oral History and Research, CCOHR) in Butler Library, and find Director Mary Marshall Clark. He explained briefly that oral history methodology is a dialogic process in which the interviewer and interviewee (also referred to as a narrator) co-create a living history of the interviewee, based on a relationship of trust. This differed from journalistic interview methods I was familiar with, in which interviews usually flowed in one direction to extract information from a source. This seemed to be a methodology that could address my concerns with other methodologies. With Professor Marable's advice ringing in my ears, I set off for the top floor of Butler Library, where I listened to an oral history with a 9/11 first responder.[3] Hearing the interviewee's voices narrate their experience while reading their transcribed words on the pages of the binder that held them together made me want to know more about this process. I went on to work closely with Mary Marshall Clark, who, as my thesis advisor, deepened my understanding that this methodology allows for multiple voices to co-exist simultaneously in order to create a more robust history. Also, since the history is co-authored, it aims to create an equitable power dynamic between the interviewer and interviewee.

As I conducted an oral history project about New York City b-girls active in the 1990s for my thesis, I not only deepened my already close relationships with my crew members, but I also learned two further things about oral history methodology. First, I learned that oral history methods support dance studies research in quite a few ways. It is a method that complements the transmission of dance through storytelling, while capturing the gestures and songs practitioners use to relive their personal experiences and share their narratives. Second, I realized that oral history has the potential to create a fuller picture of breaking history than what has commonly been depicted. This dance style, after all, is centered on the cypher and battling, and this approach extends beyond dancing. People have conflicting and contentious accounts of what happened over time. Some felt neglected that their stories weren't part of an "official" history because they didn't fit with what had been depicted in the media. A definitive history runs counter to the values of the hip hop community. Oral history methodology provided me with a way to listen to all of these stories and create a fuller picture of breaking history than had been portrayed up until that point. For example, through listening to the oral histories of New York City b-girls active in the 1990s, I learned that two women were central to the development of what some refer to as a second wave of breakin' in New York City, and around the world. I documented these histories in my MA thesis, "Dancing Like a Girl: an oral history of NYC b-girls in the 1990s" (Park 2008).[4]

Moreover, during the b-girl oral history project, I found that this interdisciplinary methodology informed by memory studies, trauma studies, history, performance, and cultural studies is particularly well-suited to hip hop dance studies. This is due in part to the varying ways that hip hop dance practitioners understand their life experiences historically, culturally, as performers, and/or survivors. Not only does oral history methodology provide a space for people's experiences to be presented in long-form quotations, but it also connects to practices from within the diaspora like griot,[5] informal storytelling, and other oral traditions.

In what follows, I share my insights on oral history: what it is, why it is particularly suited for dance research, and how it can be adapted to the dance practice being studied. As part of my writing process for this chapter, I spoke with dance researchers who incorporate oral history practices in their work, including Clare Croft, Jeff Friedman, and Cassie Mey. I also spoke with Mary Marshall Clark. These people are gracious mentors, colleagues, and leaders in the fields of oral history and/or dance. I include long-form quotes from these interviews to demonstrate how interviews can be incorporated into scholarly writing in order to "hear" the voices of these narrators, as well as to model the multivocality that oral history values. Some of these long-form quotes reflect edits made by each researcher to clarify their intentions, reflecting the collaborative process of oral history methodology. I end the chapter with a discussion of what grace shinhae jun and I term Oral History Cypher Method (OHCM), a research methodology we developed for the 2021 issue of *Conversations Across the Field of Dance Studies*, "The Cyber-Rock Mixtape: A virtual hip hop dance listening cypher," for which we served as guest editors. Imani Kai Johnson outlines five aspects of cypher theory that emerge from her observations of breakin' cyphers: call and response, improvisation, battling, relations to the other, and dark matter (Johnson 2009, 204, 212–213). These characteristics, she argues, are enacted physically in dance cyphers, but also create a "movement of movement," or a way of living. The issue features a series of conversations that we curated between five pairs of hip hop dance practitioner-theorists. By combining oral history and cypher theory as OHCM, we see researchers and practitioners, OGs and newbies alike, as co-participants in a methodological cypher. Ultimately, I invite you to sit with the ideas of deep and active listening and collaboration of knowledge production that are central to oral history methodology in hopes that it will inspire how you think about your research.

What Is Oral History?

Dance historian and theorist Clare Croft's interest in interviewing began during her time as a journalist writing about dance. However, she felt a pull to delve deeper into dancers' stories, which led her to oral history during her PhD studies at the University of Texas Austin. Currently Associate Professor of American Culture at the University of Michigan, she is the author of *Dancers as Diplomats: American choreography in cultural exchange* (2015), in which oral history interviews with dancers provide a much-needed insight into diplomatic cultural and artistic exchanges from the artists' perspective. In this passage from our interview, she highlights key points about oral history.

CLARE CROFT: I was a journalist and my experiences and interest in interviewing really grew out of writing feature articles for dance parts of daily newspapers. I just really enjoyed asking artists about what they do. I saw my role as a dance writer as someone to pull back the curtain on what it is dance people do. At that point, [I] still was doing a lot of those common pre-show or post-show Q and As, and often audience members were really curious about what dancers did all day long. I felt like I was often writing feature articles that were kind of trying to let people understand something about dance culture. At that moment, I would specifically say, sort of concert dance culture like what is training like, what is rehearsal like, how do artists have ideas, and things like that. So, to write that kind of article I really needed to interview dancers, and I did that for many years. At the point where I really wanted to go back to school to do a PhD because I felt like I wanted to write books and also just really be able to do deeper dives than

I was able to do in the course of, you know, a 1000-word article for a newspaper. […]

When I was in graduate school, I took classes from a [professor] named Martha Norkunas whose writing I super recommend for anyone interested in oral history. She was…someone who manages to turn empathy into a practice of listening. I felt like that was what she was really teaching. Also, in her work on oral history, she really emphasized it as a way to better understand racialization. She was doing a big project about African Americans who had lived their whole lives in Texas. So, I worked for her for a period of time on that project, and I feel like that's when I really started to understand the difference between the sort of just doing an interview and oral history, which I think is a more sensitive open kind of practice, and one that you know I think in the field of history has been particularly useful for telling the stories of marginalized people.

So that's kind of how I got to oral history. I also just really like talking to people and being an academic can be a kind of solitary practice. I think in some ways, I like the method, because it's, I don't know, accepted in all of my world but also lets me feel a sense of connection (2021).

Croft points here to key differences between journalistic interviewing and the practice of oral history. In journalism, an interviewee (also known as a "source") agrees to be interviewed "on the record" which means that their quotes can and will be used in a story. In the oral history interviewing process, both the interviewer and interviewee craft a narrative in which the interviewee has the power to change, redact, or add to their story. One of the main responsibilities of an oral historian is the long-form collection of a person's reminiscences. In other words, the dynamic between the people participating in an oral history process is that of co-creators, whereas in journalism, once a source states something on the record, a journalist can report it without any further input from the source.

Second, Croft reinforces the potential of oral history methods as "particularly useful for telling the stories of marginalized people." This sentiment is something that the editors of *The Oral History Reader*, Robert Perks and Alistair Thompson, include as one of the many benefits of engaging in oral history. They write,

> Moreover, for some practitioners, oral history has not just been about making histories. In certain projects a primary aim has been the empowerment of individuals or social groups through the process of remembering and re-interpreting the past, with an emphasis on the value of process as much as historical product.
>
> (1998, ix)

Cassie Mey, the Oral History Coordinator and Audio Archivist for the Jerome Robbins Dance Division at The New York Public Library for the Performing Arts, found that the oral tradition of learning dance prepared her for a career as an oral historian. After semi-retiring from dancing with Molissa Fenley's company, Mey pursued a Master's degree in Library Sciences. Her network of dancer-friends led her to a position at the NYPL where her interest in listening to dancers' stories dovetailed with working on the Dance Oral History Project. She finds it particularly useful to hear otherwise untold stories:

CASSIE MEY: It's my favorite method for dance research, in fact [...] At the end of my dance career, I was thinking a lot about, "What do I have left?" And it's memory. I think there's an importance to that, and the importance of a person's particular point of view that speaks to and speaks in contrary to the larger dance history models that get thrown out, or the way that historians construct history. [...] I really value the feminist and outsider-type angle that oral history can capture.

In dance history, especially as a dancer, I feel like the dancers' perspective and voice is often not recorded. It's often the choreographer. There's the power structure and dynamic of the choreographer and dancer, and [it's] usually the choreographer who's speaking to the artform and the work. So, I really think that the perspectives of dancers are often what gets left out of history books and silenced and I think oral history gives that a voice and a space (2021).

While oral history as a field attends to previously untold stories, it takes the careful listening of an oral historian to document it. Croft cites professor Martha Norkunas as having taught her the importance of turning "empathy into a practice of listening." One of the main responsibilities of an oral historian is the practice of deep and active listening. This type of listening leads the oral historian to become adept at following how the interviewee recalls things. Since we are not in the practice of reciting our personal histories, a narrator likely will not deliver a perfectly chronological monologue of their life. Realistically, how a person recalls their memories is not linear, as one memory might trigger another memory from their youth or something that happened the day before. This also means that sitting with the silences or the lulls in the interviewees' recollection becomes crucially important. Is this person confronting a painful or traumatic memory? Are they experiencing a particularly happy emotion that they want to remain in for a moment? Have they momentarily forgotten what they were talking about? For these reasons, the oral historian should take notes and refrain from colloquial sounds of agreement like "mmhmm," or, "yes." The objective is to be able to listen to this recording later and hear a person tell their life story with the least number of interruptions as possible. If there are moments of clarifications, the oral historian can use their judgment to help assist the interviewee with prompts like, "You spoke about ___ early in your life. Can you tell me a story about when something similar happened again?" As with any kind of qualitative interviewing, the oral historian should do their best to ask open-ended questions.

The process of transcribing and editing the interview transcript requires a different kind of attentive listening. This is one of the most time-intensive steps in the process, but it is often the most rewarding because it requires the oral historian to listen to the interviewee multiple times and work collaboratively with the interviewee to most accurately represent their life experiences in textual form. In a pure oral history interview format, once an interview is complete, the oral historian will transcribe it, either themselves or via a transcription app or service.[6] After that, they will conduct an audit-edit of the transcript, which means listening to the recording to tighten up the text to most accurately represent what the narrator has said.[7] Following this, the transcript is sent back to the interviewee for review. This step allows for the addition, edits, or redaction of any part of the transcript, as additional memories or emotions may be excavated during the interview itself. Once they've reviewed the transcript and returned it, and changes have been incorporated, the co-created document of someone's living history is complete.

However, the oral history interview and transcription process is not often the end. In fact, the completed transcription then begs the questions: how will the interview recordings and transcriptions be used? Are there narrative threads that have emerged from listening to these life histories multiple times and ways? How does this story relate to other topics? What are some connections you've seen throughout the process? How will you communicate these findings? Will it be donated to an oral history archive? Published in some form? Adapted into a performance? While oral histories have been adapted into theater regularly, adapting oral history into dance and movement provides a different kind of insight into a person's life stories.

Dance studies scholar and oral historian Jeff Friedman conducted oral histories of dancers during the HIV/AIDS epidemic in the San Francisco dance community and later completed his doctoral research on oral history and dance. He is a Professor of Dance Studies at Rutgers University and the Founding Director of the Legacy Oral History Program at the San Francisco Museum of Performance and Design. In creating the solo performance work *Muscle Memory* (1994), Friedman re-embodied oral history interviews with Frank Everett, a 28-year-old man who danced with Oakland Ballet and ODC and died of AIDS,[8] and Eve Gentry, an 84-year-old woman who danced with Hanya Holm.[9] Friedman describes a moment where Gentry recalls her Polish immigrant mother standing up to a local school official who attempts to deny Gentry school enrollment because Gentry appears too small for a six-year-old. Gentry's telling of the story implies that the school official's response is laden with xenophobia and mistrust for the immigrant:

JEFF FRIEDMAN: You learn that, when you're making choreography, that if you're true to the words of the interview, you have to embody what you think is going on there. You learn something that you would not have learned if you didn't embody it. [If] you just read the words on the page, "Oh, she had that experience that was sad," that's not enough. You have to find a way to embody it. I've learned that there are many things to learn from choreographic research that actually add to our understanding of what these interviews are.

Friedman found the process of transcription flattened the dancers' reminiscences and limited the understanding of their experience into just two dimensions. He notes that re-embodying these transcripts in performance added a layer of understanding and interpreting an oral history beyond reading a textual transcription.

Dance and Oral History

Friedman, citing French structuralist philosopher Pierre Bourdieu (1990), suggests that oral history, like dance, is embodied, temporal, and contingent. In other words, they are both practices that take place in the body (embodied), at a specific time (temporal), and are in collaboration with others (contingent) (2021). In what follows I draw on insights from interviews I conducted with fellow oral historians to point to how oral history can help us get at these aspects of dance.

While most oral history interviews are conducted as audio recordings, CCOHR Director Mary Marshall Clark believes that if the project design and budget allow, conducting both audio and video interview sessions is ideal for collecting embodied oral histories or performers and dancers. She recalls in the late 1990s her mentor Luisa Passerini's passionate charge to the field of oral history to supplement the oral/aural aspects of the field with visuality in order for the practice to thrive in a scholarly or performative way. Clark notes that for years following this, budgetary constraints limited the execution of Passerini's insight, but in 1999, she had the opportunity through the Carnegie Foundation to video record some oral history interviews.

MARY MARSHALL CLARK: We did some experimentation in South Africa, where we went to record Carnegie's mixed history there, both in terms of having unwittingly, I believe, but through a grant, supported the creation of apartheid (which is its own story and you can find that by Googling "Carnegie Corporation oral history" where we talk about that).[10] But it also allowed us to record [video] and that's the first time I realized its real significance, because we weren't in New York City recording mostly white men, with a few notable exceptions. We were recording Black leaders who had overseen – engineered – a revolution. And to watch their faces as they talked about that, especially Archbishop Desmond Tutu whose modes of expression are almost the fullest modes of expression that a human being can have. His voice goes up and down four octaves. His head moves constantly and then he stares at you like this [opens eyes wide]. He feels his sadness in his body. He feels his anger in his body, and so you could take a look at that one video and record possibly the range of emotions he had during apartheid. And that was when I became convinced that video should be the primary medium of oral history and not a secondary medium.

[…] I would say that if we're looking at power, which should be what we do in oral history, then we need to see who we're talking to. We need to not only have video interviews but visual images and objects and things that people carry with them in the process of migrating or things, concrete things. We need all the elements of documentary, really, in addition to these very focused interviews.[11]

Clark describes how, in focusing on visual documentation of embodiment in oral history, we can not only capture important information that audio recordings miss, but also – with the help of performance studies, dance studies, memory studies, and cultural studies – understand oral histories as embodied performance.

This underscores Friedman's observation of the deeply kinesthetic nature of the oral interview. Friedman uses the phrase "net narrative," to describe the embodied flow of words over time. Friedman states, "I'm looking for what are the long-form embodied cognitive metaphors and the long-form embodied experiences of our physical being that contribute to our ability to narrativize." In order to analyze what is being communicated through language and movement in an oral history interview, Friedman draws on theories from cognitive science, sociology, anthropology, phenomenology, and Labanotation.[12]

JEFF FRIEDMAN: [I]n an interview that I did with Sara Rudner at UC Riverside, [she] talked about first period [dancing] with Twyla. She literally walked her fingers down her thigh away from her while she was [beginning her discussion]. And then [later] she finally said, "…and I had to walk away from Twyla to do my own work," and that was a real thing for her. Laban would say that [the earlier gesture was] a shadow movement. People can discuss that or contend with it. People actually sometimes know things in their bodies before they say them. Sometimes they need to gesture them before they can actually connect [those embodied knowledges] enough to language them in an interview or just in the speaking world, [generally].

[...] When I did my dissertation interviews with the Twyla Tharp former dance artists, I took them into dance studios and said, "You can dance as much as you want." And that meant, at one point, that [one interview subject] decided to choreograph the entire interview. "Should we be sitting? Should I be sitting on the floor? Should [he] be sitting on the floor? Should we both be sitting on the floor? Should we face back-to-back? Should we face heel to heel? Should we stand up and do contact improvisation for the rest of the interview?" How is that [choreography] changing and embodying our experience of the interview as deeply as possible to access what she knew in her body?

For Friedman, the temporal nature of both dance and the oral history interview come together to enable stories and insights that might not otherwise come to the fore.

Likewise, Mey notes that oral history interviews often uncover contingent relationships between dancers and dance forms that audiences might not know about otherwise:

CASSIE MEY: [Oral history] counters the narrative that dance forms are so separate. Pat Catterson who's a postmodern choreographer and one of Yvonne Rainer's [dancers/collaborators] – [...] was a tap teacher and Honi Coles[13] taught her! She's not thought of as a tap dancer and having such an integral part, but Jane Goldberg was a young tap dancer in her class who brought in Honi Coles. So, there's this whole intersection where [Catterson] talks about dancers from Taylor and Cunningham coming in to watch Honi Coles teach this tap class. There are connectivities between the dance styles and forms that have yet to be uncovered.

By paying attention to the embodied, temporal, and contingent aspects of both dance and oral history, dance oral histories can open up insights not only into one dancer's story, but also into the landscape of dance more broadly.

Oral History Cypher Method

When I spoke to Friedman for this chapter, he emphasized that the logic of the research method must match the logic of the practice. In this last section, I discuss the 2021 issue of *Conversations Across the Field of Dance Studies*, which I guest-edited with grace shinhae jun, as an example of this in practice. We conceived the issue, "The Cyber-Rock Mixtape: A virtual hip hop dance listening cypher," as applying oral history methodology to the lessons we've learned in a cypher, resulting in what we've come to term OHCM. While the cypher is a literal formation where dancers exchange or battle, the epistemology of the cypher extends into how we think and navigate the world (Johnson 2009). What might it look like, then, to ask practitioners to step into a cypher with each other to discuss a specific topic, and to give space for these multiple stories, voices, and viewpoints to co-exist alongside one another? We critically considered how to include different subjective voices that would be part of this cypher. We thought about who within our crews/networks would be ideal to speak with, willing to participate in the project, and would benefit from having a scholarly publication credit. We considered a broad swath of topics ranging from local Brooklyn breakin' history, to transnational relationships, to activism and Black liberation, to the transmission and teaching of dance, to the issue of sexual harassment in the scene. We also thought about the people who would eventually interact with this publication as readers or listeners which additionally affected who, what topics, and how we presented them in the cypher.

We ultimately invited five pairs of conversants (hip hop dance practitioners) to talk for an hour via the online meeting platform Zoom. The majority of conversants are members of our found families for over two decades, so our decision-making centered on respect and care through each aspect of the process. Each pair discussed a separate pre-selected topic related to their expertise. Though these conversations were not oral histories per se, this methodology along with cypher theory affected every aspect of the project design. We generated written transcripts through Zoom, edited the rough transcripts, and then conducted an audit-edit. We became acutely aware of word choice, colloquialism, themes, and speech patterns. When did a "you know?" indicate a speech pattern and when was it seeking the other conversant's agreement? Would we transcribe the work "breakin'" exactly as it was said or would we write it as "breaking"?

When sending the transcription of the conversation to each conversant for review, we let the conversants know that we planned on publishing both the video documentation of the conversations as well as the transcripts. We also let them know that we could edit sections out of the video recording if they felt that there were parts of the conversation they did not want public. In one instance, WaAakSun, a b-boy and graf writer/aerosol artist, requested for us to blur his image and not include his government name, which we honored.

At the same time, we sent the transcripts to the conversants, they were also sent to the *Conversations* editorial board for peer review. Editorial board members gave feedback and asked for clarification, which led us to consider how much context was necessary to understand terms like "footwork" and "power" in order to understand what was discussed. At what point would we allow the language to ride in the spirit of "if you know, you know"? Ultimately, this part of the process forced us to think about how we would shape how others might listen to these stories, which informed the critical decisions we made about allowing the narrator's voices to be heard in the broader context of history. To this end, jun and I then produced annotated transcripts in addition to raw transcripts that aim to provide significant historical or cultural context to aspects of the conversation. We footnoted dates, people, places with additional research, and hyperlinked out to other resources on the web. In addition to the annotated transcripts, we asked scholars who are familiar with hip hop dance studies from the fields of ethnomusicology, ethnic studies, and dance studies to cypher with us by way of providing responses to the interviews, which we called "liner notes." Like any cypher, the exchange of energy began between the two of us guest editors, widened to include the conversants, widened again to include scholarly respondents, and again to invite audience members to engage with the information. By design, we invited readers/listeners/participants to "get down" with the knowledge produced in whatever way suits them. OHCM was conceived as a method that could be conducted during the COVID-19 pandemic when listening to peoples' histories in person was not a possibility. By necessity, we created a process that centered care for participants' time and physical safety, in a financially and (slightly more) environmentally-sustainable way. As a result, we were able to convene with people from around the world whom we might not have been able to as easily without a more substantial budget. I plan to continue using and refining OHCM in my future scholarship, particularly as it allows for more access to practitioners who wish to collaborate with me.

Conclusion

In my hip hop dance practice classes, I underscore the importance of each person developing their own style and that they should not leave my class dancing exactly the way I do. Likewise, I hope that oral history methodology, the ways that the oral historians mentioned in this chapter have applied this methodology to their artistic practices, and OHCM provide a foundation from which you will apply these methods for your own projects.

As Cassie Mey notes, "Just so much hidden history has yet to be uncovered and I think that's where dance oral history is really powerful." Oral history methodology is a way to document the stories that often accompany dance education and dance-making that can support or challenge existing narratives that center those in power. It allows for many stories to co-exist and centers care for the narrator. Applied oral history methodology in the form of OHCM provides a way to further allow the research method to match the practice, and ultimately hear the life histories of the crew and found family members I did not see in existing scholarship.

Notes

1 OG is an abbreviation for "original gangster," used colloquially to mean elders in the breakin' scene.
2 See Chang, Jeff, *Can't Stop Won't Stop: A History of the Hip-Hop Generation* (New York: St. Martin's Press, 2007) and George, Nelson, *Hip Hop America* (New York: Penguin, 2005).
3 Since then, Mary Marshall Clark and her other collaborators of the 9/11 oral history project have published their findings, see Mary Marshall Clark, Peter Bearman, Stephen Drury Smith, and Catherine Ellis, eds. *After the Fall: New Yorkers Remember September 2001 and the Years That Followed* (New York: The New Press, 2011). Hear snippets of the interviews at https://www.nytimes.com/video/us/sept-11-reckoning/100000001040144/the-moment-before-and-after.html.
4 See also MiRi Park, "Learn Your History: Using Academic Oral Histories of NYC B-Girls in the 1990s to Broaden Hip Hop Scholarship." In *The Oxford Handbook on Hip Hop Dance Studies*, edited by Mary Fogarty and Imani Kai Johnson (Oxford: Oxford University Press, 2022).
5 *Griot* refers to the people in West African societies/castes who are designated holders and interpreters of social and familial histories. See Hugo Slim & Paul Thompson, with Olivia Bennett and Nigel Cross, "Ways of Listening." In *The Oral History Reader*, edited by Robert Perks & Alistair Thomson, 114–125 (London and New York: Routledge, 1998); Alex Haley, "Black History, Oral History and Genealogy." In *The Oral History Reader*, edited by Robert Perks & Alistair Thomson, 9–20 (London and New York: Routledge, 1998); E. Moncell Durden, "Hip-Hop Dance as Community Expression and Global Phenomenon." In *Jazz Dance: A History of the Roots and Branches*, edited by Lindsay Guarino & Wendy Oliver, 184–193 (Gainesville: University Press of Florida, 2014).
6 Some free transcription apps exist, but transcription services charge fees. If you have funding for your project, you will want to determine if you have a budget to accommodate this.
7 Some oral history centers/archives like the CCOHR and The Institute for Oral History at Baylor University offer their transcription style guides/guidelines. See "Oral History Resources" at the end of this chapter for website URLs.
8 "Frank Everett," Legacy History Oral History Digital Archive, accessed August 4, 2021, https://lohpdigitalarchive.omeka.net/exhibits/show/lohp/frank-everett
9 "Eve Gentry," Legacy History Oral History Digital Archive, accessed August 4, 2021, https://lohpdigitalarchive.omeka.net/exhibits/show/lohp/eve-gentry--1909-1994-

10 A. Dunlap Smith, "South African Oral History Taped to Preserve Spirit of Movement and Its Leaders." *Columbia University Record*, 25, no. 10, December 10, 1999. http://www.columbia.edu/cu/record/archives/vol25/10/2510_S_African_Oral_History.html

11 Mary Marshall Clark (Founding Co-Director, Columbia University Center for Oral History and Research) in discussion with the author, February 3, 2021.

12 For his references to cognitive science, see George Lakoff and Mark Johnson, *Metaphors We Live By* (Chicago, IL: University of Chicago Press, 1980); for sociology, see Erving Goffman, "Presentation of Self in Everyday Life." *American Journal of Sociology*, 55 (1949): 6–7; for anthropology, see Victor Turner, "Liminality and Communitas." In *The Ritual Process: Structure and Anti-Structure*, 94–113, 125–130 (Chicago, IL: Aldine Publishing, 1969); for phenomenology, see Martin Heidegger, *Being and Time: A Translation of Sein und Zeit* (Albany, NY: SUNY Press, 1996); for Labanotation, see Warren Lamb, *Posture and Gesture: An Introduction to the Study of Physical Behaviour* (Richmond-upon-Thames: G. Duckworth, 1965).

13 Honi Coles was one half of the Vaudeville act Atkins and Coles with Cholly Atkins. See Cholly Atkins, and Jacqui Malone, *Class Act: The Jazz Life of Choreographer Cholly Atkins* (New York: Columbia University Press, 2001); Constance Valis Hill, *Tap Dancing America: A Cultural History* (Oxford: Oxford University Press, 2014); Marshall W. Stearns and Jean Stearns, *Jazz Dance: The Story of American Vernacular Dance* (New York: Macmillan, 1968).

Works Cited

Bourdieu, Pierre. 1990. *The Logic of Practice*. Stanford, CA: Stanford University Press.

Clark, Mary Marshall. Interviewed via Zoom, February 3, 2021.

Croft, Clare in discussion with Heather Castillo. Interviewed via Zoom, February 17, 2021

———. 2015. *Dancers as Diplomats: American Choreography in Cultural Exchange* Oxford: Oxford University Press.

Friedman, Jeff. Interviewed via Zoom, February 24, 2021.

Johnson, Imani Kai. 2009. "Dark Matter in B-boying Cyphers: Race and Global Connection in Hip Hop." PhD diss., University of Southern California.

Jun, Grace and MiRi Park, eds. 2022. "The Cyber-Rock Mixtape: A virtual hip hop dance listening cypher." Special issue, *Conversations Across the Field of Dance Studies* 41. https://journals.publishing.umich.edu/conversations/issue/81/info/.

Mey, Cassie. Interviewed via Zoom, February 9, 2021.

Park, MiRi. 2008. "Dancing Like a Girl: An Oral History of NYC B-Girls in the 1990s." MA thesis, Columbia University.

Perks, Robert, and Alistair Thomson. 1998. *The Oral History Reader*. London and New York: Routledge.

Smith, A. Dunlap. 1999. "South African Oral History Taped to Preserve Spirit of Movement and Its Leaders," *Columbia University Record*, 25, no. 10, December 10. http://www.columbia.edu/cu/record/archives/vol25/10/2510_S_African_Oral_History.html

Suggested Reading

Atkins, Cholly and Jacqui Malone. 2001 *Class Act: The Jazz Life of Choreographer Cholly Atkins*. New York: Columbia University Press.

Boyd, Douglas A. 2012. "Audio or Video for Recording Oral History: Questions, Decisions." In *Oral History in the Digital Age*, edited by Doug Boyd, Steve Cohen, Brad Rakerd, and Dean Rehberger. Washington, DC: Institute of Museum and Library Services. http://ohda.matrix.msu.edu/2012/06/audio-or-video-for-recording-oral-history/

Chang, Jeff. 2007. *Can't Stop Won't Stop: A History of the Hip-Hop Generation*. New York: St. Martin's Press.

Charlton, Thomas L., Lois E. Myers, and Rebecca Sharpless. 2006. *Handbook of Oral History*. Lanham, MD: AltaMira Press.

Clark, Mary Marshall. 2002. "The September 11, 2001, Oral History Narrative and Memory Project: A First Report." *The Journal of American History* 89, no. 2: 569–579.

Dougherty, Jack and Candace Simpson. 2012. "Who Owns Oral History? A Creative Commons Solution," In *Oral History in the Digital Age*, edited by Doug Boyd, Steve Cohen, Brad Rakerd, and Dean Rehberger. Washington, DC: Institute of Museum and Library Services. https://ohda.matrix.msu.edu/2012/06/a-creative-commons-solution/

Durden, Moncell, E. 2014. "Hip-Hop Dance as Community Expression and Global Phenomenon." In *Jazz Dance: A History of the Roots and Branches*, edited by Lindsay Guarino and Wendy Oliver, 184–193. Gainesville: University Press of Florida.

Friedman, Jeff. 2014. "Oral History, Hermeneutics, and Embodiment." *The Oral History Review* 41, no. 2: 290–300.

George, Nelson. 2005. *Hip Hop America*. New York: Penguin.

Gluck, Sherna Berger, and Daphne Patai, eds. 2016. *Women's Words: The Feminist Practice of Oral History*. London and New York: Routledge.

Goffman, Erving. 1949. "Presentation of Self in Everyday Life." *American Journal of Sociology* 55: 6–7.

Grele, Ronald J., and Studs Terkel. 1991. *Envelopes of Sound: The Art of Oral History*. Boston: Greenwood Publishing Group.

Haley, Alex. 1998. "Black History, Oral History and Genealogy," In *The Oral History Reader*, edited by Robert Perks and Alistair Thomson, 9–20. London and New York: Routledge.

Hay, Joanna. 2012. "Case Study: Using Video in Oral History – Learning from One Woman's Experiences." In *Oral History in the Digital Age*, edited by Doug Boyd, Steve Cohen, Brad Rakerd, and Dean Rehberger. Washington, DC: Institute of Museum and Library Services. https://ohda.matrix.msu.edu/2012/06/using-video-in-oral-history/

Heidegger, Martin. 1996. *Being and Time: A Translation of Sein und Zeit*. Albany, NY: SUNY Press.

Lakoff, George and Mark Johnson. 1980 *Metaphors We Live By*. Chicago: University of Chicago Press.

Lamb, Warren. 1965. *Posture and Gesture: An Introduction to the Study of Physical Behaviour*. Richmond-upon-Thames: G. Duckworth.

Mahuika, Nepia. 2019. *Rethinking Oral History and Tradition: An Indigenous Perspective*. New York: Oxford University Press.

Marshall Clark, Mary, Peter Bearman, Stephen Drury Smith, and Catherine Ellis, eds. 2011. *After the Fall: New Yorkers Remember September 2001 and the Years that Followed*. New York: The New Press.

Park, MiRi. 2022. "Learn Your History: Using Academic Oral Histories of NYC B-Girls in the 1990s to Broaden Hip Hop Scholarship." In *The Oxford Handbook on Hip Hop Dance Studies*, edited by Mary Fogarty and Imani Kai Johnson, 131–148. Oxford: Oxford Publishing.

Passerini, Luisa. 2003. "Memories between Silence and Oblivion." In *Memory History Nation: Contested Pasts, Memory and Narrative Series*, edited by Katharine Hodgkin, and Susannah Radstone, 238–254. Boca Raton, FL: Routledge.

Portelli, Alessandro. 2010. *The Death of Luigi Trastulli and Other Stories: Form and Meaning in Oral History*. Albany, NY: SUNY Press.

Slim, Hugo and Paul Thompson, with Olivia Bennett and Nigel Cross. 1998. "Ways of Listening." In *The Oral History Reader*, edited by Robert Perks and Alistair Thomson, 114–125. London and New York: Routledge.

Stearns, Marshall W., and Jean Stearns. 1968. *Jazz Dance: The Story of American Vernacular Dance*. New York: Macmillan.

Turner, Victor. 1969. "Liminality and Communitas." In *The Ritual Process: Structure and Anti-Structure*, edited by Victor Turner, Roger D. Abrahams and Alfred Harris, 94–113. Chicago: Aldine Publishing.

Valis Hill, Constance. 2014. *Tap Dancing America: A Cultural History*. Oxford: Oxford University Press.

Oral History Resources

Columbia Center for Oral History and Research (CCOHR):
https://www.ccohr.incite.columbia.edu

Columbia University Oral History Master's Program:
http://oralhistory.columbia.edu

Digital Omnium: oral history, archives, and digital technology:
https://digitalomnium.com/oral-history-in-the-digital-age-best-practices/

Legacy Oral History Online Collection:
https://lohpdigitalarchive.omeka.net

Louie B. Nunn Center for Oral History:
https://libraries.uky.edu/libpage.php?lweb_id=11&llib_id=13

New York Performing Arts Library, Jerome Robbins Dance Division, Oral History Channel:
https://nypl.org/dance-oral-history

Southwest Oral History Association:
https://southwestoralhistory.org

Oral History Association (OHA):
https://www.oralhistory.org

Oral History in the Digital Age:
https://ohda.matrix.msu.edu

12
To the Motion Itself

Toward a Phenomenological Methodology of Dance Research

Nigel Stewart

The Thing

In this chapter I explore a specific phenomenological methodology of dance research. Like any of the main philosophical projects of the 20th and 21st centuries, phenomenology is multi-faceted. Existential phenomenology – which subdivides into the hermeneutic ontology of Martin Heidegger (1889–1976) and the philosophy of existence of Merleau-Ponty (1908–1961), Jean-Paul Sartre (1905–1980) and Jean-Luc Marion (b. 1946) – is different from the phenomenological hermeneutics of Hans-Georg Gadamer (1900–2002) and Paul Ricoeur (1913–2005), which in turn can be distinguished from the social phenomenology of Alfred Schütz (1899–1959) or Hannah Arendt (1906–1975). However, these phenomenologies refer to, even as they depart from, the descriptive and transcendental phenomenology of Edmund Husserl (1859–1938). Accordingly, the methodology I demonstrate in the second part of this chapter is largely based on the descriptive phenomenology of Husserl but incorporates concepts by later philosophers who, in my view, improve upon Husserl's ideas.

In the first part of this chapter, I sketch some key drivers of Husserlian phenomenology. Chief amongst these is the drive to return to things *qua* things. *Zu den Sachen selbst!* ("back to the things themselves!") is Husserl's rallying cry (in Lawrence 2002, 168). What, though, is a "thing" in phenomenology? A thing is neither a factual and quantifiable object of analysis existing independently of the researcher, nor a concept that can be "applied objectively" to that object. To objectify anything in those ways is to fall foul of the "natural attitude" toward things. On the contrary, Husserl's "principle of all principles" is that a thing is the "primordial intuition," or "originary presentative consciousness"

(Moran 2012, xxxii)," of that thing "as it truly appears as itself, of itself and starting from itself" (Marion 2008, 45), and it is equally the knowledge that is immanent to and within the limits of that intuition (Husserl 2012, 43).

Secondly, a thing is intentional (Dorsey and Collier 2018, 181). At root, intentionality is the principle that consciousness is always the consciousness of something. Husserl notices two interfused aspects of intentionality. Firstly, intentionality is the noematic intuition of a thing, which is to say the manifold ways in which it presents itself within our consciousness. Secondly, intentionality is our noetic attitude toward that thing, that is, the meanings we bestow upon it and the types or "modalities of meaning" that we bestow, such as "bringing out, relating, apprehending synoptically, and taking up the various attitudes of belief, presumption, valuation, and so forth" (Husserl 2012, 184–185; see also Moustakas 1994, 69–75). Intentionality thus explicates the "primal unity" of the thing that is valued and the act of valuing that thing (Brown 2003, 11; see also Circosta 2006, 8).

Thirdly, a thing unifies the objective and subjective; indeed, this is the very "essence of phenomenology" (Moran 2000, 108). So, if phenomenology eschews objective analysis, it equally avoids "solipsist rumination," and it goes beyond "first-person reporting, mere experiential description, [...] or reflective autobiography" (Grant 2019, 21), though such tools may be useful in the early stages of an investigation. It is not interested in mere sensory "data" but meaning-making patterns of sentience (Moran 2000, 145). By grasping experiences noematically, we see how our concrete experiences of an object depend upon the concepts we bestow upon them. Reciprocally, by seizing an object noetically, we notice how those concepts are constituted through noematic experiences. Through this two-way process, the object throngs as a thing within our lifeworld.

Now "phenomenology paves the way" for all disciplines by "elucidating" this unity of subject and object (*ibid.*, 108). For instance, phenomenology might spur the geometer to comprehend a triangle, or any other spatiotemporal form, not as a universal concept objectively the same "in Tokyo and in Paris, the same in the fifth century before Christ and now" (Merleau-Ponty 1968, 31), but rather as the self-evidence of a triangle as that can be reactivated in "'coincidence' [... with] the original activity" in which a triangle was first intuited, namely, the intuition of triangular relations between bodies and "the bodily shapes of rivers, mountains, buildings" (Husserl 1970, 28).[1] Comparably, a yogi could grasp Adho Mukha Svanasana (Downward-facing Dog pose) not by imitating photographs of that triangular posture in any number of how-to books on yoga, but as a by-product of pandiculation, a reflex stimulated by yawning the armpits and inguinal creases, exhaling through the nostrils, elongating the tailbone, and so on (Sabatini 2000, 189). In similar vein, a kinesiologist might understand postural alignment, not as it can be measured biomechanically, but rather in the experience of forces flowing up and down the spinal curves (Olsen 1991, 50), or by flexing the crescent-shaped "diaphragms" that seem to float one above the other from the pelvic floor to the tentorium cerebelli (Bordoni 2020). In effect, these approaches are phenomenological in elucidating how objective knowledge appears within subjective experience.

Fourthly, the thing thrives on intersubjectivity. This brings into view the ethical basis of the relationship between subject and object, which incorporates self and other. Husserl's version of intentionality emphasizes the individual subject's intention more than the other who is intended. Sartre concludes that the other's subjectivity always escapes the subject's "I" (Barber 2018, 10). In a critique of Sartre, Schütz trumpets the "vivid simultaneity of the 'We'" within any individual's "conscious stream," on which basis he, and phenomenological sociology in general, investigates how shared meanings are produced by "consociate […] co-performing subjectivities" interacting over time within specific social situations (*ibid*, 9–10). My own position is closer to Merleau-Ponty's. Whilst acknowledging "an *écart*, […] an incessant escaping" between self and other (Merleau-Ponty 1968, 147), his key concept of the chiasm, or "intertwining," shifts attention to the "co-implication" of the subject and object "within the "flesh of the world" (Hansen 2018, 229). The realms of the sensing self and sensed other intersect, but never conflate, within an all-encompassing general Sensible: as toucher and touched within Touching, as seer and seen within Seeing, and so on. This expanded consciousness can be gained if you (the reader) and I were to move continuously palm-to-palm and with eyes closed. Even if we agree that first I (the moved) follow you (the mover) and that we then reverse those roles, we may find a point of delicious undecidability in which it's not clear who moves whom. We are sheaves moved and moving in a field of motion. Furthermore, within the noema of this chiasm is a noesis, namely, meanings that emerge from and are contingent upon the very occasion of our encounter as well as meanings consistent with our shared modes of intention (e.g. we sense each other's movement in direct perception or, alternatively, through recollection, in imagination or pure fantasy; we move for the sake of a training exercise or a late-night frolic; and so on). I contend that the kinesthetic empathy that this chiasm ensures is the condition of the possibility of phenomenological dance research. This is certainly the ground for a phenomenological approach to improvisation, particularly within environmental dance where an intertwining with the other-than-human world is paramount (Stewart 2010, 33–35; 2015, 370), but equally to the more implicit chiasmic interrelationship of spectator and dancer, researcher and dance, within a dance performance (Parviainen 1998; Stewart 2016, 2019).

Intersubjectivity does not presume a collapse of self and other. In a very different key and on a larger scale, Gadamer claims we should grasp the past not merely by reconstructing the other's "horizon of understanding," which only "mak[es] our own standpoint safely unattainable" and turns the other into a static object of knowledge; nor by "subordinating" the other to the "standards" of our own distinctly different historically evolved and culturally-specific horizon of understanding (Gadamer 1989, 305); but rather by rising to a "historically effected consciousness" (Gadamer 1989, xv, 300–307, 341–377). This is a transitional point of "agreement" in-between both horizons which clarifies and "overcomes not only our own particularity but also that of the other" (Gadamer 1989, 305). In such ways, "the path and goal of mutual understanding" is the very *Sache* (subject matter, stake, sake, and thing) of history itself (Gadamer 1989, 180). Some contemporary dance performances and rehearsal methods are explicitly concerned with this hermeneutic process (Stewart 2003, 2005b).

The thing has a fifth characteristic, namely that it (e.g. Adho Mukha Svanasana) produces its noesis, or immanent meaning, by gathering its constitutive noematic elements (e.g. different sensations of yawning and elongating) into a unity (e.g. pandiculation) through time. Heidegger gives attention to how each element of a thing "appropriates" the others into a "onefold". For instance, he meditates on how the jugness of a jug gathers the elements of earth, sky, mortals and divinities into a "round dance of appropriating" which "lightens the four into the radiance of their simple oneness": the "earth [...] receives the rain and dew of the sky" which is poured from the jug to "quench [the] thirst" and "enliven [the] conviviality" of mortals or as libation for divinities (Heidegger 1971, 178). In different ways, then, it is not the thing in general but the temporal process of "gathering" or "thinging" an object into a thing that "lays claim to thought" and most discloses the thing *qua* thing (Heidegger 1971, 172, 168).

Finally, to return to the things themselves is to return to them in their essence. All forms of phenomenology are concerned with essences (Grant 2019, 20–24), but, again, there are significant differences between them. Digging deeper than the noematic and noetic data of factually occurring specific acts of consciousness, Husserl wants to identify, from within those acts, nothing less than "pure *a priori*" noematic "essences of perception" and the "essential [noetic] meaning-intentions and interconnected meaning-fulfilments which are the "essential structures of all understanding" (Moran 2000, 108). For Heidegger, though, an essence is not a universal. As is the case with Gadamer's horizons of understanding, our experience of things, and the essences of those experiences, is always preshaped by "the finitude, worldliness, and historicity of our human predicament" (Dostal 1993, 141). For Heidegger, then, an essence is simply "what applies over the entire extent" of a set of "particular instances [...] or what lies under [them] as [their] ground" (in Grant 2019, 22, 23). Nonetheless, Heidegger's four elements of earth, sky, mortals, and divinities constitute, he intimates, the universal ground of jugness *in specie*, not a particular jug or even a genre of jugs. Again, I find that Merleau-Ponty strikes a balance. For him as for Husserl and Heidegger, essences are not pure abstractions but more like "the old term 'element'," in the sense […] of water, air, earth, and fire" (Merleau-Ponty 1968, 139). However, these are neither prescriptive nor absolute. Even if a different historically evolved set of elements are used (e.g. the five elements of Chinese Medicine), the point remains that an essence is "a general thing, midway between the spatio-temporal individual and the ideal, a sort of incarnate principle" (Merleau-Ponty 1968, 139). Physical thinking (or kinesthetic cognition) occurs when movement principles are incarnated, as is the case with Maxine Sheets-Johnstone's four components of virtual force, which I apply below, or, say, Rudolf Laban's eukinetics or Doris Humphrey's dynamics.[2]

Toward a Phenomenological Methodology of Dance Research

So how can we unplug our natural attitude to a dance? How can we return to the motion itself of that dance as danced? How can dancing be understood noematically and noetically? How do we grasp the unity of dancer and dance? How can we investigate the chiasm between researcher and dancer yet acknowledge their own horizons? How can we identify meaning-making patterns of sentience within a dance and the essential *a priori* structures of kinesthetic cognition that underpin those patterns? How does a dance gather its constitutive elements into a onefold? How can we follow the motion of meaning in and through the carnal texture of moving? I will endeavor to answer these questions through the following five-stage methodology. This is based on Herbert Spiegelberg's seven-step method in *The Phenomenological Movement* (1994) and, to a lesser extent, Clark Moustakas' "Methodology of Transcendental Phenomenology" (1994), which has had some impact on dance research (e.g. Len Deets 2015). Although I have used this methodology to generate choreographic material (Stewart 2005a; Waterton 2003), I here apply it to a phrase from José Limón's *Psalm* (1967) as danced by Stephen Pier during a demonstration I witnessed in 1996.[3] More specifically, I take the "forcetimespace" of Pier's dancing as my *Sache*, as the thing I want to investigate and to which I want to return (Sheets-Johnstone 1979, 14). Different phenomenologies of dance have defined the gathering or onefold of the theoretically distinct elements of force, time, and space as the defining characteristic of dancing in general. The "forcetimespace" of dancing is the *Sache* of dance.

Stage One: The Epoché – Phenomenological Reduction

My first move is the *epoché*: literally, the "cessation," the foundational act of "bracketing" my natural attitude (Moran 2000, 137, 147). Here I not only endeavor to disregard my habitual attitudes to dance but even temporarily suspend my belief in its actual existence so that I might return to the dance as it gives itself within my consciousness of it. For this reason, the *epoché* is to be grasped as a reduction, not in the common sense of limitation or simplification but in the older sense of restoration or return, as in the Latin *reducere*, literally "to lead back" (OED). Thus, by enacting the *epoché* continuously, I am led back from the actual dancer on the stage to my perception of that dancer and the underlying "perceptual meaning" which "belongs to the "perception as such" (Husserl 2012, 187). This perceptual meaning, "something that belongs to its essence," can outlast the dancer's ability to perform the dance (Husserl 2012, 187).

This is easier said than done because the pull of the natural attitude is constant. Here, though, I make a start by switching off, one by one, my natural attitude to force, time, and space. The performance space, I note, can no longer be a value-free and quantifiable physical entity, but rather a place of conjecture that stretches and shrinks, tears and folds within my pregiven and value-laden experience of it. Different moments in the dance cannot be sorted into a "punctiliar row of 'nows'" (Dostal 1993, 148) lined up according to the objective predicates of before, now and after (Jones 1985, 73); rather, I will investigate choreographic time as a manifold of now-points that envelop each other within my internal time consciousness. I must also hold in abeyance scientific understandings of kinetic force, such as studies by physicists of how to optimize turns in dance (Laws 2014); and I will happily set aside either the charge that force is merely an anthropomorphism when it is perceived in non-human things or that it depends upon a myth of human agency and of more-than-human forces (Spiegelberg 1994, 686, 711). Rather, I will "turn [my] full sympathetic attention to this 'myth' and […] what place the phenomenon of force has in [that] context" (Spiegelberg 1994, 712). If I do all this, I have a chance to explore

> the subjective experience of volition and free agency, and of […] alien, compelling wills. […] For the consciousness of life, the sense of vital power, even of the power to receive impressions, apprehend the environment, and meet changes, is our most immediate self-consciousness. This is the feeling of power; and the play of such 'felt' energies is as different from any system of physical forces as psychological time is from clock-time, and psychological space from the space of geometry.
> (Langer 1953, 176)

Stage Two: Describing – (Re)languaging the Dance

The next stage of phenomenological reflection is to describe this "vital power". The purpose here is to express linguistically the irreducible features of phenomena and thus "provide unmistakable guideposts to the phenomena themselves" (Spiegelberg 1994, 694). To do so, language must be used precisely and evocatively if it is to transcend habitual formulations of the phenomena. Carefully chosen metaphors and other figures of speech can be crucial. This amounts to a "re-languaging" of phenomena: a "search [for] the phrase which precisely captures the quality of the thing as it is experienced" (Sheets-Johnstone 1984, 132). This second stage, then, involves "a hard-won [linguistic] turn to a concentrated, focused perception freed from straightforward and mostly traditional understanding" (Circosta 2006, v). This is certainly the case with the main model of movement analysis on which I will now focus: the analysis of virtual force in the dance phenomenology of Maxine Sheets-Johnstone (b. 1930).

For Sheets-Johnstone, dance is experienced as an emerging "dynamic line" or "form-in-the-making which [...] appears as a revelation of force" (Sheets-Johnstone 1979, 57). She is adamant that when dancing or watching a dance "an indivisible wholeness appears before us" which can at best be written as "forcetimespace" (Sheets-Johnstone 1979, 14). Nonetheless, phenomenological reflection allows us to consider separately the temporal and spatial structures of the force that is revealed. This leads to the intuition of four *a priori* components of virtual force. Thus the "temporalization of force" can be described in terms of its fluctuating (i) "tensional" and (ii) "projectional" (e.g. abrupt, sustained, or ballistic) qualities. The "spatialization of force" can be described in terms of its (iii) "linear" and (iv) "areal" (Sheets-Johnstone 1979, 49–58) or "amplitudinal" (Sheets-Johnstone 1999, 140, 143) qualities. Linear qualities consist of a "linear design" (e.g. the curved, twisted, angular, etc., shapes that the body presents as a whole) and a "linear pattern" (e.g. the diagonal, zigzag, or other kinds of line that the body as a moving force appears to project through space). The areal qualities likewise have a design and a pattern, specifically an "areal design" (e.g. the "felt expansiveness and contractedness" of the "moving body") and an "areal pattern" (e.g. the resistant, pliant, resilient, etc., textures of the space that the dancer imagines or that the spectator perceives around the dancer) (Sheets-Johnstone 1979, 49–58).

With this, I describe the phrase from Limón's *Psalm*. Taking the natural attitude, I can say that Stephen Pier started upstage right, *traveled* along the upstage-right to downstage-left cardinal diagonal to center stage, pivoted in *reléve* by a quarter turn to the right whilst inclining his torso to left-side-high, and then *tombéd* backward to upstage left by which point he regained his balance. I observe that this phrase typifies the fall and recovery principle of Humphrey-Limón technique. Now, using Sheets-Johnstone's distinctions, let me reduce this phrase phenomenologically to the following noematic data: with increasingly expansive amplitude and centrifugal force, Pier accelerates one-two-three, one-two-three through a zestful zigzag line that unzips the whole space into two triangles. Although this force has a sustained projection and clarity of intention reinforced by the plumbline he upholds from head to tail, it soon seems that the zigzag line which Pier projects pre-exists and is unstoppable, rushing ahead and reeling him toward the opposing corner. And then, half-way along this trajectory, this force is punctured. Space is suddenly resistant and contractive. Pier is arrested abruptly by a contrary centripetal force that pulls him off-balance and winds him clockwise. Now balanced ballistically on the ball of one foot, Pier dallies with energy, letting his resistance to gravity ebb from him until the relation between body and base of support is so precarious that finally, fleetingly, he loses control. Energy plummets beneath par. He topples back. It is only when he rebounds by just catching up with himself in the ensuing reverse run that energy rises. I taste a little vertigo.

Stage Three: Watching Appearances – Time Consciousness

Having reflected through language on the constitution of forcetimespace in my originary pre-reflective perceptions of *Psalm*, I can now reflect upon those reflections. At this third stage, I go back over what I've described to review the modes of appearance and behavior of different phenomena and "paraphenomena" (Spiegelberg 1994, 706).[4] In particular, an understanding of phenomenological time, or internal time consciousness, is pivotal, for it involves reflecting on the constitution of the phenomena under investigation. Internal time consciousness as theorized by Husserl (2002) can be explained piecemeal through eight key terms: perception, impression, retention, succession, modification, protention, paradox, metacognition, and reproduction.

To begin, there is the perception of the "self-giving actual present" or "now point." This perception gives itself as a "primal impression" or "now-apprehension" (A). This "peels off" or "shades into" another primal impression (B), which "retains" that succession (A – B). This continues from one now-apprehension to the next for as long as the event lasts. Thus, within "the perception of motion" any "now-apprehension is, […] the nucleus of a comet's tail of retentions referring to the earlier now-points of the motion" (Husserl 2002, 110). Furthermore, each retention is itself retained (e.g. the succession A – B is followed by the retention A – B', which is itself retained as A – B", then as A – B''', *etc.*). Crucially, each successive retention of the shading A – B is never an exact repetition but a modification of the preceding retention and thus the primal impression. In effect, within my conscious stream, my perception of the original now point continuously mutates. Moreover, any now-apprehension is also "animated by protentions" (Husserl 2002, 120). Whereas primal impressions are real perceptions of the "now" I experience, protentions are irreal images of the "will be" I anticipate. Protentions can either be "prophetic" and "precisely [...] plan[ned]" or undetermined (Husserl 2002, 122). With both retentions and protentions, time consciousness consists of a paradox: an experience of difference (modification) within the same single "stream of lived experience" (Dostal 1993, 148; see also Jones 1985, 73).

Husserl distinguishes between time as it thus gives itself in pre-reflective perception and, on the other hand, secondary remembrance. We can also, though, exercise "a real, re-productive, recapitulative memory in which the temporal object is again completely built up in a continuum of presentifications, so that we seem to perceive it again, but only seemingly, as-if (Husserl 2002, 114). If recapitulative memory is thus cognitive of original processes of cognition, then I further contend that performance works in particular are metacognitive, that is, built from an intuition of the processes through which they will be perceived in performance and later recollected. This is no more obvious than when – as if demonstrating how retentions modify a primary impression – gestures or phrases are explicitly repeated but subtly modified to show differences within the same. In short, in researching Pier's performance of *Psalm* I do not seek to describe my process of perception when I first saw it so long ago, but rather how my recollection now of my time consciousness then, and even Limón's choreography itself, is a "presentificational modification of the process of perception with all its phases and levels, including retentions," noting how "everything has the index of reproductive modification" (Husserl 2002, 114).

This is what I recapitulate: the centrifugal force of the running steps which propel Pier to center stage is not uniform but increases in amplitude from the way that each step seems to modify the previous one into a retentive line of zigzags that trail behind him when he seems to project that line into space, but which then anticipates him when that line pulls him forward. Comparably, the sheer charge of what occurs center stage is due not just to abrupt spatial changes (*viz.*, from centrifugal to centripetal force, from sagittal to horizontal plane, from dimensional uprightness to diametral lop-sidedness, and from stability to lability), but a retention of a powerful yet unfulfilled protention within those changes, namely the zigzag run that Pier would have continued beyond that point. When the "prophetic consciousness" of the imaginary line that runs ahead in space to the opposite corner is interrupted, it is, like an imploding star, sucked within the time taken by the body center stage, galvanizing its tensional quality. Likewise, the ballistic *relevé* through which Pier then pivots for the *tombé* and the sudden rearward rush of the *tombé* itself overlap so much in my experience that he appears both retentively "here" center stage and protensively "there" upstage left even as he falls backward in between. Finally, if my recollective memory contains impressions of impulses that initiate, and pauses that punctuate, different projections of force, this occurs within a single nexus of impressions. The force through which the dance is temporalized is marked by changes of density within which time seems to distend unceasingly only to contract abruptly, but those changes nonetheless occur as fluctuations of a standing-streaming: a single temporal thing, a temporal onefold.

But if each present moment of the dance consists of the sediment of its own retentions and anticipations, then this sediment also involves the whole life of the dancer. During his demonstration, Pier spoke of how the landscape in which he grew up shaped his sense of scenic space. His first memory of dance was in choreographing a meticulously detailed route along the banks of Worrell Creek, Iowa. The contingencies of steppingstones and branches dictated a precise pattern and rhythm of movement. I sense the sprightly path of the boy by a river in the zigzag path of the man across a stage. I sense the child's fun fall in the dancer's studied *tombé*. Even if I am just imagining traces of Pier's past in his present, I am at least beginning to acknowledge Pier's own horizon of understanding and am intuiting the dance in between "points of view logically incompossible and yet really united" by the "exigency for a becoming" that is the movement itself (Merleau-Ponty 1968, 90–1).

Stage Four: Eidetic Reduction

So far, I have described the noemata of Pier's phrase, that is, the qualitative pattern or dynamic line of that phrase as it showed up in my experience. But for Husserl, that's still not enough. I must also describe my experience in a way that is "apodictic, beyond all possible doubt" (Dostal 1993, 141). This is the purpose of the fourth stage of my methodology: eidetic reduction. I must reduce the noemata further to the nuclei, or essences, of that noemata. The danger here is a kind of "hyper-reflection" in which I "disengage from the things" by reducing them to "intelligible nuclei [...] in a way that is not belied by experience but gives us only its universal contours" (Merleau-Ponty 1968, 45–46). I avoid this not just by reflecting upon my perceptions in terms of *a priori* "ideal validities" but, reciprocally, by testing those validities within the flux of what appears in those perceptions.[5] The test is advanced through what Husserl called "imaginative free variation," a kind of "thought experiment" in which I remove, modify or substitute the elements that I intuit from within the experience until "the essence comes into view and anything merely contingent drops away" (Moran 2000, 154). So, by thus testing my descriptions from the second and third stages of this investigation I propose that Pier's performance of *Psalm* boils down eidetically to two rudiments: a phase of mobilization that charges the dancer's body and a phase of demobilization in which that body discharges and passes itself over to the point in space toward which it is pulled (Spiegelberg 1994, 685). This underpins the whole eidetically and so enables me to know it apodictically.

Stage Five: Interpreting – Saturated Phenomena and the Punctum of Performance

This leads to the fifth and final stage of my Husserlian method of dance research: a hermeneutic stage in which noetic meanings are uncovered within my noematic experiences reduced to their essence. But how do I do this when the moments that seem most meaningful are, I confess, those that most forestall meaning? One such moment is when, in recollective memory, Pier's body, decentered from the vertical axis around which he pivots in *relévé*, is sucked back left low with giddy rapidity. In that moment I am bitten. I gasp. This is what Barthes, regarding the photograph, calls the punctum. This "wound, this prick, […] sting, speck, cut" (Barthes 1993, 26–27) is the bodily detail which "resists theoretical analysis […] with an intense materiality. [… N]on coded, [it …] interrupt[s] the signifying chain" (Moriarty 1991, 203–4). I experience this bodily detail as a "certain hollow […] a certain absence" (Merleau-Ponty 1968, 151): a puncture in my field of consciousness, a moment when I blank out, bliss out, taste the pure peculiarity and "sovereign Contingency" of motion itself (Barthes 1993, 4).

This is pure phenomenality. Within my recollection of my originary perception of Pier's performance, the punctum presents itself "as itself, for itself", beyond control, with the force of revelation: a gift (Marion 2008, 45). If the punctum is thus true to Husserl's principle of all principles, it follows that the punctum is a hollow that is "not nothing, being limited very precisely" to what I have "perceived" (Barthes 1993, 150). And so, I begin to intuit within this hollow not an absence of meaning but a "blindfield" of many meanings (Barthes 1993, 57). Like "the little phrase" from "Vinteuil's sonata" with which Swann is obsessed (Proust 2000, I, 203 ff., 344 ff.), Pier's phrase from Limón's *Psalm* has an authority and a power not because the sensible qualities of that phrase obliterate meaning, and certainly not because they merely prompt me to think what they might "represent," but precisely because those qualities incarnate meanings forever "in transparency behind the sensible," and that any attempt to discuss those meanings in abstract from the carnal texture of the phrase itself would produce not those meanings but only "a second version of [them], a more manageable derivative" (Merleau-Ponty 1968, 150).

Thus, the punctum returns me to the motion itself not as a noematic "power of authentication" that resists its own noetic "power of representation" (Barthes 1993, 89), but as a noematic-noetic "power of expansion" in which uncontainable meanings gush from its own carnal textures. This is close to Jean-Luc Marion's notion of the saturated phenomenon. A phenomenon is "saturated" when I am so inundated by the noematic pleasures that a thing pours over me that no number of noetic concepts I can direct toward it could ever adequately account for those pleasures. Crucially, though, Marion adds that this is "not" because "it pleases without concept, but rather because it calls for all of them, and calls them because it saturates them all" (Marion 2008, 129). This is exemplified by Merleau-Ponty in his kaleidoscopic meditation on the color red, which departs from Husserl's own attempt to reduce instances of red (including the red blotting paper on his desk) through several eidetic intuitions of redness to redness *in specie* (in Moran 2000, 134). Whereas Husserl cannot name this redness, Merleau-Ponty is more forthcoming. A red dress, he says, is a

> punctuation in the field of red things, which includes the tiles of roof tops, the flags of gatekeepers and of the Revolution, certain terrains near Aix or in Madagascar, it is a punctuation in the field of red garments, which includes, along with the dresses of women, robes of professors, bishops, and advocate generals, and also in the field of adornments and that of uniforms. [...] A certain red is also a fossil drawn up from the depths of imaginary worlds.
>
> (1968, 132)

In this vein, I won't settle for an ineffable forcetimespace *in specie*, but am emboldened to grasp the punctum of Pier's phrase, particularly the *tombé* topple, as a punctuation in a field of forcetimespace out of which meanings gush. All I can do is follow these meanings as they zigzag dialectically. I first follow the human story of the boy by the river and the man on the stage, and the mobilization and demobilization of his own forces. I then follow the more-than-human story of how it is energy *in toto*, energy itself, that rises in "a corrective action, which in turn exhausts itself in creating conditions that demand new spending" (Langer 1953, 122). When I glimpse a possible resolution of these two stories in how the human body possesses this more-than-human energy as part of an "'incarnated' human existence" (Spiegelberg 1994, 715), I'm knocked sideward by an uneasy sense of an unresolved struggle betwixt human and more-than-human powers: between the human body's projection of its own power into space against superhuman forces that claim power over that body – the latter gaining over the former in the course of the run, turn and *tombé*, the former rescuing itself as if from under the latter when, for an instance, Pier briefly catches up with himself.

At this point, I see that neither force "can ever reach the absolute maximum" for which it strives (*ibid*, 701). And then I begin to intuit, from within this endless pendulum swing between mobilization and demobilization, anticipated destruction and corrective action, falling and recovery, powers of and over the body, the kinesthetic logic through which *Psalm* incarnates the Jewish myth that inspired it: the myth of the Lamed-Vov, or 36 Just Men, whose continuous presence throughout history justifies the existence of humankind and delays the impending destruction of the world.[6] From within that pendulum swing, Pier is, through "a kind of metamorphosis," neither "separated from [him]self" as an object of the dance nor separated from the *Sache*, the subject matter that he dances (Barthes 1993, 4, 6). He becomes the thing thinging itself. In such moments, the "performer [...] is no longer producing or reproducing" the work, for the work "sings through him or cries out so suddenly that he must [...] follow" (Barthes 1993, 151). And all I can do is follow.

Conclusion

This indeed is the purpose of dance phenomenology: to follow the dance back to the motion through which it produces itself. In this respect, the methodology I have demonstrated in the second part of this chapter exemplifies the drivers of Husserlian phenomenology sketched in the first part. Chief among these is the drive to discover how the thing itself unifies what it differentiates. Firstly, my reflections on Pier's performance demonstrate the unity between object and subject and between matter and meaning, which I said is the essence of phenomenology. The final hermeneutic stage of my reflections indicated how, in surrendering to the pure phenomenality and radical materiality of motion as it "appears as itself, of itself and starting from itself" (Marion 2008, 45), it is possible to intuit noetic meanings, that is, meanings intrinsic to that motion. Crucially, this intuition occurs not so much by erasing the objective (e.g. empirical, factual) knowledge of a dance as by grasping how that knowledge is transmuted within the subjective realm. For instance, in suspending my objective knowledge of the force, time, and space of a dance, it became possible to gain a subjective knowledge – more specifically, a kinesthetic cognition – of the "forcetimespace" of Pier's dancing. Likewise, I surpassed any kind of objective account I could offer of Limón's *Psalm* not merely by ignoring such an account but by bracketing it. I did so by first demarcating the objective, empirically verifiable coordinates of the opening phrase precisely so I could then reduce them phenomenologically (step 1) to the felt noematic qualities of Pier's performance of that phrase (step 2). By then reflecting upon my reflections and particularly my retentive and protensive consciousness of the phrase (step 3), and by further reducing those spatial and temporal qualities to the eidetic nuclei of mobilization and demobilization (step 4), I was finally able to follow the motion of multiple meanings uncoiling from the motion itself (step 5). Of course, I didn't need phenomenology to realize that *Psalm* was inspired by the myth of the Lamed-Vov. But it was only through the patient application of phenomenological method that I could know subjectively how that myth is embodied in Pier's performance of Limón's choreography.

Secondly, my reflections also demonstrate how the motion itself unifies as it differentiates between self and other and between now and then. This was most keenly grasped in the third stage. Since reproductive memory consists, as I explained, of presentificational modifications of what was originally perceived, my recuperation of my time consciousness of Pier's performance guaranteed a chiasmic crisscross, but never a simple identity, between that performance then and my reflections upon that performance now. There is always a perception of a difference in the same. My most painstaking efforts to recover the past do not mitigate against this perception; rather, they guarantee it.

Finally, the above highlights the methodological importance of written description. Dance phenomenology is certainly not the only dance research method to use description strategically. Indeed, my emphasis on the punctum of performance is typical of a wider interest in description as an indispensable means of "attending to" the "eventful events" of a performance, those key "moments [...] when something *happens*" (Lepecki 2016, 22; see also Perazzo Domm 2019, 10–12). However, phenomenological description is distinctive. Since it surpasses the empirical, it is neither merely constative (presenting a true or false account of a dance event) nor reportorial (a verbal transcription of movement). On the other hand, it is neither merely personal nor narcissistic (Circosta 2006, v) since, to reiterate, phenomenology is primarily concerned not with subjectivism as such but the "mystery or paradox" of subjectivity "as the site of [the] appearance of objectivity" (Moran 2002, 2). Accordingly, written description in dance phenomenology is the systematic attempt to "come to grips linguistically" with the motion itself of the dance work as that "gives itself in experience" (Sheets-Johnstone 1984, 135). And since this hard-won perception of the motion itself discloses the meanings intrinsic to that motion, there is, finally, a unity of description and analysis: the former does not illustrate the latter, but is the very means through which the latter is crystalized.

Notes

1 This bodily intuition of spatial forms within the natural world – explored also in phenomenological geology (Raab and Frodeman 2002), archeology (Tilley 1994) and geography (Tuan 1977) – has influenced my writing on environmental dance

(Stewart 2005a, 2009) and the relation of choreography to scenography in dance theater (Stewart 2013).
2 Laban's eukinetics, or effort analysis, is concerned not so much with individual movements as the *Antrieb* – literally the "on-drive" (Bartenieff 1977) – and integrative perceptual sense of those movements as manifest in changing combinations of four essential motion factors, namely, weight (fine/firm), space (in/direct), time (sustained/sudden) and flow (free/bound) (Laban 1988). Humphrey likewise discusses different permutations of time (slow/moderate/fast), texture (smooth/sharp) and tension (slack/taut) to produce different dynamic effects (Humphrey 1987, 97).
3 Pier's demonstration was part of the tenth public session of the International School of Theatre Anthropology (ISTA) held at the Kanonhallen in Copenhagen, Denmark between May 3 and 11, 1996.
4 Some paraphenomena highlight force, such as "pressures, felt strains" (Spiegelberg 1994, 706). Others are spatial in orientation, consisting, for instance, of "felt spatial dislocations" or a dialectic between the center of vision of a thing and the fringe or halo of sensations that mark the periphery of that vision (*ibid.*, 705, 706). Others emphasize temporality, such as the trail or afterimage of a perception, or the relativity of motions of two different forces which leaves "the phenomenon of force in a strange twilight of indistinctness or reversibility" (*ibid.*, 706).
5 This is already implicit when I described the noemata of Pier's phrase in terms of Sheets-Johnstone's four *a priori* components of virtual force but equally tested their capability to describe that noemata.
6 This myth forms the basis of *The Last of the Just*, the novel by André Schwartz-Bart (2001) which was itself the main inspiration for Limón's *Psalm*.

Works Cited

Barber, Michael. 2018. "Alfred Schütz." *The Stanford Encyclopedia of Philosophy*. Edited by Edward N. Zalta. https://plato.stanford.edu/archives/sum2021/entries/schutz. Accessed October 7, 2021.

Bartenieff, Irmgard. 1977. Interviewer Ilana Rubenfeld. *Somatics* (Autumn): 9–13.

Barthes, Roland. 1993 [1980]. *Camera Lucida: Reflections on Photography*. Translated by Richard Howard. London: Vintage.

Bordoni, Bruno. 2020. "The Five Diaphragms in Osteopathic Manipulative Medicine: Myofascial Relationships, Part 1." *Cureus* 12(4): e7794. https://doi.org/10.7759/cureus.7794.

Brown, Charles S. 2003. "The Real and the Good: Phenomenology and the Possibility of an Axiological Rationality." In *Eco-Phenomenology: Back to the Earth Itself*, edited by Charles S. Brown and Ted Toadvine, 3–18. New York: State University of New York Press.

Circosta, Jo Ann. 2006. "Witness to Consciousness: Virginia Woolf and Phenomenology." PhD diss., University of Kentucky.

Dorsey, Arris and Readale Collier. 2018. *Origins of Sociological Theory*. Waltham Abbey: Ed-Tech Press.

Dostal, Robert J. 1993. "Time and Phenomenology in Husserl and Heidegger." In *The Cambridge Companion to Heidegger*, edited by Charles Guignon, 141–169. Cambridge: Cambridge University Press.

Gadamer, Hans-Georg. 1989 [1975]. *Truth and Method*, 2nd ed. Translated by W. Glen-Doepel. Revised translation by Joel Weinsheimer and Donald G. Marshall. London: Sheed & Ward.

Grant, Stuart. 2019. "The Essential Question: So What's Phenomenological about Performance Phenomenology?". In *Performance Phenomenology: To the Thing Itself*, edited by Stuart Grant, Jodie McNeilly and Matthew Wagner, 19–37. London: Palgrave.

Hansen, Mark B.N. 2018. "Performance as Media Affect: The Phenomenology of Human Implication in Jordan Crandall's *Gatherings*." In *Performance and Phenomenology: Traditions and Transformations*, edited by Maaike Bleeker, Jon Foley Sherman and Eirini Nedelkopoulou, 222–243. New York and London: Routledge.

Heidegger, Martin. 1971. "The Thing". In *Poetry, Language, Thought*. Translated by Albert Hofstadter, 163–180. New York: Perennial/HarperCollins.

Humphrey, Doris. 1987. *The Art of Making Dances*. New York: Grove Press.

Husserl, Edmund. 1970 [1936]. *The Crisis of European Sciences and Transcendental Phenomenology*. Translated by David Carr. Evanston, IL: Northwestern University Press.

———. 2002. "The Phenomenology of Internal Time Consciousness." In *The Phenomenology Reader*, edited by Dermot Moran and Timothy Mooney, 109–123. London and New York: Routledge.

———. 2012 [1931]. *Ideas: General Introduction to Pure Phenomenology*. Translated by W.R. Boyce Gibson. London and New York: Routledge.

Jones, Barry J. 1985. "Time and Time Consciousness." In *Phenomenology in Practice and Theory*, edited by William S. Hamrick, 67–99. Dordrecht, Boston and Lancaster, PA: Martinus Nijhoff.

Laban, Rudolf. 1988 [1948]. "Rudiments of a Free Dance Technique." In *Modern Educational Dance*, 3rd ed., edited by Lisa Ullmann, 52–84. Plymouth: Northcote.

Langer, Susanne K. 1953. *Feeling and Form: A Theory of Art Developed from Philosophy in a New Key*. London and Henley: Routledge & Kegan Paul.

Lawrence, Fred. 2002. "Gadamer, the Hermeneutic Revolution, and Theology." In *The Cambridge Companion to Gadamer*, edited by Robert J. Dostal, 167–200. Cambridge: Cambridge University Press.

Laws, Kenneth L. 2014 [1978]. "An Analysis of Turns in Dance." *Dance Research Journal* 11, no. 1–2: 12–19. https://doi.org/10.2307/1477841.

Len Deets, Shannon. 2015. "A Phenomenological Study of Altered Consciousness Induced Through Movement." *Dance, Movement & Spiritualities* 2, no. 2: 181–197.

Lepecki, André. 2016. *Singularities: Dance in the Age of Performance*. London: Routledge.

Marion, Jean-Luc. 2008. *The Visible and the Revealed*. Translated by Christina M. Gschwandtner. New York: Fordham University Press.

Merleau-Ponty, Maurice. 1968 [1964]. *The Visible and The Invisible*. Edited by C. Lefort. Translated by A. Lingis. Evanston, IL: Northwestern University Press.

Moran, Dermot. 2000. *Introduction to Phenomenology*. London & New York: Routledge.

———. 2002. "Editor's Introduction." In *The Phenomenology Reader*, edited by Dermot Moran and Timothy Mooney, 1–26. London and New York: Routledge.

———. 2012. "Forward to the Routledge Classics Edition." In *Ideas: General Introduction to Pure Phenomenology*, by Edmund Husserl, xiii–xxxiii. London and New York: Routledge.

Moriarty, Michael. 1991. *Roland Barthes*. Cambridge: Polity.

Moustakas, Clark. 1994. "Transcendental Phenomenology: Conceptual Framework." In *Phenomenological Research Methods*, 25–42. Thousand Oaks: Sage.

Olsen, Andrea. 1991. *Bodystories: A Guide to Experiential Anatomy*. New York: Station Hill.

Parviainen, Jaana. 1998. *Bodies Moving and Moved: A Phenomenological Analysis of the Dancing Subject and the Cognitive and Ethical Values of Dance Art*. Tampere, Finland: Tampere University Press.

Perazzo Domm, Daniela. 2019. *Jonathan Burrows: Towards a Minor Dance*. Cham, Switzerland: Palgrave Macmillan.

Proust, Marcel. 2000. *In Search of Lost Time*, 6 vols. Translated by C. K. Scott Moncrieff and T. Kilmartin. Revised translation by D. J. Enright. London: Folio.

Raab, Thomas and Robert Frodeman. 2002. "What Is It Like to Be a Geologist? A Phenomenology of Geology and its Epistemological Implications." *Philosophy and Geography* 5, no. 1: 69–81.

Sabatini, Sandra. 2000. *Breath: The Essence of Yoga – A Guide to Inner Stillness*, London: Thorsons.

Schwarz-Bart, André. 2001 [1959]. *The Last of the Just*. London: Vintage.

Sheets-Johnstone, Maxine. 1979. *The Phenomenology of Dance*. 2nd ed. London: Dance Books.

———. 1984. "Phenomenology as a Way of Illuminating Dance." In *Illuminating Dance: Philosophical Explorations*, edited by Maxine Sheets-Johnstone, 124–145. London: Associated University Presses.

———. 1999. *The Primacy of Movement*. Amsterdam and Philadelphia: John Benjamins.

Spiegelberg, Herbert. 1994. *The Phenomenological Movement: A Historical Introduction.* Dordrecht, Boston & London: Kluwer Academic Publishers.

Stewart, Nigel. 2003. "To and Fro and in-between: The Ontology of the Image in Thomas Lehmen's *Stations*." In *Stationen 3*, edited by Sven-Thore Kramm, 29–38. Berlin: Podewil/Thomas Lehmen.

———. 2005a. "Dancing the Time of Place: Fieldwork, Phenomenology and Nature's Choreography." In *Performing Nature: Explorations in Ecology and the Arts*, edited by Gabriella Giannachi and Nigel Stewart, 363–376. Bern: Peter Lang.

———. 2005b. "Understanding Understanding: Phenomenological Hermeneutics in Thomas Lehmen's *Clever*." In *Ethnicity and Identity: Global Performance*, edited by Ravi Chaturvedi, 65–77. New Delhi: Rawat Publishers.

———. 2009. "*Lune*: Dancing as Land Surveying." In *Practice-as-Research in Performance and Screen*, DVD & Catalogue, edited by Allegue, Ludivine et al. Basingstoke: Palgrave.

———. 2010. "Dancing the Face of Place: Environmental Dance and Eco-Phenomenology." *Performance Research* 15, no. 4: 32–39.

———. 2013. "Dance and the Event: John Jasperse's *Giant Empty* and the Disclosure of Being." In *Performance, Identity and the Neo-Political Subject*, edited by Matthew Causey and Fintan Walsh, 166–181. London and New York: Routledge.

———. 2015. "Spectacle, World, Environment, Void: Understanding Nature through Rural Site-Specific Dance." In *Moving Sites: Investigating Site-specific Dance Performance*, edited by Victoria Hunter, 364–384. London and New York: Routledge.

———. 2016. "Flickering Photology: Turning Bodies and Textures of Light." In *Choreography and Corporeality: Relay in Motion*, edited by Thomas F De Frantz and Philipa Rothfield, 51–66. London: Palgrave.

———. 2019. "The Erotic Reduction: Crossed Flesh in Lea Anderson's *The Featherstonehaughs Draw on the Sketchbooks of Egon Schiele*." In *Performance Phenomenology: To the Thing Itself*, edited by Stuart Grant, Jodie McNeilly and Matthew Wagner, 237–260. London: Palgrave.

Tilley, Christopher. 1994. *A Phenomenology of Landscape: Places, Paths and Monuments*, Oxford: Berg.

Tuan, Yi-Fu. 1977. *Space and Place: The Perspective of Experience.* Minneapolis: University of Minnesota Press.

Waterton, Claire. 2003. "Performing the Classification of Nature." In *Nature Performed: Environment, Culture and Performance*, edited by Bronislaw Szerszynski, Wallace Heim and Claire Waterton, 111–129. Oxford: Blackwell.

Part 4
Dance Education

13
Introduction to Research in Dance Education

New Pathways to Discovery

Lynnette Young Overby

Several years ago, I published a paper about the status of dance in public K-12 education in the United States of America (Overby 1992). The paper was informed by research, policies, and practices that existed in 1992. At the time there were no national standards for dance education, and less than 5% of K-12 public schools in the United States offered dance education to their students. Education in dance came primarily from private schools of dance and as a unit in some physical education curricula, which meant that the large majority of children living in the United States lacked access to dance education. Western and European dance forms were the accepted dance techniques. The topics discussed in the paper included the need for multiculturalism to be included in dance education, and the need for research to support assertions about the benefits and value of dance education.

Since that time, new policies and the establishment of programs and organizations have led to new developments in American dance education. In 1994, members of the National Dance Association (NDA) created the first set of National Standards for Dance Education as part of The Goals 2000 initiative, a nationwide effort to fund systematic standards reform. At the time, NDA was one of several associations under the umbrella of the American Alliance for Health, Physical Education, Recreation and Dance (AAHPERD). This reflected the reality that American public-school dance education was primarily taught as a unit in the physical education curriculum and at a few arts-centered secondary schools. In 1998, the National Dance Education Organization (NDEO) was formed. NDEO provided a forum for dance educators from many different sectors including private studios, pre-K-12th grade schools, higher education, and community dance organizations to establish dance education as separate from physical education. A three-year grant from the U.S. Department of Education enabled NDEO to identify and analyze published and unpublished dance education literature from 1926 to the present. The results of this project are reported in "Research Priorities for Dance Education: A report to the nation" (Bonbright and Faber, 2004). Pertinent to the work of this chapter is the question that was posed at the conclusion of this project: "What recommendations for the future of dance education may grow out of this project?" (ibid 2004, ii). In 2015, a new set of dance education standards were developed by a group of dance educators, including myself, as one of five National Core Arts Standards (2015). As standards were developed at the national level beginning in 1994 and again in 2015, each state Department of Education began adapting the standards to fit the needs of the particular state, a project overseen by the State Education Agency Directors of Arts Education (SEADAE).

In addition to these U.S. policy-related projects aimed at expanding access to dance education, there have been broader efforts to de-center modern and ballet as the reigning king and queen of dance technique. Scholars such as McCarthy-Brown (2017) and Guarino, Jones, and Oliver (2022) promote an expanded view of dance education as inclusive rather than exclusive. Other initiatives like the NDEO Justice, Equity, Diversity, and Inclusion audit of all organizational programming provided the opportunity for members and leaders to look deeply into their practices from staffing, to a selection of award recipients, to ensure a just and equitable organization. Furthermore, globalization has shifted U.S.-based educators' understanding of the importance of dance education beyond the borders of the United States. The recent pandemic, experienced throughout the world, promoted virtual international exchanges of dance performances, technique classes and choreographic collaborations at a level never experienced before. Once again, the need for research, advocacy, safe teaching practices, professional development transcend the borders of countries and continents. An organization that has a global focus is dance and the Child international (daCi). This organization convenes a tri-annual conference in various countries and promotes the universality of dance for all children.

As an introductory chapter to the Part on dance education research, a look back at the past helps us understand where we are today, and where we need to be tomorrow. The paper I wrote in 1992, the standards developed in 1994 and 2015, and the evolution of organizations from NDA to NDEO to many state arts organizations, as well as changing views of justice, equity, inclusion, and globalization, together provide new pathways to discovery in dance education research. Two themes, among others, have emerged that the chapters in this Part consider: (1) The need to move beyond the elevation of Western, European dance to the exclusion of all other dance forms, and (2) the continued need for research in dance education.

Expanding the Cultural Lens

Two of the chapters in this Part question a reliance on Western dance paradigms and approaches as the only path to discovery in dance education research. The first chapter, titled "Towards a Decolonial Dance Research Paradigm: Ubuntu as Qualitative Hermeneutic Phenomenology" by Alfdaniels Mabingo describes how Indigenous African knowledge systems may be used to develop a decolonial dance education research paradigm and scholarly writing. His approach to teaching and research advocates for an Afrocentric lens for exploring dance education questions. Mabingo utilizes his autoethnographic reflections to critically examine and share how he has applied the African philosophy of *Ubuntu* as a hermeneutic phenomenology to frame this vision of dance education.

The next chapter "Ethnography for Research in Dance Education: Global, Decolonial, and Somatic" authored by Ojeya Cruz Banks, draws on somatic memoirs from her ethnographic research in the Pacific, West Africa, and the United States with BIPOC (Black Indigenous & People of Color), to explore how this methodology has provided her with an opportunity to immerse herself in decolonized dance worldviews. A theme that runs through her research is understanding how mind-body-music connections are relevant to Black/West African dance pedagogies. Cruz Banks suggests ethnography to be an important vehicle for ushering globally-minded or BIPOC-centered dance education that challenges the white supremacy that pervades notions of dance and dance education. Both of these chapters highlight the need to broaden knowledge to include the assets derived from communities of color, a decolonized approach to dance education research.

Utilizing Various Research Methodologies

Three chapters in this Part provide us with examples, tools, and resources necessary to conduct qualitative, quantitative, mixed methods, and self-study dance education research. Regardless of the data gathered through (qualitative) interviews and focus groups, (quantitative) surveys or standardized tests, or (mixed methods) a combination of qualitative and quantitative, the methodology is driven by the research question. The quantitative chapter presented by Matthew Henley and myself, "Conducting an Experiment: How Quantifying Answers to a Research Question can Support Assertions of Dance Educators," describes experimental and quasi-experimental research as methodologies that answer questions about causality and generalizability in dance education. The seven steps involved in quantitative and quasi-quantitative research methodologies are described in detail with examples from undergraduate research studies conducted as part of the University of Delaware's ArtsBridge Scholars program. Quantitative data helps us reveal the impact of dance education in a format familiar to many policymakers and administrators. A goal of this chapter is to inspire dance education scholars to speak the language of dance, of research, and of the experiment.

In the chapter titled "Mixing Methods and Approaches in Dance Education Research," Matthew Henley provides guidance in conducting research that yields both qualitative and quantitative data. He describes quantitative research as an approach to better understand a phenomenon by reducing it to component parts that can be measured, analyzed, and generalized. Henley describes qualitative research as an approach that seeks to richly describe the same phenomenon as it emerges in unique contexts. He envisions dance scholars utilizing the mixed methods approach to align with and extend teaching practices and empirical research agendas to generate impactful stories and measure causal effects that will advocate for dance education as a vital practice for all students socially, emotionally, physically, spiritually, and intellectually.

Finally, we are provided with a research methodology that allows us to analyze ourselves as teachers. "Teacher Self-Study and Dance Education" by Ilana Morgan defines teacher self-study as a methodology for dance educators seeking to understand and improve their practice and their students' learning. Her personal example of self-study research as a dance teacher for youth in detention led to the question of how to reach and teach those who do not have access to arts learning. Self-study research seeks to improve an individual's teaching practice by investigating the creation and implementation of classroom strategies, practices, activities, transitions, and lessons. It is the relationship between the teacher and the student that contributes to learning. Through self-study, researchers reflect on pedagogical practices, to continue fostering excellent teaching and learning for students.

My Hopes for the Future of Dance Education

As a dance educator for 40-plus years, I have seen the focus of dance in schools and the research that followed shift several times. In the early part of the 20th century, including folk and square dancing was an integral part of many dance units taught by physical educators. The movement education approach of the 1970s opened the door to more creative approaches of movement content including creative dance. When dance moved from the physical education curriculum to consideration as a separate discipline, dance began to change again, by not only focusing on modern/creative dance methods, but also including historical, health, and interdisciplinary standards (National Dance Association 1994).

As I write this Part introduction amidst an unprecedented worldwide pandemic, and with issues of racial reckoning in the United States, dance education again is poised to change. The pandemic has forced educators to become facile in teaching on-line classes and in teaching/learning in person, while wearing masks. The need for movement for reasons beyond technique has become clear as children struggle with the social isolation of home-schooling and dancing in their living rooms. The racial reckoning that occurred in the midst of the pandemic caused much of education, including dance education, to look inwardly at racially exclusionary practices that have existed for decades.

My hope for the future of dance education research has several layers. (1) Elevate embodiment as an integral form of communication. Researchers should look upon our ability to speak through movement as an essential characteristic of dance that can be explored by dance researchers and other movement science scholars. (2) Collaborate with others throughout the world. Global approaches to dance education research will demonstrate the cross-cultural value of dance. When students gain knowledge of the vast world of dance, they gain an appreciation for cultures and begin to see the commonalities of the experiences of all human beings. (3). Make interdisciplinary research a standard practice for all educators. Problems in the world are not solved by a single discipline, but through knowledge sharing that leads to the development of new solutions. Dance education researchers can connect the essence of dance (embodiment) with other disciplinary scholars to find inventive and meaningful answers to difficult problems. Finally, (4) I see a world where there is no hierarchy in the realm of education in general, or in dance education specifically. The dance education researcher contributes new knowledge by asking and answering consequential questions. The question is related to global problems. The scholar is collaborative and works as an integral part of a team made up of community members, and other disciplinary specialists. The methods may include qualitative and/or quantitative methods. The results of this team/collaborative/global approach lead to a recognition of the value of dance for every person and society in general.

Each of the chapters in this Part on dance education research is a reflection on where we are today in dance education practices. The authors provide personal insights into a journey of discovery that informs teaching practice today and provides guidance for the future of dance education research and practice. As you read each of the chapters in this dance education research Part, continue to reflect on past practices, build on current knowledge, and through a scholarly approach, create a sustainable pathway of discovery for the future of dance education.

Works Cited

Bonbright, Jane M., and Rima Faber. 2004. "Research Priorities for Dance Education: A Report to the Nation." Office of Educational Research and Improvement: National Dance Education Organization.

Guarino, Lindsay, Carlos R. A. Jones, and Wendy Oliver. 2022. *Rooted Jazz Dance: Africanist Aesthetics and Equity in the Twenty-First Century*. Gainesville: University Press of Florida.

McCarthy-Brown, Nyama. 2017. *Dance Pedagogy for a Diverse World*. Jefferson, NC: Macfarland & Company.

National Core Arts Standards. 2015. "National Coalition for Core Arts Standards." State Education Agency Directors of Arts Education (SEADAE). www.nationalartsstandards.org

National Dance Association. 1994. "National Standards for Dance Education." National Association for Music Education (NAFME). https://nafme.org/myclassroom/standards/the-national-standards-for-arts-education-introduction/.

Overby, Lynnette Young. 1992. "The Status of Dance in Education." Office of Educational Research and Improvement. https://eric.ed.gov/?id=ED348368.

14
Toward a Decolonial Dance Research Paradigm
Ubuntu as Qualitative Hermeneutic Phenomenology

Alfdaniels Mabingo

Okwandaaza: The Introduction

In 2016, the Department of Performing Arts and Film at Makerere University in Uganda tasked me to teach a research course titled *Research Methods in Music, Dance, and Drama*. I taught the course using Anglo-European theories and methods, in which I was trained in Western universities. As classes progressed, the students inquired about how they can situate their research methods and topics in local knowledge. This encounter occurred at the same time students in universities in South Africa were advocating the decolonization of the academy. The sentiments of the students marked a turning point that sparked my orientation toward a decolonial research mindset. I started reflecting on the Indigenous African knowledge systems that could act as frameworks for research methods and scholarly writing (Battiste and Youngblood 2000).

In this chapter, I define Indigenous African knowledge systems as complex structures, logics, and processes of knowing, thinking, doing, meaning-making, being, connecting, making, and becoming that are integral to the native ways of life, logics, ethics, rationalities, integrities, and aspirations of people, their experiences, and local environments, which bear continuities and changes. I used the following questions as markers to map a decolonial convergence of dance education research and writing and Indigenous African knowledge systems anchored in *Ubuntu* philosophy: How might a researcher use Indigenous African knowledge systems such as *Ubuntu* philosophy to develop a decolonial dance education research paradigm and scholarly writing? What Indigenous African knowledge systems can anchor dance education research? How do

DOI: 10.4324/9781003145615-18

Indigenous African knowledge systems provide procedures that a researcher can use to gather, analyze, and write dance education research data? How is the positionality of a dance education researcher (re)framed when they draw on Indigenous African knowledge systems to conduct and write research? How might Indigenous knowledge systems accord local research participants agency in dance education research?

To explore the preceding questions, I examine how I have developed and applied the African philosophy of *Ubuntu* as a hermeneutic phenomenology to frame the ethics, agenda, logic, conceptualization, spirit, contextualization, and vision of my research in Indigenous dance education, and situate my reflexivity and positionality as being-in-the-world and being-with-others-in-the-world of fieldwork. In this analysis, I am not using hermeneutic phenomenology to legitimize *Ubuntu* as an Indigenous research framework. Rather, I make reference to this methodological paradigm to reveal how dominant conventional models, which are commonly elevated over Indigenous canons of intellectual inquiry, already exist in Indigenous epistemologies, ontologies, and methodologies. In this critical essay, I dissect how the *Kiganda* tradition of *okuluka omukeeka* (weaving the mat) provides a methodological formula, logic, and creed that I use to conduct fieldwork, analyze data, and write scholarly works. Whereas there are numerous Indigenous frameworks in Uganda and Africa that can be used as a basis for critical research methodological analysis, the *Kiganda* tradition of *okuluka omukeeka* provides a comprehensive epistemological, ontological, cosmological, and axiological layout, which illuminates in-depth understanding of complex experiences, environments, meanings, connections, practices, philosophies, and rationalities. Procedurally, I use the processes of *okuluka omukeeka* as a writing logic to weave the different sections of this chapter.

The Anglo-European methodological and theoretical orientations still dominate research in dance education. The dominance is also prevalent in research and writing on dance conducted in local African contexts. Although academic institutions inside and outside Africa have developed curricula that honor and integrate Indigenous African dances and music (Mabingo 2014, 2015, 2018), the methodological frameworks of inquiry and writing logics that are devoid of Indigenous thought processes continue to distort the knowledge generated from research on these dances and the people and cultures who create, celebrate, and perform them. Calls for decolonization by Indigenous dance teachers and scholars (Mabingo, Ssemaganda, Sembatya, and Kibirige 2020; Walker 2019) need to reconsider how researchers can rethink research and writing to accommodate Indigenous systems as valid knowledge.

I have titled this section *okwandaaza*, a preliminary stage in the complex process of *okuluka omukeeka*. Like the introduction, which ushers the reader into a piece of work, *okwandaaza* involves mapping the different stages of *okuluka omukeeka*. It entails reflecting on the process and, where and when possible, visiting the field to identify where the mat weaver can extract material to weave the mat. This stage marks the initial starting point – the introduction. *Okuluka omukeeka* is a detail-oriented activity. It entails identifying the need for the mat, questioning that need, conceiving the idea of weaving the mat, preparing the self, mobilizing the tools to collect weaving material, gathering, sorting, refining, and distilling the weaving material, and weaving the mat. *Omukeeka* (traditional floor rag) symbolizes knowledge, creativity, growth, complexity, life, and community connection. It is where members of families and communities sit *okuwaya* (to share stories), have a meal, welcome visitors, and many more. This ontological, axiological, and epistemological depth that the *omukeeka* (mat) embodies presents it as a resourceful anchor for a decolonial dance education research paradigm.

Okwetegeka n'okuteekateeka: De/Centering the Researcher's Positionality and Contextualizing the Research Agenda

The layout of this section follows the same logic of *okuluka omukeeka*. *Okwetegeka* (reflecting on the self) connotes the reflexivity of the mat weaver. Like in the research and fieldwork experience, constant reflection on the positionality of the self at all stages is paramount. This section de/centers my positionality in the chapter and how it plays out in research. I also draw on *okuteekateeka* (mapping the field) to review theories and literary perspectives that are essential for integrating Indigenous African knowledge systems in dance education research. In the tradition of *okuluka omukeeka*, *okuteekateeka* encompasses mapping, readying, and setting the context for different stages of weaving the mat.

Reflexivity and Positionality

Integrating Indigenous knowledge systems has continued to reframe my positionality and reflexivity in dance education research. I reflect on the identities and influences that I carry with me into fieldwork experiences. The more I reflect on these issues as an Indigenous researcher, the more I become aware of the epistemological dangers of seeking "for inclusion and recognition, which has resulted in African scholars distancing themselves from the realities on the continent as they actively seek identification with the external and distant that is often evangelized as inclusive" (wa Thiong'o 2012, 28). As a Western-trained scholar, I carry with me influences of the Anglo-European research and writing norms and procedures.

To ground me into research and writing that integrate Indigenous African knowledge systems, I have undergone the process of decolonizing my conscience (wa Thiong'o 1986). I have experienced "learning to unlearn," which Tiostanova and Mignolo have defined as "to forget what we have been taught, to break free from the thinking programs imposed on us by education, culture, and social environment, always marked by the Western imperial reason" (2012, 7). The immersive analysis of Indigenous stories, proverbs, books, articles, audio-visual recordings, paintings, folktales, and songs, among others, has been a transformational force for me as a researcher and writer. My integration of Indigenous African knowledge systems in research and writing is a radical and critical attempt to reconnect "with the buried alluvium of African memory—that must become the base for planting African memory anew in the continent and the world" (wa Thiong'o 2012, 76).

A holistic reading of Africa from multiple perspectives minimizes obsession with the exhausted Anglo-European intellectual traditions that are no longer useful in analyzing the African experiences (Ndlovu-Gatsheni 2018). For a dance education researcher and writer, it requires reading beyond the narrow scope of dance. I have engaged with broader works by Indigenous African and Black thinkers and theorists such as Ali A. Mazrui (1986), John Mbiti (1970), Valentino Y. Mudimbe (1988), Meki Nzewi (2003), Achille Mbembé (2001), Ifeanyi A. Menkiti (1984), Frantz Fanon (1967), Kwame Gyekye (1987, 1988), Odera Oruka (1990), Kwasi Wiredu and Kwame Gyekye (1992), Paulin J. Hountondji (1983), Peter Bodunrin (1981), Kwasi Wiredu (1998), Julius Nyerere (1967, 1987), Léopold Sédar Senghor (1984), George Jerry Sefa Dei (1994, 2000), Chinua Achebe (1958), Okot p'Bitek (1975, 1986), Sylvia Nannyonga-Tamusuza (2005), Walter D. Mignolo (2009), Wilfred Lajul (2014a, 2014b), Molefi Kete Asante (1996), Anthony Appiah (2001), Rose Mbowa (1999), and Kwabena Nketia (1970), among others. The works by these thinkers cover themes such as decolonization, postcolonialism, Africanity, music, African philosophies, colonization, politics, and African histories, ethics, literature, and religion. The texts grounded in decolonial Indigenous knowledge systems offer entry into a fundamental understanding of what it means to be an Indigenous researcher and the complexity of Africa as an epistemic center. The knowledge continues to create a form of power that affirms for me the validity and complexity of African and Black worldviews, being, living and intellectual interests (Wartenberg 1990).

Reflexivity as an experience in my dance education research is a continuous encounter. The multiple influences that I carry mean that I am neither an insider nor an outsider in research. Entrenching my positionality in Indigenous African knowledge systems requires acknowledging the risk for African communities to manifest global imperial designs and interests, which masquerade as emancipatory while, in reality, serving the perpetuation of coloniality (Ndlovu-Gatsheni 2018). Conducting research immersed in Indigenous knowledge systems entails seeing fieldwork not as an event or moment but as a complex experience tied to life, the people, and physical and metaphysical worlds and environments.

Beyond an Exotic "field": Contextualizing Africa as an Epistemic Center

Early research in African dance traditions was based on modernism as a paradigm of inquiry. Steered by anthropological researchers and travelers from Europe and North America, the research agenda was to discover, study, dominate, claim, homogenize, and name the exotic and fetishized Other (Smith 1999). Caricaturing the Other through research has followed a long tradition of researchers and writers framing the African people as exotic raw data and Africa as just the "field" (Abrahamsen 2017). The Anglo-European essentialism has "relegated Africa to providing raw materials ("data") to outside academics who would process it and then re-export their theories back to Africa" (Mamdani 2011, 4). As a process of decolonizing my research methods (Smith 1999), I ensure that fieldwork does not descend into what Nyamnjoh has termed as "European greenhouse under African skies" (2012, 33), a mindset that has deterred the formerly colonized Other from naming and knowing their frame of reference (Chilisa 2012).

Contextualizing Africa as an epistemic center requires acknowledging that "ever since the dawn of Euro-centered modernity, the processes of knowledge production 'for' and 'about' the Indigenous peoples of the Third World have always been characterized by a relationship of dominance and subordination and resistance" (Ndlovu 2013, 2). Methods of researching and writing about dances from and in African environments continue to be a playground for Anglo-European hegemony. To situate dance research and writing in Indigenous African knowledge systems is to critique and decenter these domineering frameworks. Application of Indigenous African knowledge systems stems from my awareness that "Pre-framing and forcing African stories into Northern theoretical frameworks is in effect a way to deny African people their authentic stories, their poesies and intellectual creativity with their stories" (Abrahamsen 2017, 27). Decolonizing the framing of the field creates space for different research perspectives to emerge, leading the researcher to multiple truths (Oelofsen 2015). Rethinking and reframing Africa beyond being just a field opens the door for developing research agendas that do not homogenize Africa as a monolithic country. Engaging Indigenous African knowledge systems can support research visions that attend to specific but complex local issues and phenomena (Ndlovu 2018). Knowledge from the research output can then reflect, respond to, and impact local communities. This chapter offers insights into the thought processes and critical actions that researchers in Indigenous dance education practices can engage to generate knowledge that is centered on Indigenous worldviews.

To make Africa a base to look at the world – a starting point for repositioning the researcher's world-sensing (Ndlovu-Gatsheni 2018), researchers have to position the research participants as interpreters, meaning-makers, collaborators, and valuable agents in research as opposed to being treated as objects to be discovered, claimed, and studied. The epistemological centeredness of Africa includes her people, ecologies, stories, experiences, cultures, and histories that form the ecosystem of Indigenous African knowledge systems (Matthews 2010). Research and writing built on Indigenous local knowledge systems flip the existing Anglo-European hegemonic approaches, which have proved cataclysmic to knowledge production.

Okutegeka: Centering *Ubuntu* as Hermeneutic Phenomenology

Navigating developing a decolonial dance research paradigm was akin to *okwetegeka*, which is one of the stages of *okuluka omukeeka*. For this stage, the mat weaver develops rationality that holds up the coherence of all other mat weaving stages. The following questions guided me to rationalize a dance education research paradigm built on Indigenous African knowledge systems: How might a researcher use Indigenous African knowledge systems to develop a decolonial dance education research and scholarly writing? What Indigenous African knowledge systems can anchor dance education research? The African philosophy of *Ubuntu* emerged as a linchpin of thought, analysis, and practical engagement in my research and writing. *Ubuntu* delineates a worldview built around interhumanness, interdependence, communalism, sensitivity to and caring for others, and individuality, which people develop, celebrate, live, and share as a community and individuals (Le Roux 2000; Letseka 2000). Represented by what Mbiti (1970) and Tutu (1999) translated as "I am because we are, and because we are therefore I am," *Ubuntu* embodies an epistemological, axiological, cosmological, and ontological ethics, logic, and loci that have people at the center. Within Ugandan Indigenous communities, *Ubuntu* drives the creativity, performance, and teaching and learning of dance, music, storytelling, poetry, and other forms of creative expression (Kibirige 2020; Mabingo 2020).

As a researcher trained in Anglo-European academic institutions, I was aware that "the hegemonic Western worldview tends to succeed in making the subjects that are socially located in the oppressed side of colonial difference, to think epistemically like the ones that are located on the dominant side" (Ndlovu 2013, 7). Bishop, Higgins, Casella, and Contos have suggested that as researchers "understanding worldviews of both the targeted community and ourselves is imperative if we are going to do more good than harm" (2002, 622). Reorienting the researcher's worldview shifts the frame of thought and reveals new ways of engaging fieldwork, valuing and understanding knowledge, and collaborating with Indigenous communities. Ndlovu-Gatsheni has emphasized that "rethinking thinking is fundamentally a decolonial move that requires the cultivation of a decolonial attitude in knowledge production" (2018, 33). Embracing *Ubuntu* as an ethics, paradigm, and lens of analysis for research in Indigenous dance education allows me to know that I do not only need to identify and define research problems as lying in communities of research but also that problems also lie in the Northern epistemologies I was trained to rely upon to do research (Abrahamsen 2017).

To shift what Gordon has termed as "the geography of reason" (2011, 95) and invoke "epistemic disobedience" (Mignolo 2009, 159), I use *Ubuntu* to "unthink" Western epistemic virtue and activate decolonial agency in dance education research (Mabingo 2020). The *Ubuntu* values and ethics of interhumanism, dignity, respect, care, empathy, inclusion, unity, and spirituality (Mangena 2016) mean "that all human beings are not only born into a knowledge system but are legitimate knowers and producers of legitimate knowledge" (Ndlovu-Gatsheni 2018, 33). As a researcher trained in Anglo-European academy, the *Ubuntu* framework facilitates immersive, relational, and spiritual fieldwork experiences and interpersonal relations. I learned that in local communities "knowledge is holistic, cyclic, and dependent upon relationships and connections to living and non-living beings and entities; there are many truths, and these truths are dependent upon individual experiences, and the relationship between people and the spiritual world…" (Hart 2010, 3).

Ubuntu is appropriate for research in Indigenous dance practices because the dance knowledge permeates people and their experiences, life, collectivities, spiritualities, and performativities. Dance exists in people's physical and metaphysical worlds. It is embodied and lived by drummers, dancers, clappers, singers, instrumentalists, peer models, teachers, learners, cheerers, and spectators before, during, and after dancing encounters. *Ubuntu*, as a frame of rationality, mutuality, and holism cuts across these creative and performative complexities.

Since hermeneutic phenomenology is concerned with the interpretation of an individual's lived experience where the researcher and research participants understand and make meaning from a phenomenon under investigation through hermeneutic circles (Annells 1996; Gadamer 1998; Heidegger 1962; Kvale 1996; Polkinghorne 1983), *Ubuntu* has all these elements experienced, lived, and shared by people. It creates a horizon that facilitates continuous questioning, which yields co-interpretations. *Ubuntu* as a hermeneutic phenomenology has revealed the following complex aspects of Indigenous dance epistemology during fieldwork:

- The research participants are co-interpreters of research experiences, realities, and encounters.
- Dance is a way to belong to, see, experience, share, connect, and live and be-in-the-world.
- Performing, learning, and teaching dance is text.
- Research is an encounter where the researcher and the research participants congregate to explore experiences.
- Dance is both a subjective and intersubjective experience.
- Dance and dancing, in whatever form, are linked to social, cultural, and historical experiences.
- Local communities have Indigenous knowledge frameworks that can act as methods of researching and logics of writing about dance.
- Dance as an investigative phenomenon transcends the act of dancing. It is a physical and metaphysical sense.
- A dancing body is a complex organism and spirit that exists in a multifaceted ecosystem.
- The symbiotic interplay between communality and individuality constitutes a source for dance experiences.
- The researcher, as an interlocutor in research, cannot distance himself or herself from subjectivity.
- Dance knowledge is held in multiple intricate epistemological points beyond the body. These act as data points.
- Dance knowledge is a holistic and circular ecosystem that is not bound by time, space, effort, and body.
- To dance is to know, think, connect, be, do, become, exist, express, and share.
- Dance, storytelling, singing, drumming, poetry, instrumentation, visual expressions, mnemonic, acting, body percussion, yodeling, and folktales are interwoven as one.
- An act of dance has more than one meaning.
- Interhumanness, dignity, care, inclusion, open-mindedness, respect, community, equity, generosity, wellbeing, and individuality are values and ethics that drive dance and music.

- Communities are laboratories and libraries of dance knowledge.
- Dance experiences and realities are not quantified in Indigenous communities.
- Spirituality is central to the practice and experience of dance.
- Dance knowledge exists in a state of flux and keeps evolving.
- The question of how research output can benefit the communities where inquiries were conducted must be the critical motivation of research.
- Embodying fieldwork experience in dance research is a fountain of meaning-making.

The abovementioned insights gained through fieldwork encounters and experiences reveal that the Indigenous communities where researchers conduct inquiries are complex and complicated. The dance practices are intricately interwoven with these ontological and epistemological aspects. These fieldwork experiences construct a reality that a researcher finds themselves entangled in. Immersing the self in worldviews and modes of reasoning such as *Ubuntu* can point the researcher to multiple ways of disentangling the complex fieldwork experiences.

By applying *Ubuntu* as hermeneutic phenomenology I was able to reconcile the "questions of ontology (what is the form and nature of reality and what can be known about it); epistemology (what is the nature of the relationship between the knower and what can be known); and methodology (how can the inquirer go about finding out whatever they believe can be known) as essential anchors of conducting and writing dance research (Lincoln and Guba 1985, cited in Laverty 2003).

Okutema ensansa: Gathering Data in Dance Education Research

I use the act of *okutema ensansa* (cutting and collecting the palm tree leaves), which is a stage in the *okuluka omukeeka*, to represent methods of gathering data. During this stage, palm tree leaves are collected from the palm trees before processing to weave the mats. This Indigenous framework guides my procedures and intentionality of navigating fieldwork and collecting data (see the subsections below). The mat weaver identifies the palm leaves suitable for weaving and cuts them using a knife or *panga*. Akin to the activity of *okutema ensansa*, the data collection in dance research is an intricate process that requires knowing the tools to use, how to use them, where to use them, and the nature of data that a researcher wants to gather.

Framing Dance Collection Methods: Why Indigenous African Knowledge Systems Matter

Developing and applying methods of data collection framed by Indigenous African knowledge systems can yield data that is representative of people and their cultures, experiences, stories, realities, and practices. Since Indigenous knowledge is relational, Indigenous research frameworks allow the research to build relationships with the people, environments, ecologies, and experiences (Wilson 2001). Dance is at the center of holistic and relational knowledge. For example, the songs, drum rhythms, storytelling, folktales, paintings, mnemonics, body percussion, make-up, costumes, props, and histories imbue relational knowing, thinking, doing, being, meaning, and becoming.

Indigenous African knowledge systems as frameworks of data collection open gates for me to apply *Ubuntu* as a hermeneutic phenomenology. From this perspective, I can appreciate that "Human lives, experiences and the world as lived (human lifeworld and its phenomena) are understood within their particular temporal, situated frame through an interpretivist epistemology, that draws upon intentionality, intersubjectivity, and hermeneutics as a theory of interpretation" (Suddick, Cross, Vuoskoski, Galvin, and Stew 2020, 2). Using *Ubuntu* as an interpretive lens, I engage in research as being-in-the-world and being-with-others-in-the-world. The relational manner of research methods "…is intertwined with the co-constituting play-process of hermeneutic interpretation, dialogue, and fusion of horizons between the researcher, participants, and the phenomenon" (Finlay 2009, cited in Suddick, et al. 2020, 4).

As human social phenomena, performing, teaching, creating, sharing, and learning dances occur in complex lived space – spatiality; lived body – corporeality; lived time – temporality; lived human relation – relationality (van Manen 1997), in which as a researcher I constantly immerse myself. The data collection methods that are ingrained in *Ubuntu* such as *okugaanira* and storytelling emphasize my reflexivity, which Sloan and Bowe have defined as "a person's reflection upon or examination of a situation or experience – [which] can help in interpreting the meanings discovered, or add value to those types of interpretations" (2014, 11). In this section, I have detailed why Indigenous frameworks matter in Indigenous dance research. The following section discusses the ethical foundations in which these frameworks can be grounded to conduct research with integrity, respect, and mutuality.

Ethical Considerations in Dance Education Research

The dignity of people is what sustains humanity and humility in Indigenous communities. *Ubuntu* imbues the value of community and a sense of respect and care that holds people together. *Ubuntu* as hermeneutic phenomenology grounds the collective humility, dignity, respect, care, consent, and support I use to explore fieldwork. Research is an interhuman experience. I do not consider myself as a know-it-all expert but embrace the research participants as knowledgeable others. I value the fact that "When Indigenous peoples become the researchers and not merely the researched, research activity is transformed. Questions are framed differently, priorities are ranked differently, problems are defined differently, and people participate on different terms" (Smith 1999, 193).

Deviating from the common practice of treating people as raw data to be studied, discovered, named, and claimed, my methods put the agency of the people at the center. I emphasize respect and safety to make the research participants feel cared for, safe, and valued. I address confidentiality in a manner desired by the research participants (Hart 2010) and seek permission to enter into spaces, experiences, and communities of practice. In Indigenous communities, spaces, activities, relationships, experiences, stories, non-human objects, and periods of time can be sacred. Consultation, listening, and following leads of the local people and elders has been key reference point for me to understand protocols, procedures, and code of behavior.

To uplift ethical conduct, I adhere to Indigenous protocols within communities, which honor principles, etiquette, and decorum that guide human existence and conduct. The protocols also orient me into the Indigenous worldviews, accord local people ownership in the research activities, guide how I can respectfully integrate the self into the cultural activities and structures of sociocultural organization, and illuminate subtle patterns of interaction in general and in dance practice in particular.

Storytelling as Hermeneutic Phenomenology

Storytelling as a practice in Indigenous communities underpins holistic interconnectedness, collaboration, reciprocity, spirituality, and humility (Kovac 2009). As a knowledge domain, it honors relational orality where the agents use the voice, vocal and body expression, intonation, verbal imagery, facial animation, context, plot and character development, natural pacing, and careful authentic recall to relay and receive information (Kovac 2010). Storytelling reveals "An awareness and connection between the logic of the mind and feelings of the heart, where both the emotional and cognitive experiences are incorporated into all actions" (Hart 2010, 10). Performing, teaching, learning, and sharing dance is storying the lived experiences. Storytelling as a data collection method unveils self-critical consciousness and awareness of positionality, forms of interaction, patterns of socialization, and sets of values (Kovach

2009). When I apply storytelling, it "becomes an interactive activity between the teller and the listener in which imagination forms the pictures" (Datta 2018, 3). The research participants claim agency to share their experiences, meanings, and reflection and interpret the world with me. As a research experience, "Personal storytelling benefits the teller as it can empower, encourage personal growth, and build resilience" (Drumm 2013, 1).

Drumm has further observed that "Storytelling influences changes in the researcher's practice. Listening to stories facilitates relationship-building between researcher and research participants. Hearing personal stories engenders greater understanding, empathy, and reflection, which is important for building rapport, trust, and care for each other" (2013, 1). As a hermeneutic phenomenology, *Ubuntu* makes storytelling a suitable method because it

> [connects] with both Indigenous ontology and epistemology: relational ontology (i.e., relational stories about human and non-human based on an I/we relationship) and relational epistemology (i.e., the knowledge that emanates from the experiences, tradition, ceremonies, and culture of the people and the environment).
>
> (Datta 2018, 1)

As a researcher, I see storytelling as an experience for the research participant to hold space with me. It is a moment for me to listen, think, process, and learn. After issuing prompts for research participants to story-tell about, I let the storyteller and stories reproduce more themes during storytelling.

Participant and Nonparticipant Observation as Ubuntugogy

Indigenous dances are complex embodied practices. Dance knowledge is composed of the seen and unseen, the physical and metaphysical. As such, participant observation becomes vital for a researcher to immerse him or herself in the embodied activities to establish relationality with experiences, reflections, environments, people, and material. Creating, performing, teaching, learning, and sharing dance intertwine doing, knowing, being, thinking, connecting, and becoming.

To collect data, I engage in participant observation as *Ubuntugogy* – a pedagogy of inquisitive embodied learning built on respectful recognition of others as a source of knowledge and knowing (Bangura 2005). Participant observation as *Ubuntugogy* underscores "respect for communal forms of living that are non-Western and creating space for inquiries based on relational realities and forms of knowing that are predominant among non-Western Other/s still being colonized" (Chilisa 2012, 3). I participate in dancing, singing, carrying and tuning instruments, drumming, instrumentation, storytelling, poetry, and nondance activities in communities to understand the research environments, feel the unseen and unheard, embody relationships, co-construct interpretations, and be-in-the-world. Nonparticipant observation entails being present in the dance scenes without active engagement in the activities. Commonly, people become nonparticipant observers momentarily when they take a rest from the rotational format of dancing, drumming, singing, poetry, storytelling, clapping, instrumentation, and other forms of performance.

Participant and nonparticipant observation for each dance environment produces rich inimitable reflections and experiences because dance practices are complex. I immerse myself in fieldwork with an open mind to learn, connect, reflect, and grow through reflective listening, questioning, and hearing through embodied being. I value materiality that is entwined to and comes out of performing, creating, learning, teaching, and sharing dance such as dust, sweat, drumsticks, and grass, among others, as a text that carries meanings.

Okugaaniira: The Indigenous Focus Group Discussions

During fieldwork, I use *okugaanira* as a focus group discussion. *Okugaanira* is an Indigenous practice of convening a village discussion forum among the Banyankore people of Western Uganda. During these fora, community members gather to reflect on issues of local interest. *Okugaanira* recognizes "interdependence and the importance of interpersonal relations for the self…and sees the individual as necessarily socially embedded and affected by context…" (Oelofsen 2015, 141). As a conversational method, *Okugaanira* reveals relational nuances and multiple perspectives. *Okugaanira* is a space for sharing where people conversationally navigate each other's worlds as thinkers, interpreters, listeners, knowers, meaning-makers, and doers. The researcher's role is to give prompts that guide the discussions around research themes with local people leading debates instead of just respondents.

Okusunsula n'okusensula: Analyzing Dance Education Research Data

Framing data analysis using Indigenous African knowledge systems invites a researcher to "focus on what the individual's specific context can offer for understanding, creating and investigating concepts" (Oelofsen 2015, 140). Mamdani has stated that "if we are to treat every experience with intellectual dignity, then we must treat it as the basis for theorization. The researcher historicizes and contextualizes not only phenomena and processes that we observe but also the intellectual apparatus used to analyze these" (2011, 9). To heed Mamdani's guidance, I use *Okusunsula n'okusensula* as an instrument for organizing and analyzing data. In weaving the mat (*okuluka omukeeka*), *okusunsula n'okusensula* (sorting and splitting the palm leaves) occurs after the leaves are collected. The mat weaver identifies the specific material and refines it into a suitable state for further processing. *Okusunsula* (sorting) is done in the field before the material is delivered home.

During the research, transcription of fieldwork data follows the logic and procedure of *okusunsula*. I start to organize and refine data from audio, visual, motion, and notebook to text. Like a mat weaver, I identify that material (data) and convert it to a state that makes it accessible and intelligible for further analysis. After *okusunsula*, the mat weaver proceeds to *okwanika* (drying the leaves) and *okufumba* (dyeing the leaves). I use these two stages to organize and streamline transcribed material by reading and re-reading texts. This immersion draws me closer to data the same way drying (okwanika) and dyeing (okufumba) draw a mat weaver closer to the material.

After *Okusensula* (splitting the palm leaves), *okwanika* (drying) and *okufumba* (dyeing) come next. The mat weaver cleaves the dried and dyed material into small pieces and visualizes relationships between different colors of dyed leaves. The split-dyed palm leaves can be grouped and refined for the subsequent stage of *okuluka* (weaving) the market. I draw on the intricate procedure and logic of *okusensula* to code, categorize, and index data into themes and map the relationships between distilled data.

Okuluka, okutobeka, n'okusona: Writing and Disseminating Research Output

The mat weaver brings the mat to being during *Okuluka* (weaving the mat), *okutobeka* (blending the colors), and okusona (stitching the weaved pieces into one whole mat). With extra attention and in a step-by-step format, the mat weaver stitches the dried, dyed, and split leaves together into smaller pieces. This tedious action-oriented exercise entails interknitting the different colors of dyed leaves into desired visual and logical patterns, which is called *okutobeka*. *Okusona* occurs after *Okuluka* and *okutobeka*. The mat weaver stitches together the different weaved pieces into a mat using *akaso* (a piece of rapia), threaded using *empiso* (threading needle). *Okuluka, okutobeka,* and *okusona* guide the way I piece together, edit, and critically discuss research finding and their attendant theories through writing, audio-visual productions, and other forms of presentation and dissemination of research output.

Abrahamsen (2017) has cautioned that the work of research(ers) can be counterproductive when research participants and their communities are merely considered as constituting research problems. The output from such research can produce irrelevant solutions or bookish solutions with little space for practical relevance to these communities. My research in Indigenous communities underscores the impact that the research output has on these communities. Together with people in these communities, we sift through the research material to identify ideas that can be collaboratively developed to improve practices and ways of living in these communities. I plow back research output into local communities through professional development workshops, discussions, and mentorship programs. I value reciprocity by sharing and presenting ideas with the intent of supporting communities (Hart 2010). Impact of research as a measure of research relevance calls for community engagement in disseminating dance education research output.

Hart has stated that "an Indigenous methodology includes the assumption that knowledge gained will be utilized practically" (2010, 9). My research informs my pedagogic practice as a dance educator. I also disseminate research through scholarly publications, practical workshops and classes, public debates, professional development activities in local communities, and communique on policy formulation and implementation. The dissemination strategy places Indigenous knowledge and people at the forefront of local and global discourses and advocates for equity, equality, anti-racism, and recognition of Black and Indigenous people.

Okusandagga: The Conclusion

Okusandagga is the concluding stage in the process of weaving the mat. It involves stitching a woven frame around the mat to hold it firm. After the mat attains the desired width and length, the mat weaver goes ahead to do *okusandagga*. It is to *kusandagga* of this chapter that I now turn.

Moving toward decolonial dance education research requires reimagining the existing domineering Anglo-European research frameworks that frequently subjugate non-Western knowledge. The Indigenous African knowledge systems suggest paradigms that a researcher can use to conduct research that reflects, responds to, honors, and illuminates the complex Indigenous dance epistemologies, ontologies, cosmologies, and axiologies. In this chapter, I have used my subjective autoethnographic reflections to reveal how the African philosophy of *Ubuntu*, as a hermeneutic phenomenology, frames the ethics, agenda, conceptualization, spirit, contextualization, and vision of my research in dance education. Furthermore, I have discussed how I use the Indigenous activity of

Okuluka omukeeka of the Baganda people of central Uganda as a methodological formula and creed to run fieldwork, analyze data, and write scholarly works. I also use *Okuluka omukeeka* as a writing logic to lay out this chapter.

Integrating Indigenous African knowledge systems clarifies the researcher's positionality and facilitates his or her reflexivity as a continuous exercise in understanding research and fieldwork. The researcher's positionality allows him or her to see Africa not just as an exotic "field" and African people not just as research objects. The Indigenous research praxis frames how the researcher can be-in-the-world and be-with-others-in-the-world during research. Immersing the self in extensive reading of works on Africa and Indigenous literature provides a starting point for a researcher to develop a research vision that centers on Indigenous knowledge, people, stories, experiences, and methods. Indigenous research frameworks offer the researcher insights and tools to develop mechanisms of disseminating research output that benefits local populations where the researches are conducted.

Works Cited

Abrahamsen, Rita. 2017. "Africa and International Relations: Assembling Africa, Studying the World." *African Affairs* 116, no. 462 (January): 125–139. https://doi.org/10.1093/afraf/adw071

Achebe, Chinua. 1958. *Things Fall Apart*. London: Heinemann.

Annells, Merilyn. 1996. "Hermeneutic Phenomenology: Philosophical Perspectives and Current Use in Nursing Research." *Journal of Advanced Nursing* 23, no. 4 (April): 705–713. https://doi.org/10.1111/j.1365-2648.1996.tb00041.x

Appiah, Anthony. 2001. "African Identities." In *The New Social Theory Reader: Contemporary Debates*, edited by Steven Seidman and Jeffrey Alexander, 362–770. New York: Routledge.

Asante, Molefi Kete. 1996. *Afrocentricity: The Theory of Social Change* (Rev. expanded ed.). Chicago: African American Images.

Bangura, Abdul Karim. 2005. "Ubuntugogy: An African Educational Paradigm that Transcends Pedagogy, Andragogy, Ergonagy and Heutagogy." *Journal of Third World Studies* 22, no. 2: 13–53. https://www.jstor.org/stable/45198556

Battiste, Marie, and James Youngblood. 2000. *Protecting Indigenous Knowledge and Heritage: A Global Challenge*. Saskatoon: Purich.

Bishop, Brian J., David Higgins, Francis Casella, and Natalie Contos. 2002. "Reflections on Practice: Ethics, Race, and Worldviews." *Journal of Community Psychology* 30, no. 6 (November): 611–621. https://doi.org/10.1002/jcop.10030.

Bodunrin, Peter O. 1981. "The Question of African Philosophy." *Philosophy* 56, no. 216: 161–179.

Chilisa, Bagele. 2012. *Indigenous Research Methodologies*. London: Sage.

Datta, Ranjan. 2018. "Traditional Storytelling: An Effective Indigenous Research Methodology and its Implications for Environmental Research." *AlterNative: An International Journal of Indigenous Peoples* 14, no. 1 (November): 35–44. https://doi.org/10.1177/1177180117741351.

Dei, George J. Sefa. 1994. "Afrocentricity: A Cornerstone of Pedagogy." *Anthropology & Education Quarterly* 25, no. 1: 3–28. https://doi.org/10.1525/aeq.1994.25.1.05x0961y.

———. 2000. "Rethinking the Role of Indigenous Knowledges in the Academy." *International Journal of Inclusive Education* 4, no. 2: 111–132. https://doi.org/10.1080/136031100284849.

Drumm, Michelle. 2013. "The Role of Personal Storytelling in Practice." Retrieved from https://www.iriss.org.uk/resources/insights/role-personal-storytellingpractice.

Fanon, Frantz. 1967. *Blackfaces, White Masks*. New York: Grove Press.

Finlay, Linda. 2009. "Debating Phenomenological Research Methods." *Phenomenological. Practice* 3, no. 1 (February): 6–25. https://doi.org/10.29173/pandpr19818.

Gadamer, Hans-Georg. 1998. *Truth and Method* (2nd ed.). New York: Continuum. (Original work published 1960.)

Gordon, Lewis R. 2011. "Shifting the Geography of Reason in an Age of Disciplinary Decadence." *Transmodernity: Journal of Peripheral Cultural Production of the Luso-Hispanic World* 1, no. 2 (Fall): 95–103. https://doi.org/10.5070/T412011810.

Gyekye, Kwame. 1987. *An Essay on African Philosophical Thought: The Akan Conceptual Scheme*. Cambridge: Cambridge University Press.

———. 1988. *The Unexamined Life: Philosophy and the African Experience*. Accra: Ghana Universities Press.

Hart, Michael A. 2010. "Indigenous Worldviews, Knowledge, and Research: The Development of an Indigenous Research Paradigm." *Journal of Indigenous Social Development* 1, no. 1A (February): 1–16. https://dev.journalhosting.ucalgary.ca/index.php/jisd/article/view/63043/46988

Heidegger, Martin. 1962. *Being and Time*. New York: Harper. (Original work published 1927).

Hountondji, Paulin J. 1983. *African Philosophy: Myth and Reality* (trans. H. Evansand and J. Rée). London: Hutchinson.

Kibirige, Ronald. 2020. "Dancing Reconciliation and Re/ integration: Lamokowang and Dance-Musicking in the Oguda- Alel Post-War Communities of Northern Uganda." PhD diss., Norwegian University of Science and Technology.

Kovach, Margaret. 2009. *Indigenous Methodologies: Characteristics, Conversations, and Contexts*. Toronto: University of Toronto Press.

———. 2010. "Conversation Method in Indigenous Research." *First Peoples Child & Family Review: An Interdisciplinary Journal Honouring the Voices, Perspectives, and Knowledges of First Peoples through Research, Critical Analyses, Stories, Standpoints and Media Reviews* 5, no. 1 (May): 40–48. https://doi.org/10.7202/1069060ar.

Kvale, Steinar. 1996. *Interviews: An Introduction to Qualitative Research Interviewing*. Thousand Oaks: Sage.

Lajul, Wilfred. 2014a. "Management of the African Knowledge System and the Future of Africa in the World." *Philosophia Africana* 16, no. 1: 43–57. https://doi.org/10.5840/philafricana20141614.

———. 2014b. *African Philosophy: Critical Dimensions*. Kampala: Fountain Publishers.

Laverty, Susann M. 2003. "Hermeneutic Phenomenology and Phenomenology: A Comparison of Historical and Methodological Considerations." *International Journal of Qualitative Methods* 2, no. 3 (September): 21–35. https://doi.org/10.1177/160940690300200303.

Le Roux, Johann. 2000. "The Concept of "Ubuntu": Africa's Most Important Contribution to Multicultural Education." *MCT* 18, no. 2 (Spring): 43–46. https://eric.ed.gov/?id=EJ607501.

Letseka, Moeketsi. 2000. "African Philosophy and Educational Discourse." *African Voices in Education* 23, no. 2: 179–193.

Lincoln, Yvonna S., and Egon G. Guba. 1985. *Naturalistic Inquiry*. Newbury Park: Sage.

Mabingo, Alfdaniels. 2014. "Teaching East African Dances in Higher Education in the US: Reconciling Content and Pedagogy." *Journal of Emerging Dance Scholarship* 2: 1–37. https://www.jedsonline.net/wp-content/uploads/2014/06/Mabingo.pdf.

———. 2015. "Decolonizing Dance Pedagogy: Application of Pedagogies of Ugandan Traditional Dances in Formal Dance Education." *Journal of Dance Education* 15, no. 4 (December): 131–141. https://doi.org/10.1080/15290824.2015.1023953.

———. 2018. "Intercultural Dance Education in the Era of Neo-state Nationalism: The Relevance of African Dances to Student Performers' Learning Experiences in the United States." *Journal of Dance Education* 19, no. 2 (December): 47–57. https://doi.org/10.1080/15290824.2018.1434527.

———. 2020. *Ubuntu as Dance Pedagogy in Uganda: Individuality, Community, and Inclusion in Teaching and Learning of Indigenous Dances*. New York: Palgrave MacMillan.

Mabingo, Alfdaniels, Gerald Ssemaganda, Edward Sembatya, and Ronald Kibirige. 2020. "Decolonizing Dance Teacher Education: Reflections of Four Teachers of Indigenous Dances in African Postcolonial Environments." *Journal of Dance Education* 20, no. 3 (September): 148–156. https://doi.org/10.1080/15290824.2020.1781866.

Mamdani, Mahmood. 2011. "The Importance of Research in a University." Retrieved from https://misr.mak.ac.ug/publication/working-paper-no-3-the-importance-of-research-in-a-university.

Mangena, Fainos. 2016. "African Ethics through Ubuntu: A Postmodern Exposition." *Journal of Pan African Studies* 9, no. 2 (April): 66–81.

Matthews, Sally. 2010. "Teaching and Researching Africa in an 'Engaged' Way: The Possibilities and Limitations of 'Community Engagement'." *Journal of Higher Education in Africa/Revue de l'enseignement supérieur en Afrique* 8, no. 1: 1–21. https://codesria.org/IMG/pdf/1-JHEA_Vol_8_1_2010_Matthews.pdf.

Mazrui, Ali A. 1986. *The Africans: A Triple Heritage*. London: BBC Publications.

Mbembé, Achille. 2001. *On the Postcolony*. Berkeley: University of California Press.

Mbiti, John S. 1970. *African Religions & Philosophy*. New York: Doubleday & Co.

Mbowa, Rose. 1999. "Luganda Theatre and Its Audience." In *Uganda: The Cultural Landscape*, edited by Ecckhard Breitinger, 227–246. Kampala: Fountain.

Menkiti, Ifeanyi. 1984. "Person and Community in African Traditional Thought." In *African Philosophy: An Introduction* (3rd ed.), edited by Richard, A. Wright. Lanham, 171–181 MD: University Press of America.

Mignolo, Walter D. 2009. "Epistemic Disobedience, Independent Thought and Decolonial Freedom." *Theory, Culture & Society* 26, no. 7–8 (February): 159–181. https://doi.org/10.1177/0263276409349275.

———. 2011. *The Darker Side of Western Modernity. Global Futures, Decolonial Options*. Durham, NC: Duke University Press.

Mudimbe, Valentin. Y. 1988. *The Invention of Africa: Gnosis, Philosophy, and the Order of Knowledge*. Bloomington: Indiana University Press.

Nannyonga-Tamusuza, Sylvia A. 2005. *Baakisimba: Gender in the Music and Dance of the Baganda People of Uganda*. New York: Routledge.

Ndlovu, Morgan. 2013. "Mobilising History for Nation-Building in South Africa: A Decolonial Perspective." *Yesterday and Today* 9 (October): 1–12. http://www.scielo.org.za/scielo.php?pid=S2223-03862013000100002&script=sci_arttext&tlng=es.

———. 2018. "Coloniality of Knowledge and the Challenge of Creating African Futures." *Ufahamu: A Journal of African Studies* 40, no. 2 (Summer): 94–112. https://doi.org/10.5070/F7402040944.

Ndlovu-Gatsheni, Sabelo J. 2018. "The Dynamics of Epistemological Decolonisation in the 21st Century: Towards Epistemic Freedom." *The Strategic Review for Southern Africa* 40, no. 1: 16–45. https://www.up.ac.za/media/shared/85/Strategic%20Review/vol%2040(1)/Ndlovu-Gatsheni.pdf.

Nketia, Kwabena J.H. 1970. "Music Education in Africa and the West: We Can Learn from Each Other." *Music Educators Journal* 57, no. 3: 48–55. https://doi.org/10.1177/002743217005700313.

Nyamnjoh, Francis B. 2012. "'Potted Plants in Greenhouses': A Critical Reflection on the Resilience of Colonial Education in Africa." *Journal of Asian and African Studies* 47, no. 2 (February): 129–154. https://doi.org/10.1177/0021909611417240.

Nyerere, Julius Kambarage. 1967. *Education for self-reliance*. Dar es Salaam: Government Printer.

———. 1987. "Ujamaa: The Basis of African Socialism." *The Journal of Pan African Studies* 1, no. 1: 4–11.

Nzewi, Meki. 2003. "Acquiring Knowledge of the Musical Arts in Traditional Society." In *Musical arts in Africa: Theory, Practice and Education*, edited by Anri Herbst, Meki Nzewi and Kofi Agawu, 13–38. Pretoria: University of South Africa Press.

Oelofsen, Rianna. 2015. "Decolonisation of the African Mind and Intellectual Landscape." *Phronimon* 16, no. 2 (January): 130–146. https://hdl.handle.net/10520/EJC189180.

Oruka, Odera H. 1990. *Sage Philosophy: Indigenous Thinkers and Modern Debate on African Philosophy*. Leiden, Netherlands: E. J. Brill.

p'Bitek, Okot. 1975. "Fr. Tempels' Bantu Philosophy." *Transition*: 3, 66–68.

———. 1986. *Artist, the Ruler: Essays on Art, Culture, and Values, Including Extracts from Song of Soldier and White Teeth Make People Laugh on Earth*. Nairobi: East African Publishers.

Polkinghorne, Donald E. 1983. *Methodology for the Human Sciences: Systems of Inquiry*. Albany: State University of New York Press.

Senghor, Lèopold Sèdar. 1994. "Negritude: A Humanism of the Twentieth Century." In *Colonial Discourse and Postcolonial Theory*, edited by Patrick Williams and Laura Chrisman, 27–35. New York: Columbia University Press.

Sloan, Art, and Brian Bowe. 2014. "Phenomenology and Hermeneutic Phenomenology: The Philosophy, the Methodologies, and using Hermeneutic Phenomenology to Investigate Lecturers' Experiences of Curriculum Design." *Quality & Quantity* 48, no. 3 (February): 1291–1303. https://doi.org/10.1007/s11135-013-9835-3.Smith, Linda Tuhiwai. 1999. *Decolonizing Methodologies: Research and Indigenous Peoples*, 1st ed. New York: Zed Books.

———. 2021. *Decolonizing Methodologies Research and Indigenous Peoples*, 3rd ed. London: Zed.

Suddick, Kitty Maria, Vinette Cross, Pirjo Vuoskoski, Kathleen T. Galvin, and Graham Stew. 2020. "The Work of Hermeneutic Phenomenology." *International Journal of Qualitative Methods* 19 (August): 1–14. https://doi.org/10.1177/1609406920947600.

Tiostanova, Madina Vladimirovna, and Walter D. Mignolo. 2012. *Learning to Unlearn: Decolonial Reflections from Eurasia and the Americas*. Columbus: The Ohio State University Press.

Tutu, Desmond. 1999. *No Future without Forgiveness*. London: Rider.

van Manen, Max. 1997. *Researching Lived Experience: Human Science for an Action Sensitive Pedagogy*, 2nd ed. London: The Althouse Press.

Walker, Ayo. 2019. "Rebalancing Dance Curricula through Repurposing Black Dance Aesthetics." *Research in Dance Education* 20, no. 1 (February): 36–53. https://doi.org/10.1080/14647893.2019.1566306.

Wartenberg, Thomas E. 1990. *The Forms of Power: From Domination to Transformation*. Philadelphia: Temple University Press.

wa Thiong'o, Ngugi. 1986. *Decolonizing the Mind: The Politics of Language in African Literature*. Oxford: James Currey.

———. 2012. *Globalectics: Theory and the Politics of Knowing*. New York: Columbia University Press.

Wilson, Shawn. 2001. "What Is an Indigenous Research Methodology?" *Canadian Journal of Native Education* 25, no. 2: 175–179.

Wiredu, Kwasi. 1998. "Toward Decolonizing African Philosophy and Religion." *African Studies Quarterly. The Online Journal of African Studies* 1, no. 4: 291–331.

Wiredu, Kwasi, and Kwame Gyekye. 1992. *Person and Community*. Washington, DC: Council for Research in Values and Philosophy.

15
Ethnography for Research in Dance Education

Global, Decolonial, and Somatic Aspirations

Ojeya Cruz Banks

The year was 1998 and I was in Nairobi, Kenya declaring that I was there to study East African dance. I was an amateur so numerous people scrunched their eyebrows when they heard the plan. They were puzzled. Finally, someone explained the confusion to me: "there is no such thing as East African dance – there is Kikuyu dance, Kikamba dance, Kiswaheli dance, and more," he said. Then, over a decade later when I was researching Indigenous dance education on the Pacific Island of Guåhan/Guam, I was told that dance is not conceptualized as an independent idea or practice. Lålai, which means to chant, can also refer to dance because they go hand and hand. At the time, I had no clue that it was fair to call these ethnographic experiences ideological revelations and interventions.

Over the years, I have continued to process the magnitude of these lessons. They brought my attention to the importance of cultural specificity and taught me to diligently identify generalizations that get in the way of understanding diverse worldviews of dance and dance education. These different cultural contexts have informed my notions of dance teaching, training, and dance artistry with distinct cultural worldviews across the globe. Places and people have taught me that how we frame dance is never culturally neutral.

The central focus of this chapter is to share how ethnography has been a methodology for advancing my thinking about dance and dance education in and out of schools. Approaches to data collection, analysis, and sharing that I employ are highlighted. I zero in on the new conceptual frameworks gained, and somatic insights acquired doing ethnographic fieldwork and analysis. Anecdotes from the Pacific continent to West Africa to the United States are shared to discuss the methodology's affordances, advantages, and challenges. Additionally, I will share how these ethnographic experiences have provided conceptual building blocks for curriculum revision at a university level. Ethnography has been a methodology for gleaning diverse dance knowledge and contributing to the evolution of teaching with decolonial and social justice aspirations. May this portrait of my ethnographic experiences provide helpful commentary about research ethics, data collection, and analysis.

The chapter is divided into five parts. The first section explores the significance of a researcher's reflexivity or standpoint. In this section, I introduce my family, dance education, and academic background. How my unique positionality informs the kind of ethnography I carry out is explained. Second, the question "what is ethnography?" is discussed. I also explain how the method's history is relevant to dance education. Third, I summarize the notions of dance and dance education that have emerged through ethnographic research. Fourth, I comment on how the ultimate goal of ethnography is about establishing relationships and respect. I also explain how I construct research questions, negotiate ethical considerations, and conduct data collection and analysis. Data collection is defined as community engagement, and I share a snapshot of how this process worked in Aotearoa/New Zealand (NZ). Then analysis is described as embodied reflection and communal think-tanking. In this section, I discuss how somatic memoirs and research participant consultation are critical analytical strategies for projects in West African and House dance. To conclude, I identify how ethnography has advanced my conceptual understanding and pedagogical approach to dance teaching; it also has inspired me to develop new university courses. Finally, I suggest ethnography to be an important vehicle for ushering globally-minded or BIPOC (Black, Indigenous, & People of Color) dance education that challenges the white supremacy that pervades notions of dance and dance education.

How I achieve ethnography is not conventional. For instance, I do not silo data collection and analysis from each other. Rather, participant observations, which I call somatic memoirs, exemplify an overlap between knowledge gathering and interpretation. Insights gained from dance practice plus consultation are at the heart of ethnographic meaning-making for me. Dance is a portal for both information gathering, analysis, and sharing back. Binaries between research standpoints, ethics, data collection, analysis, and sharing research dissolve in my research journey described in this chapter.

I draw from decolonial and Indigenous research approaches that value a holistic process that prioritizes community engagement, and cultural respect. Grounding myself in dance and somatic practices provides me the ideological leverage to center Black/African and Indigenous ways of knowledge production (Deloria

1991; Dillard 2008; Hokowhitu 2010; Kovach 2021). As Kovach (2021) asserts, for Indigenous researchers, methodology should get you home. In other words, research should anchor one in the ancestral worldviews of your people.

A Researcher's Genealogy

Family background and academic training have equally shaped my interests and aspirations as an ethnographer. A big impetus for my work is about recovering ancestral funds of knowledge related to my identity as an African/Pacific Islander (Guåhan) American woman. I also have a strong bond with Aotearoa/New Zealand, where I lived and worked for over a decade. The aspiration to research African/African diaspora along with Pacific worldviews of dance is so that my teaching and artistry are informed by the body of knowledge I call heritage.

Self-reflexivity is a virtue of ethnography. D. Soyini Madison calls reflexivity laborious and a critical practice. She writes that a researcher's positionality must strive for a "reflexivity that is willfully about the social – about the self-made gloriously and ingloriously through Others" (2011b, 136). Hence, researcher genealogy factors into research questions formed, analytical lenses employed and the ethical questions to be considered. As a dancer, I also centralize dancing, and dance community engagement, in data collection and analysis. As Frosch (1999) notes, ethnography's emphasis on participant observation is well suited for dance. Research that I have published or performed includes insights gained while dancing, teaching dance, or observing someone else teaches dance. Ethnography has exposed me to a wide range of dance pedagogy around the world.

Early in my research career, I became intrigued about the educational significance of dance in a given society. The research journey has taught me that dance generates epistemological diversity, and produces Indigenous intellect, worldview, spiritual belief systems, and more. I am interested in what Hokowhitu (2010) calls epistemic resistance or the centering of ancestral knowledge and ways of being in the face of cultural erasure by colonialism and/or racism. Hence, I call this "critical postcolonial dance recovery" work, to encapsulate how Black/African diaspora and Indigenous communities "reclaim the intellectual, spiritual and cultural knowledge" through dance (Cruz Banks 2009, 355). Moreover, my ethnographic studies champion BIPOC dance education stories that have been eclipsed by colonial, racist, and White supremacist narratives in the field of Dance Education and Dance Studies (Cruz Banks 2010a, 2016, 2019a, 2019b, 2021a, 2021b).

I am a dancer anthropologist. My disciplinary training is grounded in dance, anthropology, education, Indigenous/Pacific Studies, and Black/African/African diaspora studies. While anthropology taught me to be attuned to local knowledges and diversities of dance, being a dancer-scholar has granted me embodied data and access to kinesthetic understandings. Dance provides full-body immersion into the culture. A passport into cultural spaces, dance helps me build social rapport with the community, construct analytical frameworks, and grow artistic skills. For instance, ethnographic research in Senegal involved rigorous physical practice of sabar, a Wolof dance and drum tradition. These experiences have yielded felt, sensuous, auditory, kinetic, and somatic connections and information (Cruz Banks 2010b). Dance praxis has trained me to think in interdisciplinary ways and activate trans-Indigenous dance literacies.

A Brief History of Ethnography and The Katherine Dunham Precedent for Dance Education

Ethnography is a qualitative methodology that is defined as the descriptive study of culture. This method "pursues understanding through the layering of specific and highly complex contexts of human experience" (Frosch 1999, 258). Socio-cultural anthropologists are credited as the trailblazers of evolving the methodology. Fieldwork, participant observation, fieldnotes, interviews, collaboration, narrative writing, and social justice activism can describe the components of the methodology's tactics and mission. Martyn Hammersley and Paul Atkinson (2019) explain that ethnography (or participant observation, a cognate term) draws from "a wide range of sources of information" and involves engagement with people for an extended period of time to observe, listen, ask questions to that shed light on the research query (2019, 4).

The above synthesis of ethnography does not get into the weeds. Historically a colonial and racist project, ethnography has involved the describing of the Other using foreign and White supremacist frameworks of understanding (Smith 1999). This is why Tuhiwai Smith called research a dirty word (1999, 1). She named Western research an imperialist project in the way that it has historically essentialized and labeled Others. However, the field has evolved with BIPOC and social justice-oriented ethnographers who confront discourse inequities and value multiple and distinct Indigenous epistemologies that can be used to address injustices (Gilmore 2007; Madison 2011b; Smith 1999; Zavala 2016). Critical ethnography paired with decolonial methodologies "not only challenge epistemological foundations of colonialism but it is a project of de-linking from Eurocentric thought" (Zavala 2016, 1).

Studies of dance and dance education are part of ethnography's critical and decolonial turning point. For example, the late legendary dancer anthropologist Katherine Dunham (1909–2006) was a proponent of ethnography's reinvention, decolonial transformation, and proactive application of knowledge into educational and performative action (Chin et al. 2014; Clark 1992; Cruz Banks 2012; Dee Das 2017). Dunham respected what D. Soyini Madison calls "indigenous meanings and experiences that are in opposition to dominant discourses and practices" (2011a, 7). Dunham was recognized for her development of choreographies for the theatrical stage and movies that were informed by ethnographic observation and participation in Afro-Caribbean societies. She published this research in texts such as *Island Possessed* (1969) and *Journey to Accompong* (1946). Her ethnographic narratives plus her artistic and educational agenda work revealed Dunham's posture of somatic agility, cultural reflexivity, and a desire to decolonize anthropology (Cruz Banks 2012). Ethnographic research in Haiti assisted Dunham's development of Dunham technique. Her pedagogy sought to correct the "miseducation of the negro" as Woodson (1933) would call it, and counter racial trauma by providing socially and spiritually uplifting dance experiences relevant to people of the African diaspora in the United States. Dunham's dance pedagogies are "storehouses of Black Atlantic history" (Osumare 2010, 7).

Dunham exemplified how to use ethnographic research for dance knowledge recovery and developing culturally relevant curriculum. She showed us that ethnography is advantageous for acquiring dance worldview competencies, engaging in dance training, and developing choreographic skill sets that can inform pedagogy (Cruz Banks 2011). Ethnography can evolve theories and practices of dance education.

Notions of Dance That Emerge from Ethnography

My ethnographic research focuses on BIPOC approaches to dance education in and out of formal school contexts. I am interested in dance education that "has a long tradition of expert practitioners and dedicated advocates that date well back before the emergence of mass schooling and far into antiquity" (Robinson, 2015, xvi). Hence, I do not believe the history of dance education should start with Margaret H'Doubler or Rudolph Laban. I see them as part of a continuum of a global lineage of dance teaching and learning.

Ethnography has taught me to engage with Indigenous and/or vernacular terms that introduce different ways of knowing and conceptualizing dance and dance education. For instance, Royal (2010) once defined *haka* (Māori dance) as becoming sensorially alive in the moment. He describes *whakaahua* as an Indigenous word in New Zealand that describes the ultimate performance ideal of dance that is to become the energy of the natural world. Then, an educator speaking on purpose of West African dance for African Americans in the United States spoke of the intrinsic relationship to music and how drumming can usher in empowered realities (Cruz Banks and Jackson 2019). I have found dance to be leveraged for cultural transmission, healing from colonialism and racism, identity and community strengthening, land (re)connection, and activating spatial, somatic, and spiritual sovereignty.

Additionally, many dance artist-educators in countries such as Aotearoa, Guåhan, Guinea, and Senegal do not call themselves dance educators. One reason for this is that dance education is a Western construct that can often clash with Black and Indigenous aesthetics and terminologies (see Ashley 2013). Native linguistics often do not align with Western concepts of dance education. Some BIPOC dancers even reject association with dance education because the language is linked to what White people do. In communities I have researched across the world, dance pedagogies are described as or equivalent to oral history projects, language immersion, rites of passages, and cultural preservation work (Cruz Banks 2021b, 2019a, 2010b).

I have also found through ethnographic research that dance is not compartmentalized. Dance is often conceptually inseparable from music and communal ritual, for example. Dance can be a synchronization of music, chant, and poetry in order to create a total sensory embodiment of BIPOC literacies and subjectivities. Integrations of chant and movement such as *kapa haka* (group dance) in Aotearoa explain why dance is described as a repository of language because the dance involves hand gestures and body percussion while chanting important ancestral memories or stories. In Aotearoa, dance and chant are pedagogically bound. For instance, chant is the mouthpiece, and dance is the personification of Indigenous cosmologies. This explains why Māori use haka to teach language, breed cultural perception, and activate ethical values along with genealogical memory (Cruz Banks 2019, 2021b; Matthews 2004; Royal 2010, 2014).

Ethnographic study of Pacific and Black/African dance education worlds has elucidated to me how certain dance pedagogies are designed to submerge an individual and/or community into sonic embodiments and frequencies that "[nurture] indigenous intellectual and sensory acuity" (Perez 1997, 10). For example, in Los Angeles, West African dance educator Dr. Jeanette Jackson believes that introducing Black children to the djembe drum and dance culture is a way to divest internalized racism. For Jackson, the djembe drum culture has been a personal lifeline, and she has dedicated a career to performing and teaching West African dance. She founded African Soul International to facilitate dance programs that promote spiritual well-being for African Americans. In a publication I co-authored with Jackson, we argue that regaining cultural fluency in West African culture is a critical part of cultural, emotional, and spiritual restoration. This enables African Americans to tap into an empowering African worldview that helps us "heal from the traumatic events of forced migration, cultural dislocation, and racism" (Cruz Banks and Jackson 2019, 101).

Establishing Relationships and Respect

Ethnography is a practice of relationship building, navigating different worldviews, and critical self-reflection. Fieldwork requires postures of humility and deep respect for people at the heart of the cultural story. I call data collection community engagement and gathering of cultural information. This requires learning about the ethical protocols of making contact that exists within a community. It also involves maintaining a dialogue of collaboration, and profound respect for your research participants, their interests, needs, and perspectives (Gilmore 2007; Madison 2011a; Smith 1999; Denzin and Lincoln 2008). Community engagement should inform what data is being collected, and how it might be conceptualized, and analyzed. Research relationships should not end after the "data" has been collected; rather they should continue to grow a foundation of understanding, trust, reciprocity, allyship, and network.

Ethnographic questions – and their answers – for me have emerged from dance practice queries, community engagement, embodied reflection, and consultation with research partners from the very beginning and throughout my research process. For example, as my training in Guinea dance started to develop, queries about music and movement relationships naturally began to arise. When I started discussing my intentions to study the integral relationship of music and dance with renowned Guinea dancer Moustapha Bangoura, he encouraged me to talk to his esteemed colleague M'Bemba Bangoura, a professional djembe drummer, to get a drummer's perspective on drum-dance compositions. Understanding the music and dance equation not only fine-tuned my artistic practice, in addition to my teaching competencies, and cultural insight. I found that the development of a research question should build a dialogic relationship with a person or community. Discussing the research question or central ideas with my research partners is a way to test appropriateness, accuracy, or relevance of the query from their perspective. Inviting conversation and feedback from the people central to a project helps guide decisions about research questions, data collection, and analytical focal points.

It is important to me that my research partners value the project. This requires going beyond Institutional Review Board (IRB) approval for several reasons. For one, IRBs have historically focused on regulating biomedical research and view participants as human subjects, not research partners. Another limitation of the IRB process is that it tends to pose questions ill-suited for some social sciences, humanities, and performing arts because it was designed with medical and behavioral research in mind. However, there are IRB questions that have to do with confidentiality, consent, participation of minors that indeed warrant attention. However, Jaschik (2015) argues there is no evidence that IRB improves research or protects people. Hence, working with BIPOC or any individual or community, I simply ask permission throughout the research process. Transparency about evolving research intentions and aspirations is vital.

Data Collection Is Community Engagement: A Snapshot from Aotearoa/New Zealand

When I first migrated to Aotearoa to work at the University of Otago in 2008, I did not know very much about the local dance scene and noticed right away that the dance curriculum did not include much Indigenous content. Plus, there was not much literature specifically on Indigenous dance history or education. This was both a dilemma and an opportunity. As a dancer-anthropologist with strong inclinations toward local knowledge and cultural specificity, my instincts were to develop a conceptual framework of dance relevant to New Zealand. This is when I became attracted to the work of the Atamira Dance Company, a leading Māori contemporary dance theater whose "work embodies a unique artistic landscape shaped by the cultural identity of our people and their stories" (Atamira Dance Company). I reached out to them in 2009 and our research relationship stretched through until 2017.

To launch the research with the Atamira Dance Company I set up an introductory meeting at Café O in Auckland, where we talked family, dance, and my research interests over a cup of coffee. Situating folks genealogically is important to Māori, and during our chat, I got a chance to introduce my family-cultural background. I told them my central interest was to learn about their creative processes and decolonial aspirations. Eventually, I was given permission to observe and join their creative workshops at Unitec Institute of Technology Auckland toward the development of their work *Tāonga* that premiered in March 2009. During this project, I started to develop a significant friendship with acclaimed Māori choreographers Louise Pōtiki Bryant and Jack Gray, founding members of the Atamira Dance Company.

Data gathering strategies I used included participant observation, writing fieldnotes, informal conversation, photography, and participating in company dance classes and creative workshop rehearsals. I also carried out archival research such as reading relevant literature and performance reviews and listening to radio interviews of company members. Through the combination of experiential knowledge such as dancing with the company and listening to them, along with reviewing the text and media sources, I assembled a varied collection of information.

Participant observation is what I call being with the people. Time with them gave me the chance to get to know the company and for the members to get to know me. In addition to participating in company dance classes and creative workshops, I observed rehearsals, listening to what the choreographer and dancers discussed, and taking notes of my impressions, observations, and informal conversations. I watched them improvise, experiment, and make choreographic decisions. I paid careful attention to their bodies in motion, the qualities that permeated their movement, and the movement vocabulary they used.

Some of the best "ah ha" moments for me involved listening to Pōtiki Bryant talk about her aspirations for *Taonga: dust, water, wind* (2009). The work was based on genealogical research Pōtiki Bryant did with her Auntie Rona, born in 1924, who lived in Catlins/Kaka point, Aotearoa. She gifted Pōtiki Bryant stories of her childhood: memories of her late mum, of wind surges, fascinations with birds and more. Rona also told about deceased relatives who Pōtiki Bryant never met. The performance, *Taonga*, danced this lineage. As Frosch (1999) mentions, ethnographic objectives involve conceptualizing dance on its own terms. Therefore, listening to how Pōtiki Bryant conversed about the creative process, and what she was trying to achieve in the performance was of utmost importance to me. What I discovered was that her auntie's oral history became the choreographic framework. Each dancer personified a family member dead or alive. They even shapeshifted into birds that dwelled on Kaka point/Catlins. The company followed the *tikanga*/correct practices of artistic endeavors for Māori culture. Moko Mead (2016) articulates that art is something that deepens your connection to *whakapapa*, or in other words, genealogy and ancestral homeland.

The company followed this protocol. For instance, as part of the creative development of *Taonga*, Pōtiki Bryant spent time in Kaka point and later arranged a visit for the company to take in the smells, to see the ocean, to meet the family. The performance illuminates their movement research that kinetically conceptualizes the environmental details of Kaka point. The dancers embodied the qualities of land, sea, birds, the southerly winds, moon phases, and the ancestral memory (Cruz Banks 2017).

Fieldnotes based on participant observations were collected to "examine the creative process and dancemaking" and "chart their path of constructing a movement ethos" (Frosch 1999, 250–251). Ethnography guided my attention to not be preoccupied with the final performance but instead to give weight to why the dance is important to the artists. The research introduced me to how Atamira Dance Company's creative processes are projects of Māori epistemological renaissance. The company's decolonial mission is about creating choreographies that collate, perform, and affirm family stories and Māori cosmological orientations of the world.

Analysis: Snapshots from West Africa to the United States

In a nutshell, analysis is a rigorous examination and interpretation of the data gathered. Ethnographic analysis involves repeated reflection on the participant observations, fieldnotes, and archival data. This analysis is used to construct a narrative that focuses on the details that should elude generalization (Thomas 1993). A goal of ethnographic analysis is storytelling with cultural specificity and nuance.

A critical component of ethnographic research for me frequently involves intensive dance training and workshops that become not only data but also a critical analytical framework for the interpretation of the data. Somatic knowledge can be a rich source of ethnographic analysis. Kinetic and other sensory experiences help answer the research question with embodied insights. For instance, understanding how mind, body, and music connections are relevant to Black/West African dance pedagogies is a theme running through my research (Cruz Banks 2010a, 2012, 2019, 2021a).

The participatory information I gain through somatic memoirs is often central to analysis for me. I developed the term somatic memoirs[1] to describe "autographical movement data" that "can unearth rich experiential and kinetic information different from what might be gleaned through classical participant observation" (Cruz Banks 2017, 65). Somatic memoirs are distinct from fieldnotes because they revel in kinesthetic insights and experiential knowledge gained from dance. I situate somatic memoirs as analysis because they champion first-person memories of movement practice. They ground my analysis in embodied knowledge that is fundamental to Black/Indigenous epistemologies. Dancing immerses me in the spiritual and communal ethos of a culture. Interpretation of the movement experiences and observations, plus the reading and re-reading of fieldnotes, archives, and relevant literature help me identify themes and revelations that can advance theories and practices of dance.

At Moustapha Bangoura's *Le Bagatae* School of Dance and Drum in Guinea, West Africa, for example, I explored the pedagogical significance of the *fare ra lankhi* (dance circle) (Cruz Banks 2019). The circle is where a dancer learns to interact with a djembefola or a skilled musician of the Malian hand drum, and where one is tested to align their moves with the beat. The circle is where Bangoura taught me to identify rhythms being played and recall the corresponding movement repertoire. Personal experiences in the circle provided me with profound understandings of how musicality and movement innovation work in djembe dance traditions. Here is an excerpt of an ethnographic description, what I call a somatic memoir of being in the circle:

> I flowed eagerly into the center of the circle. My feet led me forward and I entered the round of fellow dancers and musicians. I made eye contact with the djembefola. His eyes smiled and reassured me. As I moved toward him, he punctuated my travel step with his drumming. This musical attentiveness excited me, my body rang with the beat, and I sensed the djembe soundscape becoming increasingly more dynamic as if in response to my dancing. The djembefola accented my unplanned choreography as if we had rehearsed. He drummed the rhythmic composition of my moves as if he knew what was coming. (Cruz Banks 2019a, 5–6)

My somatic memoir portrays how the circle is a pedagogical space for learning to improvise in collaboration with the music. Being in the circle also taught me to be an acute listener of the pocket of the rhythm and drum cues. In the center, I discovered that it is a dancer's job to enhance the overall polyrhythm soundscape with on-the-spot movement compositions.

The focus of somatic memoirs as analysis is to highlight bodily experiences through ethnographic narrative. Write-ups of embodied reflections describe kinesthetic and aural nuances discovered while dancing. These somatic details inform me about how dance pedagogy, creative process, and methods of movement composition are distinctly set-in motion across different cultures. The emphasis on somatic memoirs builds cultural understanding and boosts thick descriptive dance writing and artistic skills. What I learn through rigorous physical practice is a crucial analytical focal point for me for these reasons. I examine somatic knowledge through interpretations of sensory experiences and pay attention to themes and patterns that emerge.

Another significant element of analysis is what I call communal thinking. Frosch (1999) advises that ethnographers should give research partners and consultants an opportunity to guide, scrutinize, and crosscheck their analysis. I have done this by having conversations with them about interpretations that are emerging, providing them copies of drafts I want to publish or present, and humbly considering their feedback, concerns, and responses. During this phase, I often ask them again if I have their blessing to publish the work. This is helpful for ethical checks and balances on a researcher's power to define and impose labels on cultural practices.

On-going consultation with research participants and relevant colleagues has helped me find my way out of conceptual rabbit holes. We can easily become enmeshed in our research and might need to take a step back, identify the blind spots, and consider the narratives we might inadvertently be excluding. There are unavoidable research limitations, tensions, and disagreements; however, I have found that consultation is vital to processing information and constructing well-balanced and accurate analysis.

When I realized I wanted to publish my experience of studying House dance with Allison Gray of Versa Style Dance Company in Los Angeles (Cruz Banks 2021a), for example, I asked for permission and sent her a copy of the draft. I was fortunate that Gray read the draft, gave me the go-ahead, and provided me feedback for fine-tuning the analysis. The article included somatic memoirs of the dance workshops with Gray and describes how Gray taught freestyle strategies distinct from House dance. After reading my ethnographic description of freestyle as "music connection," she prompted me to think about the complexity and cultural specificity of musicality. Gray encouraged me to unpack how a dancer leverages their inherited family and ancestral rhythmic moves and grooves in the House cipher. While not all the nuances of her feedback made it into that particular publication, her comments inform my lectures, instructional language, and movement coaching.

Advancing Dance Pedagogy with Ethnography

My ethnographic journey has provided understandings of worldview, dance-making tactics, and principles of creative process distinct to Māori and other Pacific cultures plus Black/African diaspora people. BIPOC dance history, movement exercises, and approaches to teaching dance have informed the content of my pedagogy (Cruz Banks 2010b, 2016, 2017). The method has been, for me, a critical strategy for unearthing culturally relevant dance content and ascertaining artistic practices. Ethnography has advanced my epistemological reckoning of dance with global and BIPOC viewpoints that evolve my pedagogy and the curriculum content I deliver.

For example, the research I did in Aotearoa with Atamira Dance Company and Louise Pōtiki Bryant guided the revamp of all the courses I taught at the University of Otago with Indigenous perspectives. Moreover, I developed a new class called "New Zealand Dance and Global Connections," which focused on the history, evolution, and creative principles of Māori and Pacific dance. Additionally, we considered how Black/African diaspora is deployed in New Zealand. Ethnography also contributed to the design and pedagogy of a course I teach called "Global Hip Hop" at Denison University. The course was informed by the dance circle, cipher, freestyle, and House dance research I have done. Global Hip Hop explores the global roots and routes of Hip Hop and House dance. This course delves into the social history that cites legendary dancers such as Rock Steady Crew and Rockafella, Marjorie Smarth, and Ejoe Wilson. Local Ohio Hip Hop history is included, and Columbus breakin artist-educators James Alexander and Donald Isom contribute lessons. Rigorous physical practice in freestyle and improvisation within the cipher (dance circle) is emphasized in the class. Students learn the protocols of dancing in the cipher and develop Black/African diaspora dance skills in musicality.

My experiences lead me to encourage other dance educators to use ethnographic methods to engage, reflect upon different epistemologies, ontologies, and cosmologies of dance. I believe ethnography can help us reckon with McCarthy Brown's question, "who are the owners of dance" (2018, 469), which signals the need to pay attention to the whitewashing of dance teaching. I am not saying we disavow the legacies of Margaret H'Doubler, Martha Hill, or Rudolf Laban, for instance. However, at the same time, we cannot continue to tokenize or footnote the stories of BIPOC dance education. Indigenous and diaspora approaches to dance education need more equitable encounters with dominant narratives. McCarthy Brown and Schupp (2018) and Davis (2018) remind us of the need to do a better job with teacher training and curriculum development that challenge the logics, the paradigms, and assumptions of dance teaching. This means we need to become more cognizant of how dance education works around the world and why it is significant to our students, and to local and global communities. Ethnography can help realize this aspiration.

Note

1 In Cruz Banks 2010b and 2021a, and Cruz Banks and Jackson 2019, I describe how Thomas Hanna, Katherine Dunham, Adrienne Keappler, Dierdre Sklar, Martha Eddy, Jill Green and more have informed how I conceptualize somatic memoirs. One way in which I develop the notion of somatic ethnography is by situating it within Black/Indigenous worldviews, perspectives, and practices.

Works Cited

Ashley, Linda. 2013. "Dancing with Cultural Difference: Challenges, Transformation and Reflexivity in Culturally Pluralist Dance Education." *Dance Research Aotearoa* 1, no. 1: 5–23. https://doi.org/10.15663/dra.v1i1.3.

Chin, Elizabeth, Aimee Meredith Cox, Dána-Ain Davis, Anindo Marshall, Ronald Marshall, and Kate Ramsey. 2014. *Katherine Dunham: Recovering an Anthropological Legacy, Choreographing Ethnographic Futures*. Sante Fe: School for Advanced Research Press.

Clark, Veve. 1992. "Katherine Dunham: Method Dancing or the Memory of Difference." In *African American Genius in Modern Dance*, edited by Gerald E. Myers, 5–8. Durham, NC: American Dance Festival.

Cruz Banks, Ojeya. 2009. "Critical Postcolonial Dance Recovery and Pedagogy: An International Literature Review." *Pedagogy, Culture and Society* 17, no. 3: 355–367. https://doi.org/10.1080/14681360903194368.

———. 2010a. "Critical Postcolonial Dance Pedagogy: The Relevance of West African Dance Education in the United States." *Anthropology and Education Quarterly* 41, no. 1: 8–34. https://doi.org/10.1111/j.1548-1492.2010.01065.x.

———. 2010b. "Of Water and Spirit: Locating Dance Epistemologies in Aotearoa/New Zealand and Senegal." *Anthropological Notebooks* 16, no. 3: 9–22.

———. 2012. "Katherine Dunham: Decolonizing Anthropology Through African American Dance Pedagogy." *Transforming Anthropology* 20, no. 2: 159–168. https://doi.org/10.1111/j.1548-7466.2012.01151.x.

———. 2014. "West African Dance Education as Spiritual Capital: A Perspective from the United States." *Dance, Movement and Spiritualities* 1, no. 1: 163–179. https://doi.org/10.1386/dmas.1.1.163_1.

———. 2016. "Tama Wātea: Integrating Māori Perspectives into Dance Education: A Tertiary Example." In *Intersecting Cultures in Music and Dance Education*, edited by Linda Ashley and David Lines, 285–297. Cham: Springer.

———. 2017. "Haka on the Horizon." *Mai Journal* 6, no. 1: 61–74.

———. 2020. "Fare Ra Lankhi: The Circle Is an Indigenous Pedagogical and Choreographic Space for West African Dance." *Journal of Dance Education* 20, no. 4: 205–213. https://doi.org/10.1080/15290824.2019.1599896.

———. 2021a. "Stories of West African and House Dance Pedagogies: 4E Cognition Meet Rhythmic Virtuosity." *Journal of Dance Education* 21, no. 3: 176–182. https://doi.org/10.1080/15290824.2021.1942477.

———. 2021b. "Lalåi: Somatic Decolonization and Worldview Making through Chant on the Pacific Island of Guåhan." In *Perspectives in Motion: Engaging the Visual in Dance and Music*, edited by Kendra Stepputat and Brian Deitrich, 215–224. New York: Berghahn Books.

Cruz Banks, Ojeya, and Jeanette "Adama Jewel" Jackson. 2019a. "West African Dance and Spiritual Well-Being for African Americans." In *Dance and the Quality of Life*, edited by Karen Bond, 101–115. Cham, Switzerland: Springer. https://doi.org/10.1007/978-3-319-95699-2_6.

Cruz Banks, Ojeya, and Miriam Marler. 2019b. "Soil, Soul, and Somatic Senses: Memoirs of Dance in Japan and Guam/Guåhan in Postcolonial Times." In *Soulful and Spiritual Research in Dance Studies: Bodily Inscription, Self-Narrative, and Auto-Ethnography*, edited by Amanda Williamson and Barbara Sellers-Young, 343–361. Bristol: Intellect.

Davis, Crystal U. 2018. "Laying New Ground: Uprooting White Privilege and Planting Seeds of Equity and Inclusivity." *Journal of Dance Education* 18, no. 3: 120–125. https://doi.org/10.1080/15290824.2018.1481965.

Dee Das, Joanna. 2017. *Katherine Dunham: Dance and the African Diaspora*. New York: Oxford University Press.

Deloria, Vine. 1991. "Research, Redskins, and Reality." *American Indian Quarterly* 15, no. 4: 457–468. https://doi.org/10.2307/1185364.

Denzin, Norman K., and Yvonna S. Lincoln. 2008. "Introduction: Critical Methodologies and Indigenous Inquiry." In *Handbook of Critical and Indigenous Methodologies*, edited by Norman, K. Denzin, Yvonna, S. Lincoln, and Linda T. Smith, 1–20. Thousand Oaks: SAGE Publications, Inc. https://dx.doi.org/10.4135/9781483385686.

Dillard, Cynthia B. 2008. "When the Ground Is Black, the Ground Is Fertile: Exploring Endarkened Feminist Epistemology and Healing Methodologies in the Spirit." In *Handbook of Critical and Indigenous Methodologies*, edited by N.K. Denzin, Y.S. Lincoln, and L.T. Smith, 277–292. Thousand Oaks: SAGE Publications, Inc. https://dx.doi.org/10.4135/9781483385686.

Frosch, Joan D. 1999. "Dance Ethnography: Tracing the Weave of Dance in the Fabric of Culture." In *Researching Dance: Evolving Modes of Inquiry*, edited by Sondra Horton Fraleigh and Penelope Hanstein, 249–280. Pittsburgh: University of Pittsburgh Press. https://doi.org/10.2307/j.ctt5vkdz2.12.

Gilmore, Perry. 2008. "Engagement on the Backroads: Insights for Anthropology and Education." *Anthropology and Education Quarterly* 39, no. 2: 109–116. https://doi.org/10.1111/j.1548-1492.2008.00010.

Hammersley, Martyn, and Paul Atkinson. 2019. *Ethnography: Principles in Practice*. New York: Routledge.

Hokowhitu, Brendan. 2010. "Introduction: Indigenous studies; Research, identity and resistance." In *Indigenous Identity and Resistance: Researching the Diversity of Knowledge*, edited by Brendon Hokowhitu, 9–20. Dunedin, NZ: University of Otago Press.

Jaschik, Scott. 2015. "The Censor's Hand" Inside Higher Ed. https://www.insidehighered.com/news/2015/06/03/author-discusses-new-book-flaws-institutional-review-boards

Kovach, Margaret. 2021. *Indigenous Methodologies: Characteristics, Conversations, and Contexts*. Toronto: University of Toronto Press.

Madison, D. Soyini. 2011a. *Critical Ethnography: Method, Ethics, and Performance*. Los Angeles: Sage publications.

———. 2011b. "The Labor of Reflexivity." *Cultural Studies Critical Methodologies* 11, no. 2: 129–138. https://doi.org/10.1177/1532708611401331.

Matthews, Nathan. 2004. "The Physicality of Māori Message Transmission – Ko te tinana, he waka tuku korero." *Junctures: The Journal for Thematic Dialogue*, no. 3: 9–18. http://hdl.handle.net/10523/5157.

McCarthy-Brown, N. 2018. "Owners of Dance: How Dance Is Controlled and Whitewashed in the Teaching of Dance Forms." In *The Palgrave Handbook of Race and the Arts in Education*, edited by Amelia Kraehe, Rubén Gaztambide-Fernández, Stephen Carpenter, 469–487. Cham, Switzerland: Palgrave Macmillan. https://doi.org/10.1007/978-3-319-65256-6_27.

Mead, Hirini Moko. 2016. *Tikanga Māori (revised edition): Living by Māori Values*. Wellington, NZ: Huia publishers.

Osumare, Halifu. 2010. "Dancing the Black Atlantic: Katherine Dunham's Research-to-Performance Method." *AmeriQuests* 7, no. 2: 1–12. https://doi.org/10.15695/amqst.v7i2.165.

Perez, Cecelia. 1997. "Signs of Being: A Chamoru Spiritual Journey." PhD diss., University of Hawai'i.

Robinson, Sir Ken. 2015. "Introduction." In *Dance Education around the World: Perspectives on Dance, Young People and Change*, edited by Charlotte Svendler Nielsen, and Stephanie Burridge, xv–xviii. London: Routledge. https://doi.org/10.4324/9781315813578.

Royal, Te Ahukaramū Charles. "Whakaahua – An Approach to Performance." Keynote address presentation at Dancing across the Disciplines: Cross Currents of Dance Research and Performance Throughout the Global Symposium, Dunedin, New Zealand, June 29, 2010.

———. 2014. "Indigenous Ways of Knowing." http://argosaotearoa.org/work/indigenous-ways-of-knowing.

Schupp, K., and McCarthy-Brown, N. 2018. "Dancing with Diversity: Students' Perceptions of Diversity in Postsecondary Dance Programs." University of Delaware Library, Museums & Press 9. https://udspace.udel.edu/handle/19716/28722.

Smith, Linda Tuhiwai. 1999/2021. *Decolonizing Methodologies: Research and Indigenous Peoples*. London: Zed Books Ltd.

Thomas, Jim. 1993. *Doing Critical Ethnography*. Newbury Park: Sage Publishing.

Woodson, Carter. 1993. *Miseducation of the Negro*. Eastford, CT: Martino Fine Book.

Zavala, Miguel. 2016. "Decolonial Methodologies in Education." In *Encyclopedia of Educational Philosophy and Theory*, edited by Michael A. Peters, 1–6. Singapore: Springer Singapore. https://doi.org/10.1007/978-981-287-532-7_498-1.

16
Conducting an Experiment
How Quantifying Answers to a Research Question Can Promote the Value of Dance Education

Lynnette Young Overby and Matthew Henley

Introduction

As educators, we seek to facilitate, contribute to, or participate in meaningful change in students' lives. Students enter our classrooms and, over the course of x number of classes, we coordinate experiences through which students gain knowledge and skills that we hope contribute to fulfilling personal and professional lives.

When we find a strategy that seems to be working, one which leads to higher achievement, more enduring learning, deeper emotional growth, stronger social engagement, etc., we sometimes want to share our strategy with other teachers so that more students can also be positively impacted.

We want our teaching to do something and we want to reach as many students as possible. These two desires point to important ideas in educational quantitative research: causality and generalizability (Cohen, Manion, and Morrison 2018). When we seek to demonstrate that a classroom strategy leads to, impacts, or contributes to a personal or educational outcome, we are seeking causality; a relationship between cause and effect. When we seek to whom this effect applies, or to what larger group these effects might extend, we seek generalizability; a relationship between a small group and the broader population.

In educational research, causality and generalizability may be demonstrated through experimental and quasi-experimental methodologies – the topic of this chapter. In these methodologies, researchers create and implement an intervention in which they deliberately control what they propose are the causes;

these are called the independent variables. Researchers then measure the effects or outcomes of the intervention; these are called dependent variables. Often this is done by having two or more groups, one which receives the intervention, called the experimental group, and one which does not, called the control group. One set of independent variables that are important to control are the individual characteristics of the students. By randomly selecting participants from the entire population, it is assumed that any effects found from the intervention generalize to the entire population. By randomly assigning students to either the control or intervention group, it is assumed that individual differences are evenly distributed between the groups.

As an example, when Overby was teaching in an elementary school in Washington D.C. and completing her master's degree in dance education from George Washington University, she was gaining knowledge of creative dance and its many applications. Contemplating a focus for her final master's degree project, she realized that she was in a unique position to test out a hypothesis that she felt to be true – that teaching reading through creative movement (a cause or independent variable) could positively impact non-readers' ability to comprehend information (an effect or dependent variable). After consulting with the classroom teachers, she created a quasi-experimental design with two sets of lessons, one with stories integrated with movement (intervention), and one without (control). Before teaching the lessons, she gave both groups of beginning readers a pre-test on the content of the stories and specific vocabulary words to demonstrate the two groups were similar before the intervention. She then took the experimental group to a multipurpose room where they danced the stories and made shapes and movements to depict the vocabulary words. This was the intervention. She taught the control group the traditional way, by reading the stories to them and having them circle and write the vocabulary words. After the intervention, a post-test, that was similar to the pre-test, was given to both groups.

To analyze the results, she calculated how much each group, on average, improved on the dependent variable. She then used a mathematical formula called a t-test to determine if the average difference in test scores between groups was statistically significant. After analyzing the data, she was elated to see the results: the dancing experimental group had a significantly larger increase in scores than the control group! This allowed her to make the tentative claim that dance integration teaching strategies (for this group of first-grade students) caused higher reading comprehension scores in comparison to traditional teaching strategies (Young 1975).

This brief example allows us to highlight important points about causality and generalizability in experimental research. Demonstrating that dance integration improves reading scores is incredibly impactful data in advocacy for educational policy and funding that increases access to the arts. This is particularly true if the audience for the research is administrators and politicians whose job it is to make choices that impact populations. In this way, experimental and quasi-experimental designs can be powerful tools. The example also highlights the challenges a researcher faces with experimental design. Ideally, all variables would be kept the same between groups except for the independent variables of interest. As this study was done in a real-world classroom environment, not all variables could be controlled. For instance, the experimental group had reading lessons in the multipurpose room and the control group had reading lessons in the regular classroom. It is up to the researcher to demonstrate that it was dance integration and not the location that caused the differences between groups. Additionally, students should be randomly selected from the entire population to which the study hopes to generalize. Should it apply to all first-grade students in the district, city, state, nation, world? For this study, existing classes, or intact groups, were used from a single school, limiting generalizability. In education research then, this study would be considered quasi-experimental because it did not include random sampling and assignment (Shadish and Luellen 2006). Quasi-experimental design is a valuable research methodology because, though it might limit the causal and generalizable claims that can be made, these claims resulted from practices that closely resemble the real world, improving what is called ecological validity, or how well the results from the study could be applied to another context (Cohen, Manion, and Morrison 2018).

In order for Overby's experiment to be a "true" experiment she would have had to randomly select, or sample, students from all over the city, state, nation, or world, depending on the scope of her generalizability claim, and randomly assign them to either group. This is often logistically and financially impossible. She would also need to control for all variables, which would have likely meant bringing both groups to a laboratory space where all aspects, except for the movement intervention, could be held the same. Though this allows for variables to be controlled, it would be different than the children's real-world experience of going to reading class, bringing into question how applicable the findings are to the classroom given the experimental environment was dramatically different. Quasi-experimental design is an easily adoptable methodology to develop evidence about causality and generalizability in the real world and with relatively low cost and commitment.

Experimental and quasi-experimental data provide parents, educators, administrators, and policymakers with valuable tools that can be used to advocate for access and opportunities for all citizens to experience a quality dance education. The generalizability that we aim for in this research allows us to predict and advocate for practices and policies that may be effective across a wide variety of dance education settings. Moreover, the quantitative data that emerges from these types of research studies, when used in combination with qualitative data, merges to form powerful stories from real-world dance educators.

In the remainder of this chapter we will describe the seven broad steps involved in experimental and quasi-experimental research (Creswell and Creswell 2018), which are:

1. Identify an appropriate theoretical framework
2. Define variables and research questions and write the hypothesis
3. Design the experimental treatments
4. Assign participants to treatment groups
5. Run treatments and generate the data
6. Analyze and synthesize the data
7. Share the results

We will illustrate each of these steps with projects designed and implemented by ArtsBridge Scholars from the University of Delaware. ArtsBridge is an undergraduate program directed by Overby which offers undergraduate students the opportunity to develop, implement, and collect data on arts-based community engagement programs.

The Seven Steps

Identify an Appropriate Theoretical Framework

At first glance, quasi-experimental design and dance might seem to be an odd pair. Quasi-experiments operate according to a logic that assumes we can better understand experience by breaking it down into discrete namable parts, measuring and testing the relationships between those parts, then using the results to predict how those relationships will impact large groups of people. Dance on the other hand operates according to a logic in which physical, intellectual, emotional, social, and spiritual factors are inextricably intertwined and operate as procedural rather than declarative knowledge, relationships are perceived to be ephemeral and in flux, and difference is embraced within and between groups. Though change and difference are inevitable (and beautiful) parts of life, there is value in naming and defining aspects of dance experience, of making the implicit explicit, so that we can be more intentional about our practice. Theories, in essence, are an explicit description of relationships between aspects of our experience (Creswell and Creswell 2018). They provide a framework that sets the stage for the hypotheses that follow. In a research proposal or research report, theories are first described in the introduction or literature review section, followed by the hypotheses or research questions that test or verify the theory.

For instance, ArtsBridge research projects are designed to integrate arts into classroom teaching. These projects operate according to the principle that the arts "provide an alternative means to reach out to disadvantaged learners" (ArtsBridge 2022). When crafting a hypothesis and research design, a theory is needed to explain why arts integration (independent variable) positively impacts (causes) students' personal and academic success (dependent variable). ArtsBridge projects utilize both quantitative and qualitative approaches (mixed methods). However, for the purpose of this chapter, only the quantitative components will be discussed.

One theory that is central to many ArtsBridge projects is the theory of embodied pedagogy (Nguyen and Larson 2015). Whereas traditional pedagogical approaches focus on the mind as the center of cognition, embodied pedagogy acknowledges that both body and mind play a role in knowledge construction. According to this theory, embodiment facilitates learning by grounding conceptual elements in bodily and spatial sensation, uniting body and mind, and highlighting the social nature of learning.

Another theory that is centered in many of the projects as an overarching approach to arts integration is experiential learning theory. The most well-known model for experiential learning was proposed by David A. Kolb, who identified four learning stages, which are: concrete experience, reflective observation, abstract conceptualization, and active experimentation (Hedin 2010). Each of these stages of learning requires a different learning ability and individuals' strengths and weaknesses in these abilities formulate individual learning preferences. In Kolb's theory, learning occurs as experiences are grasped and transformed.

Finally, the theory of student engagement (O'Donnell, Reeve, and Smith 2012) claims that student success can be predicted from a student's observable embodiment of motivation, involvement, and commitment. This theory was used by Lucy Font in her undergraduate research project: "Adding movement to subtract monotony: The effects of a music and movement integrated curriculum on second-grade students' engagement with learning" (2016). We will come back to this theory in more detail in the next section on defining variables and writing out research questions. Broadly though, each of these theories provides an empirically-based explanation of *why* arts integration contributes to student success, one that can be tested through quasi-experimental design.

Define Variables and Research Questions and Write Out Hypothesis

Quasi-experiments measure and analyze the relationship between at least two variables (independent and dependent) for at least two different groups (control and experimental). It is therefore essential to clearly define the variables. These definitions should emerge from existing theories, which were, in turn, based on empirical evidence. Turning back to Font's study, the theory of student engagement was clearly defined according to three components:

- *Behavioral engagement* refers to a student's enduring attention, effort, and persistence throughout a learning activity (O'Donnell, Reeve, and Smith 2012, 335).
- *Emotional engagement* refers to the presence of positive emotions, such as joy and excitement, and the absence of negative emotions, such as anger or frustration. When students are emotionally engaged, they *want* to participate, rather than feeling that they *have* to participate (O'Donnell, Reeve, and Smith 2012, 335).
- *Cognitive engagement* refers to a student's use of "sophisticated learning strategies," such as elaboration, as well as his or her demonstration of critical thinking skills. Students show high levels of cognitive engagement when they paraphrase the material or relate it to prior knowledge (Font 2016, 6–7; O'Donnell, Reeve, and Smith 2012, 336).

Based on these definitions, Font was able to develop research questions about the causal relationship between arts integration and aspects of student engagement. Notice that the questions are organized according to the theoretical framework, and each question names the independent and dependent variables.

1. What are the effects of a dance-integrated mathematics curriculum on the *emotional engagement* of students from low-income homes, as indicated by enjoyment and enthusiasm?
2. What are the effects of a dance-integrated mathematics curriculum on the *cognitive engagement* of students from low-income homes, as indicated by academic understanding?
3. What are the effects of a dance-integrated mathematics curriculum on the *behavioral engagement* of students from low-income homes, as indicated by attention, effort, persistence, and conduct?

The answer to each of these questions is then articulated according to two hypotheses. The first potential answer is that a dance-integrated mathematics curriculum *will not* have an effect on engagement. This is called the null hypothesis as it proposes there will be no differences between the control and experimental groups. The second answer is that a dance-integrated mathematics curriculum *will* have an effect on engagement. This is called the alternative hypothesis and it proposes that there will be a difference between the control and experimental groups. Each of the questions ends with a clause, that is, as indicated by. This is a description of how the dependent variable was operationalized, or made measurable, in the design of the experiment, a topic to which we will return later.

Design Experimental Treatments

In most cases, the experimental treatment will be a new curriculum or approach to teaching. Part of the design of the experimental treatment, then, will be a pedagogical task. The previous step of clearly defining the independent variable will guide the design of the experimental treatment. For instance, Font designed a four-lesson curriculum that integrated Common Core Standards (National Governors Association Center for Best Practices & Council of Chief State School Officers 2010) for both math and dance. In another ArtsBridge undergraduate research project, "Consequences of our actions: Dance and transportation" (LaMotte 2018), Megan LaMotte created lesson plans that taught specific transportation concepts to two classes of fifth-grade students. Each lesson plan included the same science and social studies Common Core Standards and learning objectives to ensure the control class got a comprehensive education of the transportation content. A typical lesson for the control class would begin with some questions and answers from the students to grasp their knowledge about the topic, followed by an interactive lecture, an activity, and then time to respond to the journal prompts. The experimental group followed a similar structure but was taught through movement concepts such as locomotor, non-locomotor, level, pathway, etc.

As the exercises, lessons, units, or curricula are being developed, all variables, except the independent variable, should be kept as close to the same between groups as possible. Considering what factors, besides the independent variable, might impact the dependent variable, and designing both the experimental treatment and the control treatment to limit the impact of those factors will improve the validity of the results. For example, do the two groups: Meet at the same time of day? Meet for the same duration? Meet the same number of times? Have the same teacher? Have a similar composition of students? Have a similar teacher-to-student ratio? Do the experimental and control treatments: Have the same pedagogical approach? Have similar interactions between teacher and student? Have similar interactions between students? Any of the above could impact the outcome. Unless they are the independent variable of interest, efforts should be made to control them between groups. This, however, is not always easy in quasi-experimental design as the research negotiates ecological validity and experimental control.

After the design of the study has been established, the researchers should seek institutional approval to conduct research with human subjects. Usually overseen by Institutional Review Boards (IRB), approval ensures that practices are in place that uphold the principles of respect for persons, beneficence, and justice in research. These include, but are not limited to, seeking student assent and parental consent after a thorough explanation of the study in all appropriate languages, as well as ensuring that students and parents understand that participation is voluntary and that there will be no negative consequences either from participating or choosing not to participate.

Types of Designs

Within quasi-experimental research, there are several designs that are defined by how groups are organized and when measurements occur (Cohen, Manion, and Morrison 2018; Shadish and Luellen 2006). Some of these are: one group pretest-post-test, pretest-post-test with control group, time-series–longitudinal, repeated measures, regression discontinuity, natural experiments, correlation for experimental designs, and non-equivalent groups (see Table 16.1).

Font's study was one group pretest-post-test design. Though she ran the experiment twice in two different locations; both groups received the art-integration intervention. There was, therefore, no control group to which she could compare the results. This type of design is similar to examinations that might be given to a dance class before the content is provided, then several weeks later, a post-test is provided to determine what exactly was learned. Without a control group, causal inferences should be limited. Her results demonstrated that the students' scores improved, but without a control group, she cannot demonstrate that it was the art-integration strategy, specifically, that caused the improvement. Font also supplemented her quantitative data with several forms of qualitative data, such as teacher observations and student journaling, as a way to triangulate her findings.

LaMotte's study was pretest-post-test with control group design. Both experimental and control groups took tests on transportation. In addition, the experimental group took a test on dance concepts. Each test included multiple choice, short answer, matching, and true and false questions. Both the

Table 16.1 Common quasi-experimental designs with brief descriptions and examples from published literature in dance education

Experimental and Control Pretest-Post Test (Bayyat 2020; Lykesas, Koutsouba, and Tyrovola 2010)	There is a control group and an experimental group. A pre-test and post-test are given to experimental and control groups before and after the intervention.
Time Series/Longitudinal (May et al. 2020)	Multiple measurements are taken over time, the treatment is then introduced and the researcher continues to take multiple measurements over time. The measurements taken before the treatment are then compared to the measurements after the treatment.
Repeated Measures (Overby 1986; 1993)	A single group of participants take part in all the different treatment conditions and/or are measured at multiple times.
Correlational Design (Heiland, Rovetti, and Dunn 2012)	Multiple measurements are compared to evaluate relationships between dependent variables.
Non-equivalent Group (Ryan 2011)	The researcher chooses existing groups that appear similar, but where only one of the groups experiences the treatment.
Regression Discontinuity	An arbitrary cut-off is used to assign groups. Experimenters may use students above the cut-off as the control group, and students below the cut-off as the experimental group.
Natural Experiments	An event provides the opportunity to post-facto assess groups based on their exposure or lack of exposure to the event.

transportation test and the dance test consisted of ten questions. At the end of the unit, students took the exact same tests to measure their improvement and ensure comparable results.

Assign Participants to Treatment Groups

In a true experiment, participants volunteer for a study and are randomly assigned to intervention or control groups. In educational research, it is not always possible to randomly assign participants to different groups as studies are often conducted with intact groups in the form of existing classrooms. In LaMotte's study for instance, the experimental and control groups were existing classes at a Maryland public school. Though there might be some level of randomization when students select or are assigned to a particular class, there could be other variables that influence selection or assignment that also impact the dependent variable. For instance, college students that register for an 11 am class might have different professional or familial responsibilities than students who register for a 7 pm class. Or, given the need to accommodate other activities in students' schedules, two periods of a high school dance class might have different proportions of arts students, athletes, or AP students. In quasi-experimental design, then, where randomization does not occur, the researcher cannot automatically assume that any differences between the groups at the end of the study were caused by the independent variable and must consider what other factors might have affected the results.

Run Experiment and Generate the Data

Numerical data about human experience is not simply out there waiting to be collected like artifacts buried at an archeological site. The researcher must engage in processes of selection and transformation. Common ways to translate student experience into numerical data are the use of classroom assignments and/or existing research instruments. Classroom assignments are readily available sources of data in most classrooms that quantify learning through the assignment of a grade. When designing the assignment, test, or rubric, though, the researcher needs to carefully consider if the assignment is actually measuring what it proposes to measure as well as the possibility of grader/researcher bias. Some researcher bias can be kept in check by using existing instruments such as the Evaluation of Potential for Creativity (Barbot, Besançon, and Lubart 2011). These instruments have the benefit of being vetted to ensure that they measure the variable they propose to measure, and they often include procedures to remove researcher bias during the scoring process. There, however, are not existing instruments that measure all aspects of experience, or they might not transfer easily into educational practice in dance.

Font, for instance, had to determine a way to measure the experience of emotional, cognitive, and behavior engagement with a quantitative score. Here is where the clause from the research question, "as indicated by," becomes important (e.g. What are the effects of a dance-integrated mathematics curriculum on the cognitive engagement of students from low-income homes, *as indicated by academic understanding*?). Cognitive engagement via academic understanding was measured with pre- and post-assessments of both mathematics concepts and movement concepts. The mathematics assessment consisted of 20 items. It addressed the following math concepts: shapes, symmetry, addition, and subtraction.

Emotional engagement as indicated by enjoyment and enthusiasm was measured with pre- and post-surveys with 18 questions. Ten of these questions were used to gather emotional engagement data. Student responses to the survey were assigned a score based on the content of the response. For the first six questions, students indicated their feelings toward a variety of learning concepts by circling a smiling face, a neutral face, or a frowning face. Smiling faces were given scores of three, neutral faces scores of two, and frowning faces scores of one. The next four survey items asked students to give their opinion on a variety of statements about math and dance by circling "Y" for "yes" or "N" for "no." On these questions, positive answers received a score of two, while negative answers received a score of one. Behavioral assessment was analyzed using qualitative data.

We prefer the term data generation to data collection as it is a reminder that the researcher is an active creator, rather than a passive observer, of data. Framing the researcher as a creator of data highlights the importance of considering how the introduction of bias, even well-meaning bias, might impact the design and results of a study.

As data is being generated it is also important to consider how the groups might be affected by factors other than the independent variable. Did one or both of the groups gain or lose students? Was one or both of the groups affected by events outside of the intervention? Were the two groups separate, or was there communication between the two classes?

Analyze the Data

Statistical analyses are a way to recognize relationships among data that might not be immediately apparent. In experimental design, the analyses mirror the logic of the research design. Based on each group's average score on the dependent variable, and the distribution of individuals' scores around that average, one statistical test (t-test) answers the question: What is the probability that the difference between the groups' scores occurred by chance? To say that something is statistically significant, then, is to say that, based on the evidence, it is highly unlikely that the differences between the groups occurred by chance. Put another way, it is highly likely that the intervention caused the change in the treatment group's scores that was not observed in the control group's scores. In quasi-experimental design, when groups are not randomly assigned, different tests can be run that compensate for non-equivalency between groups.

LaMotte's study included pre- and post-scores on a test that measured students' knowledge of transportation. She analyzed if the scores from before and after the lessons were significantly different. More importantly, she analyzed whether the dance-integrated group improved their scores significantly better than the control group. Which in fact they did! This suggests that, though both lessons led to improved scores, the integrated lessons caused a larger improvement in scores than the traditional lesson for this group.

If the statistical analysis part of experimental or quasi-experimental design is daunting, we encourage interested researchers to reach out to a local College of Education or program in statistics, where there is likely a student who would be eager to apply their knowledge and assist with study design and analysis in exchange for the opportunity to be a second or third author on a resulting publication.

Synthesize the Findings

After the data have been generated, analyzed, and the results are displayed, the next step is to determine the meaning of the work. The meaning is related to the research process and answers the stated research question. In the set-up of the study, the researcher transformed an aspect of experience into numerical data. It is now the responsibility of the researcher to transform that data back into experience and tell a story about what the analysis means. LaMotte, for instance, found a significant difference in test scores between the two groups. Those test scores are meant to represent the experience of learning. Test scores are so ubiquitous in education that we often take for granted that they automatically equate to learning, but this is not necessarily the case.

In particular, experimental research attempts to tell a story about causality (did the independent variable cause a change in the dependent variable?) and generalizability (for whom would this change apply?) Because generalizability considers how applicable the findings are to the population outside the groups being studied, it is part of a study's external validity or the ability to generalize the findings to other locations and times. The researcher should ask: To what population does the sample belong? To whom do findings generalize? To whom do they not generalize? How well were the variables put into operation? Is the theory represented in the practice? How much was the experiment like the real world?

Once these questions are answered, the researcher must next provide a synthesis of the findings with connections to the theory that framed the study, past research, application possibilities, and suggestions for future studies. When a researcher makes their work public through presentation, publication, performance, teaching, or conversation, they are joining an ongoing discourse, influenced by scholars and practitioners from the distant and immediate past and influencing scholars and practitioners in the immediate and distant future. It is appropriate to both honor those who came before, and show the way for those who will come next.

Share the Results

Once the research is completed, sharing the results of the research becomes extremely important. By sharing their work, researchers contribute to the scholarly discourse on a specific topic. Finally, sharing research provides us with the opportunity to translate the research into practical information that may be used by teachers, parents, and policymakers. Dissemination may occur in many different formats. Some of these include poster and oral presentations at conferences, peer-reviewed academic journals, and book chapters. We also encourage researchers to think of other ways that their work is shared, for instance in informal conversations with students and colleagues, through vlog or blog posts, or in the development or modification of lesson plans or workshops. Each mode provides the researcher with opportunities to receive feedback and find new collaborators for future research. LaMotte presented her research at a National Dance Education Organization conference in 2017, and published her work in the *Journal of Dance Education* (2018). Both Font and LaMotte prepared lesson plans to give to the classroom teachers.

Conclusion

In this chapter, we have offered a definition of quasi-experimental design and outlined its seven steps, offering examples from ArtsBridge student scholars' dance integration research projects, and suggesting questions to consider when designing a quasi-experimental study. These rhetorical strategies point to two primary take-aways from this chapter: The first is to indicate that quasi-experimental design is within the reader's reach. Quasi-experimental research projects can begin in manageable ways that don't require large amounts of time or resources for either the researcher or the participants. They can also be very rewarding, as Font describes:

> My research experience as an ArtsBridge Scholar shaped my undergraduate experience and has ultimately made me a better educator. With the guidance of my faculty mentor, I learned how to develop and investigate a research topic and discuss it in an academic paper. The research I conducted as an undergraduate has inspired me to consider the role of dance in the classroom and ultimately made me a more dynamic and effective teacher.
> (Overby, Font, LaMotte 2019, 162)

The second strategy indicates that in the implementation of quasi-experimental research, one of the most important practices is for the researcher to ask questions at each step. Being reflective and honest about the logic of the research design and the role of researcher bias is fundamental to the execution of an ethical study.

We want our teaching to do something and we want to reach as many students as possible. These modest studies provide a foundation for future work that scales up the claims for causality and generalizability so that policymakers are informed about the value of dance education and are convinced to implement change at the system level to bring high-quality dance education to all students. As we look to the future, we see dance education scholars answering difficult questions through individual and interdisciplinary studies. The environmental scientist, or health care researcher will connect with dance education researchers through experimental studies to develop and implement research that addresses problems in classrooms and the world. All dance educators will have the facility to understand and apply the results of quality experimental and quasi-experimental research studies in their classrooms. Advocates for policy change will have a body of literature with clear quantitative data that supports the changes needed to promote dance accessibility for all citizens. In the future, dance education scholars will be able to speak the language of dance, of research, and of the experiment.

Works Cited

ArtsBridge. 2022. "ArtsBridge Home Page." University of Delaware. https://www.artsbridge.urel.udel.edu/.

Barbot, Baptiste, Maud Besançon, and Todd Lubart. 2011. "Assessing Creativity in the Classroom." *Open Education Journal, Bentham Open* 4, no. 4: 58–66.

Bayyat, Manal M. 2020. "Blended Learning: A New Approach to Teach Ballet Technique for Undergraduate Students." *Turkish Online Journal of Distance Education* 21, no. 2: 69–86.

Cohen, Louis, Lawrence Manion, and Keith Morrison. 2018. *Research Methods in Education*. New York: Routledge.

Creswell, John W., and J. David Creswell. 2018. *Research Design: Qualitative, Quantitative, and Mixed Methods Approaches*. Los Angeles: SAGE.

Font, Lucy. 2016. "Adding Movement to Subtract Monotony: The Effects of a Dance-Integrated Mathematics Curriculum on the Engagement of Students from Low-Income Homes." BA Thesis, University of Delaware.

Hedin, Norma. 2010. "Experiential Learning: Theory and Challenges." *Christian Education Journal* 7, no. 1: 107–117.

Heiland, Teresa, Robert Rovetti, and Jan Dunn. 2012. "Effects of Visual, Auditory, and Kinesthetic Imagery Interventions on Dancer's Plie Arabesques." *Journal of Imagery Research in Sport and Physical Activity* 7, no. 1: 1–24.

LaMotte, Megan. 2018. "The Integrated Approach versus the Traditional Approach: Analyzing the Benefits of a Dance and Transportation Integrated Curriculum." *Journal of Dance Education* 18, no. 1: 23–32.

Lykesas, Georgios, Maria Koutsouba, and Vasiliki Tyrovola. 2010. "Comparison of Teacher and Child-Centered Methods of Teaching Greek Traditional Dance in Primary Education." *International Journal of Physical Education* 47, no. 3: 25–33.

May, Jon, Emma Redding, Sarah Whatley, Klara Łucznik, Lucie Clements, Rebecca Weber, John Sikorski, and Sara Reed. 2020. "Enhancing Creativity by Training Metacognitive Skills in Mental Imagery." *Thinking Skills and Creativity* 38, no. 1: 1–10.

National Governors Association Center for Best Practices and Council of Chief State School Officers. 2010. *Common Core State Standards*. Washington, DC.

Nguyen, David and Jay Larson. 2015. "Don't Forget about the Body: Exploring the Curricular Possibilities of Embodied Pedagogy." *Innovative Higher Education* 40: 331–344.

O'Donnell, Angela M., Johnmarshall Reeve, and Jeffrey K. Smith. 2012. *Educational Psychology: Reflection for Action*, 3rd ed. Hoboken, NJ: John Wiley & Sons, Inc.

Overby, Lynnette. 1986. "A Comparison of Novice and Experienced Dancers' Imagery Ability in Relation to Two Body Awareness Tasks." PhD diss., University of Maryland.

———. 1993. "A Comparison of Novice and Experienced Dancers' Body Awareness." In *Dance: Current Selected Research*, edited by Lynnette Overby and James Humphrey, 57–72. New York: AMS Press.

Overby, Lynnette Young, Lucy Font, and Megan LaMotte. 2019. "Dance Education." In *Undergraduate Research in Dance*, edited by Lynnette Young Overby, Jenny Olin Shanahan, and Gregory Young, 158–164. New York: Routledge.

Ryan, Jennifer. 2011. "Math that Moves You: A Study of the Effects of a Dance Integrated Mathematics Curriculum Supplement on the Knowledge and Attitudes of Second Grade Students." In *Dance: Current Selected Research* (Vol. 8.), edited by Lynnette Overby and Billie Lepczyk, 219–258. Brooklyn: AMS Press Inc.

Shadish, William R., and Jason K. Luellen. 2006. "Quasi-Experimental Design." In *Handbook of Complementary Methods in Education Research*, edited by Judith L. Green, Gregory Camilli, and Patricia B. Elmore, 540–550. Mahwah, NJ: Lawrence Erlbaum Associates Inc.

Young, Lynnette. 1975. "The Effects of Creative Dance on the Reading Skills of Beginning Readers." MA Thesis, George Washington University.

17
Classroom as Laboratory
Teacher Self-Study and Dance Education

Ilana Morgan

Teacher Self-Study and the Nature of Dance Education

Teacher self-study involves an individual's study of themselves as a teacher and of their personal teaching practice, with an eye toward the improvement of student learning. Specifically, self-study research seeks to enhance an individual's teaching practice by investigating the creation and implementation of classroom strategies, practices, activities, transitions, lessons, and so on. Alternatively, self-study may be employed to explore specific challenges or problems in the classroom, classroom culture, policies and procedures, or the use of new curriculum. Although it may be easy to identify classroom teaching practices that one may study, teacher self-study can also research perceptions and experiences from the teacher's past or present that may relate to their identities and current actions as a teacher. It may also support inquiry into social justice issues, personal beliefs, or questions about advocacy through teaching. The intention of the research can widely vary, but the self in relation to the practice and specific arena of teaching sits at the center of the inquiry.

Within self-study, the researcher works to balance personal perception and history in relation to a delineated time and location of teaching, also defined as a situated act of teaching. This situation of teaching considers, for example, a specific set of students, curriculum, time period, or location. This balance of the personal and the situated teaching helps to position self-study as somewhere between traditional hypothesis-led research and a confessional exploration of self and practice; tipping heavily into either end of this spectrum would not result in a teacher self-study. Self-study does not include personal reflection and knowledge as a type of narcissism or intense navel-gazing. Rather, it seeks to connect a personal, situated teaching experience with published knowledge of the field at large. In this way, this type of research is both personal and interpersonal at the same time. Robert Bullough Jr. and Stefinee Pinnegar write about teacher self-study as taking place in "the space between self and the practice engaged in," with its value measured in the degree to which these two are analyzed and brought into conversation with one another. The goal, they suggest, is to "gain understanding necessary to make that interaction increasingly educative" beyond one's personal practice (2001, 15).

Because dance educators so often develop and teach their dance technique classes in private, with choreography being the product to be shared and applauded, I contend that a methodology to unearth and share these practices widely in dance is needed. John Warren, in his article on reflexive teaching and critical autoethnographic practices, discusses this private nature of teaching: "The tendency to hide our teaching is a problem that I believe has consequences for how we teach and the ability to become better at our craft. Furthermore, it means any reflexivity we do of our teaching is always done in private too" (2011, 139). He argues that we "need to reinvest in pedagogy-centered research" and to consider "a renewal in reflexive, ethnographically centered research that takes our labor in the classroom as a vital site for investigation" (2011, 140). The insight that dance educators can provide with teacher self-study is demonstrated by the ways in which we already critically analyze, discuss, and share ideas about choreographic processes that are deeply familiar in the field of dance. This processual inquiry into choreography translates easily as a tool to unbury our pedagogical moves in the classroom to improve our craft and the field.

Teacher self-study can also assist us in documenting and sharing the self and the personal expertise that is so highly valued in dance. A traditional dance pedagogical model most often views the choreographer/dance educator as the owner of knowledge who teaches from their unique performance and choreographic experience. In dance, the teacher is in many ways the teacher and the content. Parker Palmer, an educator and author, argues for the consideration of the self in research on teaching, stating that, when we teach, we teach who we are. At the same time, a "self-protective split of personhood from practice is encouraged by an academic culture that distrusts personal truth" (2007, 9). Educational reform and improvement can trend toward large quantitative programmatic assessment and wide standardized testing in order to objectively "prove" what is good for education, but this often leaves little room for the specific and sometimes messy personal experiences of teaching and the teaching self. A teacher self-study approach works against this protective split by considering reflexive pedagogy as a prime location of study and as an opportunity to question and understand the implicit knowledge of teaching and the teacher. In this process, the researcher – via the distribution of the findings from their research – makes public the reflexive and investigative nature of teaching itself while acknowledging who they are as a person.

Dance Education Teacher Self-Study: A Personal Case Study

In my own research as a dance educator, I have found teacher self-study to provide a rich and complex methodology for inquiry that bridges the theory/practice gap often prevalent in dance pedagogy research. It is easy to give weight to grand theoretical perspectives and then jump into research that "tests" these perspectives via student outcomes. However, without taking time to consider the complex processes of the specific teaching practice that arose from the theory, we are left with only part of the story. Although it seems there is no better location for investigating the practice of teaching than that of a teacher in a classroom, this location can be somewhat precarious. Self-study researchers Vince Ham and Ruth Kane colorfully and aptly describe this methodological approach as the act of

> forag[ing] somewhat nervously in the swamplands between the apparently infertile deserts of positivist detachment and the impenetrable jungles of postmodern de/con/structive self-inspection. In our interests we straddle precariously a perceived chasm between the high theory of academe and the rich chaos of situated practice.
> (2004, 103)

The description of this harrowing journey helps one to remember that straddling this chasm requires the researcher to release themselves from proving that their teaching practices "work" or are "right" and to instead choose methods that will help them to tell the story of teaching in a way that grounds theory in a practical, real-world context. In the following paragraphs, I describe my own experience of using teacher self-study to help illustrate this kind of foraging through the rich chaos of the real world in dance education.

In my research, I develop dance teaching practices and curriculum for youth in detention, and, in a larger context, I question how to reach and teach those who do not have access to arts learning. For my current project, I spent years volunteering at a detention center site before asking to embark on research that involves the students directly. For my relationship with the detention center and its staff to be strong enough for me to inquire about interviewing a population as vulnerable as detained youth, years of consistent presence and relationship-building were required. It was during this relationship-building time that I instituted a teacher self-study, which I coupled with ethnographic notes about the place, the building, and the culture of the detention center.

What arose from the relationship between this teacher self-study and the observations of the center was an understanding of how the teaching practices I created were specifically connected to the rules and culture of the center, the architecture of the building, and the ways in which youth engaged, or were allowed to engage, with the curriculum. By looking at these connections more closely – with attention paid to how and what I was teaching – I began to see specific and thematic ideas arise in my teaching practice that were related to surveillance, policing, perceptions of fear, and artistic practice as an act of rebellion. A pedagogy that negotiated between the advancement of the center's goals and the rules for the students that concurrently provided covert spaces for statements of identity and actions of agency through movement began to reveal itself. Without teacher self-study, I would not have been able to easily see these ideas as interwoven in my practice at this particular site.

As these thematic ideas arose, I further analyzed my teaching practice and continued to develop the curriculum by framing my work with published literature from areas concerning incarcerated youth, trauma-informed teaching practices, surveillance, and arts as social justice. A foundation of literature was gathered prior to my implementation of the teacher self-study, but it was the study and its thematic findings that led me back to the literature to get more specific about the theoretical frame required to continue. I moved from a generalized frame concerning aesthetic arts education and aesthetic education in relation to citizenship, to a more specific theoretical frame informed by the self-study. In this way, the self-study narrowed the project in its recursive and cyclical nature, because it honored the teaching as an unfolding and in-process research act in and of itself. The findings from the first part of this self-study led me to the next phase of the project.

I began to conduct interviews to gather perceptions of lived experiences from the students in the dance class and from staff who watched the dance class. From those interviews, exciting perceptions of dance learning arose: (1) brave choice-making was occurring via the dancemaking process as a kind of rebellion against personal circumstances and the loss of agency involving personal space, the body, and/or movement; and (2) students were learning the interpersonal skills necessary for creating dance, belonging, well-being, and positive life choices in the future. At this point in the research, it became clear that I could circle back to the curriculum and strengthen the teaching practices and activities to deliver in better ways the components that participants were identifying as important to their dance learning (leading to a possible second teacher self-study). These perceptions also pushed me to again consult the established literature to find published research that was investigating these issues of agency and interpersonal skills. What I found in this third layer of the literature review were deep connections with research in the areas of social-emotional learning and trauma-informed teaching. Currently, I am preparing the third layer of this study, in which I will add a pre- and post-dance-learning self-assessment of social and emotional skills to measure in a more concrete way the effect that dance learning might have on the development of these skills for the youth.

I share this example to illustrate the ways in which teacher self-study can circle in, around, and through the more established methods of education research, such as interviewing or ethnography, in order to improve teaching. Here, the self-study informed my selection of other research methods to include, and it directed me to gather more specific resources, which in turn helped me to connect theory to deep practice as a continual cycle of questioning. This kind of cyclical experience mirrors for many the process of dancemaking – creating, reflecting, and exploring around and through, while questioning the world of the dance being created – while also simultaneously looking and listening for what the dance is asking for next.

Without this reflective teacher self-study, I would only have created the curriculum and conducted the interviews. Although this would have been interesting, the deep and rich story of creating dance teaching practices and the actual reflection upon the acts of teaching at this site would have been lost. It would have only been a story of students' perceptions of learning, a set curriculum, and a theoretical framework; much of the why and how of the creation and institution of the discovered practices would be absent from this study.

Knowing When to Choose Teacher Self-Study

In my experience teaching graduate-level courses and advising graduate students as they embark upon dance education research, I find it necessary for students to understand when a teacher self-study is needed. If the research question can be written in the first person and if it is centered on the researcher's practice in a particular setting, then most likely a self-study is needed. Consider the following examples of these types of questions:

- How can I create and communicate classroom procedures that are intended to promote student responsibility for dance learning in new and better ways?
- How can I organize my dance studio classroom in a more welcoming way?
- In what ways do I communicate my authority when teaching dance, and how might I better implement a sense of authority in my teaching?
- What personal and significant experiences have I had as a student that might help me understand my current practice as a dance educator?
- How do I teach the concept of rhythm, and how might I improve this?
- How can I better advocate for students with disabilities in my dance classroom?

- How do I most often explain the mechanics of a dance step with students, and how might I integrate more use of imagery in these moments?
- How might I design a unit on a specific dance genre that is developed from an anti-racist and/or culturally responsive perspective?

In the above questions, we can see how the teacher and their practice are the subjects of the research. In addition, we can imagine the ways in which these questions might arise from a challenge, a problem, or an issue that emerged from a dance educator questioning their teaching practices and the effectiveness of student learning. The hoped-for outcome of the research is the improvement of learning, and the research question is specific.

Framing the Research Question with a Literature Review

After the research question is defined and before one chooses specific teacher self-study methods to employ, it is necessary – as author Anastasia Samaras offers in her book *Self-Study Teacher Research* – to "frame your research question within literature" (2011, 27). The performance of a literature review frames the question by (1) locating and defining the need in the field for the study, (2) providing guiding concepts and theories for the research and teaching actions undertaken during the study, and (3) informing or reinforcing the researcher's choice of methods. Samaras considers this an "ongoing process that you can use to continuously inform your topic and research" (ibid). This ongoing and cyclical process of returning to and working with established literature (i.e. restructuring it, switching out big ideas for other big ideas, or building a new frame all together as the study unfolds) mirrors the reflexive nature of teaching toward improvement. It is this recursive and reflexive nature – a hermeneutic lens that values a constant interpretation of and reorienting to the context and interactions as they unfold – that provides space for this frame to change and morph along with the study. The frame asks the study what needs to be considered or understood via the literature; at the same time, the study asks the frame what actions and methods the study should take. It is imperative that the study not "reinvent the wheel" or replicate already established and researched practices, so the researcher must understand what strategies, studies, and approaches to the question already exist in order to build upon already established knowledge.

Centering the Study and Choosing Self-Study Methods

After the literature review has framed the question, it is important to ensure that the teacher self-study methods chosen do in fact keep the researcher and their practice at the center of the study. Let's examine the first question from the list above: "How can I create and communicate classroom procedures that are intended to promote student responsibility for dance learning in new and better ways?" This research question might lead the teacher to first identify the procedures that are already in place and that they think are being communicated in their classroom. They may take photos of signs in the room that explain procedures or direct students, or they may record themselves communicating verbally during procedural moments in the classroom. They might make note of moments during which they hear themselves saying in the recordings things like "Don't forget to place your shoes outside the studio!" or "Can you find your way to our circle? Where should you be?"

Next, they may choose to videotape themselves while teaching. When analyzing these recordings, they can work to identify the moments when and the ways in which they communicate to students during varied procedural directions. They might notice their hand gestures directing students to line up before moving across the floor, or they may note their own facial expressions, words of redirection, or the moments in which they give feedback during class. They also might review the videos to look for moments during transitions between activities when procedures are in action and ask themselves, "What do I do? What do I say? What actions do I see that appear to promote student responsibility in some way, and are there opportunities for me to expand this?" They may take notes about the energy of the classroom during these times or make general observations regarding whether students seem to be remembering how to be ready for class.

The teacher then might take time away from the classroom to reflect upon how they define the "responsibility" of the student. What do they think this should look like in a dance classroom? What does it mean to them? How do they feel when they perceive students are or are not "taking responsibility"? Alternatively, they may write or record narratives about their own learning experiences and times when they were expected to "take responsibility" as a student. They might review their reflections and analysis with a colleague, or they may invite that colleague to watch them teach and then have a conversation about how their colleague views their communication in relation to the idea of "student responsibility." They might find that what they mean by "responsibility" is actually more related to "behaving well," which may alter the research question.

In addition, they might analyze their own written reflections and notes, identifying themes that arise about "taking," "giving," "allowing," or "telling" students what to do. They might choose to review the photos of the signs in their classroom and compare them with the themes they find in their video and audio recordings, reflections, and conversations with colleagues. The goal of the researcher is to unearth patterns, teaching actions, and personal perceptions to understand what they are doing and how they are communicating classroom procedures, all in relation to the burgeoning idea of "promoting student responsibility."

These approaches overlap and are complex, and the researcher may choose only one or two of them when conducting a self-study because of how established literature has guided them, the amount of time they have for the study, or other relevant factors. The processes are moreover recursive in nature – they weave through, back, and around – and they do not progress in a linear fashion when it comes to the use of methods, reflection, and analysis. Some consider research questions in teacher self-study as a kind of initiating a question and feel that "the process of self-study can provoke a significant change in the questions being asked. Thus, the methods selected for use in a study are not solely or inevitably driven by the nature of the research questions as is the case in more traditional forms of research" (Tidwell, Heston, and Fitzgerald 2009, xiii). However, the goal of the self-study approach remains the methodical documentation and gathering of information about the teacher and their practice, the analysis of this data, and the making of pedagogical changes as informed by the findings that arise from the analysis.

Self-Study Data Generation Methods

In this section, I offer a list of data generation methods that a dance education researcher might use when instituting a teacher self-study within a dance classroom. These approaches, procedures, and ways of collecting data can be combined or altered to fit certain types of research and to authentically capture what is under study. For dance educators, some of these methods might seem more creative and embodied, while others are more traditional with their focus on writing. Some methods offer researchers the opportunity to use the creative process in relationship to others and the environment as a site for knowledge creation and analysis.

Patricia Leavy, an arts-based researcher and author, calls for the harnessing of the creative processes in qualitative methodology: "The emerging tools [methods] adapt the tenets of the creative arts in order to address social research questions in *holistic* and *engaged* ways in which *theory and practice are intertwined*" (2015, ix, emphasis in original). Dance educators, with their choreographic and performative processes, are already well versed in creating as an act of discovery and inquiry, and they are uniquely poised to use teacher self-study to find new ways of seeing and interpreting the world around them. Some of the self-study methods mentioned here allow the researcher to free themselves from textual documentation (if they so choose) and to adopt ways to reflect upon and understand their actions in the classroom using a variety of modalities.

Photovoice

The photovoice method is borrowed from participatory research, in which participants take photos to document and reflect upon their perceived reality and lived experiences. This method can be used by educators to document their teaching spaces and moments as a type of photographic field note or to figuratively, abstractly, or metaphorically illustrate meanings and ideas that are hard to describe with words.

Collage

Collage in a teacher self-study can include collecting images and words from magazines or websites or gathering found objects that pertain to the inquiry at hand to then be arranged on a poster board or canvas. The goal is to create a visual representation of words and images that give meaning to or provide a connection between the ideas in a study. Capturing an idea in a way that words alone cannot and engaging in meaning-making through the visual are critical to collage.

Video Recordings

Video recordings can be used similarly to photography as a method for collecting visual field notes in order for a researcher to watch their teaching unfold over the course of an activity or a whole lesson. Video can also be used to watch oneself during moments in between formal teaching (e.g. in the hall, during breaks to prepare), if need be. Video can serve as a tool to analyze things such as atmosphere, sense of community, use of classroom space, how engagement ebbs and flows, or the teacher's emotional and facial expressions or bodily movements. Video can allow the researcher to widen their view of the classroom to take in the whole space "from afar," or it can narrow the focus to pinpoint moments and locations by placing the camera nearer the teacher or location being studied.

Portraiture and Landscapes

A researcher can also choose to create a portrait or a landscape in whatever medium they prefer. This could be a series of drawings or paintings created over the course of the study, or it may be a single portrait of their teaching self. This method can serve as a meaning-making tool for the researcher to see themselves in a new way, or it could be used to explore the researcher's perceptions of themselves in relation to findings through other methods in the study.

Memory Work

This method is alternately referred to as the development of memory texts, memory work, or the unearthing of memories. Because what educators do in the classroom is often built upon their memories of past experiences of teaching and learning, it may serve the researcher well to spend time thinking back and through these kinds of personal memories. In a self-study, this might look like developing questions as prompts for writing or asking a trusted teaching colleague to discuss past experiences. A researcher may include memory work (e.g. a collection of old photographs of themselves teaching, dance videos from their past) to look for metaphor and meaning arising from written and visual memories.

Storytelling

This method, which in some ways is similar to memory work, treats autobiography and storytelling as knowledge and as a way to write up findings in a study. With this method, a researcher might choose to tell a story as fictionalized, or they may make it as true to how they remember it as possible. This approach differs from memory work in that it can explore aspects of creative writing to approach knowledge that may only arise in the conceptualizing and retelling of the story itself. Particular to this method is analyzing the embeddedness of one's reality or personal identity as generated through the act of storytelling.

Journaling

With this method, the researcher journals and reflects in the moment, after each lesson, or at the end of their day in relation to the research topic. The goal is to gather the researcher's perceptions in the context and location of the research itself over time. Some self-study researchers use journaling in a very open-ended, "write anything" way, whereas others have a more directed set of reflective prompts or questions to guide their writing at the end of each teaching session. Journaling can also serve as a kind of holding place for non-objective thoughts before embarking upon the analysis of data, allowing the researcher to set aside hunches and pre-analytic ideas. This type of journaling can serve as a parallel and reflective tool for tracking the ways in which the researcher's position as the location of the study might be limiting or shading the research itself.

Field Notes

The self-study researcher may employ field notes to gather contextual information to enhance the data gathered in their study. Most often, these notes help to define the place, the time, the people involved, the power constructs, and the location in which the study unfolds. Contextual notes can also help define the energy of the classroom or school, the architectural elements of the teaching space, the general kinds of social interactions observed in the space, or the rules and policies followed or communicated at the location of study. However, the types of field notes taken are defined by the research question and the frame of the literature review.

Audio Recordings

The researcher might choose to audio record quick field notes in between teaching moments, or they might sit at the end of their day and record their thoughts and reflections about how a lesson, day, or activity went in relation to the topic under study. If the researcher is interested in their use of language, tone, volume, inflection, or means of communication, this audio method can prove especially useful for them to hear what is going on in their teaching by recording their lessons.

Reverse Interviews

With this method, the researcher prepares questions to interview themselves at key moments throughout their self-study or at the end of their research. The goal is to imagine an unknown educator as the person under study. In essence, what would it be important to know and understand about their perceptions and lived experiences in relation to the study? A researcher might audio record themselves answering each question and then transcribe and analyze the interview, or they could ask a trusted friend to serve as the interviewer and to ask follow-up questions as needed.

Movement and Dance

Educators can use dance and movement as a methodology to further their inquiry within a self-study. For example, a dance educator might identify challenges in their teaching that seem to mirror challenges in their dancemaking and then spend time exploring this perception through personal dance practice. Alternatively, a researcher might create a solo or a dance with their students as a way to explore the meaning of a particular data point or a significant finding. In the field of dance, one could choose dancemaking as the curriculum, the site, *and* the method of inquiry. This layered approach may provoke the development of new data and findings while also expanding one's teaching practice with students through the creative process. The goal is to embody and come to know the content under study that otherwise cannot be put into words or visual representation.

Analysis of the Self-Study Data

Analysis of the data collected using the methods described in the previous section can be completed in a number of ways. For more traditional methods (e.g. note-taking, journaling, audio or video recordings), one might choose to create analytical memos to make note of ideas and reflections when listening to or reading the collected data. These memos can then support theorizing toward pedagogical change and understanding. For artistic methodologies that result in creative works, the researcher might begin the analysis by viewing these works in a specific order, grouping them in a particular way, or having discussions with a trusted colleague to identify and interpret ideas that can be found in the work itself or in the process of creating. The goal is to view the work intently and then to reflect and find ideas within. This is quite like the way in which a choreographer might work with movement by arranging and rearranging to see and understand the dance in a new way, to understand its world, and its meaning. The collage, dance, photograph, or work of visual art can *be* data, or its creation can serve as a means of analyzing data through the exploration of imagery, meaning, and interpretation as the work is created.

Limitations and Ethical Considerations of the Self-Study

I offer to the reader some guiding considerations in terms of the ethics and limitations of teacher self-study. Remember that the methods described in this chapter can be in conversation with one another and that the analysis of data should attempt to connect the teaching location, context, and content being taught with an exploration of the teacher's perceptions and experiences as they relate to pedagogical improvement. Because perceptions and lived experiences can bring forth multiple ways of knowing within the same location, a definitive truth for all involved in the educator's study cannot be proclaimed. If the researcher attempts to offer a universal truth or a grand theory for all educators, then the research is likely flawed.

I urge researchers to write up their self-studies to communicate to their readers that, at its core, the study cannot be objective. They should provide space in the telling of their research to be transparent about how they wrestled with personal feelings, assumptions, and a lack of objectivity. Honestly naming and framing one's positionality and ways in which they worked to be reflexive are essential practices. The study becomes more valid and usable if the reader understands what was challenging to the researcher, what may have shaded the findings, and how the researcher dealt with these issues.

There are particular dilemmas that can arise with this type of study. Great care should be taken to be clear about how information was gathered, to clarify that the data gathering did not harm others or affect the delivery of instruction, and to state that no identifying information was obtained beyond the identity of the teacher. The care of students must be ensured. How much do we share with them about the study? Do we tell them that we are conducting research? There is no one correct answer to these questions and the ethics of student care must always be at the center of one's answer. If self-study is fully and wholly centered on the teacher (for example, a study about preparing lessons) it is not necessarily important to inform students. For other self-studies, informing students and including them as co-collaborators to get their feedback and ideas about the process as it unfolds is not only smart but ethical, especially if the study introduces practices or actions that deviate from the accepted norm. However, for some studies in which curriculum or teaching practices are being studied, informing students might alter the way the new lessons or strategies are experienced and thus the teaching situation and context can be dramatically altered. If the study is primarily about teacher action, student learning is not negatively affected, *and* the best possible instruction at the time is delivered, then it could be argued that students do not need to be informed especially if the teacher's actions under study will not disrupt students in any way. Additionally, if changes under study can be also categorized as informed personal and professional development for the teacher/researcher, informing students that the teacher is evaluating and researching their practice is not always required. In the same vein, can student work, images, or speech be examined or presented as part of the data gathered? In short, no. General observations of the class as a whole can be made (e.g. "Overall, students seemed to enjoy and laugh during this lesson"), and blanket assessments of student learning can be offered (e.g. "Most students completed the assignment and received high scores"). However, individual voices or words should never be used unless the research is approved by the Institutional Review Board.

It is also necessary for the written presentation of the research to include a description of who the teacher is and what brought them to this project. Background information pertaining to the inquiry should also be provided, such as the teacher's training and the number of years of experience, information about the study setting, and specific challenges of the class or the teacher's practice. These details help to inform the reader and may enlighten them regarding the methods chosen and how they are instituted; they also help the reader to understand how the research inquiry arose. Who the teacher is as a researcher and subject should never be hidden from the reader or the findings of the study. Situating oneself in the data increases the richness of the story being told, and it is this multifaceted approach that makes self-study research so valuable.

Conclusion

Personally, the integration of teacher self-study has provided a way for me to articulate and isolate particular changes, approaches, and orientations of my teaching practice in relationship to learning outcomes and the students who enter my classroom. I have been able to move from an intuitive and feelings-based approach of assessing "what works" to a more methodical evaluation of teaching that connects to particular education concepts and theoretical underpinnings. In this way, my teaching knowledge arises out of practice while also taking into account possible differences between my beliefs, values, and espoused theories and my actual "theories in action." This stance of teaching as inquiry helps me bridge the gap between theory and practice while seeing the larger and more complex situation of teaching.

While some may define research as requiring public dissemination and the ability to generalize to a wider population, all of which I believe are important, I contend that widening the concept of research as processual and as a way to strengthen personal practice is crucial to consider. Whether this is in the arts, teaching, or beyond, knowledge that is gained with systematic and well-defined analysis, even if centered on personal practice is valuable beyond its proof of generalizability, and even in cases in which it is not published. When we promote the betterment of practices in education we, in turn, lift the field and demonstrate to students and colleagues the importance of what Lee Shulman, an educational reformer and psychologist, calls the "wisdom of practice" (2004). There are multiple and varied ways to disseminate teacher self-study research and its findings: formal publishing, conferences, mentorship, etc. As the field opens to accept and value the researched wisdom of teaching practice, a wider knowledge base for diverse teaching situations and populations will be more available. How these become available may extend beyond formal and traditional publishing models.

The dance educator who embarks on teacher self-study and who chooses traditional methods along with arts-based methods will be able to create a study that takes advantage of their creative skills and critical awareness that has been uniquely developed through their own personal dance experiences. Combining methods in this way can help the self-study researcher understand their teaching experience as an embodied, creative, moving, and knowing individual within the complex arena of dance education. Alan Ovens and Dawn Garbett discuss creative writing and journaling as methods for self-study, and they capture the connection between the creative process as methodology and pedagogy well when they state that artistic methods offer "a means for making sense of the self-in-practice in ways that embrace the uncertainty, non-linearity, and inevitable 'messiness' that is inherent in pedagogical settings" (2020, n.p.). In my experience, no one understands the messiness of the creative process better than dance educators. We know how to choreograph curriculum, create teaching plans, guide moving bodies, and interact with many kinds of personalities and learning styles, all while facilitating dance learning as meaning-making for a room full of people. It is teacher self-study that can bend and form itself to the kind of non-linearity and beautiful messiness inherent in the understanding of an artistic and complex dance classroom.

Works Cited

Bullough, Robert V., Jr., and Stefinee Pinnegar. 2001. "Guidelines for Quality in Autobiographical Forms of Self-Study Research." *Educational Researcher* 30, no. 3: 13–21. https://www.jstor.org/stable/3594469.

Ham, Vince, and Ruth Kane. 2004. "Finding a Way through the Swamp: A Case for Self-Study as Research." In *International Handbook of Self-Study of Teaching and Teacher Education Practices*, edited by Jeffrey John Loughran, 103–150. New York: Springer Publishing.

Leavy, Patricia. 2015. *Method Meets Art: Arts-Based Research Practice*. New York: The Guilford Press.

Ovens, Alan, and Dawn Garbett. 2020. "Weaving Self-Studies through Journaling: A Systematic Review." In *Textiles and Tapestries: Self-Study for Envisioning New Ways of Knowing*, edited by Christi U. Edge, Abby Cameron-Standerford, and Bethney Bergh. Equity Press. Retrieved from https://edtechbooks.org/textiles_tapestries_self_study/weaving_self_studies

Palmer, Parker. 2007. *The Courage to Teach: Exploring the Inner Landscapes of a Teacher's Life*. San Francisco: Jossey-Bass.

Samaras, Anastasia P. 2011. *Self-Study Teacher Research: Improving Your Practice through Collaborative Inquiry*. Los Angeles: Sage.

Shulman, S. Lee. 2004. *The Wisdom of Practice: Essays on Teaching, Learning, and Learning to Teach*. San Francisco: Jossey-Bass.

Tidwell, Deborah L., Melissa L. Heston, and Linda M. Fitzgerald, eds. 2009. "Introduction." In *Research Methods for the Self-Study of Practice*, xiii–xxii. New York City: Springer Publishing.

Warren, John T. 2011. "Reflexive Teaching: Toward Critical Autoethnographic Practices of/in/on Pedagogy." *Cultural Studies ↔ Critical Methodologies* 11, no. 2: 139–144. https://doi.org/10.1177/1532708611401332.

18
Mixing Methods and Approaches in Dance Education Research

Matthew Henley

Introduction

As a teacher, I regularly receive assignments from students, which I then reduce to numerical or alphabetic scores in order to measure their demonstration of skills in, and knowledge of, dance-related content. Though these grades are important to students individually, the class's grades inform my overall perception of how students, in general, are learning, which affects the design of the course in the future. For instance, if, as a group, the class scored poorly on articulating-spine-in-the-frontal-plane during a mid-term assessment, I may pay more attention to scaffolding that skill in future iterations of the course. As a teacher, I also regularly get to know the students as individuals, each with their own unique ways of thinking, feeling, moving, imagining, and interacting. This experience of understanding the students as unique individuals also informs my perception of how students are learning and affects the design of future iterations of the course. For instance, after class, a student might tell me a story of learning to move her pelvis in figure-8 formation while dancing salsa in her grandmother's kitchen. That individual's story might affect the way I teach articulation-of-the-pelvis in future courses.

I offer these two brief examples because they encapsulate important components of mixed-methods research design, which is commonly considered a research approach that mixes quantitative and qualitative data collection and analysis (Creswell and Creswell, 2018). When I grade, I reduce an aspect of human experience, learning, to a numeric or alphabetic measurement and use that to inform my understanding of how the group as a whole engages with dance, a quantitative approach. When I engage with students individually, I come to know their unique context; their personality, learning style, academic progress, hopes for the future, etc. This context also informs my understanding of how students are engaging with dance, a qualitative approach. As many teachers know, though, grading the students and getting to know the students often feel like contradictory activities. A quantitative approach and a qualitative approach are not always easy to reconcile. Far from trying to position myself as unique, I hope these brief examples help all teachers to see that they are likely already engaged in proto-mixed-methods research. In this chapter, I will describe some of the theoretical frameworks that provide a more formal context for mixed-methods research and narrate my own experience navigating this research design. In a qualitative fashion, I would like to introduce you to myself in a little more detail.

My Story

My life in academia began as an undergraduate at the University of Arizona where I pursued degrees in Religious Studies and Dance. While I was there, people frequently commented on what a strange combination those degrees were. This, of course, points to a particular American post-Puritan view that presumes these two fields are contradictory, whereas throughout human history and across the globe currently, dance and religion are very closely tied together and their separation in the United States is an oddity, rather than the norm. I finished my undergraduate degrees and moved to New York City to pursue a career as a professional dancer in modern dance companies, dancing primarily with Randy James and Seán Curran. I later returned to academia via the MFA program in Dance at the University of Washington, and eventually the PhD in Educational Psychology, Learning Sciences, at the same university, an interdisciplinary degree deeply connected to the study of cognition and human development. Again, from a particular perspective, these degrees, Religious Studies, Dance, and Learning Sciences can seem quite separate. They generally sit in different academic traditions, humanities, arts, and social sciences respectively, each of which examines the human experience from a different frame than the others. Yet for me, they are all united in that they seek to better understand how people make meaning in their lives.[1]

The Religious Studies degree required equal credits in Eastern and Western religions, so I was exposed to the practices people engage in and the stories they tell themselves to give their lives meaning across courses in Latin American Christianity, American Judaism, Islamic Thought, Hindu Mysticism, and Native American Religions and Spirituality, among others. As a professional dancer, my favorite part of the job was to make meaning of and inhabit the world that was being built in the container of the dance. Performing was an important part, but I loved being in rehearsal and playing around with modifying my energy or my spatial or temporal relationship with other dancers and discovering how those subtle shifts lead to new revelations about the world of the dance that we were simultaneously inhabiting and co-creating. In graduate school, as I was taking courses in Educational Psychology, Cognitive Psychology, Developmental Psychology, and Neuroscience, I was learning how psychologists describe processes of meaning-making.

This was not an intentional path, nor one that I was necessarily aware of while I was in the midst of it, but it is one that I can recognize in hindsight and that I now embrace. For, though I recognize that these academic endeavors (Religious Studies, Dance, Learning Sciences) allow for an exploration of meaning-making as one aspect of the human experience, each one prioritizes culture, the body, and the mind in different ways and explores them through different research methodologies and pedagogical practices. This diversity of academic inquiry provided me with experiences of accepting different types of evidence in support of different types of knowledge claims. I now see that this kind of orientation is incredibly valuable when pursuing mixed-methods research.

What Is Mixed-Methods Research?

Mixed-methods refers to empirical research, that is research that collects or generates data about the sociomaterial world based on measurement or observation. Further, it is research that includes procedures for both quantitative data collection and analysis and qualitative data collection and analysis in order to explore the same phenomenon (Creswell and Creswell 2018). Quantitative data are generated by reducing aspects of human experience into individual variables which can be transformed into numerical data to be measured and analyzed mathematically. Qualitative data is primarily generated through transforming aspects of human experience into descriptive language, which is analyzed in theoretical and socio-historical context. A mixed-methods project would include one quantitative and one qualitative methodology.[2] Importantly, in the designation mixed-methods, there is an implication that empirical data will be collected on persons, groups, or institutions via observation, interview, or some other instrument.

This answer, though, can be made more complicated. First, it is possible to mix methods but remain in a qualitative or quantitative paradigm. Method refers to the procedures used within a methodology. The methods used to analyze data in ethnography are different from the methods used to analyze data for phenomenology. A project, therefore, which proposes to analyze data ethnographically and phenomenologically could be considered a mixed-methods project even though both aspects are qualitative. The same could be said of a project that uses both experimental design and survey. Though Creswell and Creswell

(2018) clearly define mixed-methods as a combination of qualitative and quantitative, they also use the terminology "approach" when encouraging researchers to select a qualitative, quantitative, or mixed-methods design. They explain that beyond having different procedures for data collection and analysis, each approach entails a different philosophical framework. For this reason, I sometimes use the term mixed-approach when using both qualitative and quantitative data as it reinforces the idea that the quantitative and qualitative data need to be approached from different epistemological perspectives rather than only including different procedures. Taken further, if the design includes, for instance, choreographic analysis from dance studies or choreographic explorations from dance practice research, then it extends the approach, including philosophical frameworks and methods, beyond the social sciences and into the humanities and arts respectively, in which case mixed-approach might not be a sufficient designation. Perhaps that is when the term inter/cross-disciplinary would become appropriate.

Though this might seem like hair-splitting, and I am not trying to stake a claim on new terminology, or suggest that I have arrived at the perfect (or even viable) solution, words are important, and I believe that no matter what terminology is chosen, these kinds of issues should be carefully considered when designing a research project. If we return, then, to the suggestion that mixed-approach research in education includes both quantitative and qualitative data collection and analysis, I have suggested that these two approaches are rooted in different philosophical frameworks or epistemological perspectives. Generally, quantitative research is post-positivist in nature. Positivist research seeks to reduce phenomena to individual components, called variables, in order to measure and describe the relationships between them through mathematical formulae, in order to discover universal, or at least generalizable, truths. Post-positivism adopts the first aspects of positivism, the reduction of experience to component parts in order to measure and describe their relationship through mathematical formulae, but it rejects the idea that universal truth can be found (Creswell and Creswell 2018; Merriam 2009). This is why, for instance, in most social science research, if the researcher tests the relationship between variables that they propose, what is called a hypothesis, and statistical analysis returns the results they were hoping for, they reject the null hypothesis, or the opposite of what they proposed, rather than confirm their hypothesis, or accept the relationship they did propose. This is a subtle distinction that nods to the idea that, through analysis, we can more confidently describe what is not true, while leaving what is True (capitalization intentional) open to further investigation. Qualitative research on the other hand is constructivist in nature. Constructivist research seeks to understand phenomena by richly describing how they are constructed in situated socio-historical contexts. These descriptions allow us to understand the phenomena being researched in more complicated and nuanced ways, while recognizing that the findings do not necessarily apply to everyone (Merriam 2009).

At this point, we have an important distinction. Quantitative research seeks to better understand a phenomenon by reducing it to component parts that can be measured and analyzed, and generalized, and qualitative research seeks to richly describe the same phenomenon as it emerges in unique contexts. Measuring and describing, as research outcomes, are not simply about the type of data that is collected, they reflect different underlying beliefs about how best to reveal the human experience. Connecting back to the analogy of both grading and getting to know students, they each inform a teacher's understanding of how students are learning but in very different ways.

These approaches also point to different methods of logic. Quantitative research is deductive in nature. It begins with a theory, then hypothesizes what relationships between variables would be expected to be found if that theory was correct. A research design is then set up to test those expectations. Qualitative research is inductive in nature. It begins with the observation of the phenomenon in situated contexts and after deep and prolonged data collection, themes are generated which become the foundation for a theory (Hanstein 1999). Theory testing versus theory building. Seeking patterns that generalize across a group versus richly describing an individual's or group's experience. Mixed-approach research offers the researcher the opportunity to engage in both of these activities around the same phenomenon.

I think of the modes of research in terms of two different metaphors. Quantitative research is like throwing a ball. Across the field, you can see the goal that you are supposed to hit so you organize yourself to throw the ball and hit the target. Once you release the ball you have no more control and must watch it sail across the field and either hit or miss the target. In quantitative research the hypothesis is the goal, a method for data collection is designed to reach that goal and once data collection begins, the researcher must let the process play out to see if the ball reaches the target or misses. Qualitative research is like walking around in the dark with a flashlight. As you move around and shine the flashlight in different directions, you slowly begin to build up an understanding of the space you are in and depending on what you find, you will begin to navigate the space and use the flashlight in more intentional ways. In qualitative research you might know some things about the phenomenon you seek to study but by observing, conversing, and participating you come to develop a richer and fuller understanding. Next, I'd like to tell the story of my ball-throwing and flashlight shining.

My Journey in Mixed-Methods

My inquiry began, as I suppose it often does for teachers, in the classroom. When teaching in the studio, I noticed variations in students' ability to solve the movement tasks and perform the movement sequences that I was providing. There were some students who were excellent, some who were doing a good job, and some who had lots of room for improvement. There are many potential explanations for this variation. One possible explanation is that some students are more "talented" than others: that some are good dancers and others are not. We could likely make this explanation more sophisticated and wonder if the higher achieving dancers have more developed physical competencies such as greater strength, flexibility, and/or the ability to access more complex neuromuscular patterns. These are valid explanations but they focus exclusively on output, meaning their explanation for student variation begins at the point when students start moving. I began to wonder if part of the explanation might come before movement execution, at the stage when students were observing, listening, and rehearsing; in other words, at the stage when they were making sense (again meaning-making!) of the movement material. Aha! Now I have a phenomenon: student-sensemaking in the modern dance classroom.

At the time this inquiry crystallized I was in graduate school and taking classes in psychology and educational psychology, and these fields began to frame my inquiry. I arrived at the phenomenon of perceptual-cognitive skills, or the ways that we transform sensing into knowing at the psychological and neuroscientific levels. If I had been taking classes in a different area I might have framed my inquiry in a different way. For instance, if I was in sociology I might have wondered how factors such as the students' race, class, and gender aligned with or diverged from my own, providing a form of social capital that lead to different levels of achievement. This is an excellent line of inquiry, but with a very different frame.

Being in a College of Education, I was very aware of the quantitative/qualitative divide. As I began to pursue this line of inquiry, I had to decide: Did I want to throw a ball at a target? Or did I want to shine a flashlight around? An important consideration at this point was how that target got set up, or how the hypothesis was formed. As part of the positivist/post-positivist/scientific tradition, I couldn't simply make up a hypothesis, it had to emerge from existing peer-reviewed research. Therefore, I had to determine if I could construct and defend a hypothesis based on existing studies.

The study of cognitive-perceptual expertise began with master chess players. In a series of studies (Chase and Simon 1973), expert and novice chess players were shown configurations of pieces on a chess board for 5 seconds and were then asked to recreate the configurations. It was found that the experts recalled the placement of pieces more accurately than novices, but only if the configurations were meaningful, that is, corresponded to configurations that would actually occur during gameplay. If the pieces were randomly configured the experts and novices performed the same. This suggests that experts don't necessarily have greater capacity in short-term memory, but rather that they rely on domain-specific knowledge to recognize associations between pieces. These associations allow experts to group multiple pieces into "chunks" facilitating recognition and recall. For instance, if pieces were part of a recognizable defense or attack pattern commonly used in chess, then the experts only needed to recall the placement of the pattern, not the placement of each individual piece.

These findings were replicated across different sports as experts and novices in basketball (Allard, Graham, and Paarsalu 1980), field hockey (Starkes 1987), volleyball (Borgeaud and Abernethy 1987), and rugby (Nakagawa 1982) were shown and asked to recall configurations of players on the field/court. As with chess, the experts outperformed the novices, but only with meaningful configurations. The findings were then replicated in individual sports such as tennis (Goulet, Bard, and Fleury 1989), badminton (Abernethy and Russell 1987), and karate (Williams and Elliot 1999), in which experts were able to chunk the position of an opponent's body parts in order to better predict the outcome of their behavior (e.g. where the ball, birdie, or kick would land). It was also found that musicians could recall longer sequences of random notes if particular configurations of those notes were more commonly used in music with which the musician had familiarity (Kauffman and Carlsen 1989). The paradigm was eventually adopted in dance in a series of studies that showed expert ballet dancers were better able to recall sequences of movement when the movement was "choreographed" rather than randomly ordered (Starkes et al. 1987). This result, however, was not replicated with modern dancers who recalled sequences equally between choreographed and random conditions (Starkes et al. 1990). Overall, these studies provide evidence for a theory that experience facilitates recognition and recall by chunking individual items of analysis according to domain-specific regularities. "Chunking," then, is a mechanism associated with expert perception, but according to the expertise research, it was unclear what, specifically, modern dancers were chunking. I had the beginning of a theory, but wanted more evidence before formulating a hypothesis.

At the time, I was also reading literature in neuroscience, particularly the research of Emily Cross and Beatriz Calvo-Merino who were conducting studies on neural correlates of expert perception in dance. Their studies were an extension of an earlier theory that there are two neural pathways for visual perception (Goodale and Westwood 2004). One pathway leads to the temporal cortex and facilitates object recognition, known as the "what" pathway, and a second pathway that leads to the parietal cortex and facilitates object interaction, known as the "where/how" pathway. In a variety of experiments, Cross and Calvo-Merino were able to demonstrate that when novices watch dance, neural activity occurs primarily in the "what" pathway and as an individual gains more experience in a particular dance form there is an increase in activity in the "how" pathway while watching that dance form (Calvo-Merino et al. 2006, 2010; Cross et al. 2006, 2009). Importantly, the parietal cortex has many connections to the motor cortex through what is variously called the simulation circuit, mirror neurons, or the Action Observation Network, in which action and perception resonate. Taken together, these studies suggest that as one gains experience in dance they begin to visually perceive it differently due to shifts in neural processing, which then affects how they perform via the simulation circuit, which then affects how they perceive, and on and on in a feed-forward reciprocal pattern.

These studies informed my hunch that differences in ability in the dance classroom were a function of not only physical abilities, but also of sensemaking competencies. The cognitive-perceptual evidence suggested that the skilled dancers might facilitate recognition and recall of dance phrases by "chunking" domain-specific regularities, a process that the neuroscientific literature suggests is associated with a shift in visual processing to the parietal cortex and higher activity in the Action Observation Network. The literature supported my hunch that there were sensemaking differences between novices and experts. The literature, however, did not provide me with enough evidence to justify an explanation of what, specifically, those differences were for modern dancers. I was not able to conceive of and justify how I might set up an experimental paradigm in order to measure and test those differences. In terms of my analogy, I knew what the target was but I didn't know how to organize my actions in order to throw the ball and hit the target (a statement that is generally true of me in all sports-ball-related contexts). I, therefore, picked up a flashlight.

The first round of data collection was for a final class project for a course I was taking on expertise. It was guided by the research questions: How do novice and expert dancers describe a short movement phrase? What are the similarities and differences in the descriptions of the two groups? In order to collect data, I recruited two modern dance experts (20+ years of professional experience) and two novices (less than one year of training). I put them in pairs (1 expert, 1 novice), had them watch a 30-second video of a solo dancer performing modern dance choreography, and then filmed them as they responded to the question: "What do you remember?" I transcribed the dialogue and allowed the participants to check for accuracy. After reading through the transcripts multiple times, themes began to emerge. First, the novices tended to describe the phrase as a series of discrete actions to accomplish, that is, "the dancer does a, and then b, and then c." In contrast, experts tended to describe larger structures in the movement, i.e. "in this section of the phrase, the dancer was trying to do x." Second, the language of the experts tended to be more descriptive than the novices' language. For instance, the novices used descriptions similar to "she circled her ribs" whereas the experts recalled the dancer "circling her ribs clockwise" or "circling her ribs slowly at first and then accelerating" or "circling her ribs smoothly." These descriptions could be organized in themes of space, time, and force. The first finding then, that experts grouped multiple movements into a larger phrase that has internal coherency, is a validation of the evidence that experts "chunk" information according to domain-specific regularities. The second finding suggests that those domain-specific regularities are related to the perception of space, time, and force.[3] Through qualitative inquiry, I was able to build a theory that expert dancers in this study "chunk"-ed information about action, space, time, and force to aid in recognition and recall.

My next research project (Henley 2014) sought to test if this theory applied to a larger population. This, according to Creswell and Creswell (2018), is sequential exploratory mixed-methods research. In this version of mixed methods, qualitative research comes first in order to empirically explore a phenomenon with the goal of better defining the important variables and the relationships between them. This is followed by a confirmatory phase of quantitative research. I knew what the target was and I was pretty sure I knew how to get myself organized to throw the ball and hit it. The hypothesis that drove this research was that expert modern dancers would perform better than novice modern dancers at recalling spatial, temporal, and force-based elements of a dance phrase. For this research, I recruited 12 expert and 12 novice modern dancers and asked them to watch 30 seconds of a solo modern dance phrase. They then completed a questionnaire that I created asking participants to recall spatial, temporal, force-based, and shape-based questions about the phrase. Examples of questions were:

- Shape: At the end, the dancer has one hand on her belly and one hand on her: (a) shoulder, (b) cheek, (c) forehead, (d) I don't remember.
- Space: The dancer circles her ribs and then rotates or pivots in space. What was the degree of this rotation (a) 90°, (b) 180°, (c) 270°, (d) 360°, (e) I don't remember.
- Time: The dancer wraps both arms around the front of her body, then opens the left arm to the side, and at this point, the tempo of the movement: (a)

accelerates, (b) decelerates, (c) remains the same, (d) stops, (e) I don't remember.
- Effort: While facing the side, the dancer's left arm is on her shoulder, she then moves her right arm across the front of her body to her right hip. Which verb best describes the quality of that movement? (a) Slash, (b) Float, (c) Glide, (d) Punch, (e) I don't remember.

After statistical analysis, I found that experts performed significantly better than novices on the assessment overall and on the spatial questions. There were no significant differences between novices and experts on the temporal, force-based, or shape-based questions. Though these results were promising, a major limitation existed, namely that in both the qualitative and quantitative phases, the participants were asked to demonstrate recognition and recall through verbal methods (e.g. talking about the phrase or reading and answering questions about the phrase). It could be that experts and novices had a similar recall of spatial aspects of the phrase, but the experts were better than the novices at languaging the spatial qualities.

For my dissertation (Henley 2013, 2015) then, I set out to devise a data collection instrument that would allow me to measure cognitive-perceptual differences between novices and experts while minimizing the impact of verbal mediation. This research was led by a hypothesis similar to the previous study, that expert modern dancers would perform better than novice modern dancers at recalling spatial and temporal elements of a dance phrase. Force-based elements were dropped from the hypothesis. In the previous study, force was operationalized through Laban's concept of effort, which is a framework for conceptualizing and enacting aspects of force (Newlove and Dalby 2003). Familiarity with this framework is its own kind of expertise, overlapping with, but not identical to, expertise in modern dance. In the design of the study, there was much debate among advisors and close dance colleagues about what might replace Laban's effort as a structure to analyze the perception of force and it was decided we didn't know enough at the time to inform the instrument development so it was dropped from the hypothesis.

For this study, I modified a common paradigm in psychology in which participants are presented with two stimuli and asked if there is a difference between them. If there is a difference between the stimuli, but the participant does not recognize it, then it is assumed that the participant was not attending to, or is not able to attend to, that quality (Levin and Simons 1997). A simple example is a person who is color-blind and is presented with two color patterns that are objectively different but contain colors that their color-blindness keeps them from distinguishing. They would claim "no difference" when in reality, there was. Using the same logic, I created pairs of short dance phrases in which an element of space, time, or shape was manipulated between the two phrases. Manipulations to space included, for instance, a circle of the arm clockwise in the first phrase and counterclockwise in the second phrase. Manipulations to time included altering the duration of two movements within the phrase so that the overall duration of the phrase remained the same, but the internal timing shifted. Manipulations to shape included the alteration of bodily position, for instance, a flexed elbow in the first phrase became an extended elbow in the second phrase. I recruited 40 participants (20 experts, 20 novices) who were asked to watch 32 paired phrases back to back, then indicate on a questionnaire if they noticed a difference between the two, and if so, to which category the difference belonged.

After statistical analysis, it was found that there were no differences between experts and novices at recognizing manipulations to shape, but experts performed significantly better than novices at recognizing manipulations to space and time. Though replication with a larger and more diverse sample of modern dancers would be needed before any strong claims could be made, this evidence did suggest that there were indeed cognitive-perceptual differences between novice and expert dancers; that when a novice and an expert watch a dance phrase, they "see" something different. Further, the data suggest that the domain-specific regularities that expert modern dancers use to facilitate recognition and recall through the "chunk"-ing of meaningful information are, at least in part, temporal and spatial cues.

My studies were correlational, not causational, meaning they found a relationship between years of experience and expert perception, but they did not demonstrate that years of experience caused expert perception. The causal influence could, in fact, be the opposite direction, some people might be better than others at perceiving the spatial and temporal aspects of movement and this ability facilitates success and, in turn, long careers in dance. Though the reality is likely a combination of both nature and nurture, an experiment would help determine causality. Additionally, it was unclear if the experts were aware of their expert abilities. As much of dance expertise, including expert perception, is developed through patterned practice, dance knowledge, in large part, remains procedural and implicit. We attempted to address this by including an open-ended question asking the participants to share strategies they developed across the assessment in order to be successful. This added a qualitative method to the research project, but not a qualitative approach, as the data was superficial and did not provide me with the evidence to describe the phenomenon in rich, situated context. This simultaneous mixed-methods approach, I have found, is very challenging, and I prefer to move between approaches in sequence.

Research after the Dissertation

A possible research trajectory after the initial findings of my dissertation would have been to refine and validate the data collection instrument and replicate the study with a larger and more diverse sample. However, I got a job. This affected my research trajectory in two ways. The first is that my position at Texas Woman's University (TWU), an institution that prioritizes teaching, had a very heavy teaching and service load, limiting time and capacity to engage in research. This, I know from talking to colleagues, is all too common in dance in tertiary education. The second effect that TWU had on my research was to bring the impact of culture on student sensemaking more clearly into focus. My studies up to that point were largely informed by cognitive psychology and neuroscience, fields in social science that seek to explain human experience according to general or universal principles that are moderately impacted by socio-historical context (Kagan 2009). At TWU, I became immersed in dialogue about dance that was more deeply rooted in the humanities where socio-historical context is foregrounded in explanations of human experience. I was also immersed in a culture with a student body that was culturally, geographically, and experientially diverse, calling into question the generalizability of my findings. These factors prompted me to return to qualitative inquiry, in what Creswell and Creswell (2018) would refer to as explanatory mixed-methods research. This indicates a research trajectory in which results of quantitative inquiry that speak to the quantification of an aspect of human experience at the population level are more thoroughly explained through qualitative description of the same phenomenon in a situated context.

Researching the Classroom

As I moved into my teaching position at TWU, and was more regularly in the dance practices studio, I found myself confronted with the situation that initiated this line of inquiry: some of the students were excellent, some were doing a good job, and some had lots of room for improvement. At first, I saw it as an opportunity to put into practice the implications of my research, that the development of expertise in dance was, in part, based on the development of cognitive-perceptual skills. In my previous research, I found a difference between novices' and experts' cognitive-perceptual abilities, but I didn't have an explanation for how that difference came about, nor did an existing theory support the development of a testable hypothesis, I, therefore, picked up a flashlight again and designed qualitative studies, and because my job kept me closely tied to the classroom, the studio became my lab. One study (Henley, in manuscript) was based on observational data and addressed the question: "How do students learn new concepts in the modern dance classroom?" After filming several hours of a modern dance class, I and another experienced modern dance educator closely viewed the footage for moments when students seemed to be physically grappling with movement instruction from the teacher. Though there was great variety in these responses, we noticed two patterns. In one pattern, what we refer to as top-down, the student's behavior indicated that they understood but needed time and repetition to physically integrate the instruction from the teachers. In the second pattern, what we refer to as bottom up, the student's behavior indicated that they did not understand, or were not able to address, the teacher's instruction, but through repetition and visual and verbal feedback, slowly integrated the instructions.

In a second study (Henley and Conrad 2021), I wanted to expand the form of data collection to include the students' first-person perspectives. Led by the research question "How do students describe their sensemaking experiences in the modern dance classroom?" I interviewed 16 dance majors directly after taking a modern dance class. These were semi-structured interviews guided by the questions: What happened in class today? Was anything new or challenging? What did you do when you encountered that challenge? Robin Conrad and I analyzed the interviews and identified three themes: the relationship between the teacher's pedagogy and the students' thinking, the fluid boundary between body and mind, and the attentional challenges of learning in a dance classroom. In a final ongoing study, Denise Purvis and I are combining these modalities, observing a modern dance class and collecting the students' first-person experiences via in-class assignments in order to build a more ecological understanding of student sensemaking. Though some of these projects are, at the time of publication, still ongoing, what is emerging is that whether perception or action leads the process of change; physical practice and attentional awareness are two sides of the same coin.

Grappling with Context

The second effect of my time at TWU was that I was offered the opportunity to more intentionally consider the role of culture and context in the interpretation of my dissertation research. I had demonstrated that, at least among my sample, modern dancers were better than novices at recognizing the spatial and temporal elements of a modern dance phrase. Looked at from a particular lens, this should be unsurprising, given that a good deal of the teaching of American modern dance has been influenced by Laban's theories, which foreground external spatialization (Newlove and Dalby 2003), or Maxine Sheets-Johnstone's phenomenology of dance, which she describes as an illusion of spacetimeforce (2015). These theories, in turn, reflect Euro-American metaphysics, or descriptions of reality that are based on the observation and measurement of time, space, and causality. Rather than demonstrating a general principle about the relationship between perception and production, my dissertation study demonstrated that students learned to pay attention to what they were taught to pay attention to. Or put another way, our observations reflect back to us what our culture values. This begs the question, what do other dance forms pay attention to? If, in particular cultural contexts, dance is a concentration of internal energies rather than an externalization of spatial intentions; or a channel to connect the ancestors, the living, and the yet-to-be-born rather than an illusion of spacetimeforce, then what cognitive-perceptual expertise is developed alongside the learning of those dances?

I feel very lucky to be able to explore this question more deeply with two valued colleagues. For the past six years, I have been invited as a guest teacher to the International Dance Day Festival in Lebanon, hosted by Dr. Nadra Assaf and Lebanese American University. Upon arriving in Byblos, I was immediately enamored, and have grown more so, with my loud, proud, loving, and, sometimes, volatile Lebanese friends. This disposition was present across contexts: in the classroom, at the dinner table, on the highway, walking through the *souk*, and on the stage. I could see their ways of thinking in their ways of dancing. My curiosity around this phenomenon has formalized into a collaborative ethnographic/biographical study of how Nadra developed and translated her American modern dance training to fit Lebanese bodies, personalities, and aesthetics. Put another way, how did she make sense of modern dance in Lebanese culture? In my own observations and in interviews with Nadra and several dancers who have worked with her for decades, a dance is described by and valued for its ability to express passion, to move fluidly, and to bring a community together around an important issue. Correspondingly, part of Nadra's purpose in bringing modern dance to Lebanon was to create a safe space where, in the aftermath of a civil war, Lebanese citizens across religious boundaries could come together to express their grief and find beauty in the land, in the culture, and in each other. Dancing, in this context, orients these dancers toward resilience and agency.

I have also been invited by my colleague Aadya Katikar to collaborate on the creation of a professional development curriculum for K-12 dance teachers in the National Capital Territory of Delhi, India. If, as my research indicates, patterned practice and expert perception are related, then building a curriculum around Euro-American frameworks for understanding dance would be misaligned with the practice of dance in India. We are, therefore, interviewing teachers and principals in the school system where the professional development will be offered in order to more deeply understand how dance education is enacted in that unique context. One finding emerging from these interviews is the complex task teachers are faced with when placing classical Indian forms, which are often taught through rote repetition, alongside Euro-American dance education practices, which prioritize student-centered/Laban-driven creative dance-making practices. Does altering the traditional pedagogy fundamentally change the essence of a dance? As the professional development is put into practice we will engage in an iterative process of simultaneous mixed-methods research in which we will collect quantitative and qualitative data on teachers' experiences and the effectiveness of the curriculum in order to revise the curriculum toward culturally sustaining practices.

Moving Forward

In this chapter, I have narrated how a personal interest of mine, the phenomenon of sensemaking, came into focus as a result of my conviction as a teacher that the development of expertise in dance is not solely based on a student's ability to execute movement, but also depends on their ability to make sense of what the teacher is asking of them. I have attempted to build theories of sensemaking in the dance classroom through qualitative data collection and analysis and to test if those theories apply to populations through quantitative data collection and analysis (to shine a flashlight and throw a ball, in the case of my second analogy). Across this research what is emerging is a view of dance education as a process of developing culturally situated shared patterns of attention through patterned physical practices. Or, to put it another way, dancing is a technology for developing culturally situated thinking. I, and others, will continue to develop this framing through research that seeks to understand dance education practices in diverse communities and across the lifespan, as well as research that measures and tests the impact of dance education in different populations. It is my hope that this research aligns with and extends teaching practices and empirical research agendas that generate impactful stories and measures causal effects that advocate for dance education as a vital practice for all students; socially, emotionally, physically, spiritually, and intellectually.

Notes

1 This is not the ONLY topic these fields explore, it is just the one that I chose/ended up on.
2 Within education research, quantitative methodologies are generally grouped into experimental design, correlational design, and survey. The most common qualitative methodologies are ethnography, phenomenology, case study, narrative inquiry, and grounded theory.

3 Historically and contemporarily, a good deal of philosophical and pedagogical framing of modern dance focuses on the ideas of space, time, and force. European metaphysics, in turn, is deeply concerned with space, time, and causality. This finding, then, reinforces the idea that participation in a cultural practice, such as modern dance, shapes what one attends to while engaged in that practice. Different categories would likely emerge when studying different dance practices and those categories would likely reflect the cultures' metaphysical orientations.

Works Cited

Abernethy, Bruce, and David G. Russell. 1987. "Expert-Novice Differences in an Applied Selective Attention Task." *Journal of Sport Psychology* 9, no. 4: 326–345. https://doi.org/10.1123/jsp.9.4.326.

Allard, Fran, Sheree Graham, and Maret E. Paarsalu. 1980. "Perception in Sport: Basketball." *Journal of Sport Psychology* 2, no. 1: 14–21. https://doi.org/10.1123/jsp.2.1.14.

Borgeaud, Phil, and Brace Abernethy. 1987. "Skilled Perception in Volleyball Defense." *Journal of Sport Psychology* 9, no. 4: 400–406. https://doi.org/10.1123/jsp.9.4.400.

Calvo-Merino, Beatriz, Julie Grèzes, Daniel E. Glaser, Richard E. Passingham, and Patrick Haggard. 2006. "Seeing or Doing? Influence of Visual and Motor Familiarity in Action Observation." *Current Biology* 16, no. 19: 1905–1910. https://doi.org/10.1016/j.cub.2006.07.065.

Calvo-Merino, Beatriz, Shantel Ehrenberg, Delia Leung, and Patrick Haggard. 2010. "Experts See It All: Configural Effects in Action Observation." *Psychological Research* 74, no. 4: 400–406. https://doi.org/10.1007/s00426-009-0262-y.

Chase, William G., and Herbert A. Simon. 1973. "Perception in Chess." *Cognitive Psychology* 4, no. 1: 55–81. https://doi.org/10.1016/0010-0285(73)90004-2.

Creswell, John W., and J. David Creswell. 2018. *Research Design: Qualitative, Quantitative, and Mixed Methods Approaches*. Los Angeles: Sage.

Cross, Emily S., Antonia F. De C. Hamilton, and Scott T. Grafton. 2006. "Building a Motor Simulation de Novo: Observation of Dance by Dancers." *NeuroImage* 31, no. 3: 1257–1267. https://doi.org/10.1016/j.neuroimage.2006.01.033

Cross, Emily S., David J.M. Kraemer, Antonia F. De C. Hamilton, William M. Kelley, and Scott T. Grafton. 2009. "Sensitivity of the Action Observation Network to Physical and Observational Learning." *Cerebral Cortex* 19, no. 2: 315–326. https://doi.org/10.1093/cercor/bhn083.

Goodale, Melvyn A., and David A. Westwood. 2004. "An Evolving View of Duplex Vision: Separate but Interacting Cortical Pathways for Perception and Action." *Current Opinion in Neurobiology*, no. 14: 203–211. https://doi.org/10.1016/j.conb.2004.03.002.

Goulet, Claude, Chantai Bard, and Michelle Fleury. 2016. "Expertise Differences in Preparing to Return a Tennis Serve: A Visual Information Processing Approach." *Journal of Sport and Exercise Psychology* 11, no. 4: 382–398. https://doi.org/10.1123/jsep.11.4.382.

Hanstein, Penelope. 1999. "Models and Metaphors: Theory Making and the Creation of New Knowledge." In *Researching Dance: Evolving Modes of Inquiry*, edited by Sondra Horton Fraleigh and Penelope Hanstein, 62–90. Pittsburgh: University of Pittsburgh Press.

Henley, Matthew. 2013. "Perception of Movement Qualities Associated with Expertise in Dance." PhD diss., University of Washington.

Henley, Matthew Kenney. 2014. "Is Perception of a Dance Phrase Affected by Physical Movement Training and Experience?" *Research in Dance Education* 15, no. 1: 71–82. https://doi.org/10.1080/14647893.2013.835124.

———. 2015. "Comparison of Shape, Space, and Time Judgments in Expert Dancers and Novices: Evidence That Production Enhances Perception." *Journal of Dance Medicine & Science* 19, no. 3: 103–109. https://doi.org/10.12678/1089-313X.19.3.103.

Henley, Matthew, and Robin Conrad. 2021. "'I'm Not Thinking about It to Understand It, I'm Thinking about It to Do It': Students' Sensemaking Experiences from the Modern Dance Classroom." *Journal of Dance Education*. Awaiting issue and page. https://doi.org/10.1080/15290824.2021.1884870.

Kagan, Jerome. 2009. *The Three Cultures: Natural Sciences, Social Sciences and the Humanities in the 21st Century*. New York: Cambridge University Press.

Kauffman, W.H., and J.C. Carlsen. 1989. "Memory for Intact Music Works: The Importance of Music Expertise and Retention Interval." *Psychomusicology: A Journal of Research in Music Cognition* 8, no. 1: 3–20. https://doi.org/10.1037/h0094235.

Levin, Daniel T., and Daniel J. Simons. 1997. "Failure to Detect Changes to Attended Objects in Motion Pictures." *Psychonomic Bulletin and Review* 4, no. 4: 501–506. https://doi.org/10.3758/BF03214339.

Merriam, Sharan B. 2009. *Qualitative Research: A Guide to Design and Implementation*. San Francisco: Jossey-Bass.

Nakagawa, Akira. 1982. "A Field Experiment on Recognition of Game Situations in Ball Games: In the Case of Static Situations in Rugby Football." *Taiikugaku Kenkyu (Japan Journal of Physical Education, Health and Sport Sciences)*, 27, no. 1: 17–26. https://doi.org/10.5432/jjpehss.KJ00003402664.

Newlove, Jean and John Dalby. 2003. *Laban for All*. New York: Routledge. https://doi.org/10.4324/9781315060002.

Sheets-Johnstone, Maxine. 2015. *The Phenomenology of Dance*. Philadelphia: Temple University Press.

Starkes, Janet L. 1987. "Skill in Field Hockey: The Nature of the Cognitive Advantage." *Journal of Sport Psychology* 9, no. 2: 146–160.

Starkes, Janet L., Janice M. Deakin, Susan Lindley, and Freda Crisp. 1987. "Motor Versus Verbal Recall of Ballet Sequences by Young Expert Dancers." *Journal of Sport Psychology* 9, no. 3: 222–230. https://doi.org/10.1123/jsp.9.3.222.

Starkes, Janet L., Marylynn Caicco, Cate Boutilier, and Brian Sevsek. 1990. "Motor Recall of Experts for Structured and Unstructured Sequences in Creative Modern Dance." *Journal of Sport and Exercise Psychology* 12, no. 3: 317–321. https://doi.org/10.1123/jsep.12.3.317.

Williams, A. Mark, and David Elliott. 1999. "Anxiety, Expertise, and Visual Search Strategy in Karate." *Journal of Sport and Exercise Psychology* 21, no. 4: 362–375. https://doi.org/10.1123/jsep.21.4.362.

Part 5
Dance Science

19
Introduction to Research in Dance Science

The Science of Movement and Choreography of Research – Evolving Methodologies in Dance Science

Margaret Wilson

At first glance, the term dance science could simply indicate the scientific study of movement. The measurement, prediction, recommendations, and evaluation of…a stylized turn? A slide to the floor? Yes, however, the science does not necessarily help us understand, or know, what the movement is. A scientific approach can analyze the mechanics of the movement – how it is performed, how it might be performed more efficiently, how to best train and prepare the dancer to perform the movement repeatedly, without risk to the body. And yet, the application of the information demands more than just measurement and analysis – it must apply to the situation or the population at hand. Whether complementary or contrasting, the scope of dance science – which at one time seemed to focus only on the physical demands of classical ballet – is expanding to encompass new research methodologies, focus on all dance forms and practices, and include all populations.

Historically, dance science had its roots in dance medicine – a field that developed in the 1970s (Ryan 1997). Medical practitioners wanted to understand the unique conditions they were seeing in the professional ballet dancers visiting their clinics. Demonstrating respect for the athletic nature of dance and noting the extreme demand for range of motion, flexibility, and endurance, they also came to understand the artistic elements. They made time to observe the dancers in classes and rehearsals to better contextualize the demand on the dancer's body to offer more appropriate support (Ho 2018). In addition to treating the dancers, the physicians wrote papers and presented their research findings at orthopedic and sports medicine conferences. A medical approach to studying dancers was launched.

Following this, physical therapists and sports science researchers began focusing on the causes of injury, analyzing the ways in which dancers were trained, and advocating for better medical support and physical training for dancers. For example, in the United States, The Harkness Center for Dance Injuries, West Side Physical Therapy, both in New York City and St. Francis Hospital in San Francisco not only provided specialized treatment for injured dancers but became leaders in dance medicine education. National and international dance companies brought medical professionals onto their board of directors, into their training facilities, and retained them backstage in the case of injury. Most professional dance companies, especially in Europe and the United States have support staff working to maintain the health and well-being of the dancers – for both individual and collective well-being – in their home theaters and during their touring season.

As an outgrowth of these initiatives, organizations dedicated to the health and well-being of dancers emerged: The International Association for Dance Medicine & Science (IADMS) and the Performing Arts Medicine Association (PAMA), Aus Dance (Australia), Tamed (Germany), Dance UK and Healthy Dancer Canada. Conferences hosted by these entities promoted the sharing of research and education. Bringing together medical professionals and dance companies, rehabilitation specialists and researchers, dancers and dance teachers to share information, the field expanded worldwide.

At the same time, professional dance training schools were employing physical therapists, massage therapists, nutritionists, and psychologists to focus on the health and well-being of developing dancers (of note, though not an exhaustive list: the National Ballet School in Toronto, Canada, National Ballet Schools in the United Kingdom and Australia, Riverdance, and ArtEZ in the Netherlands). In academic institutions, sport scientists and dance educators researching dance training began advocating for pre-season screening and supplemental conditioning programs. These efforts were designed to enhance the dancers' physical capacities and performance qualities, but also make the dancers more resistant to injury.

It is worth noting that dance educators, much earlier in the 20th century, were integrating health, wellness, and study of the body into their curriculum. Students of Margaret H'Doubler, who created the first dance major in the United States at the University of Wisconsin in the 1930s, had her students study anatomy, physiology, chemistry alongside Laban Movement Analysis (Brennan, Wilson, and Hagood 2007). H'Doubler emphasized the need to embed all this information into dance pedagogy and training. Her students developed dance programs throughout the United States, bringing dance into physical education programs, as well as into arts-focused degrees. Rather than trying to determine what dancers were doing wrong (ergo, becoming injured), the focus was on a more comprehensive plan of dance wellness and education. This created a grassroots home for dance science in academia. Earlier in the 20th century, somatic practitioners, such as Mabel Ellsworth Todd, F. Matthias Alexander, and Moshe Feldenkrais were working to understand and restore efficiency and ease in all movement. Their ideas and teachings, based on their scientific study, but with a "first-person experience" focus. Slowly somatics found a foothold in dance training, but in many cases, initially seemed at odds with dance science (Batson and Wilson 2014). Contemporary dance training integrated somatic principles in the technique class, especially in collegiate settings.

Around the world, professional, conservatory, educational, and recreational training facilities have become fertile ground for conducting and integrating research on dancers. University-level programs with a dance science curriculum have broadened the focus from a tight lens on injury to one that includes nutrition, biomechanics, psychology, dance for health, and dance for special populations. This effort has been aided by research presentations and publications (Durfee, Welsh, and Dunn 2004). Additionally, textbooks specific to dance, dance injuries, and dance training, grew from just a handful of books available before 2000, to a proliferation of resources focused on the health and well-being available to dancers, educators, and researchers (Ryan 1997; Redding 2019).

Over time, the development of the field of dance science has not only provided better medical understanding of the demands of dance, but has focused on optimizing performance, augmenting dance training, and promoting health and well-being. The influence from sport and exercise is undeniable, encouraging the use of a focused lens to understand and augment physical training, as well as understand the measurements we use, to find the best application for the information. The influence of somatic practices in dance and dance science has led to the expansion of the discipline to include first-person experience studies in dance, dance for health, and dance as a therapeutic modality. Incorporating both approaches has led to the integration of healthy practice and care in training – training at all levels – from community organizations to vocational and educational programs to professional dancers and the training of teachers. Organizations dedicated to the health and well-being of dancers can be found worldwide, including IADMS, OneDance UK, and Dance Health Finland, to name just a few.

The umbrella of dance science now includes a much wider range of styles and levels of participation than seen at the beginning, and there is a strong emphasis on inclusivity and dance for health. Although the language for describing the dance science varies by professional organization and continues to evolve through time, the focus on enhancing the health and well-being of dancers as well continues as it expands to using dance to benefit all populations.

In the precursor to this book, *Researching Dance: Evolving Modes of Inquiry*, Dr. Steven Chatfield (1999) introduced the scientific method and common research methodologies which could be used to study dance. In his chapter (well worth the reading!) his rich use of language and knowledge of the history of science and research methodologies are woven together beautifully to advocate for an analytical approach to understanding dance movement viewed as a creative process. With specific and controlled observation, dance movement can be analyzed to (1) better understand what is happening, (2) consider potential for injury with incorrect execution, and (3) enhance performance. Chatfield emphasized the need for intuition and reflective thinking as well as an ability to observe (the thing we wish to see) with carefully defined parameters for observation. His challenge to the reader was to look at the similarities between the scientific method in research and creation of a dance. Certainly, there are differences as the primary function of research is to describe, measure, analyze and contribute to our understanding of the mechanics of dance. Research is not dance, but as Chatfield notes, it supports dancing by asking questions, considering methodologies and approaches, acting on the question, reflecting on the outcomes, and providing answers on the outcomes of the action.

The following chapters in this book reveal some of the ways dance science research is continuing to expand its reach and evolve. The four chapters cover vast territory in terms of research focus and application and introduce new ideas about research streams and methodologies. Each author expands the definition of dance science by re-defining it within a landscape representing the breadth of the field as it matures.

The dialogue with Edel Quin documents her journey transitioning from a professional dancer with *Riverdance*, to dance science researcher, to teacher and mentor. Edel has developed a holistic approach to teaching and mentoring which is grounded in rigorous research methodology but is evolving as she is challenging the limitations of a sports science model for dance. Her current research with *Riverdance*, has brought her back to her dance roots, affirming her dance science training as well allowing her to explore new ways of conducting a comprehensive research. Along with her colleagues, she seeks to bring ecological validity to dance research – representing the real environments in which dancers train and perform. Balancing traditional methodologies and new directions in research, and learning from work with her students, she is contributing to the maturation of dance science as a discipline that can stand on its own.

Greg Youdan Jr. is a dancer, kinesiologist, and researcher working to improve research methodologies in dance for health interventions. Generously acknowledging the collaborative work he has participated in, he provides a primer on statistics, not only to be used as a tool, but as a way of thinking. With friendly and accessible language, he illustrates ways that statistics can inform our research planning, decision-making, interpret the findings and support our conclusions. He helps the reader conceptualize how mathematical precision strengthens the research endeavor by determining significance. However, he also advocates matching this objective data with observational, demographic, and patient-reports to provide a comprehensive picture. His holistic approach to understanding and sharing the complexity of statistical analysis is augmented through his declaration to make his own research accessible and applicable to as many people as he can.

Tomoyo Kawano uses a dance/movement therapy (DMT) approach for therapeutic change in the communities she works in. First, she introduces DMT and discusses the use of integrated mind-body interventions with clinical populations. Then, she identifies the ways in which traditional cultural and transdisciplinary non-verbal communication are vital to create a personal relationship within a therapeutic intervention environment. As a Japanese American, she seeks a method that provides cultural sensitivity, and which acknowledges her own presence in the research. Bracketing her own experience, she uses movement to non-verbally co-create a dance or dance ritual that serves as a basis for communication to share with her clients. Using embodied listening, her goal is to utilize inter-corporeal interactions which can best be examined in a physical practice. Challenging a traditional model of clinical accountability, Tomoyo uses a phenomenological approach, highlighting the somatic within the scientific and balancing the objective with the visceral. Proposing that movement and improvisation augments arts-based practices as a research tool, Tomoyo expands the reach of dance science as a means for connecting, communicating, and caring for her community.

Merry Lynn Morris's chapter, "Mobilizing Theory," details her personal journey researching the design, development, and implementation of mobile assistive technology. Although stemming from a personal experience with a family member using a wheelchair, her inquiry is also informed by her background as a dancer, kinesiologist, and movement analyst. Working with designers and engineers, her explorations resulted in the redesign of a mobile assistive device to better understand how technology can support and extend movement. Continued research with prototype models of chairs, wheel configurations, and redesign of the joystick was augmented by working with dancers with disabilities, referring to literature, and using Laban Movement Analysis. Her project was the basis of her doctoral studies and dissertation which expanded the framework of her research to advance a theoretical position of socio-spatiality. Detailing the qualitative research perspectives she employed, she reveals the personal and professional journey of being an advocate for differently abled bodies, while at the same keeping her sensitivity to movement, dance, and arts-based research.

Collectively, the four authors provide us with new touchstones which will lead to the growth and health of the discipline. First, each provides a call for understanding and expanding research methodologies. As researchers, we should know the methods and tools that have defined dance science research, including contributions from medicine and sport, statistics, movement analysis, and therapeutic modalities. However, embracing the complexity of movement or intervention, we need to select tools and methodologies which best represent the individuals and groups we are working with. In our analysis and description of movement, a comprehensive and situated perspective is necessary to attain ecological validity – the real-world situation being addressed.

Second, researcher reflection is vital. Rather than only considering or discussing the conclusions we attain from our tests and measures, understanding the role of the researcher in the research, and acknowledging that role, is vital. From selecting the method, statistical measure, intervention strategy, and design choice, the researcher is embedded in the research. Declaring this role validates the outcome.

Third, research should benefit the individual and the community. The goals of the researcher should be to benefit those they are studying with the clear understanding of the larger community, and their needs. Research should not be prescriptive, but a conversation.

Fourth, as we evolve as researchers, embracing the chaotic, messy, unknown outcome that our explorations and interventions provide gives us the opportunity to tell a more compelling story. Expanding the scope of our research to look at the whole is complex and difficult, but important.

Taken together, these four chapters are a part of the ongoing growth of dance science as a discipline. Honoring the historical focus on care for dancers' injuries and performance enhancement grounded only within quantitative methodologies, each author invites us to develop a broader, more inclusive frame for our inquiries. Providing examples of collaborative, situated, and reflective approaches to the collection, contextualization, and application of the "data," and expanding the range of dance forms and applications studied, the authors' research models – and honors – the recursive, reflective, and lived experience found in all forms of movement and dance.

Works Cited

Batson, Glenna and Margaret Wilson. 2014. *Body and Mind in Motion: Dance and Neuroscience in Conversation*. Bristol: Intellect Books.

Brennan, Mary Alice, John H. Wilson, and Thomas Hagood. 2007. *Margaret H'Doubler: The Legacy of America's Dance Education Pioneer*. Amherst, NY: Cambria Press.

Chatfield, Steven J. 1999. "Scientific Explorations in Dance." In *Researching Dance: Evolving Modes of Inquiry*, edited by Sandra H. Fraleigh and Penelope Hanstein, 124–161. Pittsburgh: University of Pittsburgh Press.

Durfee, Nicole, Thomas Welsh, and Jan Dunn. 2004. "Trends in IADMS Conference Presentations." *Journal of Dance Medicine & Science* 8, no. 3: 82–88.

Ho, M. 2018. "History of Dance Medicine." PhD diss., Harvard University.

Redding, Emma. 2019. "Dance Science." In *The Bloomsbury Companion to Dance Studies*, edited by Sherril Dodds, 199–217. London: Bloomsbury Academic.

Ryan, Allen J. 1997. "Early History of Dance Medicine." *Journal of Dance Medicine & Science* 1, no. 1: 30–34.

20
Mentoring Dance Science Research

Circling the Square – Edel Quin in Conversation with Margaret Wilson

Edel Quin and Margaret Wilson

Preface

Born out of conversational exchanges between the authors, this chapter highlights the recursive journey of an educator seeking scientific, embodied, and holistic approaches to mentoring the next generation of dance science researchers. Rather than being a "how to" manual, it is a reflection on the diverse experiences for dance science educator Edel Quin – as shared with fellow dance science educator Margaret Wilson. The conversations between Edel and Margaret have developed over years of working together, but were formalized in writing and over Zoom meetings during 2020 and 2021. The chapter focuses on Edel's experiences as a dance performer, dance science student, researcher, educator, and tutor – and how these have shaped a specific philosophy and approach to working with the next generation of dance science students. Detailed as an ongoing cycle of teaching, mentoring, researching, and reflecting, Edel describes her search for a holistic model for understanding the complexities and richness of dance science as it continues to develop as a field of study. In reflecting on her journey, and future pathway, she muses about how dance can be the "circle" that redefines the traditional boxes and squares in research that provide a comprehensive whole for the growth and future of dance science research.

Edel Quin is a dancer, dance scientist, and a dance science educator. She has danced professionally with *Riverdance* and was an original member of Henri Oguike's apprentice dance company. She completed a BA (Hons) in Dance, MSc in Dance Science, and is currently pursuing her PhD examining potential interrelationships between ecological dynamics and somatic-informed approaches to movement learning in contemporary dance. Edel was the program leader for the MSc in Dance Science at Trinity Laban Conservatoire of Music and Dance, UK, from 2012 to 2018, where she also taught dance science-related modules on the BA (Hons) Dance programs. She spent a period in a teaching exchange at the Hong Kong Academy of Performing Arts and is a regular contributor to Bern University's MAS in Dance Science. At the time of writing, Edel is the program leader of the BSc (Hons), integrated masters (MSci), and masters (MSc) programs in dance science at the University of Chichester in the United Kingdom, where she also contributes to the BA (Hons) Dance and BSc (Hons) Sports Science programs.

From Performer to Student

Edel's journey into dance science was unique. As she was transitioning from performer to student, she realized that she had been experiencing a systematic way of training dancers (from a sport science perspective) that she only later learned was a foundational tenant of dance science principles of conditioning and periodization – long before those terms were a part of dance science terminology.

> I stumbled into dance science. I had been a professional dancer with *Riverdance* when it was at the height of its popularity in the late 1990s. I toured the world, performing eight shows a week to packed arena audiences of between 3,000–8,000 people. It was intense, but it was also joyful. I was doing what I had always loved to do. The dancers in our company were very well looked after. We had a touring physiotherapist and masseur. We were provided with talks and information leaflets on warm-up and cool-down, nutrition, smoking, injury. We had a group warm-up session and cool-down session, immediately before going on and immediately after coming off stage. We had weekly group conditioning classes. We toured with exercise equipment (hand-held weights, rowing machines, fitness bikes) and we had a point rotation system.
>
> The point rotation system was designed to manage our workload. Each dance number within the show was allocated points based on the perceived physical intensity of that number. Every dancer in the company was trained to know every position in each dance number within the show. For any given performance, a dancer would be rotated into or assigned a set of dance numbers to perform in that show. The points associated with the assigned dance number for each show were then added up, ensuring that no dancer was performing a series of heavy or overly intense shows repeatedly, and that no dancers were repeatedly doing light shows. This kept the shows fresh for the dancer, and helped to distribute workload effectively across performance weeks and between dancers in the company.

> I was living dance science, but did not know it. At the time, I took this supportive and informed approach to dancer wellbeing for granted. It was all that I had known, and I assumed it was standard.

Edel's later dance experience as an apprentice in a contemporary dance company provided a very different experience for her. Her experience with *Riverdance* made her realize the value of what she had been introduced to, what was now missing, and how this would shape her educational journey.

> In my mid to late 20s and after five years of intense touring and performing I decided to retire from full-time dancing and pursue a degree in contemporary dance. During this time, I became more aware of the wider dance training and performance scene, beyond the one large scale and well-funded touring company I had known. I discovered that care for the dancer's wellbeing was not always so readily available, and that many contemporary dance performers are independent artists, often working in a project-based capacity. I began to realize that I had to take a more proactive role in the care and maintenance of my own body-mind because there was no one there to do it for me.

> Over time, I began to realize that my interest in optimizing my own potential through an understanding of my dancing body-mind had a collective term – dance science – and that it was possible to do a master's degree in this subject area. In 2004, I enrolled. The dance science programme at Trinity Laban Conservatoire of Music and Dance, under the leadership of Professor Emma Redding, opened me up to what I refer to as the doing-end of dance science. Previously I had been on the user-end, receiving information that others had generated, but now I was learning systematic methods that would help me to pursue some of the unanswered questions I had.

> Somewhat naïvely, at the time I thought being on the doing-end of dance science would provide me with definitive answers to my questions. I thought I would know how to measure, how to quantify, how to square my circling thoughts. As time went on, I realized that the more I learned, the more questions I had and that working towards finding answers was a journey, not a destination.

Translating and Transferring Knowledge and Experience

As a mentor and educator, Edel finds herself introducing dance science to a wide range of students who come from different backgrounds. Some come from sport and sport science (who thus need to learn about dance and theories of embodiment), and others from dance who are new to thinking about dance as a field of scientific study. She works with students from diverse dance backgrounds ranging from ballet to Irish, classical Indian to contemporary, musical theater to classical Chinese dance. Whereas the earliest research in dance science focused primarily on classical ballet dancers, other techniques present challenges to dance science as they show greater variability in style and physical demand. Contemporary, street, social, folk, and classical dance forms all place unique artistic and choreographic demands on the body. These demands will shape very different questions for the researcher and the answers to those questions may not be as generalizable across dance forms. Developing analytical tools and descriptive perspectives for a wide range of dance styles is vital for advancing the field of dance science.

> There is a general acknowledgement that dance science incorporates disciplines associated with human performance science, such as psychology, nutrition, biomechanics, anatomy, kinesiology, physiology, and motor learning (see also Eddy 1991). Yet this does not define dance science. Distinguished dance science researchers Sylvie Fortin and Emma Redding have noted a lack of clear definition for what dance science is. As a young field, dance science is still discovering its identity and therefore has not succumbed to a confining definition (Fortin 2005; Redding 2019).
>
> It is understandable, then, that dance science and sport science share disciplines. Both are exploring the functioning of the human body and mind in physical endeavors and challenging contexts. As an older field, somewhat akin to an older sibling, sport science offers examples to dance science of how human movement can be objectively examined and systemically observed in both laboratory and field settings. Sport science has paved the way for generating dance-specific tools of measurement, such as dance-specific fitness tests like the Dance Aerobic Fitness Test in contemporary dance (Wyon et at. 2003).
>
> (Wyon et al. 2003)

However, Edel notes that dance science is not simply sport science for dancers. In fact, she strongly takes issue with that premise.

> Defining dance science as "sport science for dancers" negates both the dancer as the central tenet of dance science and eclipses the particular cultural context that dance inhabits. When students first engage with dance science, they often come from the perspective of dancer – someone who dances. They have embodied knowing of what it means to dance and a lived experience of their dance training, learning, competing, and performing, to date. They are curious. They have questions, often which the act of dancing alone cannot fully satisfy for them.
>
> They choose to pursue dance science, not sport science, nor physical education, but dance science, because it resonates with their dancer identity and their desire to apply their knowledge specifically within a dance context. Thus, dance science is more than "sport science applied to dance;" it is

a way of knowing about dance through dance that embraces theoretical, scientific, and practical perspectives.

Edel's experience as a dancer and consumer of a dance science education has shaped her pedagogy in tutoring her students in direct and indirect ways. Her first introduction to research methodologies in her master's dance science program was in a model based on sport science, with a dominant focus on quantitative methodology and measurement.

First introductions to the scientific method frequently prioritize an objective, hypothesis testing, and quantifiable approach. As explained by Jill Green and Susan Stinson, "the student learns how to operationally define terms to support the pursuit of a quantifiable hypothesis, selecting a participant sample that permits generalization to a wider population, attempting to avoid error and bias" (Green and Stinson 1999, 91). Much comfort can be found in this square perspective. It offers defined rules, clear boundaries, and a refined focus.

The accepted sequential procedure provides a perceived linearity; Step 1: Define and delimit the problem; Step 2: Formulate a testable hypothesis, identifying independent and dependent variables; Step 3: Identify the method of data collection, controlling for internal and external validity; Step 4: Collect the data; Step 5: Analyze the results using appropriate statistical models; Step 6: Interpret and discuss the results. In truth, the process is never as linear as these stepping-stones imply, but the delineation provides a valuable road map to keep researchers on route towards generating relevant findings for the nature of the question(s) posed. The randomized control trial (RCT) research design is identified as the pinnacle of scientific research designs and from there everything else falls short.

From this research approach, robust research designs include attention to internal validity, reliability, and generalizability (or external validity). Internal validity refers to the extent to which the design of the study and the control of the variables eliminates alternative explanations for the results of the study. External validity refers to the extent that the findings are generalizable to a broader population beyond the sample participating in the study. The researcher has to navigate this balancing act between controlling too many variables and yet addressing the identified problem in a way that the results can be meaningful to others. Reliability is considered crucial to ensure validity. Reliability refers to the stability and consistency of the methods, thus producing repeatable results when the same variable is measured under the same conditions. Working within the scientific method, the student learns about the process of conducting research. I must emphasize that it is important that the student learn this approach as it acts as a springboard for the student thinking about research, but it is not the only method for understanding dance.

Edel feels that this approach can become overly method driven, with research questions that pursue pre-determined and often isolated outcomes. Depending on the criteria to be analyzed in quantitative research, the specificity of the method and limitations may not provide the best answers to the questions. Additionally, such an approach often forms the basis of the unease that many within the dance world feel toward scientific methods, which frequently appear overly reductive in nature, pre-defining and controlling variables to the extent that the outcomes may no longer be meaningful to the dancer or teacher. Yet, there is no denying that this approach has its place in dance science. For example, validated testing procedures and equipment adopted from sport science, such as the Wingate Anaerobic Test (WANT) (a test of anaerobic power conducted on a stationary cycle ergometer), or incremental maximal treadmill tests used to measure maximal oxygen uptake via a gas analyzer (an apparatus that is strapped onto the dancer's shoulders, and which covers the mouth and nose measuring oxygen saturation levels in respiration while the dancer) have provided useful points of departure for dance science.

> This objective gold-standard measure of maximal oxygen uptake (VO^2 max) showed that dancers were not as fit as other athletes when using this specific measure. While the results of a VO^2 max test are valuable for comparison across participant populations, the movement demands of dance, as compared to marathon running for example, are not the same, so the comparison is not always meaningful. However, realizing that cardiovascular fitness was an important training component for the dancer, and using existing sport science measures such as measuring VO^2max during an incremental maximal treadmill test protocol, led to the development and validation of dance-specific field-based measures such as the Dance Aerobic Fitness Test (DAFT) (Redding and Wyon 2003) as well as initiatives to improve training and monitoring of dancers' fitness.
>
> These existing validated means of measuring physiological demand in humans are certainly valuable in dance science, but we would be complacent to merely transpose their use from sport science without questioning the relevancy and specificity of these measures and protocols to the particular questions we wish to explore in dance.

This positivist research approach – proving or disproving, predicting outcomes, and determining measurable truths that can be generalized universally to comparable contexts – requires measurement of the dancer in a research laboratory, which is clearly very different from measuring the physiological demands of a dancer while dancing in a performance context. Dance does not happen in a lab, nor only in a studio or rehearsal venue. Dance *in* performance offers a challenge to researchers (and athletic competition to sport science researchers) as there are more variables that will influence the outcome – variables that cannot be controlled, but which should be considered.

Mentoring Student Research

As a mentor, Edel's perspective is informed by both somatics and science. Whereas science looks at a discrete phenomenon, understanding the lived experience in human movement is vital to understanding dance. Somatics introduces the experience of the researched, inviting the participant to experience and reflect on their physical self. One of the first dance science symposia, "The Science and Somatics of Dance" (Dunn and Chemlar 1991/1992), seemed to position somatics as the bridge between the science and practice of dance, but this was not well received by all. For context, many dancers were first introduced to principles of anatomy and motor learning through somatic-informed approaches to dance. However, quite soon in the evolution of dance science, critics questioned how the embodied, first-person perspective reconciles with the objective, quantifiable, third-person perspective, and this debate continues today (Batson and Wilson 2014; Fortin 2005; Green and Stinson 1999). Despite ongoing debate, over the decades somatics and science have continued to entwine, with somatics as an embodied and experiential way of engaging with the theoretical content of anatomy, physiology, motor learning, and even psychology.

> As noted by Batson, Quin, and Wilson (2012, 185), many colleagues within dance science have advocated for an integration of somatic theories and principles within dance science scholarship (e.g. Krasnow and Chatfield 1996, Geber and Wilson 2010), and many dance science courses incorporate modules that include somatics within the curriculum. The integration of somatics within dance science distinguishes dance science from sport science and is a prime example of the circles and squares that intersect within this evolving field.

Under Edel's leadership within the MSc Dance Science program at Trinity Laban Conservatoire of Music and Dance (2012–2018) an integrated psychology and somatics module, "Performance Psychology, Embodied and Perceptual Learning," was developed. The inclusion of this module expanded the research approaches students were exposed to and acknowledged the role of the first-person experience within dance science research. Edel reflects on her personal experience mentoring students experiencing a somatic approach, and how this has shaped her pedagogy.

> From my observation of dance science students over the years, some find somatics the place where the science makes sense and others are challenged by the lack of apparent logic. In both cases I value and encourage the role that somatic experiences bring to both the dance science student and the wider methodological debate within dance science.

Ultimately the aim of dance science is to advance and enhance dance practice through the application of scientific methodologies, as relevant to the nature of the inquiry. This breadth of scope supports a range of methodological possibilities and, as a mentor of dance science student research projects, my role is to help students situate their work in relation to the range of research traditions available to them; to help them to find their own research voice; and to identify questions that are meaningful, can contribute to our current knowing, and yet are feasible to conduct within the limitations of assessment criteria and time-bound frameworks of academic structures.

Somatics includes codified practices and approaches to understanding the body. In both, process is the goal, and incorporation of either of these approaches can provide an applied research perspective. Bridging science and somatics is one way the field of dance science is continuing to evolve.

Edel values different ways of knowing within dance science, proposing that within a collective search for knowledge, there is a need for both squares and circles, and, most importantly, the interactions between the two. As Edel is still actively researching, and mentoring, she is creating a link for her students to see the whole as she is collecting both qualitative and quantitative data so that both dance *and* science can be viewed and perceived from a number of perspectives. This method asks that the research also focus on the experience of both the researcher and the researched.

> The researcher is a human being who is choosing to ask a question, formulate a process by which to investigate that question, and then interpret what has been found from that process. I think there is a misconception that science is infallible. That it is somehow devoid of human error. That the person doing the scientific research is somehow detached from the process. But in every case, it is the human who is asking the questions, deciding the method, interpreting the data, and disseminating the findings to a particular audience. Humans are inherently fallible and influenced by their own lived experiences. Deane Juhan notes,

> all observation is self-observation, and all tools of clinical investigation are simply sophisticated extensions of our own perceptual facilities. These tools can expand and refine our perceptions enormously, but they can never alter the fundamental fact that it is in every instance a human being that is having, structuring, and interpreting the perceptions.
>
> (Juhan 2003, 354)

> Therefore, the myth that scientific researchers are entirely non-biased denies them their uniquely human trait. This is where qualitative and embodied methodological approaches are more enlightened. Here, there is an acceptance that the researcher is human and thus entwined within all steps

of the research process, from the decision of what to research, to how to interpret and apply the outcomes. There is recognition, too, that it is not just the researcher that is human, but also "the researched" – the participant(s). The human researcher and the human participant, accompanied by their lived experience, are valued as being central to, not detached from, the meaningfulness of both the process and the outcome of the research.

For example, Edel's own research endeavors have ranged from exploring the physiological and psychological benefits of creative dance for adolescents who would not otherwise dance (Connolly, Quin, and Redding, 2011; Quin, Frazer, and Redding 2007); to a prospective study monitoring dance exposure, well-being, and injury in collegiate Irish and contemporary dancers (Cahalan et al. 2018); to commentaries on the integration of science and somatics in dance and dance science scholarship (Batson, Quin, and Wilson 2011). Edel's research experience reciprocally shapes her philosophy in teaching research methodology to her students, and continues to evolve, as her research trajectory has evolved. Citing Lister & Wells, who propose that their field of cultural studies is a "compound field rather than discrete discipline" (in Van Leeuwen 2005, 8), Edel sees dance science as a compound field having a clear mission – to further the health and well-being of dancers. This mission is broad in its scope, evolving over time, but crucially with *dance*, and therefore with *the person dancing*, at its center.

Defining a Research Curriculum

One of the introductory modules that Edel leads in her undergraduate program at the University of Chichester is "Understanding Science and Dance Practice." This module aims to position science and dance in an inquiry-based module to lay the foundation for understanding, and undertaking, research.

> Here the developing dance science researcher is introduced to the concept of research, within the context of dance, and more specifically within the field of dance science. We identify that dance, in its broadest term, is practice-based, embodied, and enacted, taking place in a range of settings and for a myriad of purposes. We identify that science in its broadest term is the pursuit of knowing via the implementation of systematic methodologies, in order to gather evidence, often with the intention to generalize and formalize. We discuss where we currently sit on this continuum from embodied and enacted, to formalized and generalizable, and whether we see these as opposing ends of a spectrum or, in fact, a point of intersection in the middle of a continuum. We repeatedly reflect on how our position on the continuum may change across the course of the research journey. We acknowledge that dance is so much more than quantifiable feats that dancers can achieve. For many, it is an artistic pursuit, demanding a certain

degree of athleticism, and for others it is a social or recreational or health pursuit. Research that is applicable to the real world setting of dance needs to acknowledge these differing contexts.

Developing dance science researchers are often more familiar with the dance than the science. It is important for them to realize that this embodied knowledge holds value on their journey to integrating scientific methodologies with that embodied knowledge. Edel helps them understand how they can use their dance experience to develop the question that they wish to research:

> When student researchers come to me with a research intention, it often stems from personal experience or intuition. I find this a valuable starting point. From this I explore their current narrative, their reasons for wanting to pursue this research intention. In this process we identify and acknowledge inherent biased perspectives they may hold, and tease out an initial guiding research question, or series of questions, that provide an initial scaffolding for the methodological research approach.

Using this as a building block, Edel helps the students refine the nature of the question or problem. For example, if a student identifies injury as a topic they wish to investigate, she leads them through a series of generative questions that help lay the foundation for their research methodology. These questions are presented at the beginning of the process with the acknowledgment that many will not have a clear answer, as yet, but in asking these questions the seeds toward exploring the answer are sown. These questions are then frequently reviewed as the research process evolves.

- What is your topic of interest?
- What is/are your particular research question/s? How are you wording these questions?
    - Do you know of any relevant literature that relates to your research question? What domain/discipline/research perspective is this from?
    - What does the research from your literature review say? What resonates with your identified research questions (and why)? What do you reject (and why)? What do you need to research further in order to decide whether something resonates or is rejected?
    - What would be your research design and methodological approach? Does your question require an intervention or comparison of one thing (e.g. group, condition, variable, etc.) to another?
    - What might be your data collection/observation methods? How detailed can you be at this stage?
    - What specific data/mode of information will you gather from these methods (include units of measure, where quantitative)?

- Approximately how many participants would you ideally need and how would you justify this?
- Are there any particular requirements of your participant characteristics (e.g. inclusion/exclusion criteria)?
- How might you go about recruiting your participants? Is this a realistic approach to achieving your target participant number?
- What might be the ethical implications of your study and how would you mediate these?
- What is your hypothesis(es)/expected outcome(s), if the nature of the investigation supports this approach?
- What mode of analysis would you choose (consider your chosen methods of data collection, along with your research question and, if relevant, your hypothesis, to support this decision)?
- What do you think your study would contribute to dance/dance science research and practice?
- Finally, is this project feasible in the time frame, and given the resources that you and the university have access to?

With these questions, Edel provides a structure to students to understand how to conceptualize and embark upon a research journey. Her question-based format helps students identify the necessary elements in designing a study, and provides agency for the students, rather than being prescriptive, allowing them to discover their intentions in doing the research as well as understanding the need for clarity and precision in design.

As Sylvie Fortin states: "Scientific endeavors can be distinguished from artistic endeavors, but they are not necessarily opposing endeavors" (Fortin 2005, 4). Edel emphasizes that although subjectivity, perception, and process are deeply explored in the practice of dance as an art form, these are not antithetical or invalid in dance science research practice.

> As dance is central to dance science, dance science students are likely to engage with philosophical and theoretical discourses which are often more aligned with the arts and humanities (such as theories of the body and embodiment) than other human movement science students. This offers a breadth of perspective that acknowledges the important context of dance as the central entity in the research endeavor.

Identifying the stance of the researcher (why am I asking these questions, why have I selected a particular method?) is a vital component of understanding and interpreting research. Is the researcher an outside observer or an invested investigator, and how is this identified within the discussion and conclusions of the study? How does the researcher interact with and interpret the experience of the researched and provide this information as a part of the results or interpretation of results?

Edel's evolving journey as an educator and researcher has brought her to a reflective stance on the nature and future of dance science investigations. Rather than having all the answers, Edel has identified more questions.

> My personal interests within dance science research and practice frequently inhabit the messy in-between. I am interested in the confluence of perspectives, the cross-fertilization of discipline-specific knowledge, and the possibility of integrated research approaches. Not unlike David Bohm (Bohm and Peat 2010, xii), I have a desire to simultaneously understand both detail and wholeness. What excites me is the richness of possibility in exploring identified phenomena from an integrated perspective.
>
> The realization that the self-observation and perceptual facilities that first drew me towards dance science were not in opposition to, negated by, nor validated by the science, but were in fact expanded and refined because of it, has underpinned my approach to my professional career as an educator, mentor, and researcher in dance and dance science.

The greatest testament to the importance of dance science research, however, is in its application. Asking questions leads to research which leads to helping others ask questions. Asking questions about cardiorespiratory fitness has led to near worldwide emphasis on the importance of conditioning programs. Inquiries on the best ways to augment fitness have shifted the nutrition discussion within dance from dieting to fueling for performance. Questions about technique and training are now informing dance education at the entry stages in studios and schools. An organization called Safe in Dance International, of which Edel is an Associate, is dedicated to supporting, developing, and endorsing the implementation of research-informed dance science practices for dance teachers and dancers across styles, settings, and populations. Edel, along with two colleagues, Sonia Rafferty and Charlotte Tomlinson, supports this mission via their book *Safe Dance Practice* (Quin, Rafferty, and Tomlinson 2015), which translates research into recommendations, data into valuable context, and health into healthy practice. With this application, Edel is filling in spaces on an open continuum of dance practice, dance research, dance science application to pedagogy, and performance. In her mind, doing research that feeds back into practice is the most important outcome.

Returning to Her Roots with a New Purpose

In 2021 following a prolonged pause due to COVID-19, Edel was to lead a study into the physiological demands of live dance performance with her former professional dance company, *Riverdance*. As of the time of writing this chapter, the research was underway. This project represented coming full circle for Edel – returning to her first professional dance company as an established dance science researcher, combining her lived experience with scientific rigor – to understand more about the physiological demands of dance during live performance. Working together with a small team of researchers from across various departments at the University of Chichester, whose previous research expertise had centered on exploring the physiological demands of dance and military personnel (Dr. Sarah Needham-Beck), drumming (Professor Marcus Smith), and adolescent athletes (Dr. Andy West), Edel and her colleagues set about identifying specific research questions and relevant methods.

> Capturing live physiological data, when dancers are performing in front of a paying audience, is rarely – if ever – pursued in dance research. The difficulties of balancing the needs of the aesthetic intention of both the choreography and the costume with the necessary elements of robust research design and data collection are often insurmountable. As a result, there is currently no published data on the dancer's heart rate responses to live dance performance, and in particular continuous heart rate response across an entire company for the entire duration of a show, and then across multiple shows within a touring period. Whereas some data exists for rehearsal and for "simulated performance," no data exists for the actual act of performing a live show in front of a paying audience.

Working collaboratively brings in breadth, and the distinction of the research represents the strengths of all the contributing members. In this project, a close collaboration between the company director, the dance captains, and the research team resulted in multiple conversations prior to data collection about the aims and applications of the research study from the perspective of both the company and the researchers.

> It was important to the company and to the research team that the findings were, first and foremost, directly applicable to supporting enhanced training, efficient load management, and effective recovery of the dancers. It was important to the research team that we employed a robust research design and effective data collection tools, despite the constraints presented by the dancers' daily schedules and the artistic and costuming requirements of the show.

> In sport, the monitoring of such a simple variable (heart rate response) during live events is much more commonplace. My sport science colleagues were surprised to learn that to-date no such data had been published on dancers. As a team we decided to keep things simple and monitor heart rate response of the dancers via continuous heart rate recording across the

duration of the 2-hour show, analyzed relative to the dancer's individual age-predicted heart rate maximum and relative zones of intensity, and captured repeatedly at strategic intervals across the tour – first full-dress rehearsal, opening night performance, then monthly intervals until closing night of the tour, 5 months later.

We also decided to monitor rate of perceived exertion (RPE) alongside this objective heart rate data, as a means of quantifying (on a scale from 6 to 20) the subjective perceptions of intensity. These methods helped us to answer the following questions: What are the heart rate responses of dancers to a relatively set performance demand? What are the on-stage demands? What are the off-stage recovery possibilities? What are the differing demands between roles (lead and troupe, male and female) within the company? How do responses to these demands change across a tour?

In addition, the company still employed the point rotation system that was in place when I was a dancer. In discussions with the artistic director, we also included a research question about the accuracy of the point rotation system at representing actual demand of each dance number and therefore distribution of demand between dancers across repeated performances.

Because of Edel's previous association with *Riverdance* as a performer, the participants' buy-in was high from both the dancers and the company administration. Edel noted that there was a sense of doing this research *for* and *with* the dancers, not *on* the dancers. This is evidenced in the collaborative approach to identifying research questions and the importance placed on the outcomes being directly applicable to the dancers and company management. Due to the interface between the research and the researched – the science and the art – there was much the research team could not control for within this research design. Rather than the lack of internal validity being a limitation (as in a positivist paradigm), this project inhabits another type of validity, ecological validity, which looks to the applicability of research findings to the real-life context of the specific activity. Whereas previous dance research measuring the physiological demands of dance relied on rehearsals or simulated performance situations, as Kihlstrom notes, "An experiment lacks ecological validity…when the cues presented by the experimental situation lack ecological validity with respect to the real-world situation that the experiment is intended to model" (2021, 469). Edel and her team use data that represent the comprehensive experience of the dancer – cardiorespiratory demand (heart rate), physiological adaptation (changes in heart rate across time), and embodied experience (subjective perceptions of exertion) – for each individual dancer in the study. The value of this research design is that it reveals what is happening in the moment the dancer is performing their art.

Coming Full Circle

Dance is a complex movement system, and while researchers can describe specific attributes and outcomes, what a dancer experiences and the way in which the attributes shape the artistry requires different lenses for understanding, affording us the possibility to "seek multiple perspectives and meaning" (Green and Stinson 1999, 94). Here Edel circles back to sentiments expressed earlier:

> All movement is inherently complex as humans are complex dynamic systems, interacting with a complex cultural, social, and physical environment. Dance is movement in space and time, encompassing a myriad of styles, populations, contexts, and reasons for participation. Dance is at the same time describable and measurable, and yet complex in the layers of effort, intent and meaning to the point of being limited by definition.
>
> Science is one approach to knowing, to attempt to understand, and yet no single tool, method of measurement, or research approach can possibly claim to provide the complete answer to the intricate phenomena being explored.
>
> Whereas we can reduce the variables we study for measure and analysis, the challenge is often that the part can never be truly reconstituted to understand the whole, therefore dance elusively escapes the clear definitions that traditional science often seeks. The complexity of dance means that to understand what the dancer is experiencing, we must explore a range of research approaches.

Using a qualitative, embodied methodology acknowledges the ways in which researchers are entwined in every aspect of the research and yet through rigorous standards can place this into context. With her current research in collaboration with *Riverdance* and as she embarks on her doctoral work, Edel is diving deeper into the lived experience for her participants, realizing that what is measured may not be measurable outside of an ecologically valid context. She emphasizes that we need to stay open to all methodologies to be able to answer the questions at hand; the questions should drive the method, rather than the other way around. The pragmatic side of her character quickly follows that feasibility is also an essential consideration.

The application of research outcomes to education and training is an important goal for Edel, and for dance science more broadly. Edel muses that dance science does not, and should not, exist in a vacuum. With the development and intersection of research within dance studies, sociology and psychology of dance, embodied cognition, dance and/for health, practice as research paradigms, and more, Edel sees dance science as sitting in a different location on the research spectrum than its older sibling, sport science: one that is nimble enough to shift and be flexible, yet established enough to stand its ground.

> Throughout this chapter I have reflected upon what is dance science, how dance science is evolving and what methodological possibilities are afforded by that evolution. I have offered insight from my own research perspective and my years of mentoring students through their own dance science research journey. Through these reflections and insights, the value of different ways of knowing within dance science is championed.
>
> Fortin notes, "…distinguishing science from other endeavors requires focusing in particular on its methodology" (2005, 3). But just as dance science continues to evolve, science also evolves. Thomas Kuhn discusses the "paradigm crisis phenomenon, in which researchers who have been following a particular paradigm begin to find discrepancies in it. The findings no longer agree with the predictions, and a new paradigm is advanced" (1970, in Thomas, Nelson, and Silverman 2015, 14). Kuhn identifies that the old paradigm slowly fades, as many who have dedicated years to this paradigm are slow to change. Thus, these paradigm shifts emerge from a revolution, which is led by new researchers who break away from existing paradigms. Through its relatively brief, but continued maturation, dance science has experienced, and will no doubt continue to experience mini paradigm shifts, exemplified by the integration of somatics and science, and widening the research lens to observe dance as it is happening.

Edel recognizes the role her students play in these mini paradigm shifts. She comments that their curiosity, their lack of inhibition in the face of seemingly established norms or hierarchy within research methodologies, results in a vast array of research questions, often resulting in Edel reflecting on whether such a research question fulfills the dance science remit.

> The students that I have encountered over the years have also helped me to become the researcher and educator I am evolving into. It is an ever-evolving process that will most certainly continue. Students pose questions that challenge the status quo of what is understood to be, and what might not be considered "dance science." I work with Bachelor of Arts dance students who engage in rigorous quantitative analysis and Bachelor of Science dance science students who engage in embodied knowing. As a research mentor, I am not rigid about a student conforming to arbitrary expectations of research. I simply try to encourage the student to conduct rigorous research, with a clear intent, which meets the module assessment criteria sufficiently to be acceptable within their chosen program of study. I wish for each student to find the beginnings of their own research journey. My mentorship journey has made me a better researcher, has helped me to be comfortable with that messy in-between of the squares and circles that dance science frequently presents and that I seem to frequently inhabit.

Of her own book, Glenna Batson writes

> By the time this book is published, many new conversations and research initiatives will have forged ahead. Both challenge and opportunity lie before us in how we name these new initiatives, how we investigate new phenomena and how we understand dance.
> (Batson and Wilson 2014, 192)

Batson invites us, as Edel invites you, to continue this richness of discovery.

Works Cited

Batson, Glenna, Edel Quin, and Margaret Wilson. 2012. "Integrating Somatics and Science." *Journal of Dance & Somatic Practices* 3, no. 1–2: 183–193.

Batson, Glenna, and Margaret Ann Wilson. 2014. *Body and Mind in Motion: Dance and Neuroscience in Conversation*. Bristol: Chicago Intellect Books.

Bohm, David, and F. David Peat. 2010. *Science, Order and Creativity*. London and New York: Routledge.

Cahalan, Roisin, Philip Kearney, Orfhlaith Ni Bhriain, Emma Redding, Edel Quin, Lisa C. McLaughlin, and Kieran O'Sullivan. 2018. "Dance Exposure, Wellbeing and Injury in Collegiate Irish and Contemporary Dancers: A Prospective Study." *Physical Therapy in Sport* 34: 77–83.

Connolly, Mary Kate, Edel Quin, and Emma Redding. 2011. "Dance 4 your Life: Exploring the Health and Well-being Implications of a Contemporary Dance Intervention for Female Adolescents." *Research in Dance Education* 12, no. 1: 53–66.

Dunn, Jan, and Robin Chmelar. 1991/92. "Introduction." *Kinesiology and Medicine for Dance* 14, no. 2: 1–2.

Eddy, Martha. 1991. "An Overview of the Science and Somatics of Dance." *Kinesiology and Medicine for Dance* 14, no. 1: 20–28.

Fortin, Sylvie. 2005. "Measurable? Immeasurable? What are we Looking for?" In *Proceedings of the Laban Research Conference Day*: 3–14.

Geber, Pamela, and Margaret Wilson. 2010. "Teaching at the Interface of Dance Science and Somatics." *Journal of Dance Medicine & Science* 14, no. 2: 50–57.

Green, Jill, and Susan W. Stinson. 1999. "Postpositivist Research in Dance." In *Researching Dance: Evolving Modes of Inquiry*, edited by Sondra Horton Fraleigh and Penelope Hanstein, 91–123. Pittsburgh: University of Pittsburgh Press.

Juhan, Deane. 2003. *Job's Body: A Handbook for Bodyworkers*. Barrytown, NY: Station Hill.

Kihlstrom, John F. 2021. "Ecological Validity and "Ecological Validity"." *Perspectives on Psychological Science* 16, no. 2: 466–471.

Krasnow, Donna H., and Steven J. Chatfield. 1996. "Dance Science and the Dance Technique Class." *Impulse* 4, no. 2: 162–172.

Quin, Edel, Lucy Frazer, and Emma Redding. 2007. "The Health Benefits of Creative Dance: Improving Children's Physical and Psychological Wellbeing." *Education and Health* 25, no. 2: 31–33.

Quin, Edel, Sonia Rafferty, and Charlotte Tomlinson. 2015. *Safe Dance Practice*. Champaign, IL: Human Kinetics.

Redding, Emma. 2019. "The Expanding Possibilities of Dance Science." In *The Routledge Companion to Dance Studies*, edited by Helen Thomas, and Stacey Prickett, 56–67. London and New York: Routledge.

Redding, Emma and Matthew Wyon. 2003. "Strengths and Weaknesses of Current Methods for Evaluating the Aerobic Power of Dancers." *Journal of Dance Medicine & Science* 7, no. 1: 10–16.

Thomas, Jerry R., Jack K. Nelson, and Stephen J. Silverman. 2015. *Research Methods in Physical Activity*. Champaign, IL: Human Kinetics.

Van Leeuwen, Theo. 2005. "Three Models of Interdisciplinarity." In *A New Agenda in (Critical) Discourse Analysis: Theory, Methodology and Interdisciplinarity*, edited by Ruth Wodak and Paul A. Chilton, 3–18. Amsterdam: John Benjamins Pub. Co.

Wyon, Matthew, Emma Redding, Grant Abt, Andrew Head, and N. Craig C. Sharp. 2003. "Development, Reliability, and Validity of a Multistage Dance Specific Aerobic Fitness Test (DAFT)." *Journal of Dance Medicine & Science* 7, no. 3: 80–84.

21
Thinking Statistically for Dance Research

Gregory Youdan Jr.

My research is informed by my training in dance, kinesiology (motor learning), and statistics, and centers on improving research methodologies in dance for health interventions. Thinking statistically is an integral part of my process, influencing how I collect data, undertake analysis, and present results. My work is impacted by my fellowship through Mark Morris Dance For PD®[1] and my relationship with Heidi Latsky Dance,[2] a physically-integrated dance company in New York City whose mission is dedicated to the creation of relevant, immersive performance art that is accessible to all.

Statistics is a science used to analyze, interpret, and present quantitative data across genres of research. For many, statistics is stress-inducing. For me, statistics provides a logical framework that helps me understand (1) how to ask research questions and (2) what questions I can answer with the data collected. Statistics requires thoughtful consideration to ensure the validity of results. However, you do not need to be a quantitative researcher to benefit from the logic of statistical thinking. Rather, statistical thinking penetrates all aspects of the research process, going beyond the execution of a specific analysis. It instead enables a higher-level approach to methodology, allowing one to envision how statistics can help to draw thoughtful conclusions.

This chapter is not meant to teach statistics or how to run specific analyses. Rather, it is intended to provide you with (1) insight into how statistics influences my decision-making, (2) tools to develop a statistical analysis plan (SAP), and (3) clarity with respect to concepts related to statistical planning and analytical processes. For qualitative and novice researchers, this chapter provides a basic introduction to statistics and a logical framework to inform decision-making throughout the research process, thus aiding the comprehension of data and reduction of bias. Definitions for statistical jargon are defined in the footnotes. This chapter could encourage you to consider mixed methods by demystifying the quantitative side.

What Is Statistics?

Broadly speaking statistics describe what data is showing by simplifying or reducing data into meaningful summaries. Inferential statistics are used to make conclusions that extend beyond the data set at hand, and present generalizable findings. This is typically done through a statistical test on variables, which are characteristics that can be categorized or measured (e.g. age, gender, number of pirouettes, the height of jump). Descriptive statistics would be used to summarize traits of dancers who participated in a particular study whereas inferential statistics would be used to make conclusions about all dancers based on data from only those dancers who participated in that study.

When thinking about statistics, traditionally what comes to mind are data reduction,[3] hypothesis testing,[4] and threshold setting[5] to determine statistical significance,[6] all of which are related to significance-based hypothesis testing. However, proper use of statistics also helps to reduce bias[7] and/or error,[8] determine the magnitude of an experimental effect, determine a sample size, and detect differences. These are all important because they strengthen methodological approach, provide validity to results, and provide the basis for future studies. Significance-based hypothesis testing uses mathematical comparison to determine if a difference is "statistically significant" according to a threshold (i.e. significance level), which requires distinguishing between the null and alternative hypothesis. A null hypothesis is the default, where the experimental effect is equal to zero (i.e. no effect), whereas the alternative hypothesis proposes an effect. With hypothesis testing, one must consider an error. A type I error occurs when a true null hypothesis is rejected ("false positive") and a type II error occurs when a false null hypothesis is not rejected ("false negative"). To ensure accurate findings, quantitative researchers aim to reduce error and bias and be as objective as possible in their studies.

Statistical Analysis Plan (SAP)

A SAP is used to describe planned analysis for clinical trials, but no matter the size or scope, all studies should create an SAP. An SAP lays out sampling procedures; sample size and power calculations; data processes, including missing data and outlier treatment; statistical techniques; and defines statistical outputs ahead of time (all of which will be described as the chapter continues). Figure 21.1 shows the systematic of everything that goes into creating an SAP (see Figure 21.1), which I will refer to throughout the chapter.

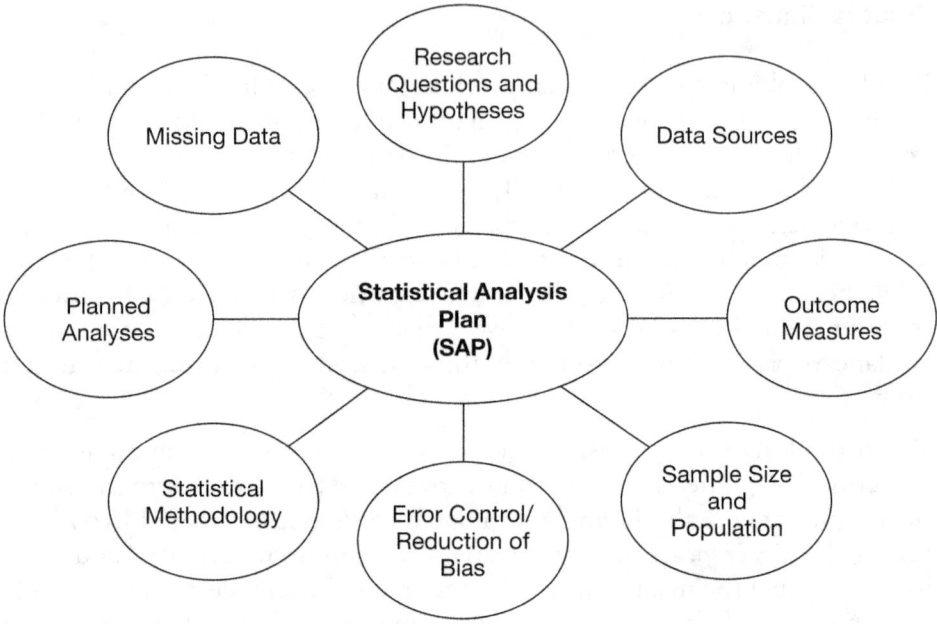

Figure 21.1 Facets of a statistical analysis plan.

Research Questions

When contemplating research questions, one of my first considerations is what type of question I'm asking. Generally, quantitative questions fall into three categories: descriptive, relational, or causal. Descriptive questions describe populations (e.g. what percentage of children are offered dance in their curriculum). Relational questions examine relationships between variables (e.g. does the starting age of dance training relate to a professional career). Relational questions are often addressed using correlations[9] but do not determine cause. Causal questions aim to determine cause and effect of one or more variables on outcome measures (e.g. does participation in a Dance for PD [Parkinson's Disease] program delay disease progression). Most of my work falls into the causal realm because my research focuses on examining the direct benefits of dance for health interventions. For instance, does a Dance for PD program lead to improvements in walking, such as increased step length?

My research questions are generated by factors including (1) observations in the studio (e.g. is the use of the mirrors beneficial), (2) the desire to develop research and language about dance for health practices to better communicate with medical professionals (e.g. why should dance for health programs be included in hospital settings), (3) the goal of improving scientific measurement of dance (e.g. quantifying dance for health interventions, such as how much time is spent balancing on one leg during a Dance for PD intervention), and (4) what is most beneficial for the community the research will impact (this requires a conversation with the impacted community). I collaborate with the community I am studying to uplift their views, needs, and stories. My best research ideas often come from conversations with community members. However, once the data collection process begins, I aim to be an impartial observer to reduce additional bias. Although, more recently I am exploring co-production methodology to better address power dynamics in knowledge production and to better honor the many ways of knowing (Mitlin et al. 2020).

The generation of hypotheses should not be driven by statistical techniques or by any specific research methodology. It is best to match statistical and research methodologies to what will best help you answer the research question, as opposed to developing a research question. Only after the research question is established should one consider how to best answer that question, what data to collect, and how to analyze that data. For example, to examine if a Dance for PD intervention improves step length, I need to consider the best method to collect step length measurements. Moreover, that method needs to be both a valid[10] and reliable[11] way to measure step length (e.g. motion capture system) both before and after the intervention. This iterative process helps ensure the use of appropriate methodologies. Moreover, one must also consider whether a larger step length is in fact a meaningful outcome (e.g. more functional) to someone with Parkinson's or if one should instead be focused on something else. Qualitative methods may be useful to capture the participant's experience and the use of mixed methods may be warranted.

Data

As a dance scientist using biomechanics and statistical methodologies to answer dance for health questions, the instruments I use for data collection and their relationship to my research question matter. In a movement science lab, I have access to equipment including:

- Motion Capture System – measure x, y, and z coordinates (e.g. Vicon, OptiTrack);
- Force Plates – measure ground reaction forces (e.g. AMTI, Hawkin Dynamics);
- Electromyography (EMG) – measure electrical activity in response to a nerve's stimulation of muscle (e.g. Delsys, Noraxon);

- Electroencephalogram (EEG) systems – measure electrical activity in brain (e.g. Neuroscan, Emotiv);
- Force Transducer – measure compressive and tensile forces (e.g. ADInstruments, ATI Industrial Automation);
- Electromagnetic Sensor – monitor movement using changes in electromagnetic field (e.g. Polhemus, 3DCoil);
- Inertial Measurement Unit (IMUs) – measure accelerations, angular rates of motion and magnetic field changes (e.g. APDM, Xsens); and
- Physical Activity Tracker – measure fitness-related metrics (e.g. Apple Watch, Fitbit).

Each tool provides different data used to answer different questions. For example, if my research question is aimed at understanding limb positions in space, I will choose a motion capture system over a force plate. I also take relevant ethical considerations into account, such as the burden on the participant to travel to the lab. This may lead me to choose more portable instruments such as IMUs, portable EMGs, or wearable physical activity trackers. Typical outcome measures I use consist of gait parameters (e.g. step length, gait speed, anticipatory postural adjustments), balance (e.g. total sway area, jerk, root mean square of acceleration), measures of muscle contraction or fatigue, and physical activity levels.

I am often not solely relying on objective data collected from these instruments. I am also interested in collecting patient-reported outcomes, clinical observational metrics, cognitive measures, and demographic or qualitative data. For instance, in a recent unpublished study examining a physical therapy intervention for people with lower limb loss, my collaborators and I collected objective (e.g. step length), subjective (e.g. clinical scales based on observation), and patient-reported measures (e.g. balance confidence scale) of motor function. Objective measures were collected using IMUs worn while performing walking and balance tasks, and a physical activity tracker attached to the prosthetic limb. Subjective clinical measures collected included the two-minute walk test (Bohannon 2017), Berg balance scale (Berg et al. 1989), and K-level (rating level used by Medicare to indicate a person's rehabilitation potential). Patient-reported outcomes included activity-specific balance confidence scale (how confident you are that you won't fall while performing X) (Powell and Myers 1995), life space questionnaire (how far you get into your community) (Stalvey et al. 1999), and prosthetic evaluation mobility subscale (patient-perceived potential for mobility using a prosthetic device) (Kaluf 2014). For a subset of the work I do, I measure cognitive improvements using tests, including Stroop Color and Word Test (reading names of colors where the font color does not match the color name (Stroop 1935), symbol-digit modality test (matching symbols with numbers) (Smith 1982), or verbal letter fluency (how many words starting with a specific letter stated in 60 seconds without repetition) (Newcombe 1969). I always collect demographic data to describe the participants in my study such as age, gender, and time passed since diagnosis or disease severity. I want to ensure my data is collected from a random representative sample of participants included (based on inclusion and exclusion criteria) and can effectively answer the hypothesis.

Statistics cannot fix poor data collection. Working primarily with quantitative data, the fidelity of data and the minimization of error (e.g. reduction of measurement error, reduction of type I and type II error) are extremely important to ensure accurate results. As such, the unit of measurement (that which is in fact being measured), and accurate measurement matter. I make sure to find literature that shows the measures to be reliable and valid in the population at hand. This means the measure is consistent and is measuring what it is intended to measure. For example, Morris et al. (2019) show APDM (Ambulatory Parkinson's Disease Monitors) wearable sensors that I use to measure gait and balance in people with Parkinson's, are a valid way to collect this data in the population of interest.

In order to develop an appropriate SAP, one must know what type of data is being collected (in statistical terms) and in which scale. The four measurement scales for quantitative data are (1) nominal, (2) ordinal, (3) discrete, and (4) continuous. Nominal data is categorical data not possessing an order, for example, color of the leotard the dancer was wearing or the gender of the dancer. Ordinal data, which is still categorical, possesses a natural ordering. Yes, you can assign numbers to these values, but no distance is conveyed. An example is grading where an A+ is better than a B-, or a scale of "dislike," "neutral," "like" for a survey. Discrete data are whole number numerical values such as the number of sautés in a certain time period or angular degree of an arabesque. Continuous data is numerical but can fall in between whole numbers such as time balanced on one leg (e.g. 15.4 seconds). Type of data is also a consideration when qualitative data is converted into quantitative data for analysis. Not all statistical techniques work with every measurement scale, and this affects the selection of a statistical test, what you are testing for, and the questions you are able to answer.

Sample Size

Part of the logic of statistics is that by looking at a small group (i.e. sample) you can draw conclusions about the whole group (i.e. population). Researchers use this logic to make inferences about large populations because it is often not realistic or feasible to survey an entire population. One consideration while using this logic is the sample size (i.e. the number of participants). The unsatisfying (but unsurprising) answer to "What is the right sample size?" is "It depends." There are, however, tools to facilitate decision-making and for use in sample size calculations. Considerations I use include:

- Population size – total number of distinct individuals in the population of interest (e.g. all dancers in world);
- Error rate – frequency of type I or type II errors in a test;
- Level of significance – probability of rejecting a true null hypothesis;
- Confidence interval – probability of a population parameter falling between a set of values if you repeat the test;
- Effect size – a quantitative measure of the magnitude of experimental effect; and
- Statistical power – probability a significance test will detect a difference if there is a true effect.

Consider the size of the entire population to which you are aiming to extend your results. For example, if my research is looking to study dancers in the United States, that is my population. However, if studying the experience of Black or indigenous or dancers of color in the United States, my population is only Black or indigenous or dancers of color within the United States. If a sample size is too small, you will not get an accurate representation of the population and the sample may include a disproportionate number of outliers, which can skew your results. A small sample limits your use of statistical tests. If a sample is too big, you can find statistical significance simply based on large numbers, and small differences become significant simply because there are so many participants (this is a type I error). Larger samples take more time to collect, increase cost, and are more complex to analyze. Thinking statistically will help you to navigate between the number of participants needed to detect change and the capacity of collecting those participants.

There is an error in any study or statistical analysis. This is not something to be feared but rather acknowledged and controlled. The probability of a type I error is generally described as a level of significance, or as the alpha level. The most common significance levels are 0.10, 0.05, and 0.01. These numbers are the equivalent of saying there is a 90%, 95%, and 99% probability that findings did not occur by chance. The most common level used for scientific literature is 0.05; however, medical research often uses 0.01 because of the implications of their results. I primarily use the 0.05 significance level but have used 0.10 in pilot studies with small samples. Significance levels are set *a priori*[12] (in advance) of conducting the research study; otherwise, you may be fishing[13] for results.

A *p*-value is used to determine whether something is statistically significant against the level of significance (alpha), in other words, the probability of finding observed, or more extreme, results when the null hypothesis is true. Using a 0.05 significance level means that a *p*-value < 0.05 is considered statistically significant whereas anything ≥ 0.05 is not significant. As mentioned, the *p*-value is also the level of chance you are comfortable accepting. Using a significance level of 0.05, a *p*-value of 0.04 rejects the null hypothesis, whereas a *p*-value of 0.051 fails to reject the null hypothesis. For example, if my hypothesis was that step length will increase as a result of dance training for people with Parkinson's, with a *p*-value of 0.04 there is enough evidence to say step length increased, whereas, with a *p*-value of 0.051, there is insufficient evidence to reject the null hypothesis. Another way of saying this is that if my threshold of acceptable chance is 0.05, then at 0.04 I would be comfortable saying these are likely not by chance and at 0.051 I would not be. You should under no circumstances change your significance level after analysis to get your results to become "significant" because you did not achieve the desired *p*-value. This is not ethical and will invalidate your findings.

Everything measured has a related margin of error, such as a standard deviation or confidence interval – which is typically reported as a range (+/.) around a point of estimate (e.g. mean, median), In detail, a confidence interval is a range around a point estimate for an unknown parameter with an associated confidence level (i.e. probability) that the range will contain the true value of the parameter given your observed data (Cumming 2012). A higher confidence level will generate a wider confidence interval (i.e. less precise). The most commonly used confidence level is 95%, although 90% or 99% are also regularly used. In terms of estimating confidence intervals or standard deviations to use for sample size calculations, you may have previous data or literature to support these estimates. If you do not have data to help you estimate a confidence interval a good starting point is 0.50 or 1.0 for a standard for deviation (based on a mean of 0). This, however, assumes that the data is normally distributed, which I cover later in the chapter. Data from disabled dancers, for example, are often not normally distributed. Finding estimates from previous literature is always recommended, regardless of the desired study population.

Additional considerations for sample size calculations include statistical power as well as effect sizes. Statistical power is one minus the probability of a type II error (beta). The most accepted percentage is 0.80. Effect sizes provide a sample-based measurement of the strength of the relationship between two variables in a population (Cumming 2012). In general, smaller effect sizes require more participants to reach the same statistical power and larger effect sizes require fewer participants to reach the same power. Estimating confidence intervals and effect sizes for sample size calculations can be based on pilot data or previous literature. Defining your significance level, effect size, desired error rates, and confidence intervals will enable you to use sample size calculators, many of which are freely available online.

Sampling

Sampling is the method of selection of participants from a larger population. When sampling, I always consider reducing bias and accounting for issues of diversity, equity, justice, and inclusion. Researchers should ensure they have a truly random sample in which all participants are equally likely to have been selected. Sampling bias can occur when certain groups are not appropriately sampled or are excluded, which leads to over- or under-estimation of statistical parameters. For example, if I were to recruit participants with Parkinson's for a study examining walking speed but only included participants in New York City, it is possible that my data may not be generalizable to those outside of New York City. This is because people in New York City may walk faster than people in other areas. Although it is nearly impossible to ensure perfect randomness, steps should be taken to ensure equitable and random recruitment and sampling. Sampling considerations include:

- Inclusion/exclusion criteria;
- Equitable and just instruments of data collection (Bahner et al. 2021; Gaddy and Scott 2020; Lee-Ibarra 2021);
- Language access (e.g. translations);
- Accessibility (e.g. Alt Text);
- Reducing barriers to participation;
- Reducing burden on participation;
- Equitable recruitment methodology;
- Compensation for participants;
- Freedom in scheduling participation;
- Data security (especially for personally identifiable data); and
- Informed consent.

Sampling error is a different construct from inclusion and exclusion criteria. For example, if you are studying hip hop dancers then non hip hop dancers are rightfully excluded from the study. If you are studying undergraduate dancers at a certain school, excluding all first-year dancers because they are more difficult for you to recruit is not an ethical exclusion. Exclusion on race or gender identity is not rightful exclusion unless it is the basis of the research question (e.g. what is the experience of Black dancers or gender non-conforming dancers in ballet schools). When recruiting, I want to ensure equitable participation and access to participation across all relevant demographics. This means the demographics of my sample should reflect the demographics of the true population and indicate that the instruments of data collection are just. In certain cases, this requires accessibility considerations, such as having study materials available in multiple languages or interpreters available, as well as finding other ways to reduce the burden and barriers for participants. I often travel to medical clinics to recruit and see participants immediately following their clinical appointments to reduce the burden of additional travel for them. Additional considerations include the method of recruitment. For instance, only recruiting digitally may exclude low-income households without digital access. If possible and appropriate, hiring research coordinators to increase accessibility (e.g. language) can facilitate recruitment and participants' understanding of the research study. When I use digital surveys, I want to ensure these surveys are accessible via a screen reader. If I am collecting data in person, I ensure the space is accessible. Accessibility begins at the first point of contact with participants and should be considered throughout the entire research process including the dissemination of results.

Data security is of vital importance, especially for undocumented participants who could experience drastic repercussions should their personally identifiable data be released. Finally, it is important to assure informed consent. In all cases, participants must be fully informed that they are voluntarily participating in a research project, told what participation means and what will be done with their data, and be advised of the project's risks and benefits.

Normality of Data

Normality is a statistical concept based on the frequency of a variable. If a variable follows a normal distribution this means the frequency follows a bell-shaped curve around the mean (Mean 0, Standard Deviation 1). If it does not follow a bell-shaped curve, it is said to be non-normally distributed (see Figure 21.2). Normality influences which types of descriptive statistics and inferential tests you should use. You may not always know ahead of time the normality of your data, and different variables may have different distributions. Normality is not something to guess. Statistical tests such as Kolmogorov-Smirnov test[14] (Chakravarti et al. 1967) and the Shapiro-Wilk test[15] (Shapiro and Wilk 1965), test for normality and provide ways to verify the normality of data. It is wise to have an SAP for normally and non-normally distributed data. There are methods to normalize non-normally distributed data, such as centering your data on the mean. However, normalizing your data requires careful consideration, as this can decrease the variation in your sample or change

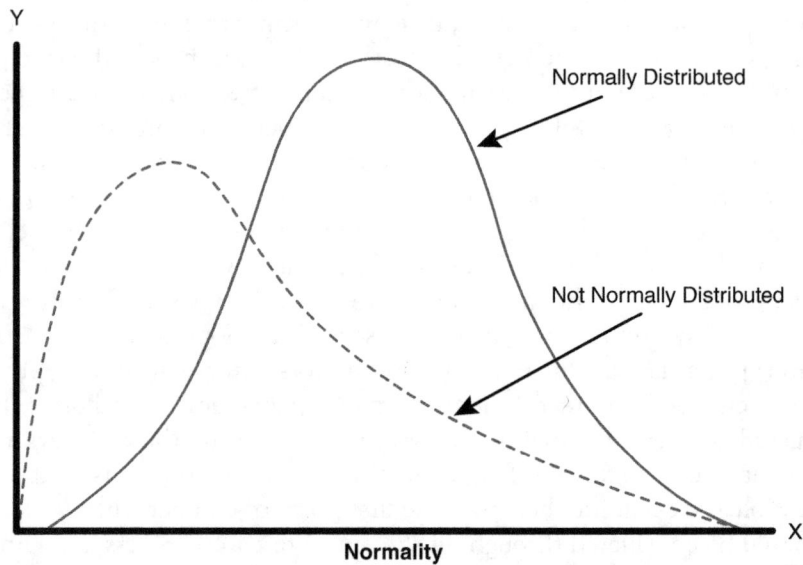

Figure 21.2 Normality. This figure shows the distribution of variable X on Y. It highlights the difference between a normal, symmetrical, bell-shaped distribution, which is represented by a solid line, and a positively skewed non-normal distribution, represented by a dashed line. This is not the only way a non-normal distribution will appear but is one representation. Anything not following the symmetrical bell shape is non-normally distributed.

your scale of measurement depending on the technique used, which can affect the interpretability of your results. Human variation in and of itself does not lead to not normally distributed data. I work with several disabled populations whose data often does not follow a normal distribution due to several different factors, including disease severity. This is often because disease severity data involves people who are functionally more or less impaired, which can lead to an asymmetric distribution. The implication of the distribution (i.e. normal or non-normal) is which statistical test you will use (i.e. parametric vs. nonparametric).

Descriptive Statistics

Three characteristics typically used to describe variables are (1) distribution (frequency), (2) central tendency (center), and (3) dispersion (spread). If analyzing multiple genres of dance, you might want to describe the frequency of dancers in each genre. Describing frequency uses distribution to characterize your sample (see Figure 21.3a). Central tendency is estimating the center of your data (see Figure 21.3b). Common measures of central tendency are mean (average), median (exact middle), and mode (most frequent). For instance, you might say that on average the participants had ten years of dance training. Common measures used to look at dispersion or spread around *center* are range, variance, and standard deviation (see Figure 21.3c). The range is the difference between the highest and the lowest values. Variance is the sum of squares, which is when you take the difference between each data point and the center and add up squared values (which eliminates the $+/\sqrt{}$). Standard deviation is the square root of variance. Descriptive statistics never drive research, but rather, they help to better understand samples and tell the story of your study. Putting these concepts together in an example, a study included five hip hop dancers, ten ballet dancers, and seven hula dancers (frequency), all of whom had ten years of dance training on average (central tendency), with ages ranging from 18 to 25 (dispersion). This begins to allow your data to tell the story of your study.

Distribution, center, and spread are, in essence, data reduction tools that provide summaries. Using data reduction, you have the potential to mask part of the data. Therefore, choices in measures arise such as the choice between mean, median, and mode. Mean is commonly used when data is normally distributed,

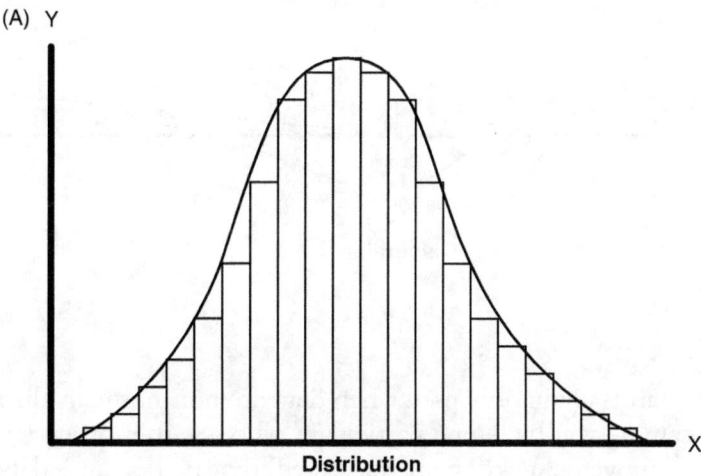

Figure 21.3 Histogram. Graph A shows a histogram highlighting frequencies of variable X on the Y axis which illustrates the distribution of the data. In this case, the data approximate normal distribution. Graph B shows a positively skewed (non-normal) distribution of variable X. This highlights the fact that although measures of central tendency do not always line up together, they are ways to approximate center. Graph C shows a schematic of two distributions that highlights dispersion (the distance from the end of the tails to the center).

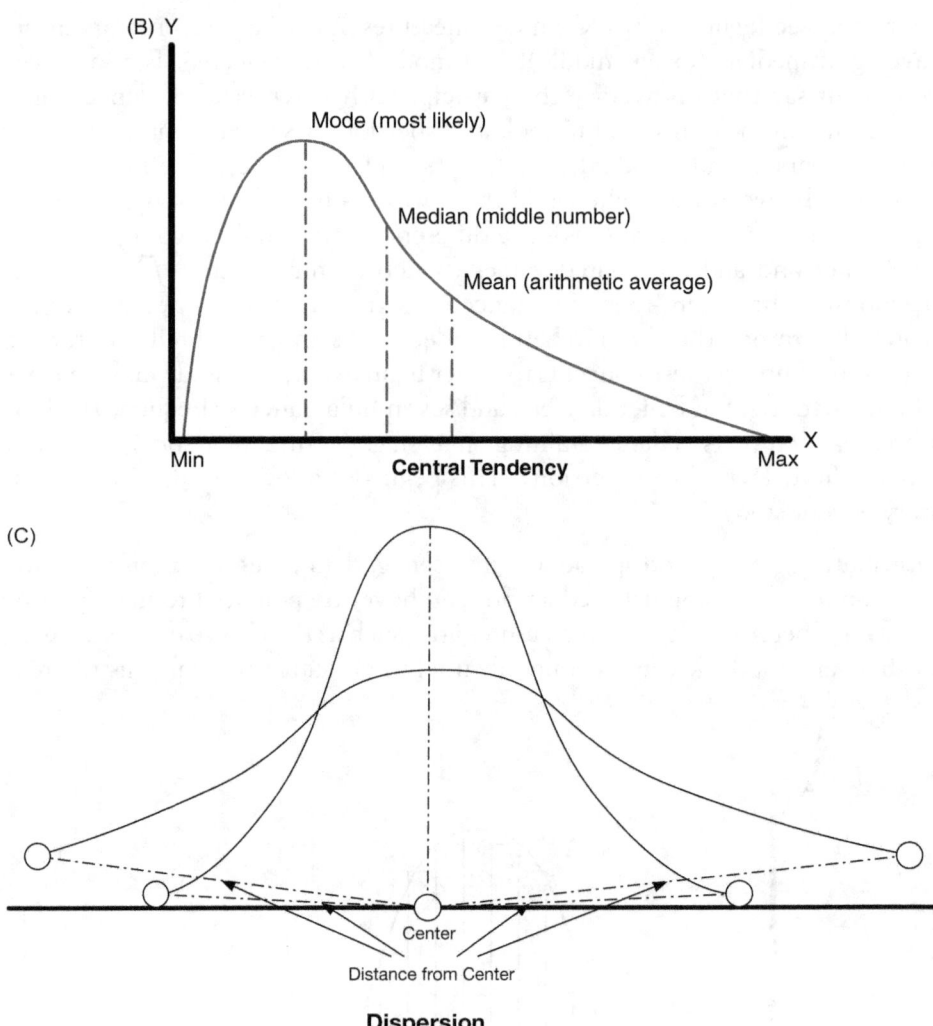

Figure 21.3 Continued

and the median is commonly used when data are non-normally distributed. If in a small sample you have one participant who is either exceptionally good or bad at the movement skill being measured, that participant's data may pull mean in one direction or another, thus falling outside of *normal* range. In this case, median is a better estimate. If your center is not the average (mean), then you want to consider a range (e.g. interquartile range) because it may not be appropriate to use standard deviation and reporting range is more useful. Any sole measurement is not a complete representation of your data. This is why using center, distribution, and spread together facilitates understanding.

Inferential Statistics

Hypothesis testing, based on testing differences in descriptive statistics (e.g. mean, median), is used to make inferences. When using inferential statistics, the first consideration should be the normality of data. This is a determining factor for whether to use parametric (i.e. normally distributed) or nonparametric (i.e. non-normally distributed) testing. The main difference between parametric and nonparametric testing is assumptions made about the underlying distribution. Parametric tests assume underlying properties based on normal bell-shaped distribution and require several conditions to be met. Nonparametric testing does not rely on an underlying distribution and can be applied when the data does not follow a normal distribution. This makes nonparametric tests more robust, meaning they can still be used even if all the assumptions are not met. For example, a traditional Analysis of Variance (ANOVA)[16] can manage a violation of normality but cannot manage the effects of outliers. Parametric testing has more statistical power,[17] meaning it will typically yield a smaller *p*-value than a nonparametric test when both are run on the same dataset.

Statistical assumptions to consider include:

- Sample size – number of participants;
- Normality – the property of the distribution of any random variable (how often they occur);
- Skewness – measures the distortion from a symmetrical bell curve of the normal distribution;
- Kurtosis – measurement used to describe the degree to which scores cluster in the tails (ends) of a distribution;
- Homogeneity of variance – an assumption that two or more group samples have similar variances or spreads (i.e. distribution around mean);
- Randomness – lack of pattern in events (i.e. not predictable); and
- Multicollinearity – high correlation between variables (e.g. measuring the same thing).

Violations of assumptions affect the validity of your findings. In some cases, statistical tests are robust vis-a-vis violations, and the intended test can still be used if statistical corrections have been made to ensure accurate results. For example, if a variable is non-normally distributed, you may try a square root transformation of the data to see if that follows a normal distribution. As mentioned above, transformations are not without consequence. Once a transformation is applied, one can only interpret data based on the transformation, which affects interpretability.

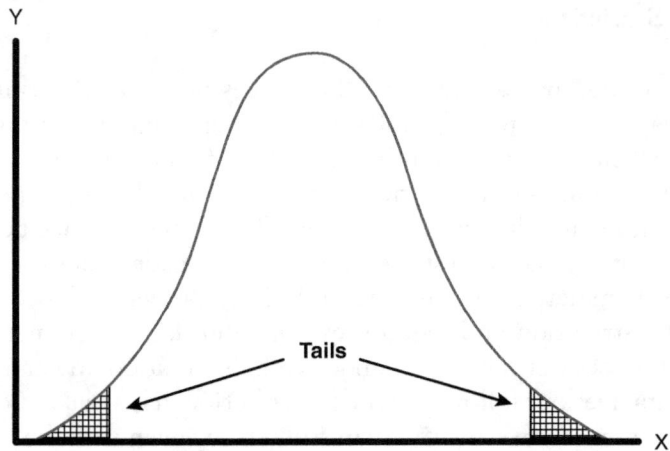

Figure 21.4 Two tails of a distribution. The distribution shown is a symmetrical bell curve, normal distribution.

Before deciding on a statistical test, I consider if my hypothesis will require a one-tailed or two-tailed test, or if it requires statistics at all. A one-tailed test checks for a relationship in one direction and ignores the possibility that the relationship may exist in the opposite direction. For example, if the null hypothesis is equal to X, a one-tailed test only checks for data that is > X or for data that is < X but not the possibility of both, whereas a two-tailed test will check if the data is either > or < than X (see Figure 21.4).

For example, if I am studying whether a dance program can increase step length, the possibility exists that step length can either increase or decrease as a result of the program, thus a two-tailed test is a warranted. If I were to wrongly use a one-tailed test, I would be ignoring the possibility that the program could in fact decrease step length. When comparing two dance programs on their ability to increase step length, I may choose a one-tailed test as I am only interested in testing the benefit (positive direction) and there is no ethical issue with ignoring the potential decrease in step length (negative direction). A one-tailed test has greater statistical power to detect significance, but it must be considered whether this is logically warranted. It is not appropriate to choose a one-tailed test simply because of increased power. Proceed with a one-tailed test if you have reason and evidence to believe the effect to be one-directional and the consequences of missing an effect in an untested direction are negligible and in no way irresponsible or unethical. In most interventional studies, you will not know the direction because the possibility of declining based on the intervention always exists, thus a two-tailed test is warranted.

Running more tests than necessary is not a best practice for research, because it increases the chances of finding a type I error by chance. Statistical methods exist to correct for this increased risk, such as a Bonferroni correction[18] (Bonferroni 1936) or Holm's method[19] (Holm 1979). I map out my planned comparisons to decide which comparisons are necessary and related to my research question. Some additional comparisons may be of interest but may not serve the study at hand.

I have covered several of my considerations for choosing a specific statistical test, including the type of data, distribution, sample size, and type of research question. An additional consideration is the number of comparison groups. For example, comparison groups would be a deciding factor between a t-test[20] (2-groups) and an analysis of variance (ANOVA) (3-groups) if all other factors, such as normality, were the same.

Many parametric and nonparametric inferential statistical tools exist, ranging from a simple t-test (used to compare two group means) to complex machine learning algorithms such as random forests[21] (Ho 1995) that are used to solve classification problems. Using more complex and advanced statistical modeling is not always better. With my background, I can use complex statistical modeling such as unsupervised machine learning;[22] however, if that makes my data more difficult to understand, decreases the interpretability of my finding, or doesn't answer my research question, then it is not the model or test to use. I always choose the simplest and most appropriate method for my research question.

Steps of Statistical Analysis

The first step after data collection is data cleaning, which is a process for fixing or removing incorrect data and making sure data is formatted correctly. During the data entry process, I use double data entry: a second person goes through and makes sure all data entered are correct. I examine ranges for all variables to make sure they fall within the appropriate range. Unsupervised machine learning uses algorithms to analyze or cluster unlabeled datasets. It allows you to find underlying patterns or groupings in your data. For example, if a scale is only 0–12 and I see a 13, this data is incorrect and investigation is needed to fix it.

This step is where I often uncover missing data. Sometimes missing data reflects a simple data entry error, and I can go back to my original data collection documents and enter the appropriate data. Other times, this data is actually missing, which requires more thought. Generally, in statistical terms, there are three types of missing data: (1) missing completely at random, (2) missing at random, and (3) missing not at random. Missing completely at random means there is no pattern in the missing data. Missing at random means there is a pattern present in the missing data but not in the primary dependent variables. Missing not at random is where the pattern affects your primary variables. Dealing with missing data also raises ethical concerns because data is being manipulated and this can introduce bias.

Common techniques for missing data include listwise deletion, average imputation, regression substitution, and multiple imputations. Deleting the participants with missing data affects your sample size and may result in the exclusion of important information. Similarly, using the mean (average) to fill in the missing data will decrease your variance and standard deviation. Regression substitution uses a regression model[23] to estimate the missing data based on your existing data. This reduces variance and increases the chance of error. Multiple imputations[24] are computationally complex and require the analysis of results across multiple imputed datasets. This is not to say one technique is better; each has its use and purpose and requires a look into the reasoning and logic. Therefore, I include steps for missing data in my SAP to minimize bias and to have a structured procedure in place before seeing the data.

After data cleaning, I analyze the data visually. I like to plot my data in various ways, including histograms,[25] Q-Q plots,[26] box plots,[27] and scatter plots.[28] During visual analysis, you may come across outliers. An outlier is not necessarily bad, and you should not jump to exclude an outlier without considering why they are an outlier and what this does to your data. Exclusion of outliers can raise ethical issues. You should not exclude an outlier simply because they do not follow the pattern that you want or because they influence results against your hypothesis. For example, if you are doing an analysis of dance education programs in the 50 states you cannot delete dance education programs in Alaska or Hawaii simply because they are geographic outliers. All outliers require research into what makes them an outlier and what their influence is. Sometimes an outlier may have substantial influence and may not match your data for a valid reason that justifies exclusion. In one study, when examining outliers I realized that a participant did not meet the inclusion criteria and should never have been collected. In this case, I did remove the participant.

Next, I begin to analyze the data using methods laid out in my SAP. The statistical techniques allow me to test underlying relationships and allow me to examine results, making sense of the information collected. However, statistical analysis is only able to indicate if variables or groups are mathematically different. It is my job as the research scientist to make sense of the data and relate this back to the literature.

There are several reasons why results may not be significant, including a too-small sample size, poorly collected data, or there actually being no real effect. All these options are plausible and only a small subset of the reasons why something may or may not be significant. Data tell a story and statistical techniques help uncover that story. Most often, there is something that the collected data can't tell me, which leads to future research questions.

Sharing of Research

There are many ways in which I share my work. Publishing in academic journals is important to document the research, ideally in open-access journals. However, publishing fees for open access are greater and often are not affordable based on funding, which means much of the research ends up behind paywalls that are not accessible to the public. Publishing rights limit the free publication of information, but many publishers do allow researchers to share their work privately by request. Conferences are also a good way to disseminate information, but similarly require expensive conference fees, making them inaccessible for many.

I strongly believe in making the research accessible to the communities for which the research is conducted. As my work involves disabled communities, I often provide lectures or community sessions for nonprofits and support groups in those communities. Translations increase costs but are important in terms of accessibility to non-English speakers. Digital accessibility is also a concern; I have yet to come across a journal that has requested Alt Text for any images or figures for people using screen readers to access articles. This book, in contrast, does use Alt Text for images. Furthermore, the digital divide means the dissemination of research in printed form is still needed. I honor any requests to share my manuscripts with those unable to access them otherwise, and I am still learning ways to make the dissemination of research more equitable and inclusive. Research requires advocacy to bring information to the community and related stakeholders. These entities can use research and data to drive change in policy and/or the interrelated dance ecology.

Conclusion

Dance research is growing, and critical views of its methodologies are essential. We need to examine how data is collected, stored, and analyzed to ensure equity with regard to whose data is collected and whose stories are told. Thinking statistically penetrates all aspects of my research and goes beyond the rote execution of a statistical test of significance, thus ensuring that I am always thinking about and refining my methodology. I believe researchers have a duty to be ethical and to use stringent methods to ensure the validity of results. Even if researchers are not working with quantitative data, a process based on logic and considerations around error, sample size, data, analysis, and reduction of bias still apply. My work in dance for health is only a small subset of the work being done, and the views presented in this chapter are my own. Good research does not happen in silos, and cross-collaboration, especially involving the impacted communities, is necessary. Equitable data collection and critical thinking about data and analyses are the first steps in advocating for meaningful policy change and change in the communities with which we are involved.

Notes

1 https://danceforparkinsons.org
2 https://heidilatskydance.org
3 Data reduction is the transformation of data into a simpler form often providing aggregate or summary statistics.
4 Hypothesis testing is a method of inferential statistics specifying which outcomes of a study may lead to rejection of the null hypothesis at a prespecified level of significance.
5 Statistical level of significance is a measure of the strength of the evidence that must be present in your sample before you will reject the null hypothesis and conclude that the effect is statistically significant.
6 Statistically significant is when results pass the threshold set by the statistical level of significance. It means that the results are unlikely to have occurred under the null hypothesis, if the null hypothesis is assumed to be true.
7 Bias is any systematic deviation between the results and the "truth."
8 A perfect statistical test would have zero false positives and zero false negatives. However, statistical tests are probabilistic and include a level of uncertainty. Type I error rate is the significance level, type II error rate is the power of a statistical test.
9 Correlation is a statistical term to quantify the degree to which two variables move in coordination with one another.
10 Reliability is the overall consistency of a measure when the measurement is repeated.
11 Validity of a measure means that it has been tested against a gold-standard and is measuring what it is supposed to be measuring.
12 *A priori* is the probability before receiving new information such as results, which is why it is always best practice to set your significance levels prior to conducting your study.

13 Fishing is also known as p-hacking, which is running multiple statistical tests and only reporting those which come back as statistically significant. This is not ethical and leads to invalid results.
14 Kolmogorov-Smirnov test for normality checks to see if a variable follows a given distribution, typically the normal distribution.
15 Shapiro-Wilk is a statistical test to see if a random sample comes from a normal distribution.
16 ANOVA is a statistical formula to compare variances across the means of difference groups.
17 Statistical power is the probability of detecting an effect (i.e., difference), if a true effect is to be found.
18 Bonferroni correction is a method to counteract the multiple-comparison problem when several tests are being performed together.
19 Holm's Method is a modification of the Bonferroni and allows for more statistical power as compared to the Bonferroni correction.
20 T-test is a parametric inferential statistic which tests for differences between two group means to determine if there is an experimental effect.
21 Random Forests is a complex machine learning algorithm using multiple regression models. It is often used to solve classification problems and is not based on hypothesis testing.
22 Unsupervised machine learning uses algorithms to analyze or cluster unlabeled datasets. It allows you to find underlying patterns or groupings in your data.
23 Regression is a statistical method that mathematically sorts out which variables do and do not have impact.
24 Multiple imputations create several plausible computationally created datasets, then combine results across those computational datasets.
25 Histogram is a bar graph-like representation of data that groups data into ranges of outcomes providing a graphical visual of a distribution.
26 Q-Q plot or quantile-quantile plot is a graphical tool used to assess data coming from some theoretical distribution (e.g. Normal). It plots two quantiles (i.e., percentiles) against one another.
27 Box plot or box and whiskers plot draws a box from the first quartile to the third quartile with a line at the median. The whiskers go from each quartile to the minimum or maximum.
28 Scatter plot is a graph in which the values of two variables are plotted along two axes.

Works Cited

Bahner, Daniel, Ariella Barker, Shoshana Bloom, Suzanne Feinspan, Valerie Feldman, Ilana Kaufman, Laurence Kotler-Berkowit, et al. 2021. "More Than Numbers: A Guide Toward Diversity, Equity, Inclusion (DEI) in Data Collection." Charles and Lynn Schusterman Family Philanthropies. https://cloudspn.tfaforms.net/266232

Berg, K., S. Wood-Dauphine, J.I. Williams and D. Gayton. 1989. "Measuring Balance in the Elderly: Preliminary Development of an Instrument." *Physiotherapy Canada* 41, no. 2 304–311.

Bohannon, Richard. W. 2017. "Normative Reference Values for the Two-Minute Walk Test Derived by Meta-Analysis." *Journal of Physical Therapy Science* 29, no. 12: 2224–2227. https://doi.org/10.1589/jpts.29.2224

Bonferroni, C.E. 1936. "Teoria Statistica Delle Classi e Calcolo Delle Probabilità." *Pubblicazioni Del R Istituto Superiore Di Scienze Economiche e Commerciali Di Firenze.*

Chakravarti, Indra Mohan, Radha Govind, and Jogabrata Roy. 1967. *Handbook of Methods of Applied Statistics*. Volume 1. Hoboken, NJ: John Wiley & Sons Inc.

Cumming, Geoff. 2012. *Understanding the New Statistics: Effect Sizes, Confidence Intervals, and Meta-Analysis*. New York: Routledge.

Gaddy, Marcus, and Kassie Scott. 2020. *Principles for Advancing Equitable Data Practice*. Urban Institute. https://www.urban.org/sites/default/files/publication/102346/-principles-for-advancing-equitable-data-practice.pdf.

Ho, Tin Kam. 1995. "Random Decision Forests." *Proceedings of 3rd International Conference on Document Analysis and Recognition* 1: 278–282. https://doi.org/10.1109/ICDAR.1995.598994.

Holm, Sture. 1979. "A Simple Sequentially Rejective Multiple Test Procedure." *Scandinavian Journal of Statistics* 2: 65–70.Kaluf, Brian. 2014. "Evaluation of Mobility in Persons with Limb Loss Using the Amputee Mobility Predictor and the Prosthesis Evaluation Questionnaire – Mobility Subscale: A Six-Month Retrospective Chart Review." *JPO: Journal of Prosthetics and Orthotics* 26, no. 2:70–76.

Lee-Ibarra, Joyce. 2021. "Data Equity: What Is It, and Why Does It Matter?" Hawaii Data Collaborative. https://www.hawaiidata.org/ideas/2020/7/1/data-equity-what-is-it-and-why-does-it-matter

Mitlin, D., J. Bennett, P. Horn, S. King, J. Mackau, and G.M. Nyama. 2020. "Knowledge Matters: The Potential Contribution of the Coproduction of Research." *The European Journal of Development Research* 32: 544–559. https://doi.org/10.1057/s41287-020-00277-w.

Morris, Rosie, Samuel Stuart, Grace McBarron, Peter C. Fino, Martina Mancini, and Carolin Curtze. 2019. "Validity of Mobility Lab (version 2) for Gait Assessment in Young Adults, Older Adults, and Parkinson's Disease." *Physiological Measurement* 40, no. 9. https://pubmed.ncbi.nlm.nih.gov/31470423/.

Newcombe, Freda. 1969. *Missile Wounds of the Brain. A Study of Psychological Deficits.* London: Oxford University Press.

Powell, Lynda Elaine and Anita M. Myers. 1995. "The Activities-Specific Balance Confidence (ABC) Scale." *The Journals of Gerontology: Series A* 50A, no. 1: M28–M34. https://doi.org/10.1093/gerona/50A.1.M28

Shapiro, S.S., and M.B. Wilk. 1965. "An Analysis of Variance Test for Normality (Complete Samples)" *Biometrika* 52, no. 3–4: 591–611. https://doi.org/10.1093/biomet/52.3-4.591.

Smith, Aaron. 1982. *Symbol Digit Modalities Test: Manual*. Los Angeles: Western Psychological Services.

Stalvey, Beth T., Cynthia Owsley, Michael E. Sloane, and Karlene Ball. 1999. "The Life Space Questionnaire: A Measure of the Extent of Mobility of Older Adults." *Journal of Applied Gerontology* 18, no. 4 (December): 479–498.

Stroop, John Ridley. 1935. "Studies of Interference in Serial Verbal Reactions." *Journal of Experimental Psychology* 18, no. 6: 643–662.

22
A Dance/Movement Therapy Approach to Interview Analysis

Tomoyo Kawano

Dance/movement therapy (DMT) is a creative arts therapy (CAT) discipline that utilizes the body and dance as knowledge and tools for therapeutic change. Implemented in a variety of clinical and community settings such as hospitals, schools, residential treatment centers, rehabilitation, and correctional facilities, as well as places of worship and at site-specific performances, the profession was established in the 1940s and 1950s through a process of trial and error experimentation in clinical practice (Chaiklin 1975, as cited in Cruz 2016). With origins from indigenous and traditional healing practices from around the world, DMT developed transdisciplinarily alongside music, drama, art, poetry, and other expressive arts modalities; as well as interdisciplinarily within pre-existing frameworks of psychological theories of health, arts, and the social sciences.

Dance/movement therapists show up in their bodies with a diversity of lived experiential knowledge. Yet, the extant knowledge base of DMT is derived from the conviction of white cis-female dancers and what is considered scientific and true in North American academia (Kawano and Chang 2019). Much of the literature and research historically reflect the perspectives of a select group of people writing for a particular audience in mind. Indigenous Māori researcher Linda Tuhiwai Smith (2021) spoke of being excluded from the focus when reading research texts, requiring her to orient herself to a text whose worldview is mostly European-American. Likewise, clinical and educational research praxis do not always account for the divergent identities of researchers. Power dynamics that are addressed in research tend to be that of the researcher and participant. The assumption is that the researcher has power, and in terms of status, this is true. However, socially ascribed memberships in certain groups impact the practitioner–researcher's positionality and engagement as well, and the discourse on such researcher identity is scarce.

In this chapter, I first describe how I developed a DMT research approach to analyzing interviews as part of my doctoral dissertation between 2013 and 2016

DOI: 10.4324/9781003145615-27

(Kawano 2017). I lay out how my embodied, cultural, esthetic background led me to want to develop an arts-based, systematized research methodology based on DMT practice. I then outline the steps of the approach itself. The DMT-based interview analysis method can be used by any researcher who has a dance/movement vocabulary and a willingness to stay open to the unknown. A possible application of this methodology is for a researcher to enact their own embodied identities to better understand the culturally situated resources they bring into their community in the forms of therapy, research, education, and performance. As part of the work of developing a critical cultural consciousness, which is a continual process, "as opposed to a learnable technique with a finite endpoint" (Azzopardi and McNeill 2016, 296), it is my wish that joining in a person's experience through a dance will bring forth better relationships with future clients and professionals, and community members to care.

The Process of Developing a DMT Practice Approach to Research

This first section tracks my process of explicating a relationship between scientific inquiry and the relational, esthetic phenomenological knowledge of DMT. In qualitative phenomenological research, verbal interviews are commonly used to explore the in-depth experiences of people. By systematizing the process of analyzing an interview using DMT practice skills such as observing, sensing, dancing, and reflecting, I hoped to share how the way that DMT practitioners come to know about a phenomenon can be applied in a research process.

Deciding What to Explore: "Who am I?" and "Who is the Research For?"

The constructivist epistemological perspective of qualitative inquiry and the interview method's focus on meaning-making align well with what happens in DMT. But qualitative research is still largely conducted in a way that separates the researcher's interoceptive bodily awareness and affective experience, as well as the researcher from their participants (Freedman and Wolf 2020). The contents of the interview, considered as data, are analyzed by the "expert" researcher, rather than collaboratively with the participants, usually through verbal means. The shared experience of the conversation may be recalled independently "where encoded information is largely abstracted beyond sensory constraints" (Chen et al. 2017, 115).

Interviewing in DMT clinical practice is a fundamental procedure to gather data about a client and begin to develop a therapeutic relationship. As a dance/movement therapist, I noticed that verbal transcripts that are commonly used in a research process were limited in their rendering of what was happening inter-corporeally in the interview interaction. Beyond pauses and other nonverbal cues, unspoken relational dynamics that reflect the systemic, social norms of peoples' ways of being, could not be encapsulated through verbal means of data collection and analysis. This inspired me to develop a DMT-based methodology to make sense of what was left hanging in a cloud, a mist, amorphous and intangible, that was not accessed in words.

An essential aspect of developing the approach was the congruency between my cultural heritage and DMT practice in the way that I embody knowledge, and with those, I wanted to engage in the research with. Thinking back to when I conducted a qualitative study for my master's thesis as a therapist-in-training, I recall how I was deeply aware of my social location as a Japanese woman living in a predominantly white neighborhood in the southwest of the United States. It was not so much that I wanted to be conscious about my racial or ethnic background, but in the suburban clinical practice where I was doing my field training, and academic institutional spaces where I was an international student, I was exoticized, being reminded daily that I was "different" in subtle but consistent ways. The invisible gap between my instinctual way of being in the world and what was being conveyed, felt larger depending on where I was and the people I was with. Feeling that a different message was being communicated from what I intended would impel me to *be* and *do* things according to Euro-American academic and professional cultural norms.

Bicultural individuals can instinctively "frame switch" (Hong et al. 2000, 710). Depending on the language that researchers use and who the researchers are, the participants will be primed to respond in particular ways (Hong et al. 2000). For social desirability, research participants with historically marginalized social locations may be cognizant of the gaze of those who hold more power and respond in a way that keeps them safe.

I decided to explore the relational differences between Japanese and Euro-American women as a way for me to engage who I was in the research process, and to learn how I may facilitate DMT in a cultural context outside of what was typically white, hetero-cis female. Interviewing bicultural Japanese women like myself in our native tongue, and listening to their stories was validating for me as the researcher, and for the participants as well. A temporary relief and a certain safety were created for the women who had similarly felt the need *to be* different. There seemed to be something relevant and important about showing care for a particular community through research, so that others might also care.

DMT Research and Ways of Knowing

DMT research shares the ethical concerns of healthcare research of informing and advancing clinical skills (Cruz and Berrol 2019). In addition to a multitude of observational case studies, increasing numbers in randomized control trials and advances in neurological and neuropsychological research in the decades since have provided quantitative and qualitative evidence for the potentiality of DMT's mind-body integration approaches for trauma treatment (Dieterich-Hartwell and Melsom 2022; Levine and Land 2016) and various other neurological and psychological conditions (Cruz 2016; Karkou et al. 2019; Koch et al. 2019). While evidence-based DMT treatment studies are needed for clinical accountability (Lyons et al. 2018), articulating what can be known via the embodied, relational, esthetic phenomenology of DMT is vital for humanizing those who engage in an exploratory process.

Typical DMT research follows traditional, academic ways of knowing and relies on verbal language and the written word that is assumed to originate in the "head/mind." The embodied neurological functions of the "head brain" are cognition, thinking, and making meaning; the "heart brain" concerns emoting, attending to one's values and relationships; and the "gut brain" is tuned into one's core identity, self-preservation, and mobilization and action (Soosalu, Henwood, and Deo 2019). These distinctions tell us that a person's worldviews, how someone might relate to others, hold their tongue, stay silent, or engage in self-care, may not come through via verbal content. In psychological gender/sex binary research, experiential, intuitive, and emotional thinking styles are associated with enacting feminine traits (Norris and Epstein 2011); women tend to locate themselves in the heart, rather than the head (Fetterman and Robinson 2013). It is curious to think about how certain types of knowledge are prioritized in academia and endorsed systemically.

Compared to "masculine," "hard" postpositivism, DMT knowledge may be gendered as "feminine" and "soft" (Meekums 2010) – sensed and abstracted, rather than concretely documented. But even in "hard" neuroscientific research, assumed to be "something rooted in dispassionate collective technique," Fitzgerald (2013) found that the autism neuroscience researchers' focus on the visceral, "gut feelings" and emotions – their emotional labor was what kept them passionately pursuing their work (2013, 10). To consider the ethical importance of balancing "our well-established cognitive, rational, 'objective,' impersonal ways of knowing with visceral forms of understanding" (Douglas and Carless 2013, 58), attending to bodies may be a step toward shedding the belief that the body and dance are adjunctive, rather than essential to accessing certain types of knowledge.

DMT Practice: Emergent Meaning and Functional Insights

Dance/movement therapists train in movement observation, assessment, and treatment and develop skills to attend to relational, nonverbal body-based processes and symbolic expression through dance, and co-create meaning with their clients. The integrated body–mind interventions utilized in DMT practice include empathic mirroring, rhythmic synchrony through body movement, and social interaction, all inherent in dance. These, incidentally, are assumed to enhance brain networks that support a person's ability to better connect intra- and inter-personally (Basso, Satyal, and Rugh 2021). Drawing on developmental theories of infant-caretaker interactions, DMT practitioners attend to body communication that includes facial expressions, as well as the acoustics of the pitch and rhythm of babbling (Loman 1998), and reciprocally moderate through mirroring and other ways of attuning, sharing in a social world (Hasson et al. 2012). Just as a good listener might be able to predict or anticipate the speech patterns of the speaker, from a neuroscientific standpoint, the "coupling" of brains that happens through nonverbals such as hand gestures, facial expressions, and environmental stimuli, leads to creating "new phenomena, including verbal and non-verbal communication systems and interpersonal social institutions" (Hasson et al. 2012, 120). From a phenomenological standpoint, attending to the bodily sensory experiences is both the process and resolution for the therapist and client's embodied, intersubjective, empathic engagement.

DMT, like dance, is also largely non-goal-oriented (Wiedenhofer and Koch 2017). DMT clients may be encouraged to tune in and listen to their own bodies, or to the bodies of others, and express themselves through a choreographed or improvised dance. In an improvised dance, the dancer has the freedom to play and organize, and become a part of the environment in space, experiencing a feeling of oneness, which may promote body self-efficacy and well-being (Wiedenhofer and Koch 2017). Displaced persons such as immigrants and refugees may not have the shared language to express their experience in words, but find an opportunity to do so through dance and movement (Harris 2009). Verbal language may be used, but articulation is not necessary. Prior dance experience for a client is optional because it is assumed that the therapist has the technical and affective skills to meet the person where they are by listening in movement and responding in kind.

Arts-Based Research: Praxis for Insights to Emanate

A research method that is compatible with the skills of DMT is arts-based research (ABR). Like DMT, ABR utilizes aesthetics as methodological tools at any stage of the research process to expand what can be known. Much like in DMT practice, the arts are used to generate questions, elicit data, analyze data, and/or represent findings (Leavy 2015) at any or all stages of the research process. Douglas and Carless (2018) identified three modes of ABR engagement: "interdependent engagement with people and place, aesthetic engagement with sense making processes, and emotional engagement with and of audiences" (2018, 156).

ABR can be perceived as an event or "praxis of relating to that which we cannot know about but are called by" (Visse, Hansen, and Leget 2019, 11). The researcher is vulnerable to communicate and represent their empirical observation as well as what they experienced and how that intersects with their experience of the research participant in an interdependent engagement with people and place. In this way, dance is the life medium to stay receptive and open to the unknown.

One of the hallmarks of ABR is the process of making meaning through the use of the arts. Although ABR is generally associated with qualitative research or a category of practice in and of itself, there are accounts of scientists testing out experimental theories in movement and using dance for scientific discovery, or representing scientific findings. For example, instead of concretizing and over-determining the temporal flow and accuracy of a process, the elastic nature of "body experiments" – playing with rhythms and molecular time – allow scientists to "use their bodies as proxies to test out the attractive and repulsive forces and tensions between atoms in a molecule" (Myers 2012, 171). According to these scientists, the main reason for using dance and movement for scientific discovery is their fluidity. Furthermore, body experiments were described as "*transductive*; that is, they can propagate forms of knowing through performative articulations that excite others into action" (Myers 2012, 178). The elastic dance renderings could then be used to educate colleagues and students in the classrooms. Myers' study provides further support for the essentiality of dynamic movement, or esthetic engagement, to keep open the possibilities for new understandings to emerge.

In ABR the researcher is not only an observer but also a dancer/performer who is emotionally engaged with the dance and with the participant(s) and/or audience. Furthermore, the arts are not only a means for data collection and representation, but a way to connect with a variety of stakeholders for "pedagogical and transformational purposes" (Visse et al. 2019, 3). An embodied and arts-based enactive approach to research is a counterbalance to conducting research from the head, using words, and being the "expert" to uncover something that is assumed to be already there.

Frameworks for Inducting the DMT Approach to Interview Analysis

My plan for systematizing the arts-based interview analysis process based in DMT was to conduct a qualitative interview study, but construct the data analysis process with an arts-based approach that I would create utilizing the practice skills of DMT. To do this, I needed a framework that allowed me to articulate the specific techniques of DMT and identify what can be known, and also bring who I am to the process.

I chose an Interpretive Phenomenological Approach (IPA) that concerns a hermeneutic interpretive circle where "researchers cannot remove themselves from the meanings extracted from the text. The researcher becomes a part of the phenomenon" (Reiners 2012, 2). The researcher interprets their own subjectivity as well as the intersubjectivity with the participant. A dual process of the interpretation of a phenomenon is to make sense of the phenomenon from the participants' point of view, after which the researcher attempts to make sense of the participant's interpretation.

Within IPA, the process of "bracketing" is a way to put forth "preunderstandings and exploiting them reflexively as a source of insight" (Finlay 2009, 13). For dance/movement therapists, this process can be done in movement. Prior to engaging in the data analysis process, I attempted to flesh out my movement preferences with a Certified Movement Analyst (CMA). At the time of my research, Laban Movement Analysis (LMA) and the Kestenberg Movement Profile (KMP) were two main movement observation and assessment frameworks that were being taught at American Dance Therapy Association (ADTA) approved DMT master's programs. In recent years, there have been many conversations on the utility and purported universality of movement classification systems based on European cultural aesthetics in a DMT education and training context. As Candelario (2021) raised, Japanese movement aesthetics values "a concentration of energy into the body" rather than "an outward focus of the body into space" (Rosemary Candelario, Comment to author, July 2, 2021). This is indeed the case for my natural movement affinity. For the purpose of inducting the approach, I felt that the CMA's analysis sufficiently offered a baseline to compare the dances I improvised for my own delight, versus the dances I would create to analyze the interviews. Somewhat unconsciously, however, for the baseline dance, I moved in a style that remained white-adjacent in my dancer-researcher identity, likely anticipating who would be analyzing my movement. This automatic adjustment was something that became second nature. I noticed this only after reading the CMA's analysis and found a lack of mention of my body – something I was made conscious about when I was training in classical ballet. Describing one's somatic form such as size and shape is common in Japan (Kanagawa, Cross, and Marcus 2001), but not generally accepted in the United States because, for instance, seeing "color" was, and is still a taboo. To see a dance is to see the bodies who dance – the tonality of the skin, the proportion of the skeletal structure, muscularity, and so on. This was an example of what is not communicated in a verbal exchange. To show my dancing body in a racialized, gendered, and ableist world is a way to begin to decolonize my own identity as a researcher in my own skin.

To create the dance and movement-based interview analysis procedure, I looked to Gilligan et al.'s (2003) *listening guide* research method and adapted it to align with my cultural views. The clear steps and the use of poetry to analyze a transcript were innovative. However, the step to create "I-poems" to differentiate self and others voices, based on the psychoanalytic premise of the "self" as an independent "I," could be limiting for those from collectivistic cultures, or for whom their primary language was not English (Japanese people seldom refer to themselves as an individual "I"). Similarly to how Japanese-American participants "found it difficult to answer so many 'I-statements' and commented on the general irrelevance of paying any attention to one's own bodily sensations in the Japanese culture," I found in applying the Multidimensional Assessment of Interoceptive Awareness (MAIA), that the instrument's "reliance on I-statements, reflects a Western individualistic cultural-specific view of the world that may not speak to other cultures and languages" (Freedman et al. 2021, 29). For the DMT approach, I modified the step to create "I–poems" to attend to the resonance and dissonance of what was being said in an embodied way.

Steps for the DMT Research Approach to Analyzing Interviews

This next section outlines the DMT approach to analysis that I developed: from data creation, analysis, to the sharing of findings. I intertwine my cultural worldviews and concepts of DMT practice with clinical and practitioner research literature to describe and substantiate my decision-making process.

Interview as Data Creation: A Relational Activity

Data is co-created in the relational activity of an interview. Engaging in interviews can be viewed as social interaction where "the perspectives of the interviewer and the respondent dance together for the moment but also extend outward in social space and backward and forward in time" (Warren 2002, 22). It is a dialogic and evolving process: what a respondent discloses in an interview conversation is relationally dependent on what is being asked and what the respondent is willing to share, consciously or unconsciously, verbally or inter-modally, with the interviewer within a particular context.

According to the Japanese philosopher Watsuji (1889–1960), the fundamental and primary significance of being human is to exist with a body in a physical space: *basho* (Kasulis and Yuasa 1987). Basho is the foundation for the relationship between the interconnection of the natural space and the human (or the intersubjective) meanings of the life-world (Kasulis and Yuasa 1987). The Japanese word for "human being" is *nin-gen*, which is composed of two characters: "person" and "time/space/between." Ningen denotes the communal and spatial nature of human beings as existing "in-between" various networks and relationships that provide social meaning in liminal time and space in a basho. Interactions between people can be seen, not as inner "thoughts" being expressed, but "of engaging in the world across space and time" (Murray and Holmes 2014, 28). The relational activity of the interview is simultaneously the data and how data is generated. Attention should be given to the set-up of the space – whether it is a virtual space or in-person in a conference room, cafe, workplace, etc. – as well as to the frequency and duration of the time together.

In a typical DMT session, the clients are the active agents. The therapist follows them into whatever themes or issues emerge as most salient (Goodill 2005). Similarly, in a research context, the interviewer may have guiding questions, but the interviewee can tell their story without sticking to a researcher's agenda. The researcher has the ethical responsibility to receive and respond to what is being offered in the moment.

It goes without saying that care must be given to the intersectional power dynamics: social locations, status, and capabilities. An often invisible aspect of this dynamic is the enactment of nonverbals between researcher and participant. Nonverbal communication is a major force in displaying and maintaining power structures (Henley 1977). While nonverbal communication can be somewhat fluid, the subtle, emotional expressions are not. Implicit biases and cultural filters and assumptions are a part of the socialization of instantly encoding the meaning of signals within a particular social system that is familiar to a person. The researcher's capacity to recognize that bodies communicate different needs differently is paramount.

Documenting the researcher's feelings, such as first impressions and the atmosphere of the interview, as well as a researcher's sensations, perceptions, and emotional reactions are necessary to track how the findings were affirmed. To avoid the time lapse between the immediate embodied experience of the researcher and later analysis of the conversation that may result in "alterations that take place between perceptual experience and later recollection" (Chen et al. 2017, 116), recording the interactions audio-visually is also essential. Recordings are additional ways to capture data visually, of the body language during the interaction; audio recordings, needless to say, amplify the breath and intervals, in addition to sounds that are present in the environment.

Analyzing an Interview: Embodied Dialectics and the Co-Creation of Meaning

The reflexive DMT analysis procedure is as follows: embodied listening to recordings; review of recordings and reflections through movement; creating a dance; sharing the dance and its meaning with the participant for feedback; integrating the feedback for more meaning-making (Tantia and Kawano 2019).

Embodied Listening: Transcribing in Movement

The DMT interpretive process begins during the interview as the interviewer engages and clarifies meaning with the interviewee. There are also cultural implications for clarifying the meaning of words. Self-regulation for Japanese Americans, for instance, is to conform to social expectations and to control oneself, rather than to focus inwardly and achieve "an individual self-comforting sense of homeostasis" (Freedman et al. 2021, 1). Yet, certain experiences cannot be put into words: "something that, ironically, poetry might accomplish in poetic terms" (Gubrium and Holstein 2002, 21). This is where movement comes in. Picking up on nonverbal signals, and relational and environmental stimuli, dancers know that thinking *in* dance can ground scientific phenomenological knowledge "in finer and deeper truths about sense-making" (Sheets-Johnstone 2011, 180). Glesne engaged in a poetic transcription to "illuminate the wholeness and interconnections of thoughts […] searching for the essence conveyed, the hues, the textures, and then drawing from all portions of the interviews to juxtapose details into a somewhat abstract re-presentation" (1997, 206). In kind, an inherent step of the DMT analysis is to listen to the interview conversation and "transcribe" in movement (Tantia and Kawano 2019). Just as one listens and re-listens to a verbal transcription, the researcher moves, and moves again while listening and/or watching the video recording of the conversation.

Review of Recordings: Introspection

Interviewing is a complex process that is not simply a way to procure information, but negotiating and generating truths (White and Drew 2011). Just as one re-reads the transcript, the researcher then reviews the video recordings. These literally provide an alternative perspective. *What resonated? Where were the dissonances?* Reflection on the written documentation of the researcher's embodied state should also happen during this time. Together, this step provides opportunities for insight to emerge. Intuitions emerge into consciousness as "bodily awareness" and "cognitive awareness," where bodily awareness comprises two first-order concepts of "gut reactions" and "feelings" (Sadler-Smith and Shefy 2004).

Creating a Dance

Based on embodying the gestures and movement phrases that emerged thus far, the researcher locates movement patterns and creates a dance. Hunter et al. (2002) claim that making meaning was the creative aspect of qualitative research, and that the incubation phase was where the "magic" (2002, 388) happened. Likening the incubation phase to "intellectual chaos," the authors and their five research subjects claimed that this nonlinear phase was where patterns emerged and conclusions were made (Hunter et al. 2002, 389). For dance/movement therapists, the incubation phase, in which chaos is transformed through an intuitive and creative process, can happen in a dance.

As Hervey (2019) indicated, the creative process of making a dance is an iterative process of trying out a movement, building on it, and then scrapping it to create anew, until there is a flutter, an insight, where something settles and feels "right." Similar to how different dance forms and body-based practices are drawn upon to create dances with the client in a DMT session, the DMT researcher applies their movement practices and dance techniques. In the words of the poet, Fujiwara Teika (1162–1241),

> An excellent poem is composed not when the author has a definite, thematic plan and clear vision of his composition, feeling he can expedite it immediately, but, rather, when a thematic plan and vision for *waka* poetry comes to him out of the blue without their initiating it.
> (as cited in Kasulis and Yuasa 1987, 101)

The style of a dance should not appropriate or mimic a dance style of any part of the intersectional cultural identity of the participants, unless done together. Just as with a client, the researcher may ask the participant about their preferences for music, determine its use, whether to elicit a particular atmosphere or feeling that was present. The length of a dance can depend on the concision factor, distilling the phenomenological data into a form that uses a minimum amount of space, time, and words (Barone and Eisner 2011).

The interpretation of nonverbal communication and resonance with esthetic choices require particular attention. A person's appearance, perceived subjectively by the researcher, may not be the internal experience of the participant. The same movement might signal gregarious passion and carefreeness to some, while courage and vulnerability to others. Such misinterpretations happen all the time, and the participant is misunderstood. They may experience re-oppression rather than empowerment. Thus, showing oneself in a body can at once be obvious, and unseen.

In the West, attention is paid to the arrangement of objects, while in Japan, attention is given to the arrangement of the *ma*: the space, or the intervals (Hall 1989). In communication, the exact amount of *ma* serves to convey the right message, which also holds true for Japanese dance and other traditional arts. What is left out has as much meaning as what is conveyed in words, and *ma* can hold esthetic value, pleasure, and satisfaction. However, this may not be immediately apparent or a shared esthetic.

Related to this idea is that of dance in ritual. Performing or witnessing a dance/ritual offers an opportunity for knowledge transmission through esthetic means. Community tensions that may otherwise not be dissipated in everyday life have a place to be resolved (Hanna 1987), and ethnic and/or cultural identity can be affirmed (Banks 2009). However, this knowledge may not immediately be clear to an outsider. Prescribed movements may only have meanings for those who share a particular cultural history. Psycho-physiologically, some gestures or facial expressions may be universal, having developed as socio-evolutionary advantages. But as with any language, "Nonverbal communication systems are interwoven with the fabric of the personality and into society itself" (Hall 1989, 82). Given that there is no consensus on interpreting or databases of emotional body gestures (Avots et al. 2019), the meanings of social signals, whether verbal or nonverbal, can only be understood within shared cultural communities, in human relationships. Instead of approaching from the lens of familiarity, body language needs to be examined through the "whole pattern in context of the individual mover having a combination of personal, cultural, and environmental experiences" (Hanna 1990, 117).

To bridge this gap, a researcher can attempt to get closer, to knock on the door, and bow down to be let in through offering to show oneself in-body, in a dance. The offering of the dance is a way to turn the lens back onto the researcher and humbly convey their experience and their experience of the research participants. Being an audience, a witness, attending to, and joining through the sharing of a dance creates an opening for people to connect beyond "understanding." In an intersectional process of attuning, the researcher should be open to not knowing, feeling uncomfortable and jolted, being in a liminal space, and relinquishing possessing the "truth."

Reflexivity: Action and Accountability

Once a dance is created, the researcher shares the recording of the dance, or possibly dances in a space where the participant is present in-person, along with a short statement. The participant then provides a response to the dance. Depending on this feedback, the researcher recreates the dance and shares it again. There is also the possibility for the participant to respond in movement or a dance if they feel called to do so.

Black feminist critical scholars emphasize that knowledge arises in dialogue (Collins 2003): "talk," or in this case, dance "between two subjects, not the speech of subject and object, [...] is a humanizing speech, one that challenges and resists domination" (hooks 1989, 131). Dialectics is a discourse approach to arriving at the truth through engaging a range of perspectives, especially those of opposing viewpoints. Dialectic thinking is pervasive in most East Asian philosophies that perceive that contradictions are inherent in everything. The spirit of a dialectic through dancing is to be radically truthful, take risks, and create new understanding and relationships in a playful, non-confrontational, and protected way, and to recognize that multiple truths can exist simultaneously.

In DMT practice, engaging in an esthetic dialectic is a way to examine how social reality works. In research, co-creating a dance can critically examine how bodies influence and enhance the understanding of researchers and participants' responses to human experiences. Even if researchers and participants may not engage in a dance-off (which might be one way to engage in a dance dialectic), the spirit of an esthetic dialectic can be a part of the research. Knowledge creation is dependent on staying engaged in the relationship, and with the afterthoughts that remain unresolved, and the conversations to be continued.

Sharing the Dance: Cyclical Accountability and Care

After the dance is shared (maybe more than once), and meaning is co-created, there can be a process of sharing the work with the larger community. This can be a communal performance or forum, academic presentation, or a publication shared through the written word. The beauty of technology is that linked videos and visuals can get to the essence of the practice and communicate what gets lost in black-and-white two-dimensional publications. Any of these ways of sharing can be opportunities to build on the interview conversations and be witnesses to the participant's lived experience. It can be empowering, but it can also make one vulnerable. The rigor is found in how the dance is received by the participant(s) first, and by the viewer and/or reader, second. Ideally, the emotion is conveyed and evoked for the audience.

There may be residual feelings that linger on, even after a presentation of the research is given. Ultimately, people can be empowered only when they "become seekers of the type of connections, interactions, and meetings that lead to harmony" (Collins 2003, 185) in the community. Dance is an animation, more than a snapshot of the encounter, dynamic in that it spans time and space and is left for deeper, varied reflection.

The Ethics of Caring and Engaging in Communal Artistic Practices

The first time I experienced something that resembled DMT was when I was dancing in an outdoor performance at Lincoln Center Plaza in the late 1990s. In this vast improvisational site work called the *Lunar Opera*, I was given only three instructions in my role as one of the many moonbeams-dancers. One was to listen to what was going on externally in the community and environment. Another was to listen to my internal feelings and sensations. The last was to move out into the space at the moment when silently called for. This experience left me with a sense of exhilaration and satisfaction. I felt I was given the permission and freedom to be who I was. The hope for the DMT approach is that participants and researchers alike can feel the freedom and permission to be themselves, and be seen and reflected back for who they are. A DMT approach to research can be an opportunity for intersectional attunement: transformative and liberatory.

It is important to note that this is just one approach to analyzing interviews, from my professional and cultural perspective, that aligns well with what DMT practitioners naturally do. By systematizing a DMT-based interview analysis process, my hope was for researchers who may be seeking to know in ways beyond verbal language to have opportunities to explore, play, and connect by joining the communities through a dance.

Finally, I believe that researchers who choose to use the arts are motivated to create dialogues with communities that can benefit from the research knowledge. The dynamism involved in the arts can evoke and mobilize individuals and communities toward new perspectives and different ways of doing/being. A dance/movement-based practitioner can move to probe the potential of research to support and enhance care for community members, to show who they are and be, and move with others in a dance. *What is research if it is not about caring for people in the community?*

Works Cited

Avots, Egils, Tomasz Sapiński, Maie Bachmann, and Dorota Kamińska. 2019. "Audiovisual Emotion Recognition in Wild." *Machine Vision & Applications* 30, no. 5: 975–985.

Azzopardi, Corry, and Ted McNeill. 2016. "From Cultural Competence to Cultural Consciousness: Transitioning to a Critical Approach to Working across Differences in Social Work." *Journal of Ethnic & Cultural Diversity in Social Work* 25, no. 4: 282–299.

Banks, Ojeya Cruz. 2009. "Critical Postcolonial Dance Recovery and Pedagogy: An International Literature Review." *Pedagogy, Culture & Society* 17, no. 3: 355–367.

Barone, Tom, and Elliot W. Eisner. 2011. *Arts Based Research*. Thousand Oaks: Sage.

Basso, Julia C., Medha K. Satyal, and Rachel Rugh. 2021. "Dance on the Brain: Enhancing Intra-and Inter-Brain Synchrony." *Frontiers in Human Neuroscience*, no. 14 (January): 586. https://doi.org/10.3389/fnhum.2020.584312

Chen, Janice, Yuan Chang Leong, Christopher J. Honey, Chung H. Yong, Kenneth A. Norman, and Uri Hasson. 2017. "Shared Memories Reveal Shared Structure in Neural Activity across Individuals." *Nature Neuroscience* 20, no. 1: 115–125.

Chaiklin, Harris. *Marian Chace: Her Papers*. Columbia, MD: American Dance Therapy Association, 52–54.

Collins, Patricia Hill. 2003. "Toward an Afrocentric Feminist Epistemology." In *Turning Points in Qualitative Research: Tying Knots in a Handkerchief* 2, edited by Y.S. Lincoln, and N.K. Denzin, 47–72. Walnut Creek, CA: Rowman Altamira.

Cruz, Robyn Flaum. 2016. "Dance/Movement Therapy and Developments in Empirical Research: The First 50 Years." *American Journal of Dance Therapy* 38, no. 2 (October): 297–302.

Cruz, Robyn Flaum, and Cynthia F. Berrol. 2019. "What's Research Got to Do with It?" In *Dance/Movement Therapists in Action: A Working Guide to Research Options* 3, edited by Robyn Flaum Cruz and Cynthia F. Berrol, 12–24. Springfield, IL: Charles C. Thomas.

Dieterich-Hartwell, Rebekka, and Anne Margrethe Melsom, eds. 2022. *Dance/Movement Therapy for Trauma Survivors: Theoretical, Clinical, and Cultural Perspectives*. New York: Routledge.

Douglas, Kitrina, and David Carless. 2013. "An Invitation to Performative Research." *Methodological Innovations Online* 8, no. 1: 53–64.

———. 2018. "Engaging with Arts-Based Research: A Story in Three Parts." *Qualitative Research in Psychology* 15, no. 2–3: 156–172.

Fetterman, Adam K., and Michael D. Robinson. 2013. "Do You Use Your Head or Follow Your Heart? Self-Location Predicts Personality, Emotion, Decision Making, and Performance." *Journal of Personality and Social Psychology* 105, no. 2: 316–334.

Finlay, Linda. 2009. "Exploring Lived Experience: Principles and Practice of Phenomenological Research." *International Journal of Therapy and Rehabilitation* 16, no. 9: 474–481.

Fitzgerald, Des. 2013. "The Affective Labour of Autism Neuroscience: Entangling Emotions, Thoughts and Feelings in a Scientific Research Practice." *Subjectivity* 6, no. 2: 131–152.

Freedman, Aaron, H. Hu, I.T.H.C. Liu, A.L. Stewart, S. Adler, and W.E. Mehling. 2021. "Similarities and Differences in Interoceptive Bodily Awareness between US-American and Japanese cultures: A Focus-Group Study in Bicultural Japanese-Americans." *Culture, Medicine, & Psychiatry* 45, no. 2: 234–267.

Freedman, Aaron, and Wolf Mehling. 2020. "Methods for Measuring Embodiment, an Instrument." In *The Art and Science of Embodied Research Design: Concepts, Methods and Cases*, edited by Jennifer Frank Tantia, 63–74. New York: Routledge.

Gilligan, C., Spencer, R., Weinberg, M. K., & Bertsch, T. 2003. "On the Listening Guide: A Voice-Centered Relational Method." In *Qualitative Research in Psychology: Expanding Perspectives in Methodology and Design*, edited by P.M. Camic, J.E. Rhodes, and L. Yardley, 157–172. Washington, DC: American Psychological Association.

Glesne, Corrine. 1997. "That Rare Feeling: Re-presenting Research through Poetic Transcription." *Qualitative Inquiry* 3, no. 2: 202–221.

Goodill, Sherry. 2005. *An Introduction to Medical Dance/Movement Therapy: Health Care in Motion*. Philadelphia: Jessica Kingsley Publishers.

Gubrium, Jaber F., and James A. Holstein. 2002. *Handbook of Interview Research: Context and Method*. Thousand Oaks: Sage Publications.

Hall, Edward Twitchell. 1989. *Beyond Culture*. New York: Anchor.

Hanna, Judith Lynne. 1987. *To Dance Is Human: A Theory of Nonverbal Communication*. Chicago: University of Chicago Press.

———. 1990. "Anthropological Perspectives for Dance/Movement Therapy." *American Journal of Dance Therapy* 12, no. 2: 115–126.

Harris, David Alan. 2009. "The Paradox of Expressing Speechless Terror: Ritual Liminality in the Creative Arts Therapies' Treatment of Posttraumatic Distress." *The Arts in Psychotherapy* 36, no. 2: 94–104.

Hasson, Uri, Asif A. Ghazanfar, Bruno Galantucci, Simon Garrod, and Christian Keysers. 2012. "Brain-to-Brain Coupling: A Mechanism for Creating and Sharing a Social World." *Trends in Cognitive Sciences* 16, no. 2: 114–121.

Henley, Nancy. 1977. *Body Politics: Power, Sex, and Nonverbal Communication*. Englewood Cliffs, NJ: Prentice Hall.

Hervey, Lenore W. 2019. "Embodied Artistic Inquiry." In *Dance/Movement Therapists in Action: A Working Guide to Research Options 3*, edited by Robyn Flaum Cruz and Cynthia F. Berrol, 200–226. Springfield, IL: Charles C. Thomas.

Hong, Ying-yi, Michael W. Morris, Chi-yue Chiu, and Veronica Benet-Martinez. 2000. "Multicultural Minds: A Dynamic Constructivist Approach to Culture and Cognition." *American Psychologist* 55, no. 7: 709.

hooks, bell. 1989. *Talking Back: Thinking Feminist, Thinking Black*. Boston: South End Press.

Hunter, Anita, Paula Lusardi, Donna Zucker, Cynthia Jacelon, and Genevieve Chandler. 2002. "Making Meaning: The Creative Component in Qualitative Research." *Qualitative Health Research* 12, no. 3: 388–398.

Kanagawa, Chie, Susan E. Cross, and Hazel Rose Markus. 2001. "'Who am I?' The Cultural Psychology of the Conceptual Self." *Personality & Social Psychology Bulletin* 27, no. 1: 90–103.

Karkou, Vicky, Supritha Aithal, Ania Zubala, and Bonnie Meekums. 2019. "Effectiveness of Dance Movement Therapy in the Treatment of Adults with Depression: A Systematic Review with Meta-Analyses." *Frontiers in Psychology* 56, no. 10: 936. https://doi.org/10.3389/fpsyg.2019.00936

Kasulis, Thomas P., and Yasuo Yuasa. 1987. *The Body: Toward an Eastern Mind-Body Theory*. Albany, NY: SUNY Press.

Kawano, Tomoyo. 2017. "Developing a Dance/Movement Therapy Approach to Qualitatively Analyzing Interview Data." *The Arts in Psychotherapy*, no. 56 (November): 61–73.

Kawano, Tomoyo, and Meg Chang. 2019. "Applying Critical Consciousness to Dance/Movement Therapy Pedagogy and the Politics of the Body." *American Journal of Dance Therapy* 41, no. 2: 234–255.

Koch, Sabine C. 2017. "Arts and Health: Active Factors and a Theory Framework of Embodied Aesthetics." *The Arts in Psychotherapy* 54 (July): 85–91. https://doi.org/10.1016/j.aip.2017.02.002

Koch, Sabine C., Roxana F.F. Riege, Katharina Tisborn, Jacelyn Biondo, Lily Martin, and Andreas Beelmann. 2019. "Effects of Dance Movement Therapy and Dance on Health-Related Psychological Outcomes. A Meta-Analysis Update." *Frontiers in Psychology* 10: 1806.

Leavy, Patricia. 2020. *Method Meets Art: Arts-Based Research Practice*. New York: Guilford Publications.

Levine, Brooklyn, and Helen M. Land. 2016. "A Meta-Synthesis of Qualitative Findings about Dance/Movement Therapy for Individuals with Trauma." *Qualitative Health Research* 26, no. 3: 330–344.

Loman, Susan. 1998. "Employing a Developmental Model." *American Journal of Dance Therapy* 20, no. 2: 101–115.

Lyons, Steven, Vicky Karkou, Brenda Roe, Bonnie Meekums, and Michael Richards. 2018. "What Research Evidence Is There That Dance/Movement Therapy Improves the Health and Wellbeing of Older Adults with Dementia? A Systematic Review and Descriptive Narrative Summary." *The Arts in Psychotherapy* 60 (September): 32–40. https://doi.org/10.1016/j.aip.2018.03.006

Meekums, Bonnie. 2010. "Moving towards Evidence for Dance/Movement Therapy: Robin Hood in Dialogue with the King." *The Arts in Psychotherapy* 37, no. 1: 35–41.

Murray, Stuart J., and Dave Holmes. 2014. "Interpretive Phenomenological Analysis (IPA) and the Ethics of Body and Place: Critical Methodological Reflections." *Human Studies* 37, 1: 15–30.

Myers, Natasha. 2012. "Dance Your PhD: Embodied Animations, Body Experiments, and the Affective Entanglements of Life Science Research." *Body & Society* 18, no. 1: 151–189.

Norris, Paul, and Seymour Epstein. 2011. "An Experiential Thinking Style: Its Facets and Relations with Objective and Subjective Criterion Measures." *Journal of Personality* 79, no. 5: 1043–1080.

Reiners, Gina M. 2012. "Understanding the Differences between Husserl's (Descriptive) and Heidegger's (Interpretive) Phenomenological Research." *Journal of Nursing & Care* 1, no. 5: 1–3.

Sadler-Smith, Eugene, and Erella Shefy. 2004. "The Intuitive Executive: Understanding and Applying 'Gut Feel' in Decision-Making." *Academy of Management Perspectives* 18, no. 4: 76–91.

Sheets-Johnstone, Maxine. 2011. *The Primacy of Movement*. Amsterdam: John Benjamins.

Smith, Linda Tuhiwai. 2021. *Decolonizing Methodologies: Research and Indigenous Peoples*. London: Zed Books Ltd.

Soosalu, Grant, Suzanne Henwood, and Arun Deo. 2019. "Head, Heart, and Gut in Decision Making: Development of a Multiple Brain Preference Questionnaire." *SAGE Open* 9, no. 1: https://doi.org/10.1177/2158244019837439.

Tantia and Kawano. 2019. "Moving the Data: Embodied Approaches for Data Collection and Analysis in Dance/Movement Therapy Research." In *Dance/Movement Therapists in Action: A Working Guide to Research Options*, 3rd ed., edited by Robyn Flaum Cruz and Cynthia F. Berrol, 171–199. Springfield, IL: Charles C. Thomas.

Visse, Merel, Finn Hansen, and Carlo Leget. 2019. "The Unsayable in Arts-Based Research: On the Praxis of Life Itself." *International Journal of Qualitative Methods* 18: 1–13.

Warren, Carol A.B. 2002. "Qualitative Interviewing." In *Handbook of Interview Research: Context and Method*, edited by Jaber F. Gubrium and James A. Holstein, 83–102. Thousand Oaks: Sage Publications.

White, Julie, and Sarah Drew. 2011. "Collecting Data or Creating Meaning?" *Qualitative Research Journal* 11, no. 1: 3–12.

Wiedenhofer, Solveig, and Sabine C. Koch. 2017. "Active Factors in Dance/Movement Therapy: Specifying Health Effects of Non-Goal-Orientation in Movement." *The Arts in Psychotherapy* 52 (February): 10–23. https://doi.org/10.1016/j.aip.2016.09.004

23
Carving an Innovative Space for Dialogic Intersections

Dance, Disability, and Design

Merry Lynn Morris

Introduction

This research encompasses the broad disciplinary areas of design, disability,[1] and dance.

When considering their intersections, these knowledge domains serve to disrupt and provoke the canons, traditions, and habitual assumptions of one another. Design might assume a normative body, environment or human condition, or a specific process; disability might be too narrowly defined or be confined by a medical lens; dance might assume a normative dancerly body and adherence to traditional practices. In the research journey I recount here, I engage questions about where the tensions of these intersections exist, where the symbiosis or congruency emerges, how one sphere creates conditions or contexts for the other, and what the nature of this conversation is.

Over the course of the multiple research phases, I have employed quantitative, qualitative, mixed methods, arts-based, and phenomenological research methods. For the purposes of this chapter, I will focus on the more comprehensive phases of the research in terms of design-related research and associated theoretical aspects.

How Did the Research Begin?

All research has an impetus, a beginning – a catalyst that propels an action or process into motion. So, where or how does this process begin? I began from a point of curiosity, a spirit of exploration, a sense of wonder, a dare to ask why, a desire to know more, to understand, to create, to connect, to explain, to change, to deepen, to reflect, to question and re-question, and question again. Research may stem from an initial observation or experience, prompting a question or series of questions.

In my case, as a dance choreographer and educator working in the area of inclusive and integrated dance, I began to question the design of assistive devices, specifically wheelchair design, in relation to human mobility and movement. This questioning was informed by my personal caregiving experience for my father who had a disability and used assistive devices over many years. I questioned the wheelchair design in both form and function, considering how other control options might enable different and potentially more expansive kinds of movement or mobility experiences. I noticed that the dancers I worked with who were wheelchair users were often unable to utilize their upper bodies/arms to the fullest extent due to the design of the chair – the main propulsion option being a hand-to-wheel or hand-to-joystick relationship. It seemed that a limited number of directional and overall spatial options existed in traditional wheelchair designs. I wondered how interactivity between people could be enhanced through additional design options. How might movement qualities in time, space, weight, and flow be maximized in the design and how might the structure visually transform to serve different creative and expressive purposes? I sought out methods for creating three-dimensional movement dynamics in the device, drawing from knowledge and experience in dance, kinesiology, and Laban Movement Analysis.

I also reflected upon questions of history such as, what were assistive devices/ wheelchairs designed to do? Who/what bodies were they designed to serve? What does the design imply about assumptions and expectations of what a person does and how? All designs make assumptions about users, from phones, to computers, to kitchen appliances, to door handles, to curriculums, to policies, to shoes, to wheelchairs. Explicitly unpacking those assumptions could help reveal the what and why of my own research process and intentions, which was informed by a dance lens.

I further observed that although sport-specific wheelchairs existed in athletics, there did not seem to be widely commercialized dance-specific assistive devices made with dance performance needs and goals in mind. This observation was confirmed through background research in assistive devices. This signaled a research gap – a place where more exploration and investigation were needed.

Extracting some of the key action words in the prior description reveals a series of thought processes involved in the research experience and suggests initial approaches to the research process: *observed, questioned, noticed, wondered, considered, sought, reflected upon*. These actions likely repeat throughout a research process from conception to realization.

Clarifying and Communicating Intent, Moving from Observation to Action

These catalyzing observations led to a path of design innovation in collaboration with engineering partners, supported initially by internal university grant funding. While the micro-level focus centered around the development of a specific "wheelchair" prototype, my thinking in directing this project maintained broader goals. One of the most challenging experiences within the project scope was to maintain the macro-level breadth that I envisioned for the project overall. For example, I had to constantly struggle against assumptions that there was a binary between notions of "disabled" and "nondisabled" bodies, and the perception that the project was medically-focused, aimed mainly at producing a technological product. The project was not meant to be strictly about "a wheelchair" or about one product outcome, or one type of body. In fact, multiple prototype developments occurred, including a small rotating, rolling, omni-directional, circular platform that transports multiple bodies through space. Negotiating the tendency for the project as a whole to be aligned with an either/or palette in media representations, grant/award opportunities, publications, or general publicity has been challenging and has required persistent effort.

My focus was on creative mobility, blending artistic and technological exploration with embodied expression to lead to multiple levels of potential applicability at both the process and product level. For example, I view choreographers as designers of form and motion. In this broad conceptual view, the intersections between the fields of dance and engineering seem undeniable. I envisioned the potential of a sustainable "Center of Excellence" in which engineers and artists worked together investigating the potential of human mobility and motion through bodily extensions and innovative technologies that would extend and support movement capacities of many forms.

Interdisciplinary Collaboration

In interdisciplinary collaborations, it is important to recognize the differences in disciplinary traditions, processes, and cultures. When the project first began, my collaborations were with mechanical engineers. There was a tendency to isolate components and identify and quantify metrics early with a goal toward prototype/product development. Given my own experiences in dance science and kinesiology, and my proclivities toward analytic thinking, I partially resonated with a technical or scientific stance. I often found myself seeking to analyze and assess possibilities from a biomechanical point of view, methodically breaking down all the elements, and delving into the physics of human motion in relation to a mobility device. Additional collaborations with physical therapists led to a continual focus on the scientific testing of the device in relation to a human body. This included analysis of muscular activation patterns and metabolic aspects (Mengelkoch, Highsmith, and Morris 2014), which could be relevant in both dance and non-dance contexts.

In my process, I worked with multiple collaborators from non-dance fields. Each of those experiences required different frameworks and suggested different goals for the research. For example, in my work with an industrial designer, a distinctly different process ensued, which was more aligned with the conceptual and creative process I had initially begun in my own journey. Abstract, image-based, more macro-level concepts in terms of aesthetics, purpose, and evolutions of the design helped organize the innovation process and produce possible design trajectories. Within an intensive four to six weeks, a dedicated classroom at the university was used for brainstorming and collaboration, using whiteboards to organize a collage of images, drawings, and short descriptions. Each collage of material was classified into different aspects of relevance (e.g. existing technologies and historical research, people, movements, application, environments, accessories, and design evolution). This experience proved pivotal for leading to additional collaborators and implementation of the larger design concept, versus pieces of the overall design concept.

In another type of experience, working with business leaders through the University of South Florida ICORPS program, the focus was on identifying a target market and customer segment(s), and analyzing pains, gains, problems, needs, and challenges. While the experience did not notably alter the project direction toward marketing and production, it provided some important insights. It created clarification and context around how value is perceived by different stakeholders, including those who work in the wheelchair industry, general wheelchair users, athletes who are wheelchair users, and dancers who are wheelchair users. It also illuminated how the project is situated within the politics of disability, systems of capitalism, and systems of healthcare.

Another consequential moment came through my efforts to research and contact local engineering companies who might be able to partner and effectively build the prototype. This felt very much outside of my comfort zone, but it became necessary in order to propel the project forward. This effort proved useful and opened up helpful collaborative opportunities that continued over the course of the project.

I would be remiss if I did not mention the significance of funding as an influential aspect in the project trajectory. Initial internal funding enabled the seeds of the project to germinate. The timeline of the project has been slowed or halted at times due to lack of funding. An external award of $40,000 from the Thatcher Hoffman Smith Prize in 2011 enabled the building of the first integrated design concept, while a sponsored research grant of $40,000 from National Seating and Mobility and Quantum Mobility, and a combination of smaller external and internal awards facilitated additional development of the device and the research to continue. Much time was dedicated to grant-writing and efforts to secure funding, with many disappointments along the way. This is a common experience for many researchers.

Working across Subfields and Methodologies

I first entered the research from a more quantitative, analytical, kinesiological positionality. At the time, I was not familiar with arts-based research methods as legitimate forms of research practice or the vast terrain of qualitative research paradigms. Yet, I was a dance practitioner, and it was movement experience and creative practice that was heavily informing my design ideas and research questions. I did not recognize those processes as "research" at the time. Sometimes as dance practitioners, we might dismiss our creative, embodied research processes, or view them as less valid. Over time, I learned to see my multiple roles as a strength, rather than some of them being less legitimate.

Working across dance medicine and science, dance education, integrated/inclusive dance, engineering, design, and health, I have been able to observe various gaps and identify possible bridges across those gaps. For example, constructions of disability have been historically shaped by a narrow, medical model, and I think this has created an artificial separation between the dance medicine community and the dance and disability community. The medical model, in its strict sense, can view a person as a specimen and view disability as a problem residing with the individual, needing fixing. While many in the medical community embrace a larger, more holistic view in contemporary times, there is perhaps distrust that dancers with disabilities feel in terms of how the medical community might approach the meaning of disability. Disability communities largely ascribe to the social model of disability, which views disability as a social construction. In fact, the communities can serve one another, given that dance medicine and science (DM&S) addresses the multi-dimensional impacts of physical and mental health in dancers, acknowledging the very real aspects of injury and unique bodily differences within a spectrum of dancers, while dancers with disabilities present opportunities for re-conceiving dance training, expanding what healthy dance practice is, and re-considering what longevity in the art form might encompass.

However, the spectrum of dancers within DM&S is still often rather narrowly conceived, with attention mostly on normative bodies and a strong focus on injury recovery (returning to an expected norm). Dancers with long-term disabilities, blindness/low vision, and/or deafness/hard of hearing (DWDBD) have received little attention in the DM&S literature in terms of specific needs for healthy dance participation (Dubon et al. 2021). An exception is that there has been some attention given to dancers with scoliosis and Ehlers-Danlos Syndrome (EDS) (Day, Koutedakis and Wyon 2011; Steinberg et al. 2021). Part of the lack of research involving DWDBD also relates to the very unique needs within the population and its small size. Additionally, dance training/practice for DWDBD is sometimes viewed exclusively as therapy, rather than as artistic preparation for participation in the field alongside non-disabled dancers.

Research Process: Theoretical Aspects

Pursuing a PhD in dance studies from 2012 to 2017 led to a significant shift in my inquiry and broadened my understanding of research. As I launched into doctoral work focused on my Rolling Dance Chair Project as a point of entry for inquiry, new ideas arose due to the influence of different facets of scholarship. This experience led me to deepen the contextual analysis for the project, expand data sources, refine the methodological approach and challenge the design development in terms of larger philosophical questions and relevant discourse in the disability, design, and dance literature. As a result, my view of what constitutes research has grown, and this has added a productive dimension to how I view, teach, and engage in research methods.

Recognizing the validity of multiple research paradigms and outcomes is important. For instance, a significant shift for me during the doctoral research experience was to value the fact that one of the primary functions of scholarly research is to generate theory (Fraleigh and Hanstein 1999), and theory generation is not exclusive to scientific research paradigms. According to dance scholar Penelope Hanstein, theory generation involves identifying phenomena, discovering characteristics, and specifying relationships (Fraleigh and Hanstein 1999, 65). Theoretical aspects from the disability, dance, and design literature coupled with participant research informed my lens and ultimately led to new theory generation.

Additionally, in my approach to teaching research methods, I embrace a wide palette, encouraging dance students to draw upon arts-based, embodied research practices, and qualitative methods in addition to quantitative methods. This can include using improvisation and choreographic processes, choreographic analysis, Laban Movement Analysis, and dance for camera tools and techniques. These are processes and tools to which the students have already been exposed throughout the curriculum.

Philosophical insights of the chair design project influenced by scholars such as Erving Goffman (1978), Michel Foucault (1995), and Michel de Certeau (1984) elicited broader questions such as how identity is shaped and challenged by interactions and attachments with material objects/structures outside of the organic body, how agency is negotiated, how meaning is ascribed, how power relationships are revealed, and what symbolic relationships emerge in this interaction. With these questions in mind, I sought to examine more closely the intimate, interwoven relationships among bodies, devices, and environments inside the domains of dance, disability, and design studies and practice.

In the literature review process, I surveyed dance, sociology, psychology, disability, philosophy, and design literature in search of theories related to bodily relationships to devices or to the environment, and vice versa. I was strongly influenced by texts such as Sherry Turkle's *Evocative Objects: Things We Think With* (2007), Mark Johnson's *The Meaning of the Body* (2007), Bruno Latour's actor-network theory (1996, 2005, 2011), Maurice Merleau-Ponty's discussions of embodiment and tool use (1962; Iwakuma 2002), Graham Pullin's *Design Meets Disability* (2009), Don Norman's design approaches/theories (2004, 2013), other design theorists writing about emotional design, interaction design, and human-centered design, and geography scholarship dealing with bodies and materiality.[2] The two main concepts that repetitively rose to the surface in the literature I reviewed were embodiment and socio-spatiality. These emergent themes opened a further line of questioning: How are these themes observed, understood, or experienced similarly and differently in the domains of dance, disability, and assistive technology design? When does embodiment occur and are there different levels of embodiment? How can notions of embodiment and socio-spatiality inform design choices?

What was emerging for me through both the scholarly readings and through dance practice was the concept of the chair itself as having agency, as being a body of its own—a dancing partner imbued with meaning, not simply an inert, neutral object assisting bodily motion. Framing the chair in this way forces a re-thinking of the design as a true partnership. Embodiment concepts brought to light the sensory, emotional, and kinesthetic aspects of the device–body-environment relationship while socio-spatial concepts illustrated the way space use reveals issues of power and reflects social norms, resistances, and conditions. This further expanded design thinking for the device-body-environment (space) relationship. For instance, designing a mobility device without height adjustment creates a hierarchical spatial relationship between standing and seated individuals, in which seated assistive device users are often "looked down upon," and overlooked or underserved in terms of access needs. Similarly, designing a mobility device that assumes only one mode of control and limits spatial directions may also enforce inaccessibility in the physical and social environment and privilege non-assistive device users over assistive device users. Relatedly, from the embodiment perspective, designing a device for a human body that needs to be responsive to a moving, expressive human body implicates more keen attention to the sensorial aspects of the device – materiality, adaptability in form and function, movement potential in time and space, and aesthetic aspects.

One decision I needed to make was the directionality from which I was approaching the theoretical analysis. Analyzing all the possible permutations between the three areas (dance, disability, design) would have been too onerous a task to move toward meaningful research in the scope of a singular research project. Thus, the line of inquiry I chose was to examine the relational effects of the disability and dance dyad upon assistive technology design.

Research Process: Data Collection

Data sources within the project over time have consisted of design research, embodied dance/movement experience, research literature, participant observations and surveys, and integrated dance performance observation. During the chair design phase, I sought to broaden the range of what my mind could comprehend in form and motion, so I inundated myself with images of chairs or chair-like structures and rolling devices of many kinds by artists and designers, focusing on innovative or unusual choices in terms of materiality, shape, and concept. Initial conceptual goals helped guide choices. I sought a design that would emphasize the visibility of the person and not occlude the organic body or access to the body. I wanted it to appear sleek and compact and integrate well with the body. Moreover, the chair needed to effectively cradle the body safely and comfortably, enable versatile seating options for different bodies, support a full range of motion, imply a sense of motion through materiality and shaping, and enable spatial movement in all directions. Design-wise, this required that the chair possess a small base and turning radius (small footprint) and an unencumbered, narrow shaft (mid-portion connecting base to seat), while enabling changes in verticality (height change), and seat rotation independent from the base. Finally, it needed to operate fluidly with bodily movement, with a hands-free option.

With these initial goals in mind, I sorted and assembled the designs that evoked a sense of curvilinear motion or flow. In order to foreground the person, not the device, I sought out transparent, blendable materials that could reflect the movement of light and emphasize the person and their movement. I specifically sought out wireless technologies and devices that enabled human body propulsion through weight-shifting or other motions beyond hand control (e.g. Segway's gyroscope technology). To explore the design goal of increasing spatial directions in the device, I investigated types of wheels, wheel designs, and rolling devices of all kinds to spur my imagination and provide points of reference for the potential of omni-directionality. I organized these source materials and evolving ideas about the design of the device via drawing and writing, and discussed these ideas with multiple engineering collaborators.

Concurrent with the aforementioned design-related research, I continued with the artistic and embodied aspects of developing and "testing" out ideas. Initial movement explorations with Segways and early prototype explorations with participants with and without disabilities were an important part of the process. For example, one of the first movement explorations involved disconnecting the joystick from a powered wheelchair and extending its reach as far as possible to approximate the notion of a mobile or wireless control in which arms/hands could move elsewhere in space, rather than on a fixed point in space to control the chair. I also tried propping the joystick in the seat itself pressed down so that it continuously circled around the studio, while I attempted to interact with it, as a dancer outside of the chair. This was a literal enactment of imagining a hands-free device in which seat sensors could enable chair motion through pressure changes (one of the first prototype iterations). It was also a way to imagine interactive potential with the chair and the environment – a smart chair, if you will. These embodied research explorations informed the prototype development in terms of establishing the viability of changing and mobilizing the locus of control to produce new dance movement possibilities and indicating the potential applicability of a responsive sensory robotic device, one which could be far more interactive and responsive to the environment and the person than existing manual chairs and the traditional, commercialized power chairs at the time. What emerged as central to these embodied explorations is that the device design is about the design of a *relationship* between the organic body and the physical and social environment. The designer(s)/researcher(s) influence the nature of that relationship in the choices and assumptions that are made.

As early as 2008, pilot IRB research was conducted with an early prototype iteration to assess the viability of having the locus of control in the seat. This involved ten participants with and without disabilities who provided feedback via surveys (dance and non-dance backgrounds). Observations were conducted by multiple viewers who were tasked with a short series of questions while viewing the participant's experience in the chair. Outcomes indicated that the design had potential but needed more stability. A pilot study was also conducted in collaboration with physical therapy colleagues to specifically measure metabolic energy expenditure comparing the early prototype with a standard manual and power chair (Mengelkoch, Highsmith, and Morris 2014). In the doctoral research journey, participant observations of eight assistive device users who were professional dancers were video-recorded. Participants worked with the more developed prototype chair and also provided their experiential feedback via a survey, consisting of open-ended and close-ended questions addressing their relationship with their assistive device and their experiences in the prototype chair (for further survey detail see Morris 2017). In some of the movement experiences with the prototype chair, I also improvised with the participants, which provided a directly embodied interactive perspective. I also observed the repertoire of well-established companies such as Dancing Wheels, Candoco, and AXIS Dance Company, as well as the individual professional performers who were also research participants, live and on video.

Data Analysis and Synthesis

Analyzing the survey data began with simple coding processes, then the grouping of these codes into larger themes. I used a similar process in coding the literature I reviewed, which I also view as part of the research data. The textual level is similar to Merriam's "open-coding" process (2009), or Saldaña's "initial coding," (2013) which entails reading all of the data and then associating a brief word or phrase to segments of data that are related. The conceptual level of data analysis (also called axial coding) encompasses theorizing about concepts, categories, properties, and themes emerging from relationships drawn between the initial codings (Groenewald 2008). I often used "in vivo coding," in which the direct words of participants are extracted as being important to emphasize (Saldaña 2013, 91–95). For example, the first survey question directs participants to describe how they experience their relationship with their mobility device. Then, the question further prompts them to address how this experience changed over time, whether dance influenced this experience and, if so, in what way. To this question, one of the participants replied:

> I have used crutches pretty much for my whole life. I have had moments where I have needed to use wheelchairs and walkers but pretty much crutches have been my go-to mobility device. As I grew more mature, I learned to accept my crutches as a part of me. I am proud of them and like to think of them as a pair of shoes almost. Dance has definitely influenced my experience with them because dance has given me the confidence to believe in myself. Dance has also shown me different ways to use my crutches.

The in vivo codes that I extracted from this excerpt were: "learned to accept," "a part of me," "proud," "as a pair of shoes," "confidence," and "different ways." The learned acceptance (over time) was echoed in other participant's responses as well and, thus, became an emergent theme for thinking about the individual's relationship to their assistive device, implicating a tension in the relationship while implying an embodiment process occurring over time. The structural code I applied to help organize the data responses to this question was "mobility device relationship."

Additionally, the in vivo codes "different ways" and "confidence" referred to the influence of dance upon the individual's relationship with the assistive device. Thus, these initial in vivo codes were categorized within a larger structural code: "influence of dance upon assistive device relationship." These organizing tools helped to collate the data into relevant chunks which were then tethered to larger research questions in the dissertation. In the theming process, several of the in vivo codes displayed a clear connection to personal identity and, thus, became associated with indicators of embodiment, such as "a part of me," "proud," and "like a pair of shoes."

Additionally, the emotive word "proud" signaled an emotional connection to the device which further aligned with embodiment theories and design paradigms, such as emotional design.

I also used "versus coding," a type of coding identifying ideas that seem to be in conflict (Saldaña 2013, 115–118). This type of coding revealed varying tensions in the data. For instance, one participant indicated experiencing a sense of freedom in the prototype chair; yet, he also noted feeling "restricted" due to feeling the need for more support and not having control, especially when another person was controlling the chair. He stated:

> I felt a sense of freedom yet restricted, as I couldn't control where I was going and although I had my hands free I spent most of the time trying to support myself to be upright and stable in the seat. As I don't have any core stability, this proves to be difficult.

Intriguingly, another participant commented that a sense of freedom emerged *because of* not needing to control the chair; instead, this participant described a sense of restriction in utilizing his usual manual wheelchair propulsion. In these two cases, the notion of freedom versus restriction was perceived in distinctly different ways. These types of conflicting statements also arose as individuals spoke about their existing devices and about their disabilities. For some, the device and/or disability was acknowledged for its restriction, limitation, or challenge; however, this was countered with newfound opportunities and possibilities (limitations versus possibilities).

Additionally, a type of coding termed "causation coding" led me to delve into the causal relationships of data segments (i.e. cause–effect relationships) (Saldaña 2013). For example, I re-examined the way participants spoke of limitations and possibilities, thus realizing that the relationship could also be viewed as a causation or directional string. One participant stated, "While my current device has limits, it also has created many movement possibilities." Thus, from the causal perspective, the initial "versus code," limitations versus possibilities, could also be understood as "limitations causing or instigating possibilities."

Whereas the first three questions of the survey were focused more generally on disability and the device used for participants, the remaining questions dealt with the prototype chair experience specifically. I sought participants' insights into how the prototype chair felt, and I coded these questions using the previously described coding techniques. For example, question four asked participants to describe their experience in the prototype chair as completely as possible, noting any feelings/sensations. Several in vivo codes arising from this question included: "not tied to a joystick," "free for expression," "more movement possibilities," "insecurity in beginning," "like floating in space," "not having control," "challenged," "looks free," and "incredible experience." The responses to this question helped me to understand what seemed important to participants or what was most prominent for them in the experience. I coupled these responses with my observations of their experience, both during the session and later upon video review of the session. Again, I further sought out connections with several major themes in the dance, disability, and design literature, to include evidence or indications of embodiment and socio-spatiality as well as meaningful design attributes (i.e. which design attributes, such as hands-free movement, the participants seemed to find most meaningful).

In the observation analyses of contemporary integrated dance choreography and of research participants' movement experiences in the dissertation work, I drew from Susan Leigh Foster's *Reading Dancing* (1986) and Laban Movement Analysis (LMA) (Bartenieff and Lewis 1980; Hackney 2003). Foster identifies five broad categories for discerning choreographic meaning: the frame, the mode of representation, the style, the vocabulary, and the syntax (1986, 59). I placed emphasis on the style (i.e. quality of movement), vocabulary (i.e. specific movements), and syntax (i.e. relationships of one movement to the next) to deduce meaning. Drawing from both Foster's approach and the LMA framework, I looked for how parts of the body were held or released, how parts were sequenced, how effort elements, such as space, time, and weight were utilized, and how the body was generally oriented in space (Bartenieff and Lewis 1980; Hackney 2003). Also important was observing how relationships were negotiated between dancers and between the dancer and the device. In particular, exploring the movement of the disabled body in performance was relevant to the dissertation goals. From descriptive observations of how the body occupied space, utilized time, initiated and sequenced movement, and enacted qualitative nuance in relation to the assistive device, inferences could be drawn. For instance, an analysis of several professional integrated dance works revealed the way the strategic use of time and space changed binary representations of ability and disability, while creatively expanding the role of the assistive device. Additionally, in observing the movement experience of one participant trying the prototype chair, I observed a tensely held unchanging torso position coupled with a gripping action on the chair seat, which seemed to indicate an initial hesitancy and apprehensiveness. Gradually, the participant began moving their arms in different spatial trajectories and with timing changes; these changes allowed the upper body to appear less rigid. I interpreted these changes to be associated with becoming more comfortable in the chair over time and developing a sense of trust to explore more possibilities – evidence of the emerging embodiment process. This observation was further validated by the participant's survey responses.

Method of Analysis for Assistive Device

While embodiment and socio-spatiality became two significant ideas that could conceptually direct design thinking and choices, I needed a more detailed movement-based framework to yield more specificity in how a design might productively evolve through a dance lens. I used LMA, which I was already familiar with through my studies at the Laban Institute for Movement Studies in New York, past coursework in LMA, and my continued application of the analysis system in teaching. Thus, I looked through the lens of embodiment and socio-spatiality while also drawing from LMA as a dance-based methodological structure for analysis. LMA was used as a means to further re-imagine future design iterations. Ultimately, I outlined a new type of design paradigm that I call embodied, socio-spatial design. The embodiment aspect highlights the central role of bodily interaction in meaning-making, acknowledging the emotional, sensory nature of experience. The socio-spatial aspect highlights the organization and design of space as imbued with meaning due to social conditions.

Fueled by a synthesis of all the data sources (participant surveys, participant observations, research literature, integrated dance performance/choreography), my organization process for the dissertation writing resulted in the following logic stream:

1. Analysis of how disability studies produces bodily conceptions;
2. Analysis of bodily conceptions in disability studies/practices in relation to bodily conceptions/enactments through dance performance;

3. The combined analysis of the disability and dance dyad in relation to assistive technology design/design theories; and
4. Distillation of bodily conceptions arising through the intersection of dance and disability as a means of prototype analysis and further design theorization for mobility devices, leading to LMA-informed Embodied, Socio-Spatial Design.

Positionality, Transparency and Credibility

Disclosing positionality is a means for establishing credibility and transparency in qualitative research. Assessing and defining positionality and stance occurs throughout the research experience and becomes a continual, evolving effort that may involve re-shaping original intentions, solidifying and advocating for an initial approach, and/or re-evaluating initial views entirely. Throughout the course of the project, a challenge continues to be evaluating my own positionality and recognizing that I have a variety of biases including being an advocate and ally for the dance and disability field, training in certain dance forms and not others, training as a non-disabled dancer, and studying/evaluating my own invention(s). I have made it a priority to listen to other perspectives and to keep a running record of what I hear. For example, early in the project, wheelchair users expressed concerns such as "what if I don't want to move sideways?" or "what if I don't want to move forward when I lean forward?" Another participant indicated the discomfort she would feel if another person were controlling any aspect of her chair's motion. Alternately, another wheelchair user described the freedom she felt when someone else controlled the spatial aspects of the chair, and she could just focus on moving and improvising with her organic body. For me, this pointed to the importance of establishing trust in any relationship or interaction between chair user and non-chair user. These types of comments encouraged me to think critically about the design and how the chair programming could accommodate a host of desires and choices for each user, attending to user agency.

From wheelchair manufacturers, I received questions about the device safety, which prompted continual consideration of what safety actually means or looks like in a dance context, where physical risk-taking is an inherent part of the practice. I also received questions about the size of the market, which pointed to a bottom-line priority of profit over any other value, a reminder of the basic realities of product development within capitalistic systems. This caused me to continually question for whom the invention could be useful, and what paths it might take beyond traditional capitalistic processes. Another comment

I received was "people in wheelchairs don't dance." This comment came from a person who was a wheelchair user at the time. When asked "according to whom?" The answer was "according to the man on the street." This pointed to the ongoing need for further advocacy, education, and visibility across different communities. Sometimes critique is difficult to hear, but I have found that it can strengthen intentionality in the research process. Learning how to analyze the value of opposing and different views, rather than simply assuming a defensive stance is an important skill in research and serves a useful purpose.

Dissemination of the Research

Choosing relevant pathways of dissemination is a key consideration in research.

It may be beneficial to ask questions such as: Who would benefit from the research? Who would be interested in the research? Can it take other forms to be transmitted across different demographics, abilities, and cultures? How can the communication spheres be enlarged to communicate across different disciplines?

Dissemination is also important from a funding and networking perspective. Being able to present your current progress and publicize your work can lead to mutually beneficial relationships, important linkages, and new resources. In my case, through the course of this project, it has been important to take visibility opportunities wherever possible in order to open up new potential support opportunities and broaden the communication reach to hear additional perspectives that could inform the research.

I have presented aspects of the research on many platforms, engaging many types of audiences and practitioners in different disciplines, including design and technology conferences and forums, dance conferences, and disability conferences and forums. Each platform has required a different type of emphasis due to the norms and expectations of that domain. I have presented at the Smithsonian Institution, where the emphasis was on the process of invention and innovation; the International Association of Dance Medicine and Science, where the emphasis was on dance performance/training potential in relation to the prototype; and the Society of Disability Studies, where the emphasis centered on how the disabled dancing body promotes radically new ways of thinking about design. I have presented for K-12 audiences, for college dance students, engineering students, architecture students, and medical students. I have presented for Americans with Disabilities Act events, disability advocacy events, for business leaders, and those in the wheelchair industry, as well as presented a TEDx talk with choreography.

The dissemination type has included live demonstrations with the technology, integrated dance choreography and speaking, poster presentations, interview formats, popular press articles, television/media appearances, journal publications, a dissertation, and patent publications. Journal publications include the *Journal of Technology and Innovation*, *Medical Problems of Performing Artists*, *Journal of Humanities in Rehabilitation*, *Physical Medicine and Rehabilitation (PM&R)*, and the *Journal of Dance Education*. I have been featured/interviewed by MSNBC, PBS, CNN, NPR's *Science Friday*, the *Reader's Digest*, and the *Inventor's Digest* (cover story). The invention has been featured at the Smithsonian Institution in Washington, DC, where I was a guest speaker and a profiled inventor (2018–2019). The design has earned five US patents. All of these types of dissemination require adaptability and re-evaluation of the target audience, purpose, and expectations.

Conclusion

In this chapter, I have provided a summation of the different aspects of inquiry involved in this interdisciplinary research project, described how philosophical and theoretical ideas emerged and contextualized the project, described how data was generated, explained the data analysis processes, and traced the ways in which different disciplinary perspectives were explored and synthesized. Challenges in the project over time have been changing collaborators, identifying appropriate industry partners, securing funding, communicating intent, navigating positionality, disciplinary differences and disability language choices, having reliable technology, and having a small study population.

To conclude, I want to emphasize that interdisciplinary collaboration in research can be immensely valuable and productive, but it is also difficult, requiring persistent efforts in terms of clear communication, transparency regarding roles, contributions, expectations and timeline, and mutual agreements regarding priority goals and objectives. Persistence and patience will be valuable characteristics to adopt when embarking upon long-term research projects.

Lastly, understand that research, by nature, leads to a continual unfolding of questions and layers to consider. While there are progress points and points of culmination and dissemination via publication, performance, etc., the thought development and unpacking will continue, offering new future opportunities.

Notes

1 In this writing, I am primarily focusing on dancers with physical disabilities who use assistive devices. I recognize there are many types of dancers with disabilities, including visible and non-visible disabilities.

2 I also examined literature from science and technology studies (STS), but material from this discipline surfaced later in the literature review, so it did not play a core role in the conceptualization process.

Works Cited

Bartenieff, Irmgard and Dori Lewis. 1980. *Body Movement: Coping with the Environment*. New York: Gordon and Breach.

Day, H., Yiannis Koutedakis, and Matthew A. Wyon. 2011. "Hypermobility and Dance: A Review." *International Journal of Sports Medicine* 32, no. 7: 485–489. https://doi.org/10.1055/s-0031-1273690

De Certeau, Michel. 1984. *The Practice of Everyday Life*. Translated by Steven Rendall. Berkeley: University of California Press.

Dubon, Mary, Rebecca Siegel, Judith Smith, Mark Tomasic, and Merry Lynn Morris. 2021. "New Directions in Dance Medicine: Dancers with Disabilities, Blindness/Low Vision, and/or Deafness/Hard of Hearing." *Physical Medicine and Rehabilitation Clinics* 32, no. 1: 185–205.

Foster, Susan Leigh. 1986. *Reading Dancing: Bodies and Subjects in Contemporary American Dance*. Berkeley: University of California Press.

Foucault, Michel. 1995. *Discipline and Punish: The Birth of the Prison*. Translated by Alan Sheridan. New York: Random House.

Fraleigh, Sondra Horton, and Penelope Hanstein, eds. 1999. *Researching Dance: Evolving Modes of Inquiry*. Pittsburgh: University of Pittsburgh Press.

Goffman, Erving. 1978. *The Presentation of Self in Everyday Life*. London: Harmondsworth.

Groenewald, Thomas. 2008. "Memos and Memoing." In *The SAGE Encyclopedia of Qualitative Research Methods*, edited by Lisa M. Given, 505–506. Thousand Oaks: Sage.

Hackney, Peggy. 2003. *Making Connections: Total Body Integration through Bartenieff Fundamentals*. New York: Routledge.

Iwakuma, Miho. 2002. "The Body as Embodiment: An Investigation of the Body by Merleau-Ponty." In *Disability/Postmodernity: Embodying Disability Theory*, edited by Marian Corker and Tom Shakespeare, 76–87. London: Continuum.

Johnson, Mark. 2007. *The Meaning of the Body: Aesthetics of Human Understanding*. Chicago: The University of Chicago Press.

Latour, Bruno. 1996. "On Actor-Network Theory: A Few Clarifications." *Soziale Welt* 47, no. 4: 369–381.

———. 2005. *Reassembling the Social: An Introduction to Actor-Network-Theory*. Oxford: Oxford University Press.

———. 2011. "Network Theory Networks, Societies, Spheres: Reflections of an Actor-Network Theorist." *International Journal of Communication* 5: 796–810. http://ijoc.org/index.php/ijoc/article/view/1094.Mengelkoch, Larry J., M. Jason Highsmith, and Merry L. Morris. 2014. "Comparison of the Metabolic Demands of Dance Performance Using Three Mobility Devices for a Dancer with Spinal Cord Injury and an Able-bodied Dancer." *Medical Problems of Performing Artists* 29, no. 3: 163–167.

Merleau-Ponty, Maurice. 1962. *Phenomenology of Perception*. New York: Routledge.

Merriam, Sharan B. 2009. *Qualitative Research: A Guide to Design and Implementation*. San Francisco: John Wiley & Sons.

Morris, Merry Lynn. 2017. "Dance, Disability, and Assistive Technology: Probing Interdisciplinary Landscapes and Re-imagining Design." PhD diss., Texas Woman's University.

Norman, Don. 2004. *Emotional Design*. New York: Basic Books.

———. 2013. *The Design of Everyday Things*. New York: Basic Books.

Pullin, Graham. 2009. *Design Meets Disability*. Cambridge, MA: MIT Press.

Saldaña, Johnny. 2013. *The Coding Manual for Qualitative Researchers*. Los Angeles: Sage.

Steinberg, Nili, Shay Tenenbaum, Aviva Zeev, Michal Pantanowitz, Gordon Waddington, Gali Dar, and Itzhak Siev-Ner. 2021. "Generalized Joint Hypermobility, Scoliosis, Patellofemoral Pain, and Physical Abilities in Young Dancers." *BMC Musculoskeletal Disorders* 22, no. 1: 1–11. https://doi.org/10.1186/s12891-021-04023-z.

Turkle, Sherry. 2007. *Evocative Objects: Things We Think with*. Cambridge, MA: MIT press.

Part 6
Dance Research beyond Disciplines

24
Introduction to Dance Research beyond Disciplines

Extending Dance-based Ways of Knowing

Rosemary Candelario and Matthew Henley

In Chapters 1 and 2 we argued that dance research is a community of practice that, despite disciplinary differences, has a great deal in common. We suggested that recognizing shared values and practices across dance research resists siloization, and that acknowledging these crossings explicitly strengthens the sense of dance research as a unique and (loosely) cohesive community of practice. Many of the authors in Parts 2 through 5 demonstrate this possibility. Though we have placed authors in specific Parts, aligning them with academic disciplines, the work, for many of them, extends beyond one discipline. In their breadth, depth, and creativity they are implementing research practices and generating knowledge that blends multiple ways of knowing, demonstrating that there is a great deal that can be shared among dance researchers.

In this Part, we turn our attention to the ways that dance research is productive beyond the community of practice of dance. While some of the authors in the previous four Parts have certainly engaged in interdisciplinary, multidisciplinary, or transdisciplinary work, the research discussed in this Part is characterized by its explicit focus on the ways of knowing and researching that are particular to dance and how this work can speak to problems outside of the field of dance. Certainly, some initiatives like adding the A to STEM to create STEAM or the competition Dance Your Dissertation acknowledge that dance has valuable contributions to make, though often as simply a means of communicating scientific research. However, the chapters in this Part assert that specialized dance knowledge and methods themselves are vital to how we approach broad problems and can contribute unique insights and frameworks not available through other modes of inquiry.

DOI: 10.4324/9781003145615-30

This kind of work is not new. For instance, Maxine Sheets-Johnstone's (1966) phenomenological analysis of the role of kinesthesis, or the felt sense of movement, began as dance scholarship but extended outward to inform the discourse on human and animal development at the individual and species level (Sheets-Johnstone 1990). Her advocacy for moving as a way of knowing and coming to know is widely cited in evolutionary biology and is now foundational to research occurring in embodied and enactive psychology. As another example, the organizers[1] of the 2013 conference Tactical Bodies: The Choreography of Non-Dancing Subjects suggest,

> Choreographers, dance researchers and others have extended the concept of choreography to works that do not necessarily involve danced movement, challenging the assumption that choreography must relate to dance and vice versa. In scholarly and other projects, the value of choreography as an approach and a means of analysis has been demonstrated across cultural sites, as well as in a variety of disciplinary domains.
> (UCLA International Institute 2013)

This conference in turn drew on publications like "Choreographies of Protest" (2003) in which Susan Leigh Foster argues that protest actions such as the Greensboro lunch counter sit-ins, ACT UP's "die-ins," and protests of the 1999 World Trade Organization meetings in Seattle can be productively read as choreography. This does not mean that she considers the protests to be dances, but rather that she employs dance studies methods to analyze the ways that protesting bodies make articulate decisions in relationship to one another in time and space based on techniques and tactics gained through training, planning, and experience. Here Foster is seeking to highlight the way that bodies, working together, create interference, enact what she calls "obstinate recalcitrance," and effectively persuade (2003, 395).

Like these precursors, the two chapters in this Part demonstrate the broad contributions dance research can make. In Chapter 25, "Strange Bedfellows: Dance Studies, Academic Disciplines, and Truth in Crisis," Janet O'Shea argues, for example, that dance studies methodologies can provide a crucial bridge between the humanities and the sciences because of their attention to the symbolic, the material, and the experiential. She writes, "By attending to the tangibilities of experience, dance studies unites humanistic 'why' questions and conventionally scientific 'how' inquiries. Dance signals that an experience can be both socially conditioned and experienced as immediate and real" (378). Working through examples like the COVID-19 pandemic and climate crisis, O'Shea argues that dance studies has the potential to intervene in these and other pressing social and political issues based in science, but which cannot be effectively addressed by science alone.

In Chapter 26, "Keeping Movement at the Center as We Dance into Interdisciplinary Research," Adesola Akinleye discusses her interdisciplinary work with architects, engineers, and others as grounded in dance movement as method. For her, this is fundamentally connected to an "ontology of co-created, responsive, transactional world" (389). Dance movement as method here has a dual purpose of revealing an embodied, transactional ontology, as well as sensing time-space within that ontology. These orientations allow Akinleye to make connections with researchers who, though they are outside of dance, prioritize moving and sensing in four-dimensional space as fundamental aspects of meaning-making.

Rather than include O'Shea and Akinleye in one of the previous four Parts, we consciously created this Part in order to point to some of the many ways that dance research has meaningful contributions and interventions to make beyond the field of dance that directly calls on the unique insights and approaches of dance research. Our goal in bringing together researchers from across the sub-fields of dance in this book is to stimulate conversation among dance researchers who may not normally interact, and thereby clearly articulate the types of knowledge and modes of knowledge-making that are unique to dance. As a result of this kind of intervention, we hope that future editions of this book will feature an expanded Part as more scholars share dance-based ways of coming to know across academic lines, and beyond the academy.

Note

1 The organizers were Alison D'Amato, Doran George, and Sarah Wilbur. The conference was presented as part of Dance Under Construction (the recurring University of California system Dance Studies conference) and as a special topics conference of the Congress on Research in Dance.

Works Cited

Foster, Susan Leigh. 2003. "Choreographies of Protest." *Theatre Journal* 55, no. 3 (October): 395–412.

Sheets-Johnstone, Maxine. 1966. *The Phenomenology of Dance*. Madison: University of Wisconsin Press.

———. 1990. *The Roots of Thinking*. Philadelphia: Temple University Press.

UCLA International Institute. 2013. "Tactical Bodies: The Choreography of Non-Dancing Subjects (Day 1)." https://international.ucla.edu/institute/event/10023. Accessed July 25, 2022.

25
Strange Bedfellows

Dance Studies, Academic Disciplines, and Truth in Crisis

Janet O'Shea

Recent years have seen multiple, large-scale crises: the COVID-19 pandemic and resulting quarantines; public health system failures; an escalation of police brutality in response to protests over police killings; and an environmental breakdown that had previously seemed decades away. The COVID-19 epidemic represented one among multiple avoidable tragedies, the worst effects of which could have been skirted if basic public health guidelines had been universally implemented and followed diligently. Instead, national and regional governments instituted measures that varied dramatically depending on their politics. Right-wing governments, such as those in the United States, Brazil, and India spread misinformation, disinformation, and outright lies that deflected attention away from the virus and toward those who reported on it and studied its trajectory. In a desperate (and self-defeating) attempt to buoy the economy, politicians at national and regional levels refused fundamental safety measures such as mask mandates, quarantines, and safer at-home measures, even as countries such as New Zealand and Taiwan that adopted strict mask, contact tracing, and/or physical distancing requirements weathered the pandemic and reopened faster. The vaccines that have the potential to end this crisis have been met with skepticism: the United States, France, South Africa, and Russia have all seen a resurgence of vaccine hesitancy.[1]

Vaccine skepticism has created the strangest of bedfellows as natural medicine advocates align themselves with anti-lockdown conservatives and white supremacists.[2] The renewal of the anti-vaccine movement comes out of conditions that are both complex and apparently contradictory. African Americans have good reason to mistrust conventional medicine because of a long history of medical racism (Gamble 1997), a distrust that extends to vaccine hesitancy (Khubchandani et al. 2021). Although women are statistically more likely to get vaccinated than men, they are also over-represented in the progressive/ alternative wing of the anti-vaxx movement (Butler 2020), a phenomenon that journalist Arwa Mahdawi (2020) attributes to the medical establishment's neglect of women's health issues. And, yet, in the United States, vaccine hesitancy is also high among white conservatives (Callaghan et al. 2020) and patriarchal Christians (Whitehead and Perry 2020). Globally, vaccine skepticism is highest in wealthy countries and lowest in poor and middle-income ones (Koslov 2021). Relatively affluent white South Africans express far more reluctance around vaccines than their low-income Black counterparts (Cocks 2021). While residents of the Global North debate the validity of the vaccine, their governments have secured the majority of doses even as their populations represent only one-fifth of the world's total (Irwin 2021). Public health experts predict that poor countries will struggle to achieve widespread vaccine coverage, rendering COVID-19, like polio, tuberculosis, and HIV/AIDS, a disease of the poor (Bengali, Linthicum, and Kim 2020). Vaccine inequality has permitted the emergence of variants and their related surges in COVID cases.

At the same time, however, the pandemic also saw the vindication of scientific research and scientific methods. In the United States, public health figures, such as Anthony Fauci and Deborah Birx, became household names and were publicly lauded, when they weren't receiving death threats. Researchers turned mRNA technology from a "scientific backwater" (Garde 2020) into a lifesaving vaccine mass-produced at speed. The same individuals who dismissed public health measures turned to medical treatment when they or their loved ones succumbed to the virus, even as some of them continued to deny the existence of the disease.[3]

The trajectory of the pandemic, then, reveals both the importance of scientific knowledge and its limits. Questions of power cut across scientific considerations such as the mechanisms for viral spread and the influence of co-morbidities on disease progression. For instance, this crisis revealed wide disparity not only in health outcomes and access to care but also in who encounters the virus in the first place. Race, income, wealth, and geography determine who works in high-risk public spaces and who can work from home. Race, income, wealth, and geography also influence who suffers from the co-morbidities that render a COVID case deadly and who benefits from the overall good health that allows an individual to withstand an infection. These concerns determine who lives in multi-generational households where the virus can easily spread. Social and political factors govern who gets sick and who doesn't; they determine who lives and who dies.

Decades of neoliberal policy exacerbated the ability of the virus to move unchecked through populations. As in other deadly pandemics, such as HIV/AIDS,

SARS-1, and MERS, the conditions of global capitalism enabled the spread of COVID-19 through frequent, high-speed, long-haul travel. Just-in-time supply lines exacerbated the crisis as frontline workers contended with insufficient PPEs and consumers confronted shortages. The neoliberal dismantling of the welfare state left individuals, communities, and small businesses directly exposed to the economic consequences of lockdown, even as corporations reaped record profits and billionaires saw their wealth increase (Beer 2021). Unable to afford even a brief gap in operations, small business owners insisted on keeping their companies open; unable to afford to stay home, low-income workers agitated for re-opening despite the evidence that this would endanger them and their loved ones.

The factors that enabled the spread of COVID-19 are questions of power, politics, economics, education, and history; they are the product of unequal systems and discriminatory institutions. The implications of these conditions cannot be fully grasped solely by understanding the etiology of the disease or the science of how it spreads. The COVID-19 pandemic is, then, a scientific problem that cannot be solved through scientific research alone. The pandemic both justifies the role of science in public life at the same time that it reveals its stark limits. As such, defending scientific knowledge means both acknowledging the validity of science while also confronting what empiricism can't fully address.

While the so-called "Science Wars" of the 1990s pitted humanists and constructivism against scientists and positivism, the relationship between disciplines is more complex. Post-positivist scholars such as Karl Popper (1959), Michael Polanyi (1958), and Thomas Kuhn (1962, 1977) emphasize consensus in scientific research, a process that is resolutely social and therefore, in some ways relative (Latour and Woolgar 1986). Although intellectual inquiry, especially in the Global North, has tended to bifurcate between materialism and idealism, this divide is not reducible to disciplinary distinctions but extends to debates within academic fields as well as between them. Similarly, scholars have long sought to trouble, analyze, and bridge this divide. Humanists, like scientists, have expressed dissatisfaction with an emphasis on discourse at the expense of the tangible while others point out that constructivism need not eschew, and indeed has not consistently neglected, the material (Ahmed 2008; Sullivan 2012).[4] Conversely, scientists and historians of science attend to the relevance of the social and, thus the discursive, to scientific analysis (Roughgarden 2013; Barad 2007; Fine 2010).

In this chapter, I suggest that dance studies, which takes physical experience as central and recognizes that the corporeal[5] is constructed in and through history, culture, and politics, can address perceived methodological gaps between humanities and scientific knowledge production.[6] Dance, by its nature, brings together the symbolic, material, and the experiential. As such, dance studies has the potential to trouble binaristic distinctions between materialism and idealism, discourse and phenomenology, and constructivism and realism. Likewise, dance studies' component methodologies, which attend to the corporeal as socially constructed, physically enacted, and subjectively experienced, can extend beyond the analysis of performance works per se and toward an understanding of other phenomena where the material, the symbolic, and the experiential merge. In this chapter, then, I suggest that dance studies as a discipline has the potential to intervene in scholarly discussions of current crises that are characterized by material circumstances created by and productive of social and political conditions.[7]

I make the case for this potential by engaging with perspectives typically absent from debates over the relationship of the sciences and the humanities – dance studies, and sport studies – as well as one arena in which scholars have engaged directly with this split: phenomenology and the philosophy of mind. I aim to show that a strategic consideration of the role of physical practice in crafting consciousness opens up avenues through which an analysis can include social circumstances, material conditions, and experiential realities while productively engaging their differences. I propose a theoretical frame that engages the social, material, and experiential, applying it initially to combat sport, a non-dance example that nonetheless operates within some of the same parameters of dance, such as intentionality, finite duration, and set parameters for action. My larger goal, however, is to suggest that a tripartite methodological frame, which attends to the symbolic, material, and experiential at once, has the potential to address a perceived split between materialism and idealism. As such, I conclude by suggesting that environmental humanities, in particular, would benefit from a consideration of physical movement and its relationship to imagination as a way of navigating a perceived division between the material and the ideal. Doing so successfully, I suggest, can begin to interrogate a politically manufactured science denial, mobilized by corporate interests and neoliberal political structures. Accordingly, I begin this discussion by tracing the history of this manufactured crisis in truth and expertise.

Veracity in an Age of Uncertainty

An inquiry into the public distrust of scientific knowledge requires a brief look at recent (and more distant) history. In the United States, the Trump administration normalized a distrust of the process of inquiry and validation. Indeed, so common was this rejection of factuality that new terms attached themselves to older conspiracy logics: alternative facts and post-truth. Notable for its paradoxical nature and its Orwellian politics, the alternative fact is, on one level, easy to dismiss: it is a cynical maneuver that diverts attention from a lie. And, yet the alternative fact is part of a larger effort to sow mistrust not only in institutions and their integrity but also in the very idea of a verifiable truth. The alternative fact challenges the notion of a stable reality that can be understood through reference to measures and standards that remain constant. Suspicion toward processes of verification has led to the emergence of the concept of post-truth, the sense that the emotional resonance of an idea matters more than its factuality. Post-truth differs from the alternative fact in its assumption of temporality: the sense of having moved *beyond* veracity and toward a differently constituted reality.[8]

One explanation for the Trump administration's attack on objective truth lies in its populism. Populist governments, whether right or left-leaning, distinguish themselves by an explicit rejection of elitism (Oliver and Rahn 2016). Populist parties, ranging from the leftist Spanish Podemos to India's far-right Bharatiya Janata Party, position "the Establishment" against the people. The Establishment includes career politicians and economic elites as well as producers of knowledge such as academics and journalists. Knowledge itself, and the accumulation of it, becomes, within populism, a cause for suspicion. Contemporary technology and economic conditions – such as the Internet's democratization of knowledge platforms and the transformation of education into a product – have accelerated such concerns, resulting in the much-discussed rejection of expertise (Nichols 2017). In the United States, the alternative fact also arises from a long history of anti-intellectualism (Hofstadter 1966), an embrace of political paranoia, and the manufacture of information (Hofstadter 1964; Berlet and Lyons 2000), which has fueled right-wing populism since early colonization (Berlet and Lyons 2000). The alternative fact is paradigmatic of this confluence of conspiracy theorizing, the intentional production of misinformation and disinformation, a distrust of verifiable claims and knowledge-producing institutions, and a cultural tendency toward anti-intellectualism.

Because poststructuralists and constructivists argued for the situated nature of knowledge leading to the widely accepted idea, at least in the humanities, that knowledge is positional (Haraway 1988) and that facts emerge through conditions that are resolutely social, political, and economic in nature,[9] the humanities came under fire (and sometimes castigated themselves) for enabling post-truthers with their relativism (Derian 2017). A broadly constructivist approach need not undercut the notion of an observable reality, however: data gathering, as Latour and Woolgar (1986) point out, is a social act; funding, a cultural and political endeavor, influences what gets studied; and, as Cordelia Fine (2010) indicates, the publications of some findings and not others determine what we perceive as fact. However, as Bruno Latour (2004, 227) argues, we've moved out of an age of certainty, where scientific fact (inaccurately) justified oppressive systems, domination of nature, and inter-societal conflict. We now live in an age of distrust in which facts and the institutions that produce them are the subject of scrutiny and subsequent rejection. If at one point, science was manipulated to support racist, sexist, and ableist agendas, to fuel the destruction of the environment, and to drive the privatization of the natural world, science denial is now used to support racist, sexist, and ableist agendas as well as to fuel the destruction of the environment and to drive privatization.

Given that the active rejection or willful ignorance of scientific expertise fuels some of the greatest crises of our time, it's worth taking Latour's critique seriously and attending to where the humanities, the arts, and the sciences converge as well as where they differ. The foundational framework of hypothesis, identification of methods, evidence, interpretation, and conclusion has been labeled the scientific method but it appears in varying forms across academic disciplines. This framework extends to creative work and even to innovation in sport and other physical training regimens. Observation and pattern recognition are not limited to the post-Enlightenment West but recur across philosophical and scientific systems and in numerous societies and time periods, including Arabic mathematical systems, indigenous astronomy, culturally specific permaculture practices, and traditional medicine systems.

Despite an attention to the positional (Haraway 1988) nature of knowledge, most scholars in the humanities nonetheless hold that material conditions govern a larger reality that our knowledge production aims to describe. Humanists, like scientists, devote themselves to the observation, description, and analysis of a reality beyond their own subjective perception. Artists, likewise, extend from their subjective perception to the creation of work that evokes images, themes, motifs, and structural devices that speak to others. Like inquiry in the humanities, scientific research can substantiate a hypothesis but any conclusion is vulnerable to disproof by future research.[10] Statistical analysis always includes a margin of error, which future analysis may show to be more influential than initially realized. Likewise, an interpretation of a statistically valid phenomenon can be shown to be erroneous and a subsequent study design can uncover new data and/or provoke contrasting conclusions. This degree of uncertainty is the source of scientific reticence, which is taken by denialists to mean that scientists haven't reached a consensus on, for instance, vaccine safety or climate breakdown. But this is an incorrect deduction as scientific consensus indicates that falsification is extremely unlikely rather than impossible.

Because no academic discipline can prove a theory for certain, debate, contradiction, and dispute are central to intellectual labor of all kinds. Anti-intellectuals and right-wing populists, with the weight of corporate interests behind them, have honed in on dispute, disagreement, and debate as evidence of the arbitrary nature of intellectual practice and findings. Examples include the effort to debunk the connections between cigarette smoking and cancer, between diet and the burden of disease, and the contribution of human activity to the climate crisis. Anti-intellectuals also tend to grasp a single counter-example (or counter-study) as evidence of the faultiness of scientific consensus. This is the basis of the self-designated science denial methodology "doubt is our product" (Oreskes and Conway 2010).

Clearly, as Latour suggests, the "targets" of critique have shifted. Scholars in the environmental humanities (EH) recognize the significance of this shift while maintaining that crises that can be measured scientifically cannot be solved through technological intervention alone (Emmett and Nye 2017, 2, 7, 55). Scholars in this field recognize the dangers of a broad rejection of scientific knowledge while suggesting that the humanities, with their eye to power, politics, context, sensation, emotion, and meaning provide insights that the sciences do not. However, the environmental humanities are largely textual in their bases, reflecting engagement from disciplines such as literature, philosophy, and history. EH scholars have made an effort to include the arts but here, too, the emphasis is on the document not on physical praxis. I suggest projects such as those within environmental humanities would benefit from attention to dance studies, as a discipline, and to the significance of movement and its material traces. Conversely, dance studies can use its interdisciplinary position to help think our way out of the political and intellectual morass in which we find ourselves because, and not in spite, of its defining contributions that differentiate it from the humanities more generally as well as from the natural sciences. In this section that follows, I offer an example of how this might work.

Combat Sport, Materiality, and Experience

By means of examining both common cause and productive divergence between academic disciplines, I invoke an inquiry I made into scientific and humanistic explanations for a practice in which material conditions, experiential reality, and symbolic meaning seem to be in tension: martial arts and combat sports (O'Shea 2017). Sport fighting can be read in ways that diverge dramatically from what it feels like from the inside. A practice that appears violent, that uses the components of conflict, can be, and often is, lived as personally empowering and generative of community (O'Shea 2019). This tension is an uneasy one: it is hard to acquire what Loic Wacquant (2004) has called the fighter's studied disinterest, the ability to separate a landed strike from its conventional meaning, rendering the pain of a punch received as a mere stimulus.

This process is both difficult and unpredictable. At any given point, the supportive but competitive relationship of the sparring match can break down into interpersonal conflict. There is always the possibility that one partner can use the aggressive appearance of sparring to take action that overrides their opponent's consent, an enactment of hiding-in-plain-sight violence.[11] Even if both fighters maintain their composure and the match remains respectful, the materiality of the strikes endure: a punch to the face aches and bruises regardless of whether one's opponent means it as a gesture of respect or ill will.

A punch indicates that there are material conditions that cannot be denied: the strike thrown with respect still lands with force. Its velocity, direction, and timing are crucially important: they determine whether the punch lands and how much it hurts when it does. And, yet, the punch received in a sparring match (usually) generates little of the shock, horror, and fury that a punch incites off the mat. Because it feels so different experientially from a punch thrown in violence, the respectful, consensual punch can't be explained by its constitutive elements alone. It shows us that materiality matters *and* that experience is not reducible to empirical conditions. Science can explain velocity, force, and direction. But it doesn't illustrate why the punch received in play registers so differently from the punch received in anger.

This question – can science account for experience? – and its corollary – does it matter if it can't? – is the source of debate in the subset of philosophy where phenomenology and neuroscience come together. Physicalists (also identified as monists, determinists, or reductionists[12]) argue that consciousness is an effect of the mechanisms of the brain. Dualists maintain that a consciousness or a will guides the activity of the brain. Consciousness, dualists insist, fundamentally differs from other phenomena and thus cannot be reduced to the brain's mechanisms.

Philosopher Thomas Nagel (1974), for instance, argues that, for an entity to have a conscious experience requires that "there is something it is like to *be* that organism" (1974, 436). This means that consciousness emerges from a first-person reality that is tied to specific physical experiences and that experience can only exist through a viewpoint (1974, 444). Nagel also insists that this gulf in perception is not an obstacle to understanding consciousness: it is the crux of the issue.[13]

Neuroscientist and philosopher David Chalmers (1996) extends this argument, maintaining that consciousness does not only consist of learning, focusing attention, and reporting on states of being. Chalmers poses such questions as why particular states produce specific experiences, a consideration that the morphology of the brain doesn't explain. Chalmers makes the argument for consciousness as distinctive from other phenomena through a thought experiment, evoking what he calls a phenomenal zombie, a being that could hypothetically learn, focus attention, and report on states while lacking the experience that we identify as consciousness. He maintains that the hypothetical possibility of such an entity means that consciousness cannot be reducible to the basic operations of the brain (1996, 97). For these reasons, Chalmers claims that physical explanations can address the easy problems of consciousness – *how* a phenomenon works – but not the hard problems: *why* it does so (with the caveat that the easy questions are not, in reality, all that easy).[14] These debates, alongside their physicalist counterparts, constitute a field of inquiry known as the philosophy of mind.

Philosopher Hyjin Lee (2011) takes the dualist argument a step further by attending to Nagel and Chalmer's neglect of the body. She argues that the phenomenal zombie is conceivable not only because an organism could theoretically function without consciousness but also because neurologically inscribed habitual movement, which she calls muscle memory, enables behavior. She goes on to illustrate the "sensual muscle imagination" that inheres in the process of physical training, wherein learning new movement patterns requires envisioning what that movement looks and feels like. Lee calls the sense of accomplishment and satisfaction that accumulates in this process "enhanced vitality" (2011, 201).

Dance studies scholars have, of course, long been aware of the neglect of the body that philosophers such as Lee identify. Indeed, dance studies scholars have made the case for understanding the body as part of willed action for a long time, even if they have not identified this effort in exactly these terms.[15] While dualists in neuroscience might see recourse to the body as replicating physicalists' assumptions that the mind is reducible to physical structures, dance studies challenges the underlying association of the body with automaticity. Dance studies thus provides the means of conceptualizing the body as part of intentionality, enriching the possibilities for what Lee names a philosophy of mind and body.

An additional gap in the philosophy of mind, beyond the neglect of the physical that Lee identifies, is the privileging of consciousness and subjective experience over the influence of the social. By contrast, dance studies, with its emphasis on power, identity, difference, and history, illustrates that subjectivity develops through the physicalization of the social. In order to address this body-subject-social complex, dance philosopher Philipa Rothfield (2021) draws together the disparate intellectual trajectories of Merleau-Ponty and Nietzsche to argue for a consciousness rooted in subjective experience, in the forces of the social, and navigated through the body.[16] Blending these approaches produces an approach that might be characterized as a philosophy of the mind and the corporeal.[17]

Such considerations explain the apparent paradox of the respectful punch. It's difficult to acquire the aplomb that Wacquant describes as "studied disinterest" because there is a materiality to the punch. It's unpleasant, painful, and distracting.[18] And yet, fighters do it all the time: they separate the sensation of the punch from its usual effects of flinching or mindless retaliation. They are able to do so because of a shift in consciousness that occurs through willed effort. This suggests that there is something that, to paraphrase Nagel, it is *like* to be a sport fighter. Physical training produces a consciousness that is specific and contingent.[19] The social sets parameters for the emergence of fighter selves, so that prior experiences of violence or subjugation may render studied disinterest harder to achieve for some participants than others; some may retreat from combative play while others may gravitate to it readily, depending on prior experiences of aggression off the mat. Such differences are, in turn, influenced by economics, race, gender and gender identity, sexual orientation, regional and national origins, and ability. The social also allows this training and facilitates the self that emerges such that contrasting types of sport fighters – focused and self-possessed versus gratuitously violent – emerge from different training environments.

These insights may address the contained problem of martial arts and their relationship to violence but what are the implications of such a recognition of the importance of materiality and an acknowledgment of its limits beyond this example? How might they challenge scienticism's reduction of all questions to morphological ones while also countering science denial's rejection of projects of veracity? What implications does this hold for dance studies, the humanities, and interdisciplinary thought?

One point at which the humanities can intervene in the space between scienticism and science denial is in questioning the question. As Cordelia Fine (2010) points out, scientific questions often indicate a bias toward an expected answer. Biologist Frans de Waal (2016), in writing about animal intelligence, illustrates that our grasp of scientific facts is only as solid as the tool we use to measure them. In de Waal's research, the crux of the problem is that we may be so lacking in the arenas in which other animals excel that we struggle to design a measure of their intelligence (de Waal in Garces 2019, 21). Philosopher Gary Gutting (2013) illustrates a potential tautology: if we are convinced that only science can solve our most important questions, we are left with the questions that only science can answer.

The humanities can address what Chalmers identifies as hard questions: why does a phenomenon operate the way it does? Why does it feel the way it does? Why does it matter? Because of this focus on questions of why, humanities speak to considerations of meaning, experience, context, and change. For this reason, Martha Nussbaum (2010) argues that the humanities are central to the workings of democracy. The ability of analysis and interpretation to upend conventional wisdom has led Elizabeth Freeman to argue that the humanities offer a "shock to common sense" (2005, 93). Judith Butler (2004, 12) argues that the structure of the address is of crucial importance in moments of political upheaval.

The humanities, as Jane Desmond (2016) argues, operate in and through the work of the imagination. The humanities, Desmond suggests, do not merely reflect how we live. Rather they allow us to map out how we want to live. Intellectual work in the humanities can allow us to envision new possibilities, determining what kind of future we contribute to when we create knowledge, deploy categories, and mobilize ideas. Imagination, as Kelley (2002), Srnicek and Williams (2016), and Klein (2017) point out, precedes action: in order for a new way of living to become possible, it must be thinkable. Ruth Levinas (2013) argues that new ways of living already operate in existing elements of society as well as in both concrete aims and imaginative desires for the future, suggesting that attending to what is possible necessitates attending to what already exists.

Physical practices, in their immediacy, allows us to live out other ways of being beyond what we see in front of us (O'Shea 2019). While a range of art forms such as literature, visual art, music, and film allow us to imagine other ways to live and some of them render this imagination tangible, physical practices such as dance enable this effort to become both concrete and relational. When we enact something corporeally, it becomes part of our life experience; it becomes real in a way that renders imagination more plausible. When it happens in conjunction with the efforts of others, imagination instantiates itself as resolutely social. Dance studies, like the phenomenon it analyzes, has the potential to vivify and concretize imagination by linking the experiential, social, and material.

By attending to the tangibilities of experience, dance studies unites humanistic "why" questions and conventionally scientific "how" inquiries. Dance signals that an experience can be both socially conditioned and experienced as immediate and real. By illustrating that physicality and physical practice operate as creative effort[20] dance studies has the potential to extend the notion of imagination beyond visual or narrative registers and toward lived realities. By analyzing practices along the lines of experience, networked relations, and the tangibility of spaces, in addition to understanding their discursive and representational meaning, dance studies can trouble a binaristic split between materialist and idealist perspectives.

The Politics of Truth and the Climate Crisis

I conclude with an example far more pressing than that of sport fight's consolidation of subjectivity through enhanced vitality: the climate crisis. Environmental breakdown, like the COVID-19 pandemic, requires an acceptance of scientific truth *and* an engagement with factors that cannot be understood through science alone. The climate emergency is a clear example of the consequences of the social on the material world. Industrialization, capitalism, and globalization have prompted the "hockey stick" increase in emissions. The global popularity of the combustion engine, the appeal of the private car, and aviation, all driven by both a demand for luxury and the pressures of an ever faster-paced world propels environmental breakdown (Emmet and Nye 2017, 101). Industrial agriculture is driven by a rising global demand for animal products as markers of middle-class status and by the globalization of chemical fertilizer use, which, in turn, emerged out of a need to find a market for surplus materials of war (Shiva 2016, 3).

The climate crisis thus illustrates how social action yields material consequences. Humans build cars and sell them and create freeways and parking structures to accommodate them, thus releasing carbon dioxide into the air while also destroying the plant life and the soil that could sequester it. Humans breed animals in captivity and build businesses around them and, in the United States, rely upon government subsidy for those businesses (Simon 2013). These practices produce methane, a gas with 28 times the warming potential as CO_2. The crops that feed these animals rely on industrial fertilizers that wash into waterways causing dead zones. Humans cut down rainforests to create products for global industries ranging from fast food to packaged snacks to construction. Scars in the soil and the husks of burnt trees evince the physicality of the political and the economic.

And, yet, the materiality of these effects exceeds their social production. Environmental feedback loops show us that the physical impacts of economic policy cannot be reduced to or contained within the category of the social. A heating climate causes drought, which dries out the forest, which becomes more likely to burn, putting more carbon into the atmosphere, which further heats the earth's climate. Intensifying weather patterns demand intervention in the form of immediate aid and rebuilding, which requires resources. Feedback loops are a tragic illustration of how the material both emerges from and exceeds the social and the political.

Addressing the climate crisis requires a defense of scientific knowledge and yet its conditions, effects, and solutions cannot be reduced to scientific problems.

The most important questions pertain not only to how climate crisis works but also to why we are allowing it to happen (Emmet and Nye 2017, 79); they concern not only how to fix it technologically but also why we might want to invest in a more equitable world. Addressing environmental breakdown hinges on more than understanding the facts. The climate crisis is an existential threat that demands immediate, focused attention and, paradoxically, measured reflection; it requires a consideration of how to reduce production and consumption without replicating, or worsening, existing disparities. Action against the climate crisis is political, but it is also cultural, social, and economic; the industries that drive the environmental emergency have come into being because of assumptions about how we want to live.[21] This makes the climate crisis tragically difficult to address but it also means that it demands the engagement of the imagination. It raises the deceptively simple question of what kind of world we want to live in.

Action against environmental degradation begins but cannot end with acknowledging scientific truth. Taking action against the climate crisis hinges on understanding criteria for accomplishment, group affiliation, and social convention. It requires redefining desire, self-identity, community interaction, and notions of success and failure so that we can envision different futures. Science isn't equipped to address these questions because these are matters of interpretation and imagination.

Addressing climate change means rethinking our American notion of busyness that we have exported to the rest of the world through neoliberal economics. It requires a historical and cultural understanding of a Calvinist investment in work as a symbol of moral worth, in a culture that has jettisoned Calvinist ideas of frugality and celebrates conspicuous consumption. To face down climate change requires confronting the economic interests that have excessive political control in the United States, in particular, but also globally. Altering a seemingly endless cycle of continual labor and continual consumption is a matter of politics and economics but also an act of reflection, suggesting a rethinking of individual worth and social accomplishment. The climate emergency requires being able to envision something else beyond what we have in front of us. It requires an ability to picture other ways of living and relating.

The climate crisis cannot be fully acknowledged as an emergency through a mere recitation of the facts. Nor will it be countered only by measuring its impacts or even by researching the relative merits of, for instance, solar versus wind power or cell-based versus "free range" meat. Rather, it requires a consideration of the tangible that also investigates questions of power. It likewise calls for an engagement of the imagination: a willingness to consider what currently seems impossible and to reflect on its physical realization.

The claim I put forward here aligns with that of the environmental humanities. Scholars in a range of humanistic and social science disciplines urge attention to the social, political, cultural, historical, and economic factors that drive environmental breakdown, arguing that we already know how to address the climate crisis technologically but that we struggle to engage its harder questions, which are social and political in nature. However, the environmental humanities have largely ignored the importance of physical effort and movement, tending more toward analyses of texts and visual images. I have suggested, here, that addressing the crises of our moment – the COVID-19 pandemic and climate breakdown, among others – requires an understanding of the material, the symbolic, and the experiential; it includes grasping how the immediacy of experience is crafted through the social. It demands uniting materialist and idealist perspectives (while also recognizing that their differences can be productive). It necessitates reflecting on the centrality of imagination and how physical practices concretize imagination.

I do not mean to suggest that dance studies automatically does all these things. In both its subject of analysis and its constituting methodologies, however, dance studies brings together concerns that, in other disciplines, sit at odds. The crises of our moment demand a dynamic engagement between and across disciplines and methodologies. Dance studies, with its ability to concretize imagination, unite the social and the experiential, and link the material and the ideal, is well placed to answer this call.

Notes

1 Notably, however, the number of Americans who are vaccine skeptical has been declining. Current estimates place it at 25% of the adult population (Kelley 2021).
2 This alliance is both unlikely and expected at once. Mesch and Schwirian's (2015) study suggests that those who mistrust the government are more likely to forego vaccination. Mistrust in government spans the political spectrum and includes a range of races, genders, and economic classes.
3 Emergency room nurse Jodi Doering narrated jarring and poignant examples of COVID-denial even among those dying from the disease (Villegas 2020).
4 In performance studies, some of the most influential theorists of discourse make their arguments to suggest that iteration becomes material rather than to claim that the material is reducible to the iterative. Thanks to Anurima Banerji for pointing this out.
An additional factor here is the perceived "crisis in the humanities," which may further skew perceptions of the utility of science versus a superfluity of the humanities. Although the modern university was constructed around the humanities (Giersdorf 2009), late capitalism/neoliberalism has eroded the traditional university structure

(Readings 1996). Student enrollment in both undergraduate and graduate humanities degrees has declined steadily since the 1990s (Schmidt 2018).

5. Here, I use the term corporeality as a mediator between the experiential and the social, a point elaborated by Philipa Rothfield (2010). In doing so, I am indebted to Susan Foster's (1995) theorization of the term as well as DeFrantz's and Rothfield's (2016) elaboration on the concept.
6. Sally Ann Ness (2011) makes a compelling case for the utility of philosophical theories that attend specifically to bodily motility for dance studies.
7. I explore this idea in my current research project, which focuses on physicality and emotion in social justice movements.
8. This idea seems to have reached its apotheosis in Rudy Giuliani's 2018 assertion that "truth is not truth." (Morin and Cohen 2018).
9. This idea emerged in part through the Foucauldian (1995) power-knowledge critique and in part via science and technology studies' insistence upon science as a social practice. Examples of the latter include Latour and Woolgar (1986), Haraway (1988), and Traweek (1992).
10. https://www.forbes.com/sites/startswithabang/2017/11/22/scientific-proof-is-a-myth/?sh=1f7729fe2fb1; and https://theconversation.com/forget-what-youve-read-science-cant-prove-a-thing-578
11. Veronika Partikova (2016) calls this hidden violence in martial arts training.
12. These terms are usually used interchangeably in philosophy of mind discussions. However, as Hyijin Lee points out, perspectives within physicalism, such as emergentism, exhibit dualistic tendencies (2012, 197).
13. I have laid out this argument in detail elsewhere (2017) so I provide only a brief summary of these debates here.
    Nagel's argument parallels that of ethologist Frans de Waal (2016), who argues that we cannot grasp non-human intelligence without acknowledging the *umwelt*, or subjective world, of particular animals.
14. Psychiatrist Jeffrey Schwartz and Sharon Begley (2002) pose a still more fundamental question: if consciousness is just an after-effect of something firing off in our brains, why do we care about what it is and how it works?
15. The emphasis in dance studies and performance studies on what dancing and performing do, as well as what they mean, constitutes, to my mind, a consideration of how willed action engages with the social. See for instance Candelario (2016), Kondo (2018), and Foster (2021).
16. Dance studies is, of course, not alone in its attention to the confluence of the cultural and the subjective. Phenomenological ethnography, such as works by Thomas Csordas (1994) and Greg Downey (2005) also examine the consolidation of the cultural via experience.
    Rothfield's uniting of Merleau-Ponty and Nietzsche's seemingly disparate perspectives on subject formation is distinctive but her efforts to place physicalized subjectivity in a social context have antecedents. A subfield of phenomenology concerns itself with the accumulation of physical skills as part of a socially configured subjectivity. For example, see Young (1980), Sobchack (2005), and Downey (2010).

17 I draw my understanding of corporeality as mediating between subjective experience and social conditions from Foster (1995) and DeFrantz and Rothfield (2016).
18 Admittedly the materiality of sport fighting differs in some key ways from violence. Gloves and mouth guards produce a qualitatively different experience from real-world conflict: the dull ache of a gloved punch differs from the sharp sting of a bare-knuckled fist. Mouth guards protect against broken teeth and bitten lips.
19 This process of physical training involves creating a new repertoire of possible behaviors, which can be understood through Pierre Bourdieu's (1977) notion of the habitus. Scholars such as Martha McCaughey (1997) and Loic Wacquant (2004) have investigated the process through which physical training allows participants to create a new habitus.
20 I expand upon the idea of physical practice as creative effort elsewhere (forthcoming 2023).
21 As evidenced, for example, in George H. W. Bush's 1992 remark at the first Earth Summit in Rio de Janeiro that "the American way of life is not negotiable." See, for example, "A Greener Bush" (2013) for a discussion of this quote and its significance.

Works Cited

Ahmed, Sara. 2008. "Some Preliminary Remarks on the Founding Gestures of the 'New Materialism.'" *The European Journal of Women's Studies* 15, no 1: 23–29.

Barad, Karen. 2007. *Meeting the Universe Halfway: Quantum Physics and the Entanglement of Matter and Meaning*. Durham, NC: Duke University Press.

Beer, Tommy. 2021. "Report: American Billionaires Have Added More Than $1 Trillion in Wealth during the Pandemic." *Forbes*. January 26, 2021.

Bengali, Shashank, Kate Linthicum, and Victoria Kim. 2020. "How Coronavirus – A 'rich man's disease' – Infected the Poor." *LA Times*, May 8, https://www.latimes.com/world-nation/story/2020-05-08/how-the-coronavirus-began-as-a-disease-of-the-rich.

Berlet, Chip and Matthew N. Lyons. 2000. *Right Wing Populism in America: Too Close for Comfort*. New York: The Guilford Press.

Bourdieu, Pierre. 1977. *Outline of a Theory of Practice*. Richard Nice, trans. Cambridge: Cambridge University Press.

Butler, Judith. 2004. *Precarious Life: The Powers of Mourning and Justice*. London, New York: Verso.

Butler, Kiera. 2020. "The Anti-Vax Movement's Radical Shift from Crunchy Granola Purists to Far-Right Crusaders." *Mother Jones*. June 18, https://www.motherjones.com/politics/2020/06/the-anti-vax-movements-radical-shift-from-crunchy-granola-purists-to-far-right-crusaders/.

Candelario, Rosemary. 2016. *Flowers Cracking Concrete: Eiko & Koma's Asian-American Choreographies*. Middletown, CT: Wesleyan University Press.

Callaghan, Timothy, Ali Moghtaderi, Jennifer A Lueck, Peter Hotez, Ulrich Strych, Avi Dor, Erika Franklin Fowler, Matthew Motta. 2020. Correlates and Disparities of COVID-19 Vaccine Hesitancy. August 5. Available at SSRN: https://ssrn.com/abstract=3667971 or http://dx.doi.org/10.2139/ssrn.3667971.

Chalmers, David. 1996. *The Conscious Mind: In Search of a Fundamental Theory*. Oxford: Oxford University Press.

Cocks, Tim. 2021. "As Vaccines Arrive, South Africa Faces Widespread Scepticism over Safety." *Reuters* February 8, https://www.reuters.com/article/us-health-coronavirus-safrica-anti-vacci/as-vaccines-arrive-south-africa-faces-widespread-scepticism-over-safety-idUSKBN2A81WJ.

Csordas, Thomas. 1994. *The Sacred Self: A Phenomenology of Charismatic Healing*. Berkeley: University of California Press.

DeFrantz, Thomas and Philipa Rothfield. 2016. *Choreography and Corporeality: Relay in Motion*. London: Palgrave Macmillan.

Derian, James Der. 2017. Trump Demands a Post-Post-Truth Response. *The Conversation*. May 30, https://theconversation.com/trump-demands-a-post-post-truth-response-77563.

Desmond, Jane. 2016. *Displaying Death and Animating Life: Human-Animal Relations in Art, Science, and Everyday Life*. Chicago: University of Chicago Press.

Downey, Greg. 2005. *Learning Capoeira: Lessons in Cunning from an Afro-Brazilian Art*. Oxford: Oxford University Press.

———. 2010. "Throwing Like a Brazilian: On Ineptness and a Skill-Shaped Body." In *Anthropology of Sport and Human Movement*, edited by Robert Sands, 297–326. Lanham, MD: Lexington Books.

Emmett, Robert S., and David E. Nye. 2017. *The Environmental Humanities: A Critical Introduction*. Cambridge, MA: MIT Press.

Fine, Cordelia. 2010. *Delusions of Gender: How Our Minds, Society, and Neurosexism Create Difference*. New York: W. W. Norton.

Foucault, Michel. 1995. *Discipline and Punish: The Birth of the Prison*. New York: Vintage Press.

Foster, Susan Leigh. 1996. *Corporealities: Dancing Knowledge, Culture, and Power*. London: Routledge.

———. 2021. "What Dancing Does." UCLA Senate Faculty Research Lecture. April 14, https://www.youtube.com/watch?v=WUzLjvjwm5U.

Freeman, Elizabeth. 2005. "'Monsters, Inc.': Notes on the Neoliberal Arts Education." *New Literary History* 36, no. 1: 83–95.

Gamble, Vanessa Northington. 1997. "In the Shadow of Tuskegee: African Americans and Health Care." *American Journal of Public Health* 87, no 11: 1773–1778.

Garde, Damian. 2020. "The Story of mRNA: How a Once Dismissed Idea became a Leading Technology in the Covid Vaccine Race." *Stat*. November 10.

Giersdorf, Jens. 2009. "Dance Studies in the International Academy: Genealogy of a Disciplinary Formation." *Dance Research Journal* 41 no. 1: 23–44.

"A Greener Bush." 2013. *The Economist*. February 13, https://www.economist.com/leaders/2003/02/13/a-greener-bush\.

Gutting, Gary. 2013. "Science's Humanities Gap." *New York Times*. September 18.

Haraway, Donna. 1988. "Situated Knowledges: The Science Question in Feminism and the Privilege of Partial Perspective." *Feminist Studies* 14, no. 3: 575–599.

Hofstadter, Richard. 1964. "The Paranoid Style in American Politics." *Harpers*. November, https://harpers.org/archive/1964/11/the-paranoid-style-in-american-politics/.

———. 1966. *Anti-Intellectualism in American Life*. New York: Vintage.

Irwin, Aisling. 2021. "What Will It Take to Vaccinate the World against Covid-19?" *Nature*. March 25.

Kelley, Alexandra. 2021. "1 in 4 Americans Refuse to Get Covid-19 Vaccine." *The Hill*. March 10.

Kelley, Robin D.G. 2002. *Freedom Dreams: The Black Radical Imagination*. Boston: Beacon Press.

Khubchandani, Jagdish, Sushil Sharma, James H. Price, Michael J. Wiblishauser, Manoj Sharma, and Fern J. Webb. 2021. "COVID-19 Vaccination Hesitancy in the United States: A Rapid National Assessment." *Journal of Community Health* 46: 270–277.

Klein, Naomi. 2017. *No Is Not Enough*. Chicago: Haymarket Books.

Kondo, Dorinne. 2018. *Worldmaking: Race, Performance, and the Work of Creativity*. Durham, NC: Duke University Press.

Koslov, Max. 2021. "COVID Vaccines Have Higher Approval in Less-Affluent Countries." *Nature*. July 22, https://www.nature.com/articles/d41586-021-01987-9.

Kuhn, Thomas. 1962. *The Structure of Scientific Revolutions*. Chicago: University of Chicago Press.

———. 1977. *The Essential Tension: Selected Studies in Scientific Tradition and Change*. Chicago: University of Chicago Press.

Latour, Bruno. 2004. "Has Critique Run out of Steam? From Matters of Fact to Matters of Concern." *Critical Inquiry* 30: 225–248.

Latour, Bruno and Steve Woolgar. 1986. *Laboratory Life: The Construction of Scientific Facts*. Princeton, NJ: Princeton University Press.

Lee, Hyijin. 2011. "Zombies and Muscle Memory: Rethinking Somatic Consciousness and the Mind-Body Problem." *Human Movement* 12, no. 2: 196–202.

Mahdawi, Arwa. 2020. "If Women are Hesitant about the Vaccine, It's because the Health Industry Hasn't Earned Their Trust." *The Guardian*. December 19.

Martin, Randy. 2012. "A Precarious Dance, a Derivative Society." *TDR; The Drama Review* 56, no. 4: 62–77.

McCaughey, Martha. 1997. *Real Knockouts: The Physical Feminism of Women's Self-Defense*. New York: New York University Press.

Mesch, Gustavo S., and Kent P. Schwirian. 2015. "Social and Political Determinants of Vaccine Hesitancy." *American Journal of Infection Control* 43, no. 11: 1161–1165.

Morin, Rebecca and David Cohen. 2018. "Giuliani: 'Truth isn't Truth.'" *Politico*. August 19, https://www.politico.com/story/2018/08/19/giuliani-truth-todd-trump-788161.

Nagel, Thomas. 1974. "What Is It Like to Be a Bat?" *The Philosophical Review* 83, no. 4: 435–450.

Ness, Sally Ann. 2011. "Foucault's Turn from Phenomenology: Implications for Dance Studies." *Dance Research Journal* 43, no. 2: 19–32.

Nichols, Thomas. 2017. *The Death of Expertise: The Campaign against Established Knowledge and Why It Matters*. New York: Oxford University Press.

Nussbaum, Martha. 2010. *Not for Profit: Why Democracy Needs the Humanities*. Princeton, NJ: Princeton University Press.

Oliver, J. Eric and Wendy M. Rahn. 2016. "The Rise of the *Trumpenvolk:* Populism in the 2016 Election." *Annals of the American Academy of Political and Social Science* 667, no. 1: 189–206.

Oreskes, Naomi and Erik Conway. 2010. *Merchants of Doubt: How a Handful of Scientists Obscured the Truth on Issues from Tobacco Smoke to Global Warming*. New York: Bloomsbury.

O'Shea, Janet. 2017. "It Matters How You Move: An Ethnographic Memoir of a Collaboration between Dance and the 'Hard' Sciences." *Dance Research Journal* 49, no. 3: 6–**23**.

———. 2019. *Risk, Failure, Play: What Dance Reveals about Martial Arts Training*. New York: Oxford University Press.

———. Forthcoming 2023. "What Is Kali? You Are Kali: Choreography, Creative Relationality, and Improvisation in Filipino Martial Arts and Bharata Natyam." In *The Oxford Handbook of Indian Dance*, edited by Anurima Banerji and Prarthana Purkayastha. New York: Oxford University Press.

Partikova, Veronika. 2016. "'Your Partner is Not your Enemy': Confronting Hidden Violence in Martial Arts Schools." *LoveFightingHateViolence.com*. December 16, http://lfhv.org/2016/12/16/your-partner-is-not-your-enemy-confronting-hidden-violence-in-martial-arts-schools/.

Polanyi, Michael. 1958. *Personal Knowledge: Towards a Post-Critical Philosophy*. Chicago: University of Chicago Press.

Popper, Karl. 1959. *The Logic of Scientific Discovery*. London: Hutchinson.

Readings, Bill. 1996. *The University in Ruins*. Cambridge, MA: Harvard University Press.

Rothfield, Philipa. 2010. "Differentiating Phenomenology and Dance." In *Routledge Dance Studies Reader*, edited by Alexandra Carter and Janet O'Shea, 2nd ed., 303–318. London: Routledge.

———. 2021. *Dance and the Corporeal Uncanny: Philosophy in Motion*. Abingdon, Oxon and New York: Routledge.

Roughgarden, Joan. 2013. *Evolution's Rainbow: Diversity, Gender, and Sexuality in Nature and People*. Berkeley: University of California Press.

Schmidt, Benjamin. 2018. "The Humanities are in Crisis." *The Atlantic*. August 23, https://www.theatlantic.com/ideas/archive/2018/08/the-humanities-face-a-crisisof-confidence/567565/.

Schwartz, Jeffrey M. and Sharon Begley. 2002. *The Mind and the Brain: Neuroplasticity and the Power of Mental Force*. New York: Harper Perennial.

Shiva, Vandana. 2016. *Who Really Feeds the World? The Failures of Agribusiness and the Promise of Agroecology*. Berkeley, CA: North Atlantic Books.

Simon, David Robinson. 2013. *Meatonomics: How the Rigged Economics of Meat and Dairy Make you Consume Too Much – and How to Eat Better, Live Longer, and Spend Smarter*. San Francisco: Conari Press.

Sobchack, Vivian. 2005. "Choreography for One, Two, and Three Legs (A Phenomenological Mediation in Movement)." *Topoi* 24: 55–66.

Srnicek, Nick and Alex Williams. 2016. *Inventing the Future: Postcapitalism and a World Without Work*. London and New York: Verso.

Sullivan, Nikki. 2012. "The Somatics of Perception and the Matter of the Non/Human: A Critical Response to the New Materialism." *European Journal of Women's Studies* 19 no. 3: 299–313.

Traweek, Sharon. 1992. *Beamtimes and Lifetimes: The World of High-Energy Physicists*. Cambridge, MA: Harvard University Press.

Villegas, Paulina. 2020. "South Dakota Nurse Says Many Patients Deny the Coronavirus Exists – Right Up Until Death." *The Washington Post*. November 16.

de Waal, Frans. 2016. *Are We Smart Enough to Know How Smart Animals Are?* New York: W. W. Norton.

Wacquant, Loic. 2004. *Body and Soul: Notebooks of an Apprentice Boxer*. Oxford and New York: Oxford University Press.

Whitehead, Andrew L., and Samuel L. Perry. 2020. "How Culture Wars Delay Herd Immunity." *Socius Sociology Research for a Dynamic World* 6. https://journals.sagepub.com/doi/full/10.1177/2378023120977727.

Young, Iris Marion. 1980. "Throwing Like a Girl: A Phenomenology of Feminine Comportment, Motility, and Spatiality." *Human Studies* 3, no. 2: 137–156.

26
Keeping Movement at the Center as We Dance into Interdisciplinary Research

Adesola Akinleye

In this chapter, I discuss how I have come to position dance-movement within the activity of research. I am drawing on my own dance-based research process, which often involves interdisciplinary collaborations with people whose first expression is not dance (such as architects, engineers, musicians, fine artists, and designers). Yet the distance in dance-exploration between myself and a non-dancer is less about our respective ability to move with competence and more about our shared notion that movement has meaning beyond the design of a pleasant esthetic. Colleagues in other disciplines whose practices derive from an ontology of co-created, responsive, transactional world, reflect my own determination of dance as an expression of the interaction of self with world. We share a predisposition to find meaning in the experiential. For instance, I have been so warmed by how readily someone from an engineering discipline lunges into dancing with the belief my experience as a choreographer will help guide us both through a process of non-verbal meaning-making. Thus, I have also felt the weight of the responsibility of being the facilitator or even a *representative* of dance, among an interdisciplinary group of researchers. I am charged with checking I am not just leading people into a hedonistic romanticizing expression, thereby missing the progression of any meaning our dancing together might divulge.

In these interdisciplinary collaborations, where we are exchanging processes and methodological approaches, it is made clear to me that the question "why am I using dance?" needs to yield more of a response than just "because I am a dancer." Such a response at the very least takes for granted how dance contributes to knowledge-making, at worst it assumes a homogenization, a monocultural relationship with movement. This has led me to reflect on what dance is doing within a research activity. In this chapter, I identify two important positions for movement when dancing into interdisciplinary research. Firstly, dance-movement as a *method* for revealing an embodied methodology that

DOI: 10.4324/9781003145615-32

constructs the world as responsive, interactive, and experiential, stemming from an ontology reflected in many Indigenous and Africanist worldviews. Secondly, within that ontology, dance-movement as a *method* for registering awareness of the sensation of time/space. That is, seeing movement as a means for bringing attention to the syntax of a transactional world.

Methodology: Coming into Being of Place

I stand, eyes closed, feeling the spread of weight on cool floor reach across the soles of my feet to my heels. I notice the outer edge of my little toes, the slant of my ankle caused by the instinctive moderation of weight attending to the outside line of my foot reveals. My knees, bones nestled, sitting: the loving hug of condyle and meniscus. The fabric of my sweatpants touching parts of my thigh. A habitual flexion pulls my abdomen in toward my spine as I trace my presence into my pelvis and up to my ribs. I relax and sigh, a breath out; my focus is interrupted by my self-consciousness: a flicker of detachment. But breathing-in, I feel into the mildly tight, resting sensation of my shoulders, bringing me back to the tri-balance of my feet. My neck feels long, humming, back broadening. Fingers twitch as I notice the descent of my arms, elbow slightly bent. I hover suspended between the pull to subject-centered, self-consciousness, and the physical sensations of being... My attention is drawn to the hairs on my forearms reaching out to the walls around. As I reach forward with my arms, the shift in my spine moves my head forward and I am brought into noticing the daylight splashing across my closed eyelids as the window blinds dally in a slight breeze from the open window. I feel the difference in temperature between my arms; one closer to the window holding the knowledge of breeze, the other basking in the flood of refracted sunlight. I open my eyes and hear my heartbeat, the crackle of the hum of the room, a voice outside. I start to notice the colors around me. The twitch of my fingers as I sense into the white walls shaping this room, the deep black of the table in front of me. I lift my arms, ribs expand, neck arches back, I find my eyes are closed again; cheekbone leading eyes to the warm strip of sunlight flooding in through the window – balance altered as I lean into the light – leg extended out to counterbalance arms reaching forward, a long sense of suspending. In my next breath, I am pushed backward onto my extended leg by the sound of a car passing. I twist my shoulders around the spongy mooring of weight that is my knee. Arms swinging around as if elongating to the walls that frame the room, I float on the moment of being in Place, belonging to the assemblage of sensation that is this moment. My dancing body is the sensory responsiveness for being in Place, for being of the assemblage of now. *I am, because we are*, the African philosophy of Ubuntu articulates how my sensing comes into form through being in relationship with that about me (Bstan 'dzin rgya and Tutu 2016). The Lakota language also honors this inter-connectedness with the confirmation and prayer *Mitákuye Oyásin*, which means *all my relatives/we are all related* (Chipps and Chiat 2003). This relational ontology takes reality away from the Western metaphysics of elements to be measured (Smith 1999). Instead, the world is an inter-connected web (Deloria Jr. and Wildcat 2001), the transactional nature of which is described by Chief Seattle:

> Whatever befalls the earth befalls the sons and daughters of the earth. Man did not weave the web of life; he is merely a strand in it.
> (Seattle, Gifford, Cook, and Jefferson 2005, 58)

Speaking over 150 years ago, Chief Seattle's knowledge is often simplified into later *discovered* Western concepts of ecosystems and environmental cycles, but he makes the larger point that we are inextricably *of* it all: a part of the assemblage of the moment of Place. Tongan social anthropologist Hūfanga 'Okusitino Māhina and other Pacific Elders and philosophers of tāvāism also explain this through the tā-vā philosophy of reality, that we cannot step out of the sum of everything (Ka'ili and Māhina 2017; Māhina 2004; Māhina et al. 2021). Pragmatist John Dewey, living in North America in the late 1800s, also convinced we emerge from our surroundings, echoes the Indigenous philosophy around him through his notion of *transaction*. In the Dewian lexicon *transaction* denotes that we are constituted in the changing relations with natural/cultural/social world and natural/cultural/social world is inextricably realized through us (Dewey, Boydston, and Lavine 1989). This is contingent on understanding the world is not a single entity but a multiplicity of relationships, which have histories and futures – agency in the widest sense.

The ontological view I am describing is made apparent to me when I dance. Movement becomes a way to be aware of flow, relationship, transaction; I am not suggesting dance makes transaction happen, as if it was possible to be suspended from being a part of everything until one "mastered" being related through dance. Rather that dance-movement brings this transactional ontology into focus through engaging the full range of human experience along the spectrum of thought, reflection, sensation, and immediacy of the empirical. My transactional awareness of Being comes into sense (wisdom/awareness/feeling) when I approach meaning through the embodied dialogue of dance-movement. Thus, explaining his experiential ontology in *Art as Experience*, Dewey describes me dancing when he writes:

> …when the savage is most alive, [s]he is most observant of the world about [her]him… [Her]his senses are sentinels of immediate thought and outposts of action…
> (Dewey 2005, 18)

I claim the "savage," and following the nuanced elegances of Indigenous and Africanist epistemologies, dance-movement has meaning because it brings my perception of "me" into relational dialogue. I blur the boundaries of my perceived edges through knitting time and space in the embodied moment of movement. As I move to dance, entanglements/relationships (flesh, floor, music, temperature, reflection, window, and car passing by) become intrinsic to the form and content of my presence. This is in part because dance is simultaneously across what I am doing (dance), being (dance), and in (dance). Because I am moving, my realization of being a part of it all is not contained in fixed events, the dance itself makes meaning from the non-fixed flow of movement (changing relationships). It is this quality of dance-movement that offers insight into the ontological paradigm of a transactional world. I am noticing the in-betweenness, the flow as I move because the meaning, decision-making that is birthed into movement, is a response to the shifting nature of world. Things/moments are acquiring meaning through my moving body passing through them, belonging to them, combining, re-arranging as inner experimentations.

In Western society, it is not uncommon to think of the world without a knower or a knower without a world (Dewey, Boydston, and Lavine 1989). But within this Western context thinking is often conflated with verbal language. As if thinking was the action of verbalizing, as if to think of the world is to verbalize the world into reality. But from my embodied dance perspective, the act of moving in responsive, situated, integration of the assemblage I am a part of *is thinking* (Manning and Massumi 2014). Here *thought* lives across and through my skin in the ever-shifting relationships my dance movement traverses. Karen Barad draws on quantum physics to describe this relational ontology, using the term intra-action.

> "intra-action" signifies the mutual constitution of entangled agencies...it is important to note that the "distinct" agencies are only distinct in a relational, not an absolute, sense, that is agencies are only distinct in relation to their mutual entanglement; they don't exist as individual elements.
> (Barad 2007, 33)

Weight hollows back in the camber of my spine, sacrum catching my pelvis into a tilt, arms thrown forward, my history of Martha Graham classes flung beyond my fingertips. A surge in my right side transforms the curve of my spine into twist, releasing my left leg. Leg thus becomes the stern around which my torso turns, floor partnering my spiral, window bathing me in strips of sunshine, the sounds of cars dissolving. My dance movement slows the roar of sensation down to cruder, more recognizable, calmer, packages of memory. So that I can grasp at meaning to drag it beyond the mosaic of felt sensation into a continuity that has spatio-temporal form. Thus, dance creates form and content for a knowability of *now*. Allowing me to communicate or articulate my sense of presence in the intra-action of the assemblage of now. Movement is my articulation of how this moment is known to me – through the felt responsiveness of being *a part of it all*.

I am not indulging in the Cartesian doubting of my own existence by suggesting dance helps me find mySelf in what is around me. Rather I am merely underlining the intra-action, indigenous worldview that "I" am changed when my relationships change (Deloria Jr. and Wildcat 2001; Ka'ili and Māhina 2017; Māhina 2004). This centralizes experience: a transactional ontology. Dance can demonstrate how the world the dancer is discovering and responding to is a world the dancer is co-creating (Sheets-Johnstone 2009). Dewey sums up for us in *Knowing and the Known*:

> Our position is simply that since man as an organism has evolved among other organisms in an evolution called "natural," we are willing under hypothesis to treat all of his behavings, including his most advanced knowings, as activities not of himself alone, nor even as primarily his, but as processes of the full situation of organism-environment.
> (Dewey, Boydston and Lavine 1989, 97)

Dance-movement emerges from the *full situation* of the moment of organism-environment. During interdisciplinary collaborations, I have found colleagues are articulating the same transactional ontology that dance reveals to me. Of course, a collaboration does not begin with the ability to clearly articulate one's ontological worldview! We all have felt how the nomenclature of our discipline can leave us tongue-tied in the initial stages of collaborative research. But where a group of people from different backgrounds accept (or even invite) dance as part of a research activity, there seems to be an innate propensity toward the experiential as a central component to meaning-making. To some colleagues, this is embedded in their understanding of the world through cultural knowledges (Māhina 2004), to some through other forms of making such as music (Sennett 2009) or architecture (Pallasmaa 2005; Rasmussen 1959), and to some through the quantum physics of studying the mechanics of the world (Barad 2007). As I talk to and read reflections from people with a transactional worldview from outside of the field of dance, I find them grappling with the same explorations as me, for instance, Rasmussen suggests:

> Architecture as something indivisible, something you can not separate into a number of elements... It is something else and something more. It is impossible to explain precisely what it is – its limits are by no means well-defined. On the whole, art should not be explained; it must be experienced.
> (Rasmussen 1959, 9)

The shared ontology of a transactional world has led me to work within a range of interdisciplinary collaborations. I suggest one's ontology is not subject-specific but has more to do with one's worldview (and perhaps cultural upbringing). However, for those who see the nature of being as experiential and relational the activity of dance seems to exemplify the wider transactional nature of their understanding of the world. I feel there is more opportunity for research and exploration across shared ontologies, than across shared subjects/specialties. It seems seeing dance-movement as a useful part of the research process relies less on the shared subject specialism of being a *dancer* and more about the importance of having a compatible worldview, congruent ontologies. I have more language, meaning-making, and questions in common with someone who perceives the *reality* of the world as I do, than I have in common with someone who can do a triple pirouette as I do. For instance, I go into the studio and start to bend my knees. A practice of plié: I have done this movement-intention hundreds of thousands of times. Each of these executions of plié is meaning-making because I am part of a different assemblage of moments every time. Plié is a way of naming the event of bending my knees in the dance studio, but the experience is different each time. For Sammy, also a dancer, but who does not share my transaction-based ontology, the very fabric of the reality of "plié" is different when they bend their knees. Thus, when Sammy and I stand in the studio together and plié, our methodological framework determines what we are doing. What we are doing differs, because the meaning of what we are doing differs: we are responding to different worlds (ontologies) even though the mechanics of the event of executing a plié might look relatively the same. Within my methodological framework, I am using plié as a method for exploring my intra-action world, Sammy is using plié to affirm their Subject on the object of the floor (for instance). The significance of the movement, even what is felt by doing the movement, and possibly the cellular make-up of the movement, does not remain the same regardless of what we envision we are doing (Abraham et al. 2020; Franklin 2019; Garfinkel et al. 2015).

In Community

Recently I have been researching how moving through the city reveals the materiality and relationships between form and social construct that become part of the everyday choreography of what it is to be human in a community. I have been exploring with architects, engineers, musicians, fine artists, and designers who also perceive the multiplicities and co-creation of the moment of *now* (that for me is revealed by dancing). What has been fascinating is how within their specialties colleagues come to the same ontology as I have gathered through my specialty of dancing. Methodologically we have developed frameworks informed by our respective disciplines. It is this exchange of methodology (process) that I find extremely valuable about interdisciplinary work. I have come to know the world (ontology) through moving; this has led to the responsive, sensing body being a part of my methodological framework. Then, sharing an ontology of sorts, the interdisciplinary collaborations I have been involved with have revealed that our methodological standpoints have some alignment too. When I bend my knees with an architect colleague, we are both interested and open to how doing this together tells us about an intra-active ontology. That is how we have been able to start to understand each other outside of the subject-based language and techniques that mark the parameters of our practices. There is a like mind-ed-ness that allows for shared meaning to be possible and thus gives us the possibility of communication. But what has been unique across collaborations is that my dance-movement has offered a distinct language that collaborators feel is missing from the verbal and visual languages they are accustomed to exchanging with. The physicalized nature of dance seems to offer a mode of exploration and expression that is particularly useful in highlighting the transactional. I am proposing that in this interdisciplinary arena, movement has been the method through which we have come to be able to investigate the syntax of time/space. Therefore, I offer dance-movement as a mode within the research process for noticing Being-in-Place with *specific questions*, at *a specific time* (Akinleye 2021; Casey 2009).

Method: Knowing (at least) Four-Dimensional Distance

I am seeing movement as a method within my methodological framework, informed by the ontology revealed by dance discussed earlier. This embodied, transactional, experiential methodology is given form and content through locating things in time/space. We use at least time/space to locate experience (we can experience in more levels of reality than time/space but not less, because of the corporality of our bodies). As corporeal beings we cannot be present in space without a time or be present in time without a space: we understand our presence in terms of a spatial and temporal equilibrium.

> Ontologically, time and space are an abstraction of the form and context of things commonly existing in one level of reality… In ontological terms, time and space are the common medium in which all things are, in a single level of reality, spatio-temporally or four-sided dimensionality.
> (Māhina 2002, 303)

I have been seeing movement as a method for being aware of the operation of entanglement; the syntax of the fabric of an ever-changing time/space reality. I stand, feel the spread of weight on my toes to my heel. The fabric of my sweatshirt dripping down my shoulders. Sound of cars passing outside, white of the wall beside me, black table, I reach my left arm upward unfolding from the elbow and extend my right arm downward unfurling my fingers toward the brown wood of the floor. At the peak of the extension of my arms my weight transfers to my right leg: opening arms, rock forward, close arm rock back to my left leg. I repeat the movement – open-rock-forward, close-rock-back, open-rock-forward, close-rock-back. Each execution is different, not least because it is preceded by the experience of the action before. I have set an alarm for ten minutes. Open-rock-forward, close-rock-back, open-rock-forward, close-rock-back… The sensation changes as one arm starts to fatigue, I miss-step back and readjust my weight, close-rock-back. I open my arms with the sound of the car getting closer to my window, open-rock-forward. The sun comes in and out of clouds sometimes shining on my fingertips close-rock-back, open-rock-forward. The movement becomes a measure of being here, the mode through which I am experiencing the texture of *now*, I feel my presence in space, the accumulation of rocking back and forth. Movement measures distance in time and space, because movement becomes a method for being present, of being aware of the composition of time and the arrangement of space. Movement evolves into a process for making recognizable the flow of transactional change. Movement becomes the method for knowing four-dimensional distances (spatial-temporality).

A group of student-architects and I explore notions of movement, methodology, and method. Opposite the building where I am teaching a class for this group of student-architects, there is a big supermarket. Between our classroom building and the supermarket is a covered courtyard. It is a big concrete space that people are walking through to get to the school, do their shopping, or simply to move from the north side of the building complex to the south. As a class, we go out and walk through the courtyard. This is a 20-minute *choreography* where each dancer-architect is walking at their own pace, some very fast, some very slowly, some barely covering ground using their movement to merely lift their leg in the first step. After this, back in the classroom, we describe the space using architectural drawing. The sense of how big the space is, how fast the 20 minutes went by, are all contingent on the type of movement the dancer-architect undertook. The movement is a filter for understanding the size of the courtyard and the size of the 20 minutes. The movement of the body is the filter through which comprehension of being in the spatial-temporality is deciphered. As a group, we play with the kinds of movements we do (not just fast or slow, using formal and informal dance moves) to notice how the space and time of the courtyard are comprehendible. Dance-movement is the method of perception of the time/space of the courtyard in the assemblage of the 20 minutes.

We go out again this time adding a new improvisational aspect to the choreography. The dancer-architects can interrupt the direction/tempo (space/time) of their own walk to move in response to another dancer-architect's movement. This could be through an encounter of crossing paths or visually seeing another dancer-architect from a distance. The dancer-architects also respond to avoiding elements of the more general purpose of the time/space of the courtyard in 20 minutes (bike stands, people carrying shopping, the security guards). Comparing previous experiences of the courtyard, with the 20 minutes of the movement we just completed and the 20 minutes of movement we are about to dance, we are interested in what happens to our individual perception of the time/space of the Place of the courtyard. This plays with responsiveness using movement to slow the roar of sensation down to *cruder and more recognizable packages of memory*, that are the events of encountering the Place of being in the courtyard. The social construct of time and space is made evident within the dance-movement offering a different vessel through which to experience Being in the Place of the courtyard. Generalized social constructs for public time and space are usurped when the students use dance-movement, which by its nature is using a different logic than the general logic of public space (including using some of the responsive rules of the improvisation we are dancing). The students' dance-movement becomes the conduit through which the courtyard and the 20 minutes are perceived.

Watching the students with my choreographic eye, the entanglements the dancer-architects experience become interesting schemas for generating further movement. As a choreographer, I find these new perceptions fascinating entries into exploring movement composition. But in research terms, I would suggest what we are doing in the courtyard and the 20 minutes is using movement as a method to gather "data." What the students do later to inform their design proposals (analysis) draws on the meaning and connections revealed across the embodied experiences of the dance moving (data). At this point of having generated "data" through movement, an interdisciplinary colleague, such as student-architects, might return to the expressive form of their own practice to analyze how the movement-generated knowledges informs their wider research. For me as a choreographer, I continue to use movement to explore the data/ideas/experiences. I draw on knowledge of dance to interrogate ideas through choreographic practices and the physicality of my own body.

The last stage of a research process is another point where movement knowledges can be presented in another expressive form to be disseminated (such as through dance performance). That is, having been through the choreographic analysis process I could write about what I found, or I could continue with the method of movement and choreograph a dance. Just as a musician colleague could write or compose a music score about moving in the courtyard and 20 minutes, or an engineer could write or design a structure about the courtyard and 20 minutes. Thus, I am suggesting seeing movement as a method.

Movement as a method is not limited by dance, I am seeing the smallest flick of the architect's pencil as a possible responsive movement. Seeing movement as a response in the musician's fingers, the singer's breathing. Within my practice, I am seeing all these as notations of time/space that generate comprehension and dialogue within the intra-action of being present. Movement is a conduit for learning, making, and remembering the emergence of *now* amid the construction of the past and the anticipation of the future. The first-person narrative of dance-movement in time/space allows for positionality within the web of the present. We can tantalizingly trace the permanence of change in the material of our moving dancing-bodies. We can become aware of the multiple agencies of intra-action through the mapping of the movement in and around us.

Dancing in Interdisciplinary Research

I am aware I have ironically, brutally separated the notion of method from the notion of methodology to write a chapter that is primarily about intra-connection and fluidity! Working in multidisciplinary collaborations has led me to interrogate my own dance-based methodological practice. The importance of dance-derived ontological and epistemological grounding has been made particularly evident when working in interdisciplinary contexts where colleagues do not arrive with *scholarly* dance education notions of what dance looks like, feels like, or can manifest from. Recent collaborations have left me articulating dance-movement as a mode for engaging with four-dimensional distances, a mode for noticing the nuances of time/space reality; in which the interactive nature of dancer with the world can become an illustration of the transactional make-up of the world. Interdisciplinary colleagues who want to collaborate with my dance practice often see dance as an exciting medium for meaning-making and communication even if they are not trained in dance themselves. But within the excitement of including dance in multi-disciplinary research design, I feel a concern that we in the dance field can be less attentive to the philosophical imperatives of dance than someone from a different discipline. In the interdisciplinary setting particularly, this can leave dance-researchers being co-opted into representing a narrow interpretation of what movement means constructed from outside the field rather than from the dance-researchers own ontological position. As Sheets-Johnstone suggests:

> ... a heightened or greater philosophical awareness on the part of the dancer might provide sounder critical grounds... This keener awareness is particularly vital because dancers are sometimes all too ready to embrace immediately the views of any philosopher who pays attention to them...

[with the dancer's keener awareness] Thinking and doing are not then polarized but mutually illuminating; dancers are not mindless, any more than philosophers are disembodied.

(Sheets-Johnstone 1984, 127–128)

As a dance-based researcher it is important I do not unwittingly assume dance shares the same meaning across time/space, and the experience of the people I am dancing with (and of course across the methodologies of other dance-based colleagues). I am reminded dance carries philosophical meaning-made knowable through cultural, historical, and social filters at different times and in different geographic locations. Dance-movement conveys different meanings across and within the flesh of different bodies of experience. As we shed colonial frameworks, it is clear there is not a single interpretation or history of dance. Thus, dance is framed through the ontology of the researcher's practice and this needs to be explicit. For me, this has been to keep movement as a central *method* for exploration when dancing into research.

Works Cited

Abraham, Amit, Eric Franklin, Carla Stecco, and Robert Schleip. 2021. "Integrating Mental Imagery and Fascial Tissue: A Conceptualization for Research into Movement and Cognition." *Complementary Therapies in Clinical Practice* 40: 1744–3881. https://doi.org/10.1016/j.ctcp.2020.101193

Akinleye, Adesola. 2021. *Dance, Architecture and Engineering*. London: Bloomsbury Publishers.

Barad, Karen. 2007. *Meeting the Universe Halfway: Quantum Physics and the Entanglement of Matter and Meaning*. Durham, NC: Duke University Press.

Bstan'dzin rgya, Mtsho and Desmond Tutu. 2016. *The Book of Joy: Lasting Happiness in a Changing World*. New York: Penguin Random House.

Casey, E.S. (2009). *Getting Back into Place: Towards a Renewed Understanding of the Place-World*, 2nd ed. Bloomington: Indiana University Press.

Chipps, Victoria, and Susan Chiat. 2003. *Pray from Your Heart: Teachings of a Lakota Elder*. Seattle, WA: Morningstar Pub. Co.

Deloria Jr., Vine. and Daniel R. Wildcat. 2001. *Power and Place: Indian Education in America*. Golden, CO: Fulcrum Publishing.

Dewey, John. 2005. *Art as Experience*. New York: Penguin.

Dewey, John, Jo Ann Boydston, and Thelma Z. Lavine. 1989. *John Dewey: The Later Works, 1925–1953* (Vol. 16: 1949–1952, Essays, typescripts, and Knowing and the Known). Carbondale: Southern Illinois University Press.

Franklin, Eric. 2019. *Grow Younger Daily: The Power of Imagery for Healthy Cells and Timeless Beauty*, 2nd ed. Minneapolis: OPTP.

Garfinkel, Sarah N., Anil K. Seth, Adam B. Barrett, Keisuke Suzuki, and Hugo D. Critchley. 2015. "Knowing Your Own Heart: Distinguishing Interoceptive Accuracy from Interoceptive Awareness." *Biological Psychology* 104: 65–74. https://doi.org/10.1016/j.biopsycho.2014.11.004.

Kaʻili, Tēvita O., and ʻOkusitino Māhina. 2017. *Marking Indigeneity: The Tongan Art of Sociospatial Relations*. Tucson: The University of Arizona Press.

Māhina, ʻOkusitino. 2002. "'Atamai, fakakaukau and vale:'mind', 'thinking' and 'mental illness' in Tonga." *Pacific Health Dialog* 9, no. 2: 303–308.

———. 2004. *Art as Tā-Vā 'Time-Space' Transformation*. Auckland, New Zealand: Center for Pacific Studies, University of Auckland.

Māhina, ʻOkusitino., Pd'utu-'O-Vava'u-Lahi, Adriana Mahanga Lear, Kolokesa Uafa Mdhina-Tirai, Sione Lavenita Vaka, Maui-Tā-Vā-He-Ako, and Tevita O.Kaʻili. 2021. "Atamai-Loto moe ʻAonga-Fakaʻofoʻofa: A Tā-Vā Time-Space Philosophy Mind-Heart and Beauty-Utility." *Pacific Studies* 44, no. 1–2: 1–12.

Manning, Erin, and Brian Massumi. 2014. *Thought in the Act: Passages in the Ecology of Experience*. Minneapolis: University of Minnesota Press.

Pallasmaa, Juhani. 2005. *The Eyes of the Skin: Architecture and the Senses*. Chichester: John Wiley & Sons.

Rasmussen, Steen Eiler. 1959. *Experiencing Architecture*. London: Chapman & Hall.

Seattle, Chief, Eli Gifford, Michael Cook, and Warren Jefferson. 2005. *How Can One Sell the Air?: Chief Seattle's Vision*. Summertown, TN: Native Voices.

Sennett, Richard. 2009. *The Craftsman*. London: Penguin.

Sheets-Johnstone, Maxine. 1984. *Illuminating Dance: Philosophical Explorations*. Lewisburg, PA: Bucknell University Press.

———. 2009. *The Corporeal Turn: An Interdisciplinary Reader*. Exeter: Imprint Academi.

Smith, Linda. T. 1999. *Decolonizing Methodologies: Research and Indigenous Peoples*. London and New York: Zed Books.

Part 7
Creative Workbook

27
A Creative Workbook for Rehearsing Ethics, Orientations, and Practices

Rosemary Candelario and Matthew Henley

Introduction

In Chapter 2, we describe the ethics, orientations, and practices that we find vital to the development and implementation of responsible and rigorous dance research. In this workbook, we expand on those topics by providing the reader with multiple activities to deepen their engagement with ethics, orientations, and practices in their own research practice, as well as in the teaching of research methods to novice researchers. Consistent with the book's focus, the workbook does not address activities found in many other methodology texts such as how to write a research question, purpose statement, or literature review. Instead, this workbook encourages the development of processes that cultivate modes of participation conducive to research that guide decisions about methodological design and enactment. Following sections with activities related to ethics, orientations, and practices is a final section, "Putting It All Together," in which we offer activities that promote thinking systematically across ethics, orientations, and practices and multi-step activities for research design, including activities by some of the contributors to the book.

The activities in this workbook engage different learning styles and disciplines. They do not privilege writing, but rather include it as one of many modes of knowing and learning, including kinesthetic, aural, figural/imagistic, quantitative, and spatial. Accordingly, readers will find activities that provide opportunities for movement, writing, talking, working with objects, teaching/lesson plans, and more. Moreover, we encourage readers to engage the activities as written, or to put them into another mode. Finally, readers will notice that many of the activities we propose below need to be done with others. Wendy L. Belcher tells us that writing is social (2019); we propose that research, too, is social. These social activities could happen in a formal classroom setting or among an informal group of people at the same stage of the research process.

We encourage users to see activities in the workbook as porous, malleable, and interconnected. Just as we suggested earlier that the research process is not linear, so too do we encourage readers to find their own pathways through this workbook, and even to connect back to previous chapters. For instance, after completing the activity "Putting chapters into practice" you could complete a "Beneficence and justice timeline" for the same project. The activities "Connecting the chapters" and "Putting the chapters into practice" offer the reader opportunities to return to earlier chapters in the book to synthesize, analyze, and apply lessons from the authors' narratives.

Ethics

Situating the Researcher

1. Create a list of the different communities of practice in which you are a participant: studio, school, family, work, faith group, dance club, etc.
2. For each community, draw a circle, label it and place yourself at the center (see Figure 27.1).
3. Following Bronfenbrenner's Ecological Systems Theory (1992), nest each of those circles in larger circles that represent the systems in which they are embedded (see Figure 27.2).
4. Consider: What does it mean to create and share knowledge in your communities of practice?
    - What are the rules for how people relate to each other, both inside and outside the circles?
    - What kinds of things does the community pay attention to? What does it not pay attention to?
    - How does the community share new ideas or practices? What kind of evidence is used? How does the community determine if an idea or practice is good/valid/beautiful? Who gets to be a knowledge maker?

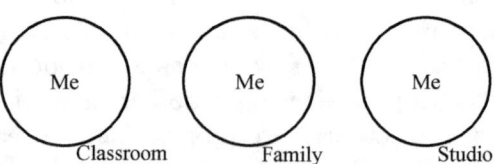

Figure 27.1 Three communities of practice in which researchers might situate themselves.

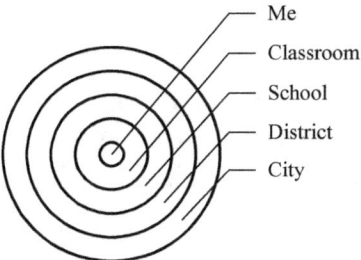

Figure 27.2 Nested communities of practice.

5. Consider how these circles overlap. What happens when the ethics, orientations, and practices of two different communities of practice which you are a part of operate at the same time?

Situating the Phenomenon/Population/Participant

1. Create a list of the different communities of practice that impact your phenomenon: locations, cultures, institutions, historical eras, etc.
2. For each community, draw a circle, label it, and place the phenomenon at the center.
3. Following Bronfenbrenner's Ecological Systems Theory (1992), nest each of those circles in larger circles that represent the systems in which they are embedded.
4. Consider: What does it mean to create and share knowledge in these communities of practice?
    o What are the rules for how people relate to each other, both inside and outside the circles?
    o What kinds of things does the community pay attention to? What does it not pay attention to?
    o How does the community share new ideas or practices? What kind of evidence is used? How does the community determine if an idea or practice is good/valid/beautiful? Who gets to be a knowledge maker?
5. Consider how these circles overlap. What happens when the ethics, orientations, and practices of two different communities of practice that impact the phenomenon operate at the same time?
6. Consider the relationship between Situating the researcher and Situating the phenomenon. Where is there resonance and dissonance between your ethics, orientations, and practices, and those of the communities you intend to study? What does this imply for research design?
7. What assumptions about your topic do you bring that your participants might not hold?

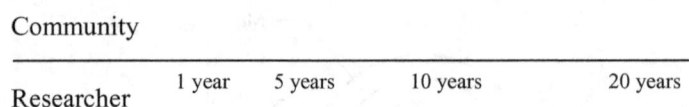

Figure 27.3 Beneficence and justice timeline.

Beneficence and Justice Timeline

Create a timeline and brainstorm potential benefits and risks that might occur because of your research. Consider this for both the researcher and the phenomenon/population/participant over a 20-year period (see Figure 27.3). Make a list of pros and cons/benefits and risks:

- How does this research benefit you? What risks does it pose?
- How does this research benefit the participants? What risks does it pose?
- Do the benefits/risks change at different stages of the research and sharing? For example, being able to use the written product to promote their work, doing panels together before and after publishing, being invited to give compensated workshops at your university, etc.

Orientations

Connecting outward to Communities of Practice

Naming the Participants in Your Community of Practice

Similar to "Situating the researcher" above create a figure of nested circles that names peers, advisors, artists, or scholars who directly or indirectly influence your work. The first circle is you, the second circle might be the names of peers who are exploring topics similar to yours, the third circle might be advisors with whom you work or artists or scholars with whom you have a relationship, the fourth circle might be artists or scholars you admire but have not had a chance to interact with yet. Who is missing? Who is over-represented? Put two or more individuals in the same tier, or across tiers, in conversation with each other based on what they have said, written, or demonstrated. How would they resonate? How would they dissonate?

Engaging in Conversation with Your Community of Practice

D. Soyini Madison describes "being part of an interpretive community" (2012, 22) as an important part of the research process. Far more than just conducting a literature review, Madison sees this as building an active relationship with an interpretive community, knowing what they are saying or doing, and being able to critically engage, apply, and extend others' work, even that which you don't admire.

Imagine you are gathering your interpretive community together around a conference table, in a lab, or in the studio to work on your research questions. Who would you gather and why? Who is missing from this group? Who might be over-represented? Who do you not want to invite but should really be there? Write an agenda for the gathering.

Imagine this same group is at a dinner party together; write a script for how the conversation would unfold.

Imagine you have gathered several of the members of the group as part of an academic panel; compose questions that would engage the panelists, and then answer the questions in their voices.

Working from Curiosity

An Invitation to Move

What am I interested in? What questions/ideas/themes/situations do I keep coming back to over and over again? What kinds of things do I like to do?

An Invitation to Journal

What am I interested in? What questions/ideas/themes/situations do I keep coming back to over and over again? What links do I have saved in my bookmarks? What books are on my shelf or in my wish list? What kinds of things do I like to do? (Talk to people, look through papers, find documents, analyze.)

An Invitation to Relate

Ask someone else: What are you interested in? What questions/ideas/themes/situations do you keep coming back to over and over again? What kinds of things do you like to do?

You could also ask someone else: What do you think I'm interested in? What questions/ideas/themes/situations do you see me coming back to over and over again?

Carefully Questioning Assumptions and Engaging in Self-Reflexivity

Making the Implicit Explicit

Respond to the following prompts in movement, written word, spoken word, images, etc.:

I believe dance _____
I believe good dancers _____
I believe "real" dancers_____
From my perspective, the dance form I practice
- Is characterized by the following qualities/traits: _____
- Has the following history: _____
- Has the following internal debates/controversies: _____

I know all this because _____
I sometimes have doubts about _____ in the dance form I practice.
I respect practitioners and scholars such as _____, _____, and _____ because _____.
I disagree with practitioners and scholars such as _____, _____, and _____ because _____.

Share these responses with friends and colleagues from different communities of practice. Where is there resonance? Where is there dissonance? Where were you surprised? Where were they surprised?

Set a reminder on your calendar to repeat this process in six months, a year, two years, etc. What has changed? What has stayed the same? Why? And why is it important?

Valuing Care, Intuition, Spirit, Affect, Relationality, Emotion

Prioritize Wellness

Research projects have many moving parts that operate over long periods of time. It is quite common for researchers to lose themselves while striving for results and deadlines. After the COVID-19 pandemic and the United States-based racial uprisings of 2020–2022, it is more important than ever to prioritize wellness, our own and that of our communities. Make a habit of asking yourself: How am I today? What have I done to support my health and well-being? Make a habit of asking your community, including participants: How are you today?

And, as Matthew's old boss Seán Curran would say at the beginning of every class: Don't just hear, but really listen. Don't just listen, but really hear.

Emotion/Spirit/Relation Memos

The practice of "memo-ing" often attends to emergent synthetic or analytic thoughts during the data generation process. In this activity, however, we suggest that you create memos that record your emotional state during data generation, insights that are connected to intuition or spirit, and/or relational dynamics between you and the community. While taking field notes or writing post-class/rehearsal observations, divide a piece of paper in half. On one half, record your observations of the community. On the other half, record your emotion/spirit/relation memos. Afterward, look for relationships between the two sides of the paper.

"Memo That Sh*t"

Memoing–through writing, moving, and talking–alongside all of the stages of the research process–is an important way to be in touch with your intuition. Having a dedicated notebook, notes program, voice memo folder, or video album close at hand to record insights, questions, ideas, random thoughts, worries, gut feelings, concerns, etc. about the research is a vital way to tap into a different kind of thinking. Reviewing memos can reveal proto-analytical thoughts, un-examined questions, and fruitful new pathways. For some researchers, spontaneous memoing comes naturally. If you find that you are not often memoing, try instituting an intentional daily practice of writing/moving/talking for three minutes about your research. Review your memos periodically and/or when you're feeling stuck or unsure. Share your memos with an advisor or trusted colleague to hear their insights.

Critically Observing

Coffee Shop Observation

1. As a group go to a coffee shop, student union, some social area where you can all sit separately yet in proximity to one another and observe for 20–30 minutes.
2. Take notes and notice how your position in the room, or your interests impact what/how you observe.

3. Share what you noticed. What did you learn from others' observations? What did you learn about your own skills of observation?
4. If possible repeat the observation one more time with these insights in mind.

Noticing and Articulating (adapted from Rosenwasser and Stephen 2019)

1. Select a streaming/video dance to watch. Decide ahead of time if you will watch the whole dance without taking notes or take notes while watching.
2. Either during or after the dance, complete the phrase "I noticed that…" These should be short descriptions of what you saw. If working on your own, push yourself to generate as many as possible. If working in a group, take turns with each person completing the phrase and try to go around the group as many times as possible. The descriptions do not need to be sophisticated. Simple descriptions are effective (e.g. I noticed the dancers clapped at different times. I noticed the dancer fell to the floor. I noticed the woman touched the other woman's face.) Pay attention to when descriptions become interpretations (e.g. I noticed the dance was about friendship) and evaluation (e.g. I noticed the dancers had really good technique).
3. After one round of viewing and "I noticed…" watch the dance again and repeat the process two, three, or even four times.
4. How did the process of viewing the dance change after practicing "I noticed…"? How did the descriptions of the dance change throughout the process? What patterns began to emerge across the descriptions? Why are these patterns important to the dance?

This process can be repeated with a dance class, a painting, a written text, a meal, etc.

Being Willing to Try out Different Lenses and Scopes

Troubling the Binaries

Use these questions, posed in Chapter 1, to guide a movement improvisation, freewrite, or group discussion:

- Ephemerality/Persistence: In what ways does the dancing disappear as it is being danced and in what ways does the dancing remain?
- Universal/Situated: What in your dancing is shared with all other dancers and what is unique to your community or even you alone?

- Subject/Object: In what ways do you conceive of yourself or another as being a body and in what ways do you conceive of yourself or another as having a body?
- Everyday/Rarified: How is dancing embedded in and intertwined with all aspects of life and how is dancing a unique and rarified experience?
- Mundane/Sacred: In what ways is dancing of the earthly world and in what ways is dancing of the spiritual world?
- Discursive/Non-discursive: How is dancing part of ongoing public and private discourse and how does dancing resist participation in public and private discourse?
- Agent/Instrument: In what ways is dancing empowering through invited spectatorship and in what ways is dance disempowering through unwanted spectatorship?

Change Your Perspective or Scope

Sometimes we look at something for so long that we lose sight of what it is, or we become convinced that our view is the only correct one. Practicing changing our perspective can bring new insights. Try out these activities:

- Inspired by Banyai's book *Zoom* (1998) draw your research topic from multiple levels of a zoom lens: from a microscopic, almost abstract, level, to the subject itself, to the subject in its immediate context, a broader context, all the way up to a macro or planetary view.
- As performers, we are often faced with the challenge at a certain point in the rehearsal process to "face away from the mirror." Similarly, we may need to adjust our spacing to a proscenium stage, a gallery space, an outdoor plaza, etc. What would it mean to do this with your own research, either literally or figuratively? Try out at least three options.
- The dancers Eiko & Koma in their workshops and some performances like *Husk* (1987) work with "eye angle," that is, looking at the dance from an intimate and perhaps unexpected angle, for example from lying on the floor. Try looking at your data while "lying on the floor" with it. What do you see differently?

Three Lenses

Choose a short dance, and analyze it from the perspective of three different theories. Notice how the different theories may call for different writing styles, or may lead you to focusing on different aspects of the dance.

Dis-Order/Re-Order

In various stages of research, including but not limited to analysis and writing, dis-ordering and re-ordering can provoke new insights.

- Create a reverse outline from a piece of writing by tagging each paragraph with a descriptive word or phrase, and numbering it in terms of section and paragraph. Write these tags and numbers onto a big piece of paper with colored markers (size and color also help you see your work differently!) Then go through and notice if there are tags that need to be moved to different sections, if there are similar tags spread out that need to be brought together, or if there are tags that don't belong. Then re-order all the tags and use them to reorganize your writing. (You can also do this by printing out a copy of your text, cutting all the paragraphs out, re-ordering them, and taping them back together.)
- Borrow another artist's process, for example, Merce Cunningham's chance operations or Brian Eno's oblique strategies, to introduce another kind of order or process into your research.

Noticing When to Slow down and When to Leap

Researcher, Know Thyself

Oftentimes we get so wrapped up in what we "have to" do, seeing research methods as a series of discipline-based hoops that we're required to jump through, that we forget that research is something we "get to" do. You have made space in your life to nurture your inclinations toward curiosity and sense-making about the practice of dance. Your personal strengths and opportunities for growth are with you throughout the process. Being explicitly aware of them will aid you in your journey.

Engage in an ongoing practice a freewriting about yourself as a researcher: Are you someone who reserves judgment, who slowly and carefully gathers and synthesizes information? How can you create opportunities to be bold and share tentative claims and practices? Are you someone who reaches and shares conclusions very quickly? How can you create opportunities to slow your process and check your assumptions? Are you more productive in the morning, afternoon, or evening? Do you need silence or background noise when you read? What parts of the research process give you anxiety? In what parts do you experience a sense of flow?

Losing Your Rush

Inspired by Höfling's use of the Brazilian phrase, practice "losing your rush" in your daily life. What would your coffee taste like if you sat down to drink it, rather than getting it to go? What could you notice on your commute if you walked rather than drove or took public transportation? Similarly, if you "lost your rush" in your research, what could you notice?

Practices

Set up

Discerning Your Interests and Position

Gather up the questions you have, the things you are drawn to doing, the intervention you want to make, the population you want to work with. You could do this by writing these out by hand in columns on a piece of paper, by typing them up in a document, or by writing them on post-its and putting them on the wall. Notice where they line up and where the discrepancies are. Your research questions, purpose, data streams, and analysis tools have to have an internal consistency, and be connected into a disciplinary framework. What doesn't fit; what could replace it? Are you doing it because it sounds cool, or because it's really going to help you answer the questions you have?

Reviewing the Literature and Other Forms of Disciplinary Discourse

In order to identify literature and other forms of disciplinary discourse on their own terms, complete the following matrix (see Table 27.1). This could be done with published literature (i.e. articles and books) but it could also be done with streaming video lectures or knowledge shared as part of an oral tradition. You could also do a "literature review" of dances that speak to your interest. Answer each question to the best of your ability, completing the matrix for one source at a time. As we argue in this book, different academic traditions attend to these practices in different ways and to different degrees. For some sources, the answers will be explicitly available, for others, answers will need to be inferred from the source. Most answers will require more space than suggested here; either redraw the matrix leaving more room or recreate it in a spreadsheet. Repeat the process for multiple sources, noticing as you go the themes that are developing, as well as similarities and differences in definitions of key terms, methods, etc.

Table 27.1 A matrix for reviewing and comparing sources

	Source 1	Source 2	Source 3
What is/are the phenomenon/focus of inquiry/relevant variables?			
What existing conversations are being referenced?			
What worldview does this inquiry sit in?			
Who are the people involved?			
What are the places that are involved?			
How are data/practices generated?			
How do the authors sort and connect?			
How do the authors elaborate?			
How do the authors share their work?			
How do the authors establish validity/believability/beauty?			
What are the limitations of this work?			
What is the impact of this work?			

Making a Plan

The questions below, shared in Chapter 2, were offered to the book's contributors to consider while writing. Here we offer them to the reader as a way to think systematically about how practices in a research design fit together. As you plan your research, answer each of the questions below.

- Set up
  - What disciplinary practices or conversations inform your research?
  - What counts as knowledge? What themes pervade?
  - How is your work in conversation with the work of others?
  - How do you decide what to explore?
  - How do you position yourself in relation to the inquiry?
  - What ethical issues arise during the setup phase of the inquiry?
- Generate
  - What counts as data/practice?
  - How is it generated, collected, and documented?
  - What ethical issues arise during the generation phase of the inquiry?

- Sort and Connect
  - How do you make sense of the information you've collected or practices in which you've engaged?
  - How do you test, perceive, or generate relationships in and among the practices and/or data you've collected?
  - What ethical issues arise during the sort and connect phase of the inquiry?
- Elaborate
  - How do these processes lead to new explanations, practices, and/or questions?
  - How do you ensure your work is good/valid/believable?
- Share
  - How do you share your work?
  - What ethical issues arise during the sharing phase of your inquiry?

Generate

Getting Used to Generating

Before needing to generate practices or data for a specific research project it is helpful to develop the skills and build the muscles for generating. Find time to engage in practices that produce artifacts based on your actions, observations, or thoughts. Some of these include:

- Improvising
- Freewriting
- Freetalking into a recorder
- Drawing/doodling
- Collage making
- Map-making
- List-making

Begin to pay attention to how practices in which you already engage are data generation practices:

- Little dances around your kitchen and melodies you sing to yourself are proto-artistic practices
- Conversing with a friend is a proto-interview
- Conversing with your class is a proto-focus group
- Journaling or taking notes after rehearsal is proto-participant observation

An Improvisational Score for Data Generation

Move
Feel
Look
Listen
Smell
Taste
Relate

Descriptive Writing

This interactive activity will help you evaluate the quality of your field notes, movement description, or rehearsal notes. It works best in a class or with a group of at least three people. Choose a sentence from your notes that describes an action taking place. Have your peers enact what they understand from your sentence. This works best when one person enacts the sentence and the others comment on or coach the person enacting the description. Compare what they did to the original. Workshop together on how to get your written description closer to the action.

Sort and Connect

Connecting Chapters

- Mabingo and Zaccarini both use the metaphor of weaving to refer to the research process: describe how these metaphors work. What other metaphors for research appear in the chapters? What metaphor might work for you?
- Stewart and Quin and Wilson argue that dance forces us to deal with both theory and practice: describe this tension in their words. How do you grapple with this tension in your research?
- Kawano and Pollitt both advocate for the value of pausing. What do they claim is found in the pause? What can be found when you pause?
- Cruz Banks, Youdan, and Chillemi and Fortuna describe research ethics: where do they resonate? Where do they dissonate? How do you describe your approach to ethics?
- How does putting Mabingo's use of Ubuntu and Zaccarini's idea of FutureBlackSpace in conversation situate research between historical tradition and future possibility? In your own work, what traditions do you bring with you? When and how do you create space for you or your community of practice to generate knowledge on its own terms?

- Pollitt and Akinleye describe their research in the temporality of *presence*. How does this *presence* disrupt objective positionality in research? What are the challenges in articulating and verifying the importance of *presence* in research?
- Kawano's interpretive phenomenological, arts-based methodology allows for interactive movements between researcher and research participants for embodied data reporting and reflective meaning-making. It aligns with Quin and Wilson's understanding of the *human* researcher and the *human* participant, accompanied by their lived experience within the research process and its outcome. How do observation and participation of the researcher merge? What are the benefits and challenges of researcher self-reflection in research processes and how do they intersect with generalizable knowledge?
- Morgan, Youdan, and Morris work with communities who, according to procedural ethics, require special care and attention. What ethical practices do they suggest when working with these populations? What lessons can be applied to communities with whom you work?
- Henley and Quin and Wilson describe the value and practice of mixed-methods research. Where do they resonate? Where do they dissonate?
- Höfling and Overby and Henley describe research methods that need to be modified to better meet "real-world" circumstances. Describe these modifications and why they are made. Consider what deviations from "standard" practice might need to occur in your own research.
- The concept of *horizontalidad* (horizontality) in Chillemi & Fortuna and Zaccarini's interracial dialogues in institutions interrogate the relationship between research and "the institution." How does change occur on a relational and organizational level? How can institutional equity and inclusion be further strengthened in research?
- Morris, O'Shea, and Akinleye write about productive tensions of working across disciplines. How do they navigate these crossings? Make a list of other fields that may also have an interest in your research area. How might the worldviews of your fields lead to different questions? Or, how might they lead to different methods to investigate the same questions? If you like, take this a step further and reach out to colleagues in other departments to chat about your ideas.
- Bench et al and Quin and Wilson address how the pedagogy of their methodology has deepened their engagement with it. Where do they resonate? Where do they dissonate? How would you teach a methodology or method you are using? Develop a lesson plan or syllabus for a course or workshop, specifying for whom the class is designed.
- Otake and Cruz Banks both emphasize daily, repeated work in their chapters. For Otake this is about practicing and experimenting – whether on her own or with a collaborator, while for Cruz Banks, this entails building

relationships and respect with the community. What are the ongoing, daily aspects of your research?
- Park and Pollitt both perform their methodology within their writing as well as describe it. How can you perform your methodology in your presentation of your work?

Making Groups

Part 1

1. Gather together something you have a collection of, such as books, records, t-shirts, socks, spices, etc.
2. Place all of the items into three separate groups and describe the organizational logic. Is it based on color, function, age, or genre?
3. Scramble the collection and organize according to a different logic. Describe the new organization.

Part 2

1. Choose a topic and complete a literature search to find 20–25 sources
2. Print the abstracts and organize them into three piles (piles could be conceptual, chronological, methodological, etc.).
3. Write down a description of each of the piles and a description of the logic for the overall organization.
4. Shuffle the abstracts and repeat the process according to a different logic.
5. Shuffle the abstracts and give them to a classmate or peer and have them repeat the process. Compare systems of organization.

Elaborate

What Does That Look Like? Why Is That Important? (Adapted from Rosenwasser and Stephen 2019)

As we begin to find connections between data or practices, our thoughts are often positioned in the middle of a spectrum between the concrete and the abstract. For instance, after watching a hypothetical dance several times, I might conclude that, in a section of the dance, the woman was chasing the man. This interpretive statement invites elaboration in order to become both more concrete and more abstract. "What does that look like?" offers an opportunity to be more concrete and describe the movement evidence that leads to the conclusion. "Why is that important?" offers an opportunity to be more abstract and explore the implications of the conclusion. Return to a piece of your writing–possibly one developed as part of one of the other activities in the workbook in response to a text, theory, practice, datum–and practice asking yourself "What does this look like?" and "Why is that important?" Think of these not as single questions but as chains. "What does that look like?" is repeated multiple times as "What else does that look like?" "Why is this important?" is repeated multiple times as "Why is 'what's important' important?"

The Outlier

An outlier is a practice, data point, or theory that doesn't seem to fit with the rest of the practices, data, or theories. It is unexpected, and we often, therefore, remove it to create a more orderly pattern. The outlier, though, invites us to consider that there is a pattern we do not see. The outlier might belong if we could perceive a different pattern, or it might open insights to the nature of the pattern, or the types of patterns we are trained to see. The next time you encounter a data point that doesn't belong (e.g. a very low or very high score on a student's test, a strange comment from an interviewee) or a practice that doesn't belong (e.g. a movement phase or spatial relationship that doesn't fit with the rest of the dance), instead of simply removing it, ask yourself: If viewed from another perspective, why might this be here?

An Improvisational Score for Data Analysis

Dance the data.
Take a walk.
Call a friend.
Take a bath.
Stomp around.

Share

Many Ways of Sharing

Share your research or literature review findings in a variety of creative formats that encourage you to respond to audience and scope. Here are some suggestions:

- Academic journal article of 5,000–8,000 words
- Academic presentation lasting 20 minutes
- Academic poster
- Community presentation

- Dance or improvisational score
- Lesson plans for different age groups
- Grant proposal of 1,500 words
- Pecha Kucha (www.pechakucha.com)
- Documentary film
- Vlog, blog, or website
- Spoken word performance
- Haiku
- Drawing or painting
- Visual collage
- Mindmap
- Song
- Letter written to a friend
- 30-second elevator pitch
- Explanation to family and friends at a meal

Putting It Together

Just Start

Notice something you pass every day and research it. Track your own pathway through the steps:

- Set up
- Generate
- Sort and Connect
- Elaborate
- Share

Make or learn a dance or improvisational score. Track your pathway through the steps:

- Set up
- Generate
- Sort and Connect
- Elaborate
- Share

Across these experiences, consider the situational, relational, and procedural ethics that emerge. Attend to the orientations (starting from curiosity, carefully questioning assumptions, engaging in self-reflexivity, etc.).

Putting Chapters into Practice

Part 1

Choose a phenomenon/practice/population/participant, for instance, a first-year hip hop technique class in a BA program. Based on Midgelow, DeFrantz, Overby, and Wilson's introductory chapters: What questions could be asked from each of the subdisciplines? What disciplinary frameworks inform each inquiry?

Part 2

Choose one chapter and use it as a guide to design a hypothetical research project related to that first-year hip hop technique class. How would you set up, generate, sort and connect, elaborate, and share? Select a second chapter (possibly from another Part of the book) and repeat the process. Compare the two. How does the selection of different methodologies lead to different theoretical frameworks, research questions, types of evidence gathered, modes of analysis, and pathways for sharing?

Part 3

Choose a different phenomenon (e.g. a Dance For PD®[1] class, a queer burlesque performance, a religious ritual) and repeat the process. How do research methods need to adapt to meet the needs of the community of practice that is being investigated?

Adapting Methodologies and Methods to Meet the Needs of Specific Projects

A number of the chapters in this book discuss how the author adapted to the needs or interests of participants or the dance (e.g. Bench et al., Cruz Banks), or to new information, new events, and new contingencies (e.g. Höfling, Morris). Some even discussed discovering an issue not addressable by standard methodologies (e.g. Mabingo, Kawano). Don't be constrained by what's written in methodology and methods books (including this one!). In fact, Johnny Saldaña, author of a widely used text on coding, actually encourages researchers to come up with their own codes (2015). If something is not working, pause and notice it. Memo about it and/or talk to a colleague. If you have an intuition about something else that might work, memo about it and/or talk to a colleague. Try out your new idea and see what happens.

Scaffolded Inquiry

This exercise should happen in parts over multiple days or weeks. It begins with the premise that we are naturally sense-makers but that often the sensemaking that we do is fast, implicit, and influenced by preconceived notions. The exercise, therefore, is set up to slow down the sensemaking process, make it explicit, and ask you to reflect on the relationship between what you think is happening and what is actually happening.

1. Select a phenomenon in your personal or professional life that you interact with regularly, that you have already come to some conclusions about, and that you have a hunch that if you slowed down and looked at it more closely that you might come to a more nuanced or complicated understanding about. It is most productive to frame a how or why question around this phenomenon.
2. Set Up: Begin by articulating bias (i.e. What do you think the answer is?) and describing the context (i.e. What are the important physical and social "actors" that impact the phenomenon?).
3. Generate: Engage in a series of at least three freewrites about this topic that each last at least 30 minutes. These are your thoughts about the phenomenon. It is not about answering or proving anything. It is about making your implicit thoughts explicit, to reveal your fast, often unconscious, thinking to yourself. These should happen with some time in between each session to allow new or different ideas to emerge. Throughout this step, it is worthwhile to continually return to articulating bias and describing the context (i.e. What biases are revealed in your freewrites? What new "actors" emerge in the writing process that were not initially described?)
4. Sort and Connect: Take a step away from being the author of the freewrites and re-approach them as if they were data, written by someone else. Read through them several times trying to get a sense of what the "author" is trying to say. Can certain statements be grouped together by theme, chronological unfolding, or some other structure? Are there patterns, contradictions, or revelations?
5. Elaborate and Share: Synthesize the themes and patterns to create a new, possibly more nuanced or complicated, understanding of the phenomenon. This can all be put together in a format that can be shared with someone. Begin by describing the context (who and what does the reader need to know about understand the inquiry?), articulate your bias (what preconceived notions did you have about this topic?), describe the data (what did you learn from the data?), and describe the possibilities for future inquiry (what questions do you still have?).

After gaining familiarity with this process, repeat the steps but this time, instead of freewrites as data, the researcher can interview 1–3 people who also have familiarity with the phenomenon.

Outline of a Statistical Analysis Plan (Contributed by Gregory Youdan Jr.)

This is a general outline for an SAP. Not all aspects may make sense for every study. Therefore, you will need to use the statistical thinking gleaned from Youdan's chapter to make judgment calls on what will best serve your study.

1. Introduction.
    a. Abbreviations used.
2. Objective of study.
3. Research question and hypotheses.
4. Outcome measures.
    a. Type of data.
    b. Scale.
5. Data sources.
    a. Valid and reliable methods for data collection.
6. Methodology.
    a. Study design.
    b. Inclusion/exclusion criteria.
    c. Variables of interest.
7. Sample size.
    a. Calculation used.
8. Statistical methodology.
    a. Normality.
    b. Planned analyses.
        i. Assumption checks.
    c. Handling of missing data.
    d. Error control/reduction of bias.
        i. Significance level.

Mini-Oral History (Contributed by MiRi Park)

In Park's dance history courses, she requires her students to conduct a research project that includes both primary and secondary sources. She encourages them to take the opportunity to speak with their parents or that auntie or cousin who always seems to "go off" when a certain song is played at family gatherings/parties. The difference in this kind of project from a larger book/dissertation or public project is that this may be a narrower scope than a full life history. This can mean that this is subject-oriented. In this case, the oral historian might begin with the prompt: "Tell me about a song that you love to dance to." In this setting, the budding oral historian should employ the principles outlined for the oral history interview process, recapped here in list-form:

- Allow the interviewee to tell their story
- Practice deep-listening
- Make space for silences
- Transcribe/edit the interview
- Send back to interviewee for feedback and approval
- Write up the analysis
- Organize for the final form of output: paper, presentation, or website

Writing/Dancing (Contributed by Jo Pollitt)

1. **Dance yourself into writing**
   Dance for four minutes and, while maintaining momentum and energetic state, continue this dancing as writing on the screen or page
2. **Write yourself into dancing**
   Begin writing with pen or keyboard, and write for as long as it takes until the writing can only be continued in movement off the page
3. **How long is the life of a movement?**
   a) Attempt to dance the length of the life of a movement /// // / do this for a continuous period of time notice differing lengths and lives. b) Attempt to write the length of the life of an idea, thought, or energetic shift. //// / /// / do this for a continuous period of time notice differing lengths and lives on the page.
4. **Writing with shifting focus**
   (a) write with an internal focus for one minute, (b) write with a focus on the surface of the body for one minute, (c) write while focusing beyond the horizon for one minute, (d) write while maintaining focus in the room for one minute, and (e) write with all of the foci states at once.
5. **Resistance**
   Begin writing with your dominant hand then switch to your non-dominant hand and continue this compositional state into dancing that inhabits the attention of the non-dominant.
6. **Spot-lit solo**
   Practice entering the screen or paper page as a spot-lit stage and perform a three-minute solo there.

7. **Write like you dance**
   "these are not words to hide behind" (Winterson 1995, 95).

Note

1 See https://danceforparkinsons.org

Works Cited

Banyai, Istvan. 1998. *Zoom*. New York: Puffin Books.

Belcher, Wendy Laura. 2019. *Writing Your Journal Article in Twelve Weeks*, 2nd ed. Chicago: University of Chicago Press.

Bronfenbrenner, Urie. 1992. "Ecological systems theory." In *Six Theories of Child Development: Revised Formulations and Current Issues*, edited by Ross Vasta, 187–249. London: Jessica Kingsley Publishers.

Madison, D. Soyini. 2012. *Critical Ethnography: Method, Ethics, and Performance*, 2nd ed. Los Angeles: Sage.

Rosenwasser, David and Jill Stephen. 2019. *Writing Analytically*, 8th ed. Boston: Cengage.

Saldaña, Johnny. 2015. *The Coding Manual for Qualitative Researchers*, 3rd ed. Thousand Oaks: Sage.

Index

Note: Page numbers followed by "n" denote endnotes.

Abrahamsen, Rita 205
Abreu, Frede 145n2
Adeniji, Anna 79, 87
African dance traditions 187, 195, 212, 215, 217–218, 222
African Soul International 218
Ahmed, Sara 26–27
Alexander, F. Matthias 281
Alim, H. Sami 122
"alternative facts" and post-truth 371–372, 387n8
American Dance Therapy Association 332
archives 110; in Brazil 135–144
arts-based research (ABR) 330–331, 349, 350, 417
ArtsBridge 231, 232, 234, 240
Asian American Studies 128–129
Assaf, Nadra 272
assistive technology design 283, 346–360
Assunção, Matthias Röhrig 135
Atamira Dance Company 219–221, 223
attending 20–21, 27, 48, 49, 51, 54, 87, 177, 329–330, 366, 378
authorship 126, 141–142, 144

Bacon, Jane 55
Bailarines Toda la Vida *see* Dancers for Life
Balanchine, George 115, 144
ballet 111, 115, 118, 127, 144, 186, 279, 289, 333
Bangoura, M'Bemba 218
Bangoura, Moustapha 218, 222
Banyai, Istvan 31, 411

Barad, Karen 392
Barthes, Roland 115, 174
Batson, Glenna, et al. 292, 302
Behar, Ruth 30
Belcher, Wendy Laura 9, 403–404
Belmont Report 23
Beltran, Myra 122
b-girl dance *see* break dancing
Bimba, Mestre 138–139, 140, 141
Bishop, Brian J., et al. 197
Black Indigenous & People of Color (BIPOC) 187, 213–217, 223, 224
Black Studies 80, 85, 88, 93n1
blackness 42, 79–80, 83, 84, 89–91, 93n1
Bohm, David 297
Bourdieu, Pierre 78n7, 154, 387n19
Brasília, Mestre 142, 143
break dancing 110, 129, 147–150, 157–158
Butler, Judith 51, 378

Cajete, Gregory 30
Calamels, Daniel 68
Caldwell, Linda 31
Calvo-Merino, Beatriz 265–266
cancel culture 127
Canjiquinha, Mestre 137–143
capoeira 110, 124, 134–144
care, choreography and 120, 124
Carnegie Foundation 154–155
Castoriadis, Cornelius 71
Catterson, Pat 156
causality and generalization in quantitative research 228–229, 239, 241

centering 66
Chalmers, David 375–376
Chatfield, Steven 282
choreographic analysis 113–130
choreography, non-dance forms of 366
Clark, Mary Marshall 148, 154–155
Clifford, James 31
climate crisis 49, 50, 111, 124, 373–374, 379–381
coding 115, 354–356
Coles, Honi 156, 163n13
collaboration 189, 347, 347–349, 360, 389, 393–398
collective creation 45, 61–66, 69, 71–76
colonialism (and coloniality) 44, 114, 120, 123, 185, 217; ethnography and 215; *see also* decolonization
combat sport *see* martial arts
commas 52–54, 57–58
Common Core Standards 234
communal thinking 88, 222–223
community dance 44, 61–76, 337
"communities of practice" 11–15, 406–407
Conrad, Robin 271
consciousness 375–377
constructivism 14, 262–263, 327, 370–371, 372
COVID-19 pandemic 25, 64, 98, 120, 158, 186, 189, 297, 366; mishandling of 368–370, 379
creative writing 252, 257, 424; freewriting 412, 415
Creswell, John W. and J. David Creswell 261–262, 267, 270
critical race theory 107, 109–110, 117, 129
Croft, Clare 57, 149–152
Cross, Emily 265–266
Cunningham, Merce 115, 156, 412
curiosity 4, 28–29, 301, 345, 407
Curran, Seán 260, 409

D'Houbler, Margaret 216, 224
Dance Aerobic Fitness Test 291
dance and the Child international (daCi) 186
dance criticism 126
Dance for PD programs 304, 306–307
dance medicine 279–280; dance medicine and science (DM&S) 349–350
Dance Oral History Project 152
dance science: development of 279–284, 289; sports science and 14, 287, 288–290, 291, 301; subjectivity in 293–294, 296–297
dance studies 26, 107–112, 113–114; contributions to other fields by 366–367, 370, 376, 378, 381
dance/movement therapy (DMT) 283, 326–339
Dancers for Life (Bailarines Toda la Vida) 44, 61–76, 78n4
data analysis 34, 170, 203–204, 221–223, 238–239, 254, 335–337, 354–357; choreographic analysis 114–116; statistical analysis and 307–313, 319–321
data collection 26, 32, 199–200, 290, 295, 296, 298–299, 352; as "community engagement" 213, 214, 218–219; data cleaning 319–320; data generation 238, 415; Henley on 261–263, 266–271, 273; as social act 372; storytelling as 202; *see also* interviews
Datta, Ranjan 202
Davis, Crystal U. 224
de Certeau, Michel 351
de Wall, Frans 377, 387n13
decolonization 30, 88, 90, 110, 120–125, 127, 187, 191–196, 205, 213, 215–216
DeFrantz, Thomas 116, 117, 122
Delanty, Gerald 69
Desmond, Jane 378
Dewey, John 391, 393
dialectic thinking 338
disability (and ableism) 23, 125, 345, 346, 347, 349–358
Do the Right Thing (film) 3
double consciousness 81, 83, 85–87, 89
Douglas, Kitrina and David Carless 331
Drumm, Michelle 202
DuBois, W.E.B. 79
Dumit, Joe 51
Duncan, Isadora 144
Dunham, Katherine 216

ecological validity 230, 235, 282, 284, 299
Eiko & Koma *see* Otake, Eiko
Ellis, Carolyn 22, 24–25, 125
Elo, Mika 41
embodiment 51, 66, 189, 294, 351–352, 357; embodied pedagogy 232; in oral history 154, 155

empathy 62, 70, 74, 151; in Ubuntu 196, 197
Eno, Brian 412
environmental humanities (EH) 371, 374, 381
ephemerality of dance 14, 410
epistemology 10, 199, 200, 202
equity 17, 21, 25, 144, 186, 205, 321, 417
ethics 9, 21–26, 37n1, 201, 404–406, 416; of choreographic analysis 125–127; of self-study 254–255; rehearsal ethics 25–26
ethnography 26, 31, 109–110, 111, 125, 134–135, 187, 212–224; autoethnography 187; history of 215–216
experiential research theory 232
Expresión Corporal Danza 66–68, 72

fat phobia 125
Feldenkrais, Moshe 281
feminist theory and practice 48–58
Fine, Cordelia 373, 377
Floyd, George 25, 44, 80
folkloric shows 137, 141, 142–143
Font, Lucy 232–234, 235, 237, 240
Forti, Simone 55
Fortin, Sylvie 289, 296, 301
Fortuna, Victoria 73
Foster, Susan Leigh 17, 35, 54, 110, 128; essays by 123–124, 366; *Reading Dancing* 114–119, 121–22, 127, 356
Foucault, Michel 115, 351, 387n9
Fraleigh, Sondra Horton 4, 6
Freeman, Elizabeth 378
Friedman, Jeff 149, 153–154, 155–156
Frosch, Joan D. 214, 220, 22
funding 12, 16, 230, 321, 347, 348–349, 359, 360, 372
FutureBlackSpace (FBS) 44, 79–91, 416

Gadamer, Hans-Georg 164, 167
Galloway, Terry, et al. 75
gender 309, 329
Geni, Mestre 142, 143
Gentry, Eve 153–154
George, Doran 118, 119
Giersdorf, Jens Richard and Yutian Wong 113
Gilligan, Carol, et al. 333
Global North 114, 121, 123, 124, 127, 128
Global South 110, 129; research in 134–144
Goffman, Erving 351

Goldberg, Jane 156
Gordon, Lewis R. 197
Gottschild, Brenda Dixon 116
grading 259
Graham, Martha 115, 144, 392
Gray, Allison 223
Gray, Jack 219
Green, Jill and Susan Stinson 290
grief, stages of 79, 86
Grimes, D. Sabela 122
griot 149, 162n5
Grupo Corpo 118, 128
Grupo Semente do Jogo de Angola 134–135
Guarino, Lindsay, et al. 186
Guillemin, Marilys and Lynn Gillam 22
Gutting, Gary 377

H'Doubler, Margaret 216, 280–281
Ham, Vince and Ruth Kane 245
Hammersley, Martyn and Paul Atkinson 215
Hansen, Pil 43
Hanstein, Penelope 5, 7, 19n3, 350
Haraway, Donna 54
Hart, Michael A. 205
Hay, Deborah 115
Heidegger, Martin 164, 167–168
hermeneutics 167, 174, 176, 248, 332; *see also* phenomenology
Hervey, Lenore 336
Hijikata, Tatsumi 101
Hill, Martha 224
Hilton, Becky 50
hip hop (dancing and culture) 28, 117, 122, 128, 147–150, 157–158, 224
HIV/AIDS 153, 369
Hokowhitu, Brendan 214
Holmes, Toubab 87
Hope, Cat 52
horizontality 45, 63–64, 70, 71, 75, 417
Hosoe, Eikoh 101
House dance 213, 223, 224
humanities 107–109; *see also* environmental humanities; and under science
Humphrey, Doris 168, 171, 181n2
Hunter, Anita, et al. 336
Husserl, Edmund 110, 164–168, 171–174, 175

imagination 66, 166, 202, 353, 371, 378, 380–381; collective 75; physical 51–52, 56–57, 376
improvisation 48–57, 66, 72–73, 142, 224, 350; phenomenological approach to 166
inclusive/integrated dance 349
indigenous peoples 26, 111, 122, 391–392; First Nations 26, 43, 52, 55
innovation and novelty 9, 138, 222, 347, 359, 373
Institutional Review Boards 219, 235, 256
integrated research approach 297
interdisciplinary research 13–15, 32–35, 108, 111, 149, 189, 347–349, 360, 367, 374, 389–399, 404
interhumanism 196, 197, 198, 201
International Association of Dance Medicine and Science 359
interviews 8, 150–151; arts-based analysis of 332; body language during 335, 337; DMT analysis of 327–328, 332–336; interviewing techniques 152–153; for self-study 253; *see also* oral history
"intra-action" 392–393, 398
intuition 8, 27, 30, 164–165, 170, 172, 176, 181n1, 282, 295, 409, 421

Jackson, Janette 217–218
Japanese dance aesthetics 95, 332–333, 337; butoh 114, 118
Jaschik, Scott 219
Johnson, Imani Kai 150
Johnston, William 96, 101
Jonas, Joan 95, 100
Jones, DonChristian 97
Joy, Jenn 41–42
Juhan, Deane 293
jun, grace shinhae 149, 157–158
justice, principle of 24; *see also* racial justice; social justice

K–12 dance education 185, 272
Kagan, Jerome 10, 11–13
Katikar, Aadya 272
Keali'inohomoku, Joann 141–142, 144
Kestenberg Movement Profile 332
Khan, Akram 128
Kihlstrom, John F. 299

kinesthetic cognition 168, 176, 213, 221–222, 366
knowledge: ancestral 214; DMT and 329, 338; forms of 10; Indigenous African systems of 187, 191–206; Otake on producing 95–97, 101–103; populist suspicion of 372
Kolb, David A. 232
Kramer, Paula 43, 52
Kuhn, Thomas 301, 370
Kuppers, Petra 77n1

Laban Movement Analysis (LMA) 16, 115, 280, 283, 332, 346, 351, 356–357
Laban, Rudolf 52, 155–156, 216, 224, 268, 271; eukinetics of 168, 181n2
Labanotation 155
lability 51
Lacan, Jacques 81
LaMotte, Megan 234, 235, 238–239, 240
Langer, Susanne K. 169
Latour, Bruno 351, 372–373, 374
Lave, Jean and Étienne Wenger 11, 15, 17, 20
Leach, Paea 55
Leavy, Patricia 250
Lee, Hyjin 376
Lerman, Liz 31
Levinas, Ruth 378
liminal spaces 56, 334, 337
Limón, José, Psalm 168, 170–177, 181n6
listening 127, 147, 151–153, 409; DMT and 328, 330, 335, 339; empathy and 151, 152
Lister, Martin and Liz Wells 294
literature review 8, 27, 32–34, 135, 148, 230, 232, 246, 348, 253, 266, 295, 311–312, 351, 354, 413–414
Locsin, Agnes 122
Longley, Alys 55
Lorde, Audre 90

maculelê 137, 141, 145n4
Madison, D. Soyini 27, 30, 214, 216, 406–407
Mahdawi, Arwa 369
Māhina, 'Okusitino (Hūfanga) 391, 395
Mamdani, Mahmood 203–204
Mandradjieff, Mara 125
Māori dance 216–217, 219–221, 223–224, 326
Marable, Manning 145

Marin, Maguy 125
Marion, Jean-Luc 164, 175
martial arts 124, 371, 374–375, 377, 387n18–19; *see also* capoeira
Martin, Randy 116
materialism *vs.* idealism 370–371
Mauro-Flude, Nancy 55
McCarthy-Brown, Nyama 186, 224
McCloughan, Iris 97, 98
Mead, Hirini Moko 220
meaning-making 261, 327, 331, 336, 394
memoing 409, 421
mentoring student research 286, 288–296, 301
Merleau-Ponty, Maurice 164, 165, 166, 168, 175, 351, 376
Mey, Cassie 149, 152, 156, 158
mid-embodiment 43, 50, 54, 56–57
Midgelow, Vida 50, 55
Mignolo, Walter 123
Mirabal, Robert 95
mirroring 70–71
Misa, Stephanie 43
Mitákuye Oyásin 391
mixed-methods research design 259–273
Moustakas, Clark 168
multiculturalism 185
Myers, Natasha 51, 331

Nagel, Thomas 375, 376, 377
National Dance Association (NDA) 185, 186
National Dance Education Organization (NDEO) 185–186, 240
Ndlovu-Gatsheni, Sabelo J. 197
non-violence 75
Norkunas, Martha 151, 152
not-knowing 48–49, 51–52, 54, 57–58, 337
Novack, Cynthia 116
Nussbaum, Martha 378
Nyamnjoh, Francis B. 195

objectivity 29, 31, 164–166, 176, 244, 255, 283, 290, 292, 308, 329, 372
Ohno, Kazuo 101
ontology 125, 199, 389–392, 394–395, 399
oral history 26, 110, 111, 147–159, 423–424
Oral History Cypher Method 149–150, 156–159

Otake, Eiko 42, 94–103; as Eiko & Koma 7, 94, 95, 102, 119, 411
outliers 305, 310, 317, 320, 419
Ovens, Alan and Dawn Garbett 257

Palmer, Parker 244
paradigm shifts 301
Paraha, Tru 56
Passerini, Luisa 154
Pastinha, Mestre 138–139, 140, 141
Perez, Rosie 3–4
performance enhancement 284
Perks, Robert and Alistair Thompson 151
phenomenology 164–166, 187, 192, 197–198, 371, 375, 387n16; in dance research 164, 168–177; Interpretive Phenomenological Approach; phenomenal zombie 376; *see also* Ubuntu
Pier, Stephen 168, 170–177
Pigram, Dalisa 55
place: "being in Place" 390, 395, 397; politics of 64, 65; *see also* spatial-temporality
Polain, Marcella 53
Polanyi, Michael 370
Popper, Karl 370
populism 372
positionality 22, 29, 192–194, 206, 213, 214, 255, 326, 349, 358, 398, 417; emotional 95; historical 118, 126; knowledge and 372, 373; Western 43, 52; *see also* reflexivity
positivist *vs.* post-positivist research 262
Pōtiki Bryant, Louise 219–220, 223
Practice-as-Research (PaR) 41–45, 46n1
"practice" term 42
presence 48–58
Preston, VK 26
psicomotricidad 68
publication of research 321, 338
Purvis, Denise 271
puxada de rede 141, 146n5

quantitative *vs.* qualitative approaches 29, 34, 187–188, 259–260, 261–263, 270, 276n2
quasi-experimental design 230–241
queerness 55, 57, 111

racial justice 44, 62, 74, 81, 218
Rafferty, Sonia 297

Ramos, Petrona 123
Rasmussen, Steen Eiler 393
Rasta, Mestre Lua 142, 143
reading scores and dance 229–230
Redding, Emma 288, 289
reflexivity 29, 193, 194, 213, 214, 216, 244, 338; quiz on 408
Rego, Waldeloir 140–141
relationality 27, 49, 52, 65, 127, 200, 202; in community dance 70, 72
Research Excellence Framework (UK) 46n2
research: defined 6–10; design process of 345–360; orientations 26–32, 406–413; Otake on 94–96, 102–103; practices 32–35, 413–420; *see also* ethics
resonance 109, 333, 337, 347, 372
Reyes-Aquino (aka Reyes-Tolentino), Francisca 122, 123
Ribeiro, Djamila 126
Ritchhart, Ron, et al. 33, 38n8
ritual dances 337
Riverdance 282, 287–288, 298–300
Rodrigues, Lia 126
Rosenwasser, David and Jill Stephen 31, 410, 418
Rothfield, Philipa 376
Royal, Te Ahukaramū Charles 216–217
Rudner, Sara 155–156
Ryan, Trevor 55

Safe in Dance International 297
Saldaña, Johnny 31, 421
Samaras, Anastasia 248
Sanchez-Colberg, Ana 80, 87
Santiago, Richard "Break Easy" 147
Sartre, Jean-Paul 164, 166
Savigliano, Marta 65, 123–124
Schilder, Paul Ferdinand 67
Schupp, Karen 224
Schütz, Alfred 164, 166
science: distrust of 368–74, 380; humanities and 11, 370–371, 372, 377–378, 386n4
Scott, Kim 55
Seattle, Chief 391
sensoperception 66, 68
"sensual address" 41–42
sexuality 22
Sharpe, Christina 89

Sheets-Johnstone, Maxine 110, 168, 170–171, 271–272, 366, 398–399
Shulman, S. Lee 256
Sinatra, Jonathon 48
Sloan, Art and Brian Bowe 200
Smith, Linda Tuhiwai 326
Snow, C.P. 11
social justice 45, 65, 111, 213, 215
socio-spatiality 284, 351, 356, 357
somatics 118, 119, 187, 212, 292–293; "somatic memoirs" 221–223
Soto, Merián 98, 100
Soul Train 4
Soulja Boy 122
spatial-temporality 44, 260, 396–398; in Japanese culture 334
Spatz, Ben 42
Spielberg, Herbert 168
spirituality 111, 199, 260, 411
sports studies 371
statistical analysis 34, 238–239, 262, 283, 304–322, 373; Statistical Analysis Plan (SAP) 304, 305–306, 309, 313, 320, 423
Steup, Mattias and Ram Neta 10
Stokoe, Patricia 66
storytelling 149, 201–202; for self-study 252
student engagement theory 232–233
subjectivity 62, 66, 71, 74, 82, 165–166, 177, 198, 296, 332, 371, 376

Taylor, Diana 53
Taylor, Paul 156
teacher self-study methodology 188, 243–257
Teika, Fujiwara 336
Tharp, Twyla 155–156
theory generation 350
"three cultures" distinctions 11–13
Tiostanova, Madina and Walter D. Mignolo 194
Todd, Mabel Ellsworth 281
Tomlinson, Charlotte 297
tourism 140–141, 142–143
transaction, Dewey on 391
Trump administration 120, 371–372
Tutu, Desmond 155
typewriting 50, 424

Ubuntu 187, 191–192, 196–203, 390–391, 416; Ubuntugogy 202–203

universality 16, 85, 114, 121, 165, 186, 255, 262–263, 270, 291
Upward Turn 79, 83, 85

Van Heut, Vicky 55
Vázquez, Rolando 127
violence: in Argentina 44, 62–63, 74; against Blacks 80, 84, 89; in martial sports 375, 377, 307n18

WaAakSun 157
Wacquant, Loic 374, 377
Wallensteen, Hanna 87, 88
Warren, John 244
Watsuji, Tetsuro 334
wellness 23, 280, 281, 408

Western dance paradigms 186–187, 192, 195, 197, 217, 272–273, 326
whiteness 44, 79–81, 87–91; "white gaze" 79, 81, 83, 85, 88; white supremacy 25, 89, 187, 213–215, 368
Winmar, Roma 48, 52, 57–58
Winnicot, Donald 75–76
Wittgenstein, Ludwig 6
Woodson, Carter 216
Woolgar, Steve 372
Wright, Michelle M. 93n1
writing as dancing 43, 49–57, 424–425

Young, L. Martina 55

Zaccarini, John-Paul 44
Zuroski, Eugenia 29